ATHLONE
IN THE
VICTORIAN ERA

GENERAL VIEW OF ATHLONE DURING THE VICTORIAN ERA

ATHLONE
IN THE
VICTORIAN ERA

JOHN BURKE

ATHLONE
THE OLD ATHLONE SOCIETY
2007

The Old Athlone Society, Athlone, Ireland
email: oldathlone@online.ie
Author email: victorianathlone@googlemail.com

ISBN 978 0 9503428 6 3

Printed in Ireland by Alfa Print Ltd., Athlone

ACKNOWLEDGEMENTS

A work of this size will always require many people to help bring it to fruition. I would like to thank my parents, John and Carmel, and the other members of my family, for financial and emotional support during my time in college, and for their help and advice throughout the publication process.

To Gearóid O'Brien, a Trustee of the Old Athlone Society and Executive Librarian in the Aidan Heavey Public Library, I am very grateful. He shared his considerable knowledge of local history with me. He was most generous with his time (which I took a lot of!) and his advice, which, allied with his enthusiasm for the topic, helped improve the text immeasurably. Dr. Patrick Murray, a member of the Society Council, and editor for this publication, provided continuous support and encouragement throughout, making valuable comments and suggestions. He always remained a positive influence on the entire project, and without his assistance, guidance and support this book may not have seen the light of day. I owe another kind of debt to Dr. Harman Murtagh, whose *Athlone History and Settlement to 1800* provided a model and an inspiration for my own work which, I hope, reflects some of the qualities I found in Dr. Murtagh's. I am also grateful to my publisher, The Old Athlone Society, especially to those among its membership who encouraged my project from the start, read and commented on various drafts and, in the cases of George Eaton, President of the Society, and Finian Corley, Honorary Secretary, saw it through the press.

During the printing process, I was in frequent contact with members of the staff at Alfa Print Ltd., especially Jimmy Kenny and Damien Wheatley, both of whom responded patiently to my queries and suggestions. I should also mention the guidance provided by my M.A. supervisor John Tunney at the Galway-Mayo Institute of Technology, and the Head of the Department of Humanities there, Mary MacCague. Without their help and patience I would have found finishing the degree a more difficult task.

I have tried to ensure that my account of Athlone in Victorian times is an accurate one. Whatever errors or omissions may be discovered are to be attributed solely to me, and will be rectified in any future edition.

John Burke
March 2007

CONTENTS

LIST OF ILLUSTRATIONS

LIST OF FIGURES AND TABLES

ABBREVIATIONS

The following abbreviations and conventions are used for sources cited more than once in the footnotes:

A.M.	*The Athlone Mirror*
A.S.	*The Athlone Sentinel*
Addenda 1841	*Addenda to the Census of Ireland for the year 1841; showing the number of houses, families and persons in the several townlands and towns of Ireland* (Dublin, 1844)
Athlone 1945	*Athlone Civic Week 1945* (Athlone, 1945)
Athlone 1947	*Athlone Civic Week 1947* (Athlone, 1947)
Athlone 1950	*Athlone Civic Week 1950* (Athlone, 1950)
Atkinson, Norman,	Atkinson, Norman, *Irish Education – a history of educational institutions* (Dublin, 1969)
Banim, Mary	Banim, Mary, *Here and There Through Ireland* (Dublin, 1892)
Best, Geoffrey	Best, Geoffrey, *Mid-Victorian Britain 1851-75* (London, 1979)
Bourke, Eoin	Bourke, Eoin, "'*The Irishman is no lazzarone*' German travel writers in Ireland 1828-1850", *in History Ireland*, Vol. 5, No.3, Autumn, 1997 (Dublin, 1997)
Census 1851, part 1	*Census of Ireland for the year 1851, part I; showing the Area, Population and Number of Houses by Townlands and Electoral Divisions* (Dublin, 1852)
Census 1851, part IV	*Census of Ireland for the year 1851, part IV; showing the Area, Population and Number of Houses by Townlands and Electoral Divisions* (Dublin, 1853)
Census 1861, Report	*Census of Ireland for the Year 1861, Part V – General Report* (Dublin, 1864)
Census 1871, Vol. 1	*Census of Ireland 1871, Part 1 – Area, houses and population: also the, civil condition, occupations, birthplaces, religion and education of the people, Vol. 1, Leinster* (Dublin, 1873)
Census 1871, Vol. 4	*Census of Ireland 1871, Part 1 – Area, houses and population: also the, civil condition, occupations, birthplaces, religion and education of the people, Vol. 4, Connaught* (Dublin, 1873)
Census 1881, Part II	*Census of Ireland, 1881, Part II, General Report with Illustrative Maps and Diagrams, Tables and Appendix* (Dublin, 1882)
Census 1881, Vol. 1	*Census of Ireland 1881, Part 1 – Area, houses and population: also the, civil condition, occupations, birthplaces, religion and education of the people, Vol. 1, Leinster* (Dublin, 1881)

Census 1881, Vol. 4	*Census of Ireland 1881, Part 1 – Area, houses and population: also the, civil condition, occupations, birthplaces, religion and education of the people, Vol. 4, Connaught* (Dublin, 1881)
Census 1891, Vol. 1	*Census of Ireland 1891, Part 1 – Area, houses and population: also the, civil condition, occupations, birthplaces, religion and education of the people, Vol. 1, Leinster* (Dublin, 1891)
Census 1891, Vol. 4	*Census of Ireland 1891, Part 1 – Area, houses and population: also the, civil condition, occupations, birthplaces, religion and education of the people, Vol. 4, Connaught* (Dublin, 1891)
Census 1901	*Census of Ireland 1901, Part 1 – Area, houses and population: also the, civil condition, occupations, birthplaces, religion and education of the people, Vol. 1, Leinster* (Dublin, 1901)
Clarkson, L. A.,	"Population History, 1700-1921", in Graham, B. J. & Proudfoot, L. J. (Eds.), *An Historical Geography of Ireland* (London, 1993)
Collins, Tom,	Collins, Tom, *Athlone Golf Club 1892-1992* (Athlone, 1992)
Comerford, R. V.	Comerford, R. V., *The Fenians in Context – Irish Politics & Society 1848-82* (Dublin, 1998)
Conmee, Rev. John S.	Conmee, Rev. John S. (S.J)., *Old Times in the Barony* (Dublin, 1979)
Connolly, S. J.	Connolly, S. J., *Religion and Society in 19th Century Ireland* (Dundalgan, 1987)
Crossman, Virginia	Crossman, Virginia, *Local Government in 19th Century Ireland* (Belfast, 1994)
Cullen, Louis M.,	Cullen, Louis M., *An Economic History of Ireland since 1660* (London, 1972)
Currivan, P. J.	Currivan, P. J., "Athlone as a Railway Centre", in *Journal of the Irish Railway Record Society*, Vol. 4, No. 20, Spring, 1957 (Ballyshannon, 1957)
Daunton, Martin	Daunton, Martin, "Society and Economic life", in Matthew, Colin, *Short Oxford History of the British Isles – The Nineteenth Century* (Oxford, 2000)
Delany, Ruth,	Delany, Ruth, "Athlone navigation works, 1757-1849", in Murtagh, H. (Ed.), *Irish Midland Studies*, (Athlone, 1980)
Edwards, R. Dudley & Williams, T. Desmond	Edwards, R. Dudley & Williams, T. Desmond (eds.) *The Great Famine – Studies in Irish History 1845-52* (Dublin, 1994)
F.D.J.	*The Faulkner's Dublin Journal*
F.J.	*The Freeman's Journal*
Fitzpatrick, Jim,	Fitzpatrick, Jim, *Three Brass Balls – The Story of the Irish Pawnshop* (Cork, 2001)

Forbes, John, M. D.	Forbes, John, M. D., F. R. S., *Memorandum made in Ireland in the Autumn of 1852* (London, 1853)
Gailey, Andrew	Gailey, Andrew, "Unionist Rhetoric and Irish local government reform, 1895-9", in *Irish Historical Studies,* Vol. 24, No. 93 (Antrim, 1984)
Gazetteer	*The Parliamentary Gazetteer of Ireland, Adapted to the new Poor Law, Franchise, Municipal and Ecclesiastical arrangements and compiled with special reference...* Vol.1 A-C (Dublin, 1844)
Geary, Frank	Geary, Frank, "Regional industrial structure and labour force decline in Ireland between 1841 and 1851", in *Irish Historical Studies,* Vol. 30, No. 118 (Antrim, 1996)
Grannell, Fergal	Grannell, Fergal, O.F.M., *The Franciscans in Athlone* (Athlone, 1978)
Griffiths, A. R. G.	Griffiths, A. R. G., *The Irish Board of Works 1831-1878* (London, 1987)
Guinnane T.	Guinnane, Timothy W., "The Vanishing Irish - Ireland's population from the Great Famine to the Great War", in *History Ireland,* Vol.5, No.2, Summer, 1997 (Dublin, 1997)
Harrison, J. F. C.	Harrison, J. F. C., *Early Victorian Britain, 1832-51* (London, 1971)
Hart-Davis, Adam	Hart-Davis, Adam, *What the Victorians Did for Us* (London, 2001)
Hoppen, K. Theodore,	Hoppen, K. Theodore, *Elections Politics and Society in Ireland 1832 – 1885* (Oxford, 1984)
Hoppen, K.T.	Hoppen, K. Theodore, *Ireland Since 1800 – Conflict and Conformity* 2nd ed. (Longmans, 1999)
Horn, Pamela	Horn, Pamela, *Pleasures and Pastimes in Victorian Britain* (Sutton, 1999)
Howarth, Janet,	Howarth, Janet, "Gender, domesticity and sexual politics", in Matthew, Colin, *Short Oxford History of the British Isles – The Nineteenth Century* (Oxford, 2000)
Inglis, H.D.	Inglis, H. D., *A Journey Throughout Ireland during the Spring, Summer and Autumn of 1834* (London, 1834)
Irish Crisis	*The Irish Crisis of 1879-80, Proceedings of the Dublin Mansion House Relief Committee 1880,* (Dublin, 1881)
Kane, Robert,	Kane, Robert, M. D., *The Industrial Resources of Ireland, 2nd Ed.* (Dublin, 1845)
Keenan, Desmond	Keenan, Desmond, *The Catholic Church in Nineteenth Century Ireland – A Sociological Study* (Dublin, 1983)
Kennedy, David	Kennedy, David, "Education and the People", in McDowell, R. B., *Social Life in Ireland 1800-45* (Cork, 1979)

Kennedy, L &
  Kerrigan, Colm

Kennedy, L & Clarkson, L. A., "Birth, Death and
Exile: Irish Kerrigan, Colm, *Father Mathew and the
Irish Temperance Movement 1838-1849* (Cork, 1992)

Kinealy, Christine

Kinealy, Christine, "Food Exports from Ireland 1846-
47", in *History Ireland,* Vol. 5, No.1, Spring 1997
(Dublin, 1997)

Land Owners in Ireland

*Land Owners in Ireland - Return of owners of land of one
acre and upwards in the several counties, counties of cities,
counties of towns in Ireland in 1876* (Baltimore, 1988)

Langrische, Rosabel

Langrische, Rosabel Sara, "Athlone in the 1880s –
Being extracts from the journal of Rosabel Sara
Langrische", in *Journal of the Old Athlone Society,
Vol. II, No. 7 (2004)*

Lee, Joseph

Lee, Joseph, *The Modernisation of Irish Society
1848-1918* (Dublin, 1973)

Lenehan, Jim

Lenehan, Jim, *Politics and Society in Athlone
1830- 1885 – A Rotten Borough* (Dublin, 1999)

Lewis, Samuel

Lewis, Samuel, *A Topographical Dictionary of Ireland*
(London, 1837)

Lowe, W. J.,

Lowe, W. J., "The Irish Constabulary in the Great
Famine", in *History Ireland,* Vol.5, No.4, Winter, 1997
(Dublin, 1997)

Lyons, John Charles,

Lyons, John Charles, *The Grand Juries of the County of
Westmeath from the year 1727 to the year 1853 with an
Historical Appendix, Vol. 1* (John Charles Lyons, 1853)

Mahony, Jas.

Mahony, Jas., *Hand-Book to Galway, Connemara and the
Irish Highlands* (Dublin, 1854)

Malcolm, Elizabeth &
  Jones, Greta

Malcolm, Elizabeth & Jones, Greta, *Medicines and the
State in Ireland 1650–1940* (Cork, 1999), p.102.

Malcolm, Elizabeth,

Malcolm, Elizabeth, *Ireland Sober, Ireland Free – Drink
and Temperance in Nineteenth Century Ireland* (New
York, 1986)

Malcolm, *Irish temperance*

Malcolm, Elizabeth, "The catholic church and the
Irish temperance movement, 1838-1901", in *Irish
Historical Studies,* Vol. 23, No. 89 (Antrim,1982)

Mason, Tony

Mason, Tony, *Sport in Britain* (London, 1988)

Matthew, Colin

Matthew, Colin, "Public life and politics" in
Matthew, Colin, *Short Oxford History of the British Isles
– The Nineteenth Century* (Oxford, 2000)

Matthew, *Introduction*

"Introduction: the United Kingdom and the
Victorian Century", in Matthew, Colin, *Short Oxford
History of the British Isles – The Nineteenth Century*
(Oxford, 2000)

McDowell, R. B.

McDowell, R. B., "The army", in McDowell, R. B.,
Social Life in Ireland 1800-45 (Cork, 1979)

Abbreviations

Morash, Christopher   Christopher, Morash, *A History of Irish Theatre –
1601-2000* (Cambridge, 2002)

Murphy, Brian   Murphy, Brian, *A History of the British Economy
1740-1970* (London, 1973)

Murray, A. C.   Murray, A. C., "Nationality and local politics in late
nineteenth-century Ireland: the case of County
Westmeath", in *Irish Historical Studies,* Vol. 25, No. 98
(Antrim, 1986)

Murtagh, *Athlone to   Murtagh, Harman, *Athlone History and Settlement to
1800*   *1800* (Athlone, 2000)

Murtagh, H.   Murtagh, H., *Irish Historic Towns Atlas Volume VI –
Athlone* (Dublin. 1994)

Murtagh, Harman,   Murtagh, Harman, "Old Athlone", in Keaney, M. &
"Old Athlone"   O'Brien, G., *Athlone - Bridging the Centuries*
(Mullingar, 1991)

Murtagh, Harman,   Murtagh, Harman, "Athlone", in Simms, Anngret &
"Athlone"   Andrews, J.H., (Eds.), *Irish Country Towns* (Dublin,
1994)

Newsinger, John,   Newsinger, John, *Fenianism in Mid-Victorian Britain*
(London, 1994)

Newsome, David   Newsome, David, *The Victorian World Picture* (London,
1997)

O'Brien, Brendan,   O'Brien, Brendan, "They once Trod the Boards in
Athlone", in *Journal of the Old Athlone Society* Vol. II,
No.5 (Athlone, 1978)

O'Brien, Gearoid   O'Brien, Gearoid, *St Mary's Parish, Athlone – a History*
(Longford, 1989)

O'Brien, Municipal   O'Brien, Brendan, "Some Aspects of Municipal
Government in Athlone", in Keaney, M. & O'Brien, G.,
Athlone - Bridging the Centuries (Mullingar, 1991)

O'Brien, *Workhouse*   O'Brien, Brendan, *Athlone Workhouse and The Famine*
(Athlone, 1995)

O'Connor, John   O'Connor, John, *The Workhouses of Ireland – The fate
of Ireland's poor* (Dublin, 1995)

O'Donoghue, Bernard,   O'Donoghue, Bernard, *Oxford Irish Quotations*
(Oxford, 1999)

O'Donovan, John,   O'Donovan, John, *Ordinance Survey Letters for
Longford,* 27th May 1837, NLI.

O'Farrell, Padraic Col.   O'Farrell, Padraic Col., "Athlone – A Garrison
Town" in Keaney, M. & O'Brien, G., *Athlone -
Bridging the Centuries* (Mullingar, 1991)

O'Farrell, Patrick   O'Farrell, Patrick, *England and Ireland Since 1800*
(Oxford, 1975)

O'Tuathaigh, Gearoid,   O'Tuathaigh, Gearoid, *Ireland before the Famine 1798
– 1848* (Dublin, 1990)

Papers 1848	*Papers relating to Proceedings for the relief of the distress and State of the Union and Workhouses in Ireland 5th Series 1848* (London, 1848)
Paseta, Senia	Paseta, Senia, *Before the Revolution – Nationalism, Social Change and Ireland's Catholic Elite, 1879-1922* (Cork, 1999)
Pelling, Henry	Pelling, Henry, *Popular Politics and Society in Late Victorian Britain 2nd Edition* (London, 1979)
Proudfoot, L. J.,	Proudfoot, L. J., "Regionalism and Localism: Religious Change and Social Protest, c.1700 to c.1900", in Graham, B. J. & Proudfoot, L. J. (Eds.), *An Historical Geography of Ireland* (London, 1993)
Quane, Michael	Quane, Michael, "The Ranelagh Endowed School, Athlone", in *Journal of the Old Athlone Society* Vol. I, No.1 (Athlone, 1969)
Report 1841	*Report of the Commissioners appointed to take The Census of Ireland for the year 1841* (Dublin, 1843)
Report Industries	*Report of the Select Commission on Industries – Ireland* (London, 1885)
Report into Municipal	*Report of the Commissioners appointed to inquire into the Municipal Corporations in Ireland* (London, 1835)
Report of Fairs	*Report of the Commissioners appointed to inquire into the State of Fairs and Markets in Ireland* (Dublin, 1855)
Report on Outrages	*Report of the Select Committee on Outrages (Ireland)* (London, 1852)
Ritchie, Leitch	Ritchie, Leitch, *Ireland Picturesque and Romantic,* (London, 1838)
Roche, Desmond	Roche, Desmond, *Local Government in Ireland* (Dublin, 1982)
Royal commission, 1868	*Royal commission of inquiry, primary education (Ireland), Vol. VI, Educational Census. Returns showing the number of children actually present in each primary school on 25th June 1868...* (Dublin, 1871)
Saint, Andrew	Saint, Andrew, "Cities, architecture and art" in Matthew, Colin, *Short Oxford History of the British Isles – The Nineteenth Century* (Oxford, 2000)
Sheehan, Jeremiah,	Sheehan, Jeremiah, *South Westmeath – Farm and Folk* (Dublin, 1978)
Shiman, Lillian	Shiman, Lillian, Lewis, *Crusade against drink in Victorian England* (New York, 1988)
Sime, William	Sime, William, *To and Fro, or Views from Sea and Land* (London, 1884)
Slater's	*Slater's National Commercial Directory of Ireland* (London, 1846-94)

Spiers, E. M.	Spiers, E. M., "Army Organisation and Society in the nineteenth century", in Bartlett, Thomas & Jeffrey, Keith, (Eds.), *A Military History of Ireland* (Cambridge, 1997)
Statement as to the decline of Trades	*Statement as to the decline of Trades and Manufacturers since the Union 1834-43*, NLI, MS 13629 (5)
Stokes, G.T.	Stokes, George T., *Athlone, the Shannon and Lough Ree, with a local Directory edited by John Burgess* (Dublin, 1897)
Strean, Annesley,	Strean, Annesley, Rev. "St. Peter's Parish, Athlone", in Mason, William Shaw, *A Statistical Account or Parochial Survey – Drawn up from the communications of the clergy, Vol. III* (Dublin, 1819), p.44.
The W.I.	*The W.I., and Midland Counties Advertiser Almanac 1890* (Athlone, 1891)
Thom's	*Thom's Official Directory of the United Kingdom of Great Britain and Ireland* (London, 1837-1901)
Thomson, David	Thomson, David, *England in the Nineteenth Century <1815-1914>* (London, 1950)
Trevelyan G.M.	Trevelyan, G. M., *Illustrated English Social History: 4* (London, 1964)
Turner, Michael,	Turner, Michael, *After the Famine – Irish Agriculture 1850-1914* (Cambridge, 1996)
Vanston, George T. B.	Vanston, George T. B., *The Law relating to Municipal Towns under the Towns Improvement (Ireland) Act 1854* (Dublin, 1900)
Vaughan & Fitzpatrick	Vaughan, W. E. & Fitzpatrick, A. J., *Irish Historical Statistics – Population 1821 - 1971* (Dublin, 1978)
Vaughan, W.E.	Vaughan, W. E. (Ed.), *A New History of Ireland V – Ireland under the Union 1, 1801-70* (Oxford, 1989)
Venedy, Herr J.	Venedy, Herr J., *Ireland and the Irish During the Repeal Year, 1843* (Dublin, 1844)
W.I.	*The Westmeath Independent*
Weld, Isaac	Weld, Isaac, *Statistical survey of the County of Roscommon.* (Dublin, 1832)
White, Harry	White, Harry, *The Keeper's Recital – Music and Cultural History in Ireland, 1770 - 1970* (Cork, 1998)
Wiley, Miriam	Wiley, Miriam M., "Housing, Health and Social Welfare", in Kennedy, Kieran A., *From Famine to Feast – Economic and Social Change in Ireland 1847-1997* (Dublin, 1998)
Wilson, A.N.	Wilson, A. N., *The Victorians* (London, 2002)
Wohl, Anthony S.	Wohl, Anthony S., *Endangered Lives – Public Health in Victorian Britain* (London, 1983)

CHAPTER I

Athlone,
foundation to Victorian

The town of Athlone is situated at 53.25N latitude and 7.56W longitude in the centre of the low-lying midlands of Ireland in south County Westmeath. Traditionally considered as one of the probable locations for the centre of Ireland the town has been, for many centuries, one of the main fording points on Ireland's longest river, the Shannon. It is surrounded by bogland to the east and west, Lough Ree to the north and the callow floodplains to the south. The eskers that were deposited during the last Ice Age elevate certain parts of the town, and those who settled there used them to help define the town's streetscape. The eskers themselves were used in times past as the main transport routes when people were travelling from east to west and vice versa; their low levels of woodland rendered them far easier to traverse than the surrounding boggy land. At Athlone, as at Clonmacnoise further south, the presence of the esker provided the communications needed for a settlement to establish itself and thrive.

There are three popular etymologies for the name Athlone; the first is that *Áth Luain* translated into English means the 'Ford of the Moon'.[1] In a related etymology the Rev. Annesley Strean, the Church of Ireland reverend for St. Peter's parish on the west side of the town, noted in 1819 that local people sometimes referred to the town as 'Balladusnashaghtina'. Apparently this was also related to the moon with a possible Irish version, according to Strean, being 'Baile 'tus na seacht meina [seachtaine].' Basically this meant 'the town at the beginning of the week', Moonday, later known as Monday.[2] One of the more popular etymologies for the name Athlone comes from the great Irish Epic *An Táin Bo Cuailigne*, which relates how the loins or haunches of the *Finnbheanach*, or white bull, were dropped at the ford where Athlone grew, providing the area with a name 'The Ford of the Loins'. The most

---

1   Lewis, Samuel, *A Topographical Dictionary of Ireland* (London, 1837), p.85.
2   Strean, Annesley, Rev. "St. Peter's Parish, Athlone", in Mason, William Shaw, *A Statistical Account or Parochial Survey – Drawn up from the communications of the clergy, Vol. III* (Dublin, 1819), p.44.

popular possibility is that an innkeeper called Luan used to operate a ferry and perhaps act as a guide at the ford for those wishing to cross the Shannon at Athlone or 'The Ford of Luan'.[3]

Athlone itself began to grow as a settlement from the 12th century (though there is evidence of earlier ecclesiastical habitation) when Toirrdelbach O'Chonchobair erected his first bridge there around 1120 after his defeat of the Munster tribes at the ford. He also built a wooden castle there in 1129, though it only lasted two years when it was destroyed by a bolt of lightning. The castle and bridge were to be replaced on a number of occasions during the 12th century due to the fighting between Toirrdelbach and the Ua Mael Sechlainn clann from Meath.[4] Athlone's importance as a ford and strategic settlement site grew considerably during this period, with the Cluniacs, a religious order, founding their only church in the country there in the same century.[5]

The arrival of the Anglo-Normans in Ireland in 1169 was to see the town grow even further. Having reached the ford in the years just prior to 1200 the Normans decided that Athlone was to be the staging-point for their expansion into Connacht. Recognising the importance of the location, Bishop John de Gray completed construction of a stone bridge and castle at Athlone in the second decade of the 13th century.[6] Evidence also suggests that a wall was built around the town in the same century. The castle was the administrative centre of Athlone from where the river was monitored and the crossing over the Shannon was guarded. Neither was its importance lost on some of the English monarchs, as in the case of Henry III, who would not grant the castle to either his son when he granted him dominion over Ireland nor to Richard de Burgo when he was granted the whole of Connacht.[7] The town expanded rapidly and soon straddled the river.

Evidence of growth during the 13th century is indicated by the establishment of a Franciscan Friary in the town some time in the middle of the century and as well as this, the town was said to hold an eight-day fair and markets.[8] Those who had settled at the ford began to run what were Athlone's first real businesses. Boat builders and fabricators of waterwheels, probably for grinding corn, are believed to

3 Murtagh, Harman, "Old Athlone", in Keaney, M. & O'Brien, G., *Athlone - Bridging the Centuries* (Mullingar, 1991), p.11.
4 Murtagh, H., *Irish Historic Towns Atlas Volume VI - Athlone* (Dublin. 1994), p.1
5 Conlan, Patrick, "The medieval priory of Saints Peter and Paul in Athlone", in Murtagh, H. (Ed.), *Irish Midland Studies* (Athlone, 1980), pp.74-75.
6 Murtagh, H., p.2, Murtagh, Harman, "Old Athlone", pp 11-15.
7 Lewis, Samuel, p.85.
8 Grannell, Fergal, O.F.M., *The Franciscans in Athlone* (Athlone, 1978), p.5, Murtagh, H., p.2.

have been present in the town during the century. Athlone's strategic position caused the O'Connors of Offaly, afraid of the invading Anglo-Normans, to burn the town on a number of occasions. The bridge was almost totally destroyed in the late 13th century and its replacement erected in 1306 did not last long, with repeated attacks from the surrounding Gaelic clans. Eventually a ferry had to be used to move people from one side of the town to the other. This situation appears to have persisted right up to the sixteenth century, when a stronger garrison at the town provided the security needed to build and protect the bridge.[9]

The east side of the town is thought to have grown at a faster rate than the west side with a reference to the bridge, from the 14th century, describing how it connected the Castle to 'the town'. The Gaelic resurgence of the same century caused the grip that the Anglo-Normans had on Athlone to be tenuous at best with communications between it and Dublin hard to maintain. A large fire engulfed the town in 1315, and such was the damage that the Normans abandoned the settlement for a time. However, development still continued; tower houses may have been built and the religious orders remained in the vicinity of the ford. The orders in Athlone were described as Gaelic at the start of the 16th century, though the accession of the Tudors in England was to see the town again targeted by the crown, and a change in the status of the religious orders in Ireland.[10]

Tudor forces retook the castle in 1537 and the Dissolution of the Monasteries Act ensured that the land to the south of the castle, formerly in the possession of the Cluniacs, could be used for any expansions that were deemed necessary. In 1559 Athlone Castle became the seat of the President of Connacht as well as the headquarters of the provincial government. The Earl of Essex, a suitor to Queen Elizabeth, also resided in the castle for a short time during her reign.[11] Between 1566-7 a new stone bridge was constructed under the orders of the Lord Deputy. This led to Athlone growing again as an economic base. Markets were set up on both sides of the river, mills were built and a market house was constructed. Already very important to the town, eel fisheries grew in number and became the backbone of the local economy. By the late 16th century the town wall required restoration, for it had degenerated badly, and extra fortifications were added in the form of new gatehouses at the main entrances to the town.[12]

9   Murtagh, H., p.2.
10 Ibid.
11 Lewis, Samuel, p.85.
12 Murtagh, Harman, "Old Athlone", p.16.

Athlone was given its first known charter in 1599 due to the number of merchants present, though there is evidence of burgesses in Athlone as far back as the 13th century. Under the reign of James I in 1606 the town boundaries were established, along with a municipal corporation and Athlone's right to send a representative to parliament. The borough sent two MPs to parliament prior to the Act of Union after which it sent just one.[13] By the year 1620 the town's population was roughly 1,300 with a mix of Old English, Welsh and Gaelic Irish living within its walls. Most of the inhabitants were Roman Catholic, though the number of Protestants did grow after the Cromwellian invasion of the mid-17th century. Interestingly the area of Athlone called 'Irishtown' changed from the west side of the town to the east side after this event.[14]

An estimate of 200 houses has been given for the town around the year 1622 and the number was to grow with grants secured by the locals from the President of Connacht These grants were used in the construction of houses from bricks '*in the English manner*'. A number of years later Athlone was described as '*a fine English town*' for it had been raised '*...from the form of a poor naked village to a formal shape and fashion of a civil corporation*'.[15] The new development happened, for the most part, on the east of the town and though the facades were attractive the interiors were, according to reports, haphazardly designed.

The Catholic insurrection of 1641 reached Athlone and manifested itself as a 22-week siege on the castle, where the President of Connacht, Lord Ranelagh, resided.[16] There was an attack on the town itself by a large number of Westmeath men but they were eventually driven out after a small level of success. It took a number of weeks for reinforcements to come from Dublin to help lift the siege but by this time Lord and Lady Ranelagh had secured safe passage from the town and garnered help for the English who remained there. When the reinforcements eventually arrived they encountered a severely depleted army on the brink of starvation. A number of years after this siege the walls on the east side of Athlone were reinforced by Cromwellian engineers with new bastions added to deter any would-be attackers.

These 17th century fortifications greatly influenced the growth and layout of the town. Settlement was beginning to occur outside the town walls, space within was scarce and usually occupied by better off citizens. The dwellings outside of the walls were almost certainly those of the poorer native Irish.

13 Lewis, Samuel, p.87.
14 Murtagh, H., pp.2–3.
15 Ibid., p.2.
16 Lewis, Samuel, p.85.

Athlone lost most of its importance as an administrative centre in 1672 when the Presidency of Connacht was abolished. Religious non-conformists entered the town during the same century, mainly the Anabaptists and the Quakers.[17] By the year 1690 the town, by virtue of its growth, was listed in the top ten towns in the country. However the Jacobite war of the late 17th century was to see it sustain heavy damage.

Athlone was severely affected in the year 1690 when a large portion of the town was burnt and the bridge badly damaged. In 1691 the west side took a tremendous hammering from over 12,000 cannonballs as well as other ordnance. Even after the war the town's fortunes did not improve with another disaster, lightning striking the castle's powder store in 1697, seeing a large area on the west side take heavy damage. Despite this Athlone appeared to recover and was described as a '*handsome large town*' by the year 1709. The destruction of the Roscommon side in the late 17th century paved the way for a military barracks to be constructed beside the castle. The town also gained a '*right good*' stagecoach service to Dublin in the early 1700s that ran on a weekly basis.[18]

The improvements to the Shannon navigation in the 1750s saw a new canal created on the western fringes of Athlone; this was used by boats to bypass the hazardous conditions that were present on the river's course and enabled them to travel through the town for the first time.[19] Though the local people had suffered during the Famine of 1740, the population was estimated at 2,500 in the mid-18th century, a figure that was to grow steadily over the next few decades.

The garrison grew throughout the late 18th century with facilities expanding from the original quarters and stables. The Athlone barracks became the headquarters for the Western Command in 1796, securing the town's military importance up to the present day. During the Napoleonic Wars in Europe the castle was refortified and a series of batteries established on the west of the town. Other important buildings constructed in the town during the 18th century were the Tholsel, Ranelagh Endowed School as well as two new Roman Catholic churches, one on each side of the river, erected in the 1790s. A small number of classical schools established in the town during the 18th century survived into the 1800s.[20]

---

17 Murtagh, Harman, "Athlone", in Simms, Anngret & Andrews, J.H. (Eds.), *Irish Country Towns* (Dublin, 1994), p.159.
18 Ibid., p.161.
19 Delany, Ruth, "Athlone navigation works, 1757-1849", in Murtagh, H. (Ed.), *Irish Midland Studies* (Athlone, 1980), p.193.
20 Murtagh, Harman, "Athlone", p.159.

With the establishment of the Grand Jury system, the roads leading to the town were modernised thus improving Athlone's economic situation. The Tholsel was the venue for a number of social functions and the river provided an attractive backdrop for a number of parties. The town was said to have roughly sixty merchants during the 18th century though the detail of their trade is incomplete. Industries in the town included a brewery, a number of malt houses, a famous felt hat industry and four small whiskey stills. Also present for a number of years during the same century was a linen market. There is evidence that a bank was established in the town around 1750. However, despite the appearance of growth the levels of investment in Athlone were relatively low and its national importance fell rapidly; it was rated outside the top twenty-three towns in the country by the year 1798.[21]

Its geographical position did not favour the development of Athlone during the 18th century whereas the port and coastal towns expanded greatly over this period with international trade links growing. The town never appears to have been able to compete on an agricultural level with other towns in the region such as Moate or Ballinasloe. The land surrounding Athlone was of an inferior quality and the market itself was not well managed; regulation of the fair did not happen until well into the Victorian era. Markets were held on both the east and west sides of the town during the 18th century with the shambles situated adjacent to the market street on the Connacht side. The streets where the markets took place were called Connaught Market St. and Leinster Market St.[22]

Millers who had set up on the Elizabethan bridge were producing large quantities of flour during the closing decades of the 18th century; some of the flour was sent to Dublin due to overproduction. There were four large scale mills that produced 5,300 barrels of wheat and 1,300 barrels of oats collectively per annum on the west side of the town along with a large brewery owned by William Le Poer Trench, Thomas Evans and William Oliver Stephens that produced 8,000 barrels of porter a year.[23] Also on the bridge was a tuck mill, used for finishing cloth. The mill could have assisted in the manufacture of friezes in the town, which by the early 19th century was the main non-farming occupation around Athlone, taking over from linen making. In the Athlone district it was estimated that '…*the linen trade gave employment to at least from 4 to 5,000 from about 1776 down to about 1812.*'[24] The trade fell off in importance

21 Murtagh, H., p.3.
22 Murtagh, Harman, "Athlone", p.160.
23 Strean, Annesley, p.81.
24 *Statement as to the decline of Trades and Manufacturers since the Union 1834–43*, NLI MS 13629 (5).

'*immediately after the Peace*', following the end of the Napoleonic campaign.[25]

As to the quality of the dwellings in the town, Sherrard's survey from 1784 provides an indication. Drawn up for the Incorporated Society for the Promotion of Protestant Schools in Ireland, it was the most comprehensive survey of the town's housing until the census of the 19th century. Excluding those lands owned by Irwin McMullen, a local landowner who inherited a number of properties on the east of the town, statistics were collected that help show the types of houses on both sides of the river. The Roscommon side of the town had forty-seven dwelling houses, four dwelling houses in bad repair, fifty-eighty cabins and twenty-three cabins in bad repair or ruin. For the Westmeath side of the town the figures were forty-eight dwelling houses, six dwelling houses in bad repair, thirty-four cabins and one cabin in bad repair or ruin. These figures provide some evidence as to which side of the town was more prosperous; the Westmeath side had twenty-four fewer cabins and, significantly, twenty-two fewer cabins in bad repair or ruin.[26] So prior to the start of the Victorian era it appears that the Westmeath side of the town was the more prosperous side, basing this assessment on the quality of houses to be found there.

By 1800 the population of Athlone was estimated at 4,000 people, trade had improved due to the better infrastructure and the town had begun to see inns established in larger numbers to cater for the growth in the number of travellers. Many who visited may have noted a number of newer houses on some streets but also a haphazard layout to the dwellings, as did Rev. Strean:

> In the town [St. Peter's Parish] there have been built many new houses of late years, some in the old streets and more in a situation which before was a receptacle for dung and other nuisances...The other parts of the town on both sides of the river, are not built on any general plan, the proprietors of plots in the town, which are numerous, having let them to tenants who have erected buildings of various descriptions, each to suit his own private convenience, equally regardless of the regularity of the streets, proportional height of houses, or uniformity of fronts, and still less of public advantage.[27]

However, most of the visitors to the town were less than impressed by what they were greeted by, and almost all noted how dirty, run down and inhospitable a place Athlone was.

25 Ibid.
26 Murtagh, H., p.3.
27 Strean, Annesley, p.49.

Local trades appeared to suffer in the early decades of the 19th century with an influx of goods from Britain. Strean noted that this influx had provided Athlone with an abundance of shopkeepers, while most people living around the town were employed in agriculture.[28] A number of the small-scale cottage industries disappeared with the spread of these imports, though the arrival of steamboats on the river in the 1830s was to provide some impetus for the town's economy to grow again. The education facilities for the Church of Ireland congregation received a boost in 1826 when a school was established in the town.[29] In most of the small schools in the town the syllabus was '...*the rudiments of English, writing and accounts.*'[30]

Samuel Lewis' *Topographical Dictionary of Ireland*, published in 1837, provides the best information on Athlone at the start of the Victorian era. He stated that Athlone '...*retained much of its character as a military station.*' Most of the town walls were extant on the east of the town with access to the urban area gained via a gate in the wall. The western part of the town did not have any substantial remains of the walls or gates. One of the bridges over the canal on the same side of the town was falling asunder with the other two protected by palisades. The barrack was believed to be capable of holding 267 artillery, 592 infantry and 187 horses in the year Lewis visited, with a number of ancillary military buildings including a hospital located within its grounds. He describes the narrow Elizabethan bridge as having a passage that '...*is often attended to with difficulty*'. The presence of mills on the structure also slowed the flow of human traffic across it with its narrow supporting arches and accompanying eel weirs slowing the flow of the river itself.

The town had a total of 1027 houses, roughly five times more houses than in the 1600s, of which 546 were slated and 481 thatched. Most of the dwellings were made of limestone, the most plentiful local stone. However, a good brick factory in Clonown south of the town and a long tradition of brick making on Brick Island, on the river, meant that a number were constructed from that material. Steamboats, which had recently begun trading, appeared to be faring well connecting Athlone to Dublin via the Grand Canal and the river.

The town market was held under the walls of the castle on Tuesdays and Saturdays with animals and crops on sale. The town shambles near the Connacht market Lewis described as being '...*abundantly supplied with provisions of all kinds.*' The Athlone fair occurred on four occasions

28 Strean, Annesley, p.100.
29 Murtagh, Harman, "Athlone", p.159.
30 Strean, Annesley, p.78.

during the year in January, March, April and August, though these dates could vary – all the fairs were supposed to last three days.[31] During the 1830s Athlone's famed felt hat industry, noted in the writings of Jonathan Swift, was in decline even though felt hats had been the town's most famous export throughout the 18th century.[32] Indeed one letter noted that the hat industry in the town started on a downward trend *'immediately after the Union'*, in 1800.[33] Linen products as well as friezes were still manufactured in the town though, as already noted, on a far smaller scale than previously. The other industries in the town included *'two extensive distilleries'*, two tanneries, two soap and candle manufactories, two public breweries *'on a large scale'* as well as several corn mills.[34]

The facilities in the town for justice were quite inadequate. The Tholsel, which was also the courthouse, was knocked in 1837 and the borough prison in the Castle was considered so bad that offenders were interred only for a few hours until they were placed elsewhere.

Religious buildings in the town included a Church of Ireland church built in 1804 in St Peter's parish on the west side of the town. The same parish also had three small chapels and a failing Augustinian religious house. The Church of Ireland church in the parish of St Mary's on the east bank of the Shannon was rebuilt in 1826 by a grant of £2,300 from the Board of First Fruits. That parish also had a late 18th century church for the Roman Catholic congregation along with a Franciscan chapel that was re-edified in 1825. Baptist and Methodist houses of worship existed on the east side of the town.

On the west side of the town Ranelagh Endowed School was still in operation, though Lewis thought it was about to fail. As well as this there were three other schools, one for boys, one for girls and a Sunday school. The east side had a school for boys, another for girls and again also a Sunday school. There was *'the abbey'* school for the sons of Roman Catholics as well as a mixed school part-sponsored by the Baptist Society. Excluding the Sunday schools there were 371 pupils attending these schools, 218 boys and 153 girls. A number of private schools in the town catered for 550 other children.

From a survey of the development of Athlone over the centuries it is obvious that the town's position was the most important factor in affecting its fortunes. Straddling the River Shannon at a crossing point

---

31 Lewis, Samuel, p.87, *Traveller's New Guide through Ireland* (Dublin, 1815), p.182.
32 Murtagh, Harman, *Athlone History and Settlement to 1800* (Athlone, 2000), pp. 183–184.
33 Statement as to the decline of Trades.
34 Lewis, Samuel, p.87.

of great antiquity the town's value as a military centre appears to have been its most important feature. Indeed, the town seems to have grown mainly due to this fact; its highest position amongst the rankings came in the 17th century, a time when it was heavily re-fortified. The subsequent abolition of the Connacht Presidency downgraded the town's importance as an administrative centre and after this the industry and trade developments appear to have slowed and Athlone began to lose its significance as a commercial centre. Few educational facilities appear to have been present before the 19th century; the main one, Ranelagh Endowed School was believed to be in terminal decline. At the start of the Victorian era Samuel Lewis confirmed the town's importance as a military post; perhaps Athlone would have struggled to survive without the presence of a large garrison. He also noted a number of industries in the town, many of which were in decline. Certainly the picture provided is not one of a town that was undergoing great advances in industry, education, or infrastructure.

CHAPTER 2

Demographics and housing
1831-1901

DEMOGRAPHICS

The study of Ireland's demographics during the 19th century has been a thorough and informative one. The country as a whole saw unprecedented growth in its population in the late 18th and early 19th centuries, though the Famine and its effects were to see the trend reversed. Study of the demographic information for Ireland during and after the Famine has illustrated that the country lost a huge number of people to starvation, disease and emigration, and roughly 2 million fewer people resided on the island in 1861 than in 1841. The migration of many of these people to Britain, America and Australia has been the subject of numerous reports, histories and novels; Irish demographic history in the 19th century is massively relevant to explaining how this country, and indeed many other countries, developed in the late 19th and early 20th centuries. Something that is so important on a national scale cannot but have similar resonance on a local level and Athlone's demographic history will now be explored to assess if it too followed the national trend.

The main source used to achieve this are the census returns from 1831-1901, which were compiled every ten years during that period. However, when one is using the census statistics it must be remembered that as one seminal work noted: '[the] *slippery nature of municipal statistics*' means that all material dealing with Athlone must be treated with caution.[1] It should also be remembered when using the census returns that the information recorded and the rules for recording it changed over the decades. Some statistics included in certain years may have no direct equivalent in the subsequent census, e.g. death rate statistics in 1871 noted how many people died each year from 1861 to 1871, whilst the 1881 statistics noted an overall figure for the decade only. Bearing these points in mind an attempt will now be made to first present and

---

1 Vaughan, W. E. & Fitzpatrick, A. J., *Irish Historical Statistics – Population 1821 - 1971* (Dublin, 1978), p. xix.

then assess the demographic history of Victorian Athlone as accurately as possible.

Prior to the Victorian era there was a considerable growth in the number of people living in Athlone. A massive rise occurred between 1800, when the population was roughly 4,000 people, and the 1830s.[2] Rev. Annesley Strean noted of the local population in 1819:

> ...[that] there is no doubt it has increased from the influx of military since the garrison has been augmented by extensive additional barracks...as many families of the troops accompany and many followers attach themselves to the several regiments.[3]

According to the census returns for 1831, 11,046 people, including the military, lived in Athlone, showing a rise of over 7,000 on the 1800 figure. For this census, the commissioners used Athlone Borough, as the measure of the town itself. Whilst these figures appear straightforward, it is not until one consults the census returns of 1841 that some confusion arises. In that year the figure estimated as representing the actual population of the town was 6,393, excluding the military. On the face of it, it appears as if there was a massive fall in population. However, when the results are qualified it becomes obvious that the 1831 census had recorded those people living in a far larger area than the 1841 census.[4] The reason for this was that the actual boundary for the '*town*' had not been defined for the purposes of the census by 1831. In 1832 a boundary was defined for the Athlone Borough and was described as:

> All that whole circuit and extent of land and water, lying within the compass of one mile and a-half from the middle of the bridge over the Shannon, commonly called the Bridge of Athlone, directly forth in a right line every way round except the castle of Athlone and the precinct thereof.[5]

As part of establishing a borough, quoted as 4,522 acres, another survey of the town's population was carried out in 1832. The population of urban Athlone, an area of 485 acres, was included as part of this report which provided an estimate of 6,161 people, a more reasonable estimate of the number of inhabitants.[6] Using this information it appears that in the decade between 1831 and 1841 the actual population of the town

2 Murtagh, H., p.7.
3 Strean, Annesley, p.67.
4 *Addenda to the Census of Ireland for the year 1841; showing the number of houses, families and persons in the several townlands and towns of Ireland* (Dublin, 1844), pp. 116-117 (Athlone, Co. Westmeath), pp.406-407 (Athlone, Co. Roscommon).
5 *The Parliamentary Gazetteer of Ireland, Adapted to the new Poor Law, Franchise, Municipal and Ecclesiastical arrangements and compiled with special reference...* Vol.1 A-C (Dublin, 1844), p.99.
6 *Parliamentary representation: boundary reports* (Ireland), H.C. 1831-32 (519), xliii, 23, p.5.

was growing. This is confirmed by the fact that the area used in 1841 was less than that of the boundary report. Subsequent to the 1832 report the actual acreage of Athlone for the purposes of the 1841, 1851 and 1861 census was set at 440 acres. This reappraisal of the area of Athlone led to a situation where a far more accurate figure for the population of the urban area was reached (*Fig. 1*).

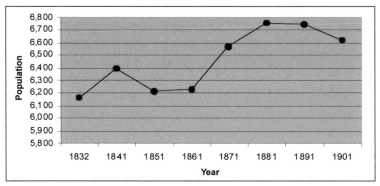

FIG.1: ATHLONE'S DEMOGRAPHIC HISTORY 1832-1901

As to the class of people who were living in and around Athlone in 1841, previous to the Famine, information received by the commissioners brought them to the following conclusions:

> It was ascertained that Athlone and its neighbourhood are much resorted to by a numerous class of small attuitants, pensioners, etc. who have been attracted by certain local advantages afforded by that part of the country.[7]

The high number of both small landholders and elderly people living around the town meant that substantial losses were certain to materialise during the Famine, losses that are confirmed by the census for 1851.

Unfortunately, the census of that year actually proves quite problematic when one attempts to find the figure for Athlone's population. The total returns quoted exclude all those in the garrison, (for which no figure was given) the workhouse, 1,766 (705 males and 1,061 females) and Bridewell, four. What must be remembered is that the town was split between two counties and two provinces, which undoubtedly caused some confusion when the statistics were being compiled. Interestingly, the actual census data from the two reports, which dealt with Athlone, those for Leinster and Connacht, presents two possible figures for the total returns – 6,218 or 6,207.[8] However,

7 *Report of the Commissioners appointed to take The Census of Ireland for the year 1841* (Dublin, 1843), p.xix.
8 *Census of Ireland for the year 1851, part 1; showing the Area, Population and Number of Houses by Townlands and Electoral Divisions* (Dublin, 1852), pp. 260, 184.

when one adds up the totals from these reports for each side of the town a figure of 6,214 is arrived at. Perhaps even more interestingly a figure of 6,199 for the entire town can be arrived at by taking the figures quoted in the *Census of Ireland for the Year 1851, Part VI – General Report*, published after the original census reports, for each side of the town and adding them together. Incidentally, the original census reports also differ from the later general report on the number of people in Athlone, Co. Roscommon; the earlier report cites it as 2,701 and the latter as 2,686, a difference of fifteen.[9] So in fact the population of Athlone could reasonably be estimated as being within a range of 6,199 to 6,218 for 1851.

One thing that is certain is that the figure, whatever it was, is less than that of 1841. While the obvious reason for this population decline was of course the effect that the Famine of 1845-1851 had on the local inhabitants, one must also bear in mind that many people actually entered the town in search of work during the Famine when the Shannon navigation works were underway. This may have actually bolstered the numbers that were included in the census, hiding a greater decline in the local population. The confusion over the actual figures does not obscure the overall demographic trends too much. However, the decline continued into the 1860s.

The census material for 1861 quotes a figure of 5,902 people in the town excluding some 323 people in the workhouse and two others in the Bridewell; again the garrison, numbering 825 persons, is not included in the totals. The slight population rise reflected by the census returns can be accounted for by a number of factors. The decade 1851 to 1861 has been generally accepted as being one of moderate agricultural growth in Ireland.[10] The improved level of economic security when spread out over the entire decade may have led people to defer emigrating from the town and as well as this the agricultural upturn would have ensured a better food supply, lowering death rates.[11]

The population of Athlone by the year 1871 was 6,565. However, in a departure from previous form this figure *does* include those who were in the workhouse, 325 and in the garrison, 618.[12] What one has to bear in mind is that the acreage used in the census for 1871 was almost two-

9   *Census 1851, part 1, p.184, Census of Ireland for the Year 1851, Part VI – General Report* (Dublin, 1853), p.584.
10 Cullen, Louis M., *An Economic History of Ireland since 1660* (London, 1972), p.137.
11 *Census of Ireland for the Year 1861, Part V – General Report* (Dublin, 1864), pp.100-101 (Athlone, Co.Westmeath), pp.420-421 (Athlone, Co.Roscommon).
12 *Census of Ireland 1871, Part 1 – Area, houses and population: also the, civil condition, occupations, birthplaces, religion and education of the people, Vol. 1, Leinster* (Dublin, 1873), p.901, *Census of Ireland 1871, Part 1 – Area, houses and population: also the, civil condition, occupations, birthplaces, religion and education of the people, Vol. 4, Connaught* (Dublin, 1873), p.473.

and-a-half-times that of the previous three census returns, standing at 1,099 acres. Taking this into account what is obvious from the figures is that the town was certainly seeing a declining population, most probably due to emigration. The methods and criteria under which the census returns were compiled require quite a lot of qualification when it comes to assessing trends and an attempt has been made to do this in the case of Athlone. *Table. 1* shows the town's total population including (*Row A*), and excluding (*Row B*), all inmates, soldiers, etc. for the years 1851 to 1901 in an attempt to make the trends and changes in demographics clearer.[13]

Year	1841	1851	1861	1871	1881	1891	1901
Acreage	440	440	440	1,099	1,129	1,129	1,198
A) Population incl. of inmates, etc.	----	----	7,672	6,565	6,755	6,742	6,617
B) Population excl. of inmates, etc.	6,393	6,209*	5,902	5,622	5,308	5,184	5,717[†]

TABLE 1: POPULATION NUMBERS 1841-1901

* An average of the range 6,199 and 6,218.

† Summerhill Industrial School, which was noted in the two previous census returns, and still in operation in 1901, was not noted as included.

In 1881 the population figure quoted in the census was 6,755 and the acreage of the town was estimated at 1,129 acres. Again this figure is inclusive of inmates of the workhouse, 310, the members of the garrison, 1,032 and, for the first time, those attending Summerhill Industrial School, 105.[14] The figure, again when viewed without these three statistics (*Table. 1*) shows a further decline in the town's population. The bad harvest of 1879 and 1880 caused considerable hardship around Athlone at the time, accounting for a rise of roughly 1,176 deaths in the Athlone Barony for 1881 compared with 1871.[15] Also one must bear in mind that the area used to define the town had grown by thirty acres for the 1881 census, highlighting the fact that the decline in the local population was even greater than it first appears.[16]

In 1891 there was an overall decrease in the population of Athlone, with the numbers of people living within the town boundaries falling to 6,742. At the time of this census the numbers in the workhouse were

13 *Census 1871, Vol. 1*, p.866, *Census 1871, Vol. 4*, p.426.
14 *Census of Ireland 1881, Part 1 – Area, houses and population: also the, civil condition, occupations, birthplaces, religion and education of the people, Vol. 1, Leinster* (Dublin, 1881), p.901, *Census of Ireland 1881, Part 1 – Area, houses and population: also the, civil condition, occupations, birthplaces, religion and education of the people, Vol. 4, Connaught* (Dublin, 1882), p.473.
15 *Census 1881, Vol. 1*, p.901.
16 *Census 1881, Vol. 1*, p.866, *Census 1881, Vol. 4*, p.426.

285, in the garrison 1,076, and Summerhill Industrial School had 197 people in total.[17] While a further decline in the population of the town is again apparent, though the trend was certainly slowing considerably; the decline between 1881 and 1891 was roughly half that over the previous two intercensal periods (*Table. 1*). This time the acreage used is the same as that for the 1881 census, making the decline far easier to compare.[18]

By the year 1901 the population of Athlone stood at 6,617, down once more on the previous census. The figures used for 1901 again include the inmates of the workhouse, 258 and those men and their families stationed at the garrison, 642; though still in existence Summerhill Industrial School was not treated separately as before.[19] The fall in numbers can be accounted for by the fall in those stationed at the garrison, down 434, fewer inmates at the workhouse, down twenty-seven, and the possible exclusion of the industrial school. This would actually mean that the town's basic resident population actually grew by almost 550 in the decade from 1891 to 1901.[20] One contributing factor to this rise was that the town boundaries were expanded yet again to 1,198 acres in total. As well as this the trend of declining numbers that was certainly slowing by 1891 may have slowed even further, highlighting a change in fortune for the town and its inhabitants.

ATHLONE, THE GROWTH OF TWO TOWNS

Athlone's development has often been seen as occurring at different rates on each side of the Shannon. The east side had for centuries previous to the Victorian era been viewed as the more affluent and attractive side of the town, with the west invariably seen as less developed and less modern. Up to 1901 Athlone was split between two counties and two provinces meaning that a larger number of census returns had to be consulted to ascertain the town's complete demographic history. This split means that in fact Athlone has perhaps a more detailed census history than many towns in Ireland, a history that can be used to assess development more accurately on a local level. In 1901 the amalgamation of the town placed it wholly in Leinster though the two wards into which it had been split were still extant and equated

17 *Census of Ireland 1891, Part 1 – Area, houses and population: also the, civil condition, occupations, birthplaces, religion and education of the people, Vol. 1, Leinster* (Dublin, 1891), p.901, *Census of Ireland 1891, Part 1 – Area, houses and population: also the, civil condition, occupations, birthplaces, religion and education of the people, Vol. 4, Connaught* (Dublin, 1891), p.473.
18 *Census 1891, Vol. 1*, p.866, *Census 1891, Vol. 4*, p.426.
19 *Census of Ireland 1901, Part 1 – Area, houses and population: also the, civil condition, occupations, birthplaces, religion and education of the people, Vol. 1, Leinster* (Dublin, 1901), p.51.
20 *Census 1901*, p.2.

to, in the case of St. Mary's ward, Athlone, Co. Westmeath and in the case of St. Peter's, Athlone, Co. Roscommon.

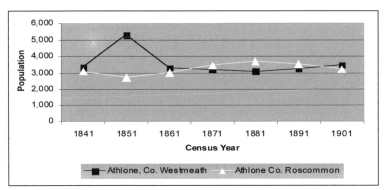

FIG.2: POPULATION LEVELS OF BOTH SIDES OF ATHLONE INCLUDING
ALL SOLDIERS AND INMATES

Fig.2 above illustrates the changing demographics on both sides of the river in Athlone using the figures quoted in the census returns. The differences between the inclusion and exclusion of the garrison are qualified throughout the text as well as in another graph (*Fig.3* below).

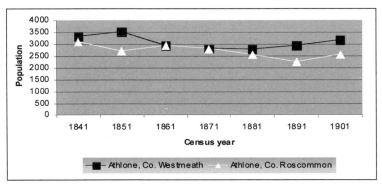

FIG.3: POPULATIONS EXCLUDING THE MILITARY AND INMATES OF THE
WORKHOUSE, BRIDEWELL AND SUMMERHILL INDUSTRIAL SCHOOL

In 1841 the Westmeath side of Athlone had 250 more people living there than on the Roscommon side of the town. Neither the workhouse nor the garrison was included in these figures. The acreage of each portion of the town was also different from the other, with *Fig.4*, showing the changes over the decades. The Roscommon side constituted 198 acres in 1841, some fifty-six less than the Westmeath side of the town and this would certainly help to account for the sizeable difference in population, the exclusion of the garrison bringing the acreage down.[21]

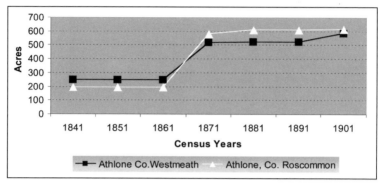

FIG.4: ACREAGE USED FOR CENSUS RETURNS ON BOTH SIDES OF
THE RIVER

By 1851 there was again a definite difference between the two sides of the town. The Westmeath side saw a small growth in numbers of almost 200, whilst the Roscommon side saw a fall of almost 400 people. Both the garrison and workhouse were excluded from these figures. One conclusion that could be drawn from this was that the Famine had a far greater effect on the Roscommon side of the town. The fact that the acreage used for the census remained the same makes the comparison far easier and conclusions drawn far more likely. Again, as can be seen from the total town figures, the differences in figures provided for the census in 1851 complicate matters (in the case of the Roscommon side of the town two figures are quoted, 2,701 and 2,686) though the trends are still easily discernible.

The census returns for 1861 are interesting, for they show a virtual parity in numbers on both sides of the river. The better fortunes of the decade must have assisted the Roscommon side in gaining some extra residents, for the population stood at 2,952, actually just two people more than the Leinster side, though neither the army on the Roscommon side nor the 323 inmates of the workhouse on the Westmeath side were included in these figures. The number of houses had grown on the west side of the river almost to pre-famine levels and whilst the east side may have had more houses, fewer people lived in them. The acreage for both sides of the town for the 1861 census remained the same as in the previous two.[22]

21 *Addenda 1841*, pp. 116–117 (Athlone, Co.Westmeath), pp.406–407 (Athlone, Co.Roscommon).
22 *Census 1861, Report*, pp.100–101 (Athlone, Co.Westmeath), pp.420–421 (Athlone, Co.Roscommon).

By 1871, with the inclusion of the army and workhouse in the total figures, an increase in the populations of both sides of the town and their acreage was recorded. The Roscommon side grew to be sixty-three acres larger than the Westmeath side, measuring 581 acres. The fact that there were only 325 people in the workhouse but 618 in the garrison helped give the Connacht side a numerical superiority of 291 over the Leinster side, its total population comprising 3,428 persons. Also with the inclusion of the garrison the number of houses on the west side of the town had for the first time exceeded that on the east side.[23] The inclusion of the army in the figures only serves to disguise a decline in the population of the Roscommon side of the town as evidenced in *Fig.3*.

By 1881 another slight increase in acreage saw the Roscommon side of the town grow slightly larger again than the Westmeath side. The fact that the Land War was still being waged in 1881 meant that the garrison was very large in that year, numbering more than 1,000. This, coupled with over 100 people in the Summerhill Industrial School and the fall in numbers in the workhouse on the Leinster side of the town, meant that the Roscommon side had a total of 611 more people living there than on the opposite side of the river, in total 3,683 people.[24] Again referencing *Fig.3* it is obvious that the decline in the population of the west side of Athlone was continuing with an actual drop of almost 300 people. The Westmeath side of the town appeared to be holding its own, with a far smaller drop in numbers, just fifty people fewer than in the previous census.

By the last decade of the 19th century a trend towards greater growth on the Westmeath side of the town can be seen. Even though the garrison and Summerhill had slightly more people in 1891 than in 1881, the population difference, bearing in mind no change in area, was far less, standing at just 262 in favour of the west side of Athlone.[25] *Fig.3* shows that indeed the Westmeath side of the town was starting to grow in its population, almost up 200 on the 1881 figure, whereas the Roscommon side was witnessing a decline. This time a fall of over 300 people was recorded.

In 1901 the acreage again changed with the Roscommon side of the town still having a slightly greater area than the Westmeath side. The numbers stationed at the garrison had fallen considerably, almost 500 down on the 1891 figure. The numbers of people on the Leinster side

23 *Census 1871, Vol. 1*, p.866, *Census 1871, Vol.4*, p.426.
24 *Census 1881, Vol. 1*, p.866, *Census 1881, Vol.4*, p.426.
25 *Census 1891, Vol. 1*, p.901, *Census 1891, Vol.4*, p.473.

of the town outnumbered those on the opposite side by a margin of 225. However, the growth in the population was now being mirrored on the west of the town which gained over 300 people since 1891, though one must remember that its size had increased by sixty-six acres. Indeed, the growth on the east of the town had actually slowed, even taking increased acreage into account, to record a gain of just over 200 people. The economic growth of the previous decade appeared to have had a positive effect on both sides of the town. Most remarkable was the growth on the Roscommon side of Athlone, which showed that a forty-year trend of decline had been reversed, perhaps heralding a positive change in fortunes for that side of the river.

Taking the town either as a whole or in two separate parts, there is no doubt that overall, once the statistics are qualified, the Victorian era was one of population decline in Athlone. The early 19th century before the Famine had been one of great population growth in the town; the local farms were productive enough to allow this growth to occur and support the new citizens. Also there was the national trend, reflected at local level, of people marrying at a young age, having more children with a consequent rise in population.

The census figures for 1841, after the urban boundary had been set, show, in comparison with the 1832 boundary survey figures, a population that was still experiencing a high rate of growth. The census of 1851, the first post-Famine census, shows the effect that the humanitarian disaster had on the local inhabitants. Overall the town's population fell by around 200 people with the losses all on the Roscommon side of the town – the Westmeath side actually saw a marginal rise in numbers. The Famine more than anything else initiated a trend of population decline across the nation, though locally this was not readily apparent. Whilst in Athlone the population figures appeared to show growth, the huge changes in the area of the town masked the reality of the situation. The presence of the garrison in the town also obscured what was actually happening, especially on the Roscommon side. Again, qualification of these numbers and those in the workhouse assist in painting a more realistic picture of the town's demographic history throughout the period.

The effects of the Famine reversed a trend of population growth and precipitated great decline for most of the Victorian era in the town. It was only when some semblance of economic growth and stability came to Athlone in the form of new industries and better social conditions that the town again began to grow. By 1901 Athlone appears to have reversed the trend of decline which was already slowing by 1891.

Though the numbers living there, exclusive of those in the garrison, were still almost 1,000 less than they were in 1841, even with the far larger area, a trend of population growth had begun, which continued into the 20th century.

DOMESTIC HOUSING

The economic prosperity of a nation's people can often be well represented in the quality of their dwellings. Additionally, the condition of houses in towns is indicative of differences in prosperity between the social classes. In this section the changes in the housing stock of Athlone during the Victorian era is analysed with a view to providing further evidence on the development of the town. As related in the preceding chapter, prior to the start of the Victorian era it appears from Sherrard's Survey that the Westmeath side of the town was by far the more prosperous; better quality houses were to be found there. For the purposes of this section, census statistics, Griffith's Valuation and contemporary observations of houses and buildings on both sides of the town will be used in an attempt to map the changes that took place and assess if progress was made.

Prior to the Victorian era in 1831 the figures that dealt with houses in Ireland grouped them under just three headings; 'Inhabited', 'Uninhabited' and 'Building'. In relation to Athlone, as with the population statistics, the 1831 census covered a far larger area, 4,522 acres, than any subsequent one and as such can only be used to show very general trends. Isaac Weld, the statistician, who visited the town in 1832, stated that the type of construction in the town exhibited: '...a *total lack of symmetry...whether in reference to the style of the houses or the alignment of the streets, and a mixture of poor and indifferent houses with those of better description.'* He went even further, saying that he believed the only houses that approached a reasonable construction and quality were those on the Leinster side of the town.[26] The houses on the Connacht side were '*cabins of the meanest description*' whose occupants '*gave indication of the lowest state of civilisation*'.[27] Indeed, the poor construction of the town in general led the travel writer H. D. Inglis to state in 1834: '*Athlone is a remarkably ugly town. So deficient is it in good streets that after I had walked over the whole town, I still imagined I had seen only the suburbs.*'[28] John O'Donovan of the Ordinance Survey went further to state, in 1837, that '*Athlone is the ugliest town in Europe.*'[29] These powerfully

26 Weld, Isaac, *Statistical survey of the County of Roscommon.* (Dublin, 1832), p.547.
27 Ibid., p.548.
28 Inglis, H. D., *A Journey Throughout Ireland during the Spring, Summer and Autumn of 1834* (London, 1834), p.337.
29 O'Donovan, John, *Ordinance Survey Letters from Longford*, 27th May 1837, N.L.I.

descriptive comments appear to back up Sherrard's late 18th century survey findings as well as Rev. Strean's observations; the Connacht side of the town was of an inferior build to the Leinster side. Also in 1837, when a more reasonable area had been defined, Lewis' survey of the town found that the roofs of houses were roughly evenly split between slate and thatch at 546 and 481 respectively, giving a figure of 1,027 houses in the town.[30] Slating was becoming more common, and thatching became indicative of a poorer dwelling. Generally, opinions of Athlone's construction and form during the 1830s were very negative – another visitor to the town in 1838 called it *'irregularly built'* and *'confused'*.[31]

HOUSING STOCK 1841-51

By the time of the census of 1841 the urban boundary had been fixed, and far more useful information was available as to the class of houses in Ireland. They were then rated under four main headings, '1st Class', '2nd Class', '3rd Class' and '4th Class'. The system that the census commissioners had drawn up to rate the quality of the houses (the same system was used throughout the 19th century except for a small departure in 1871) was described thus:

> We adopted four classes, and the result was, that in the lowest, or fourth class, were comprised all mud cabins having only one room – in the third, a better description of cottage, still built of mud, but varying from 2 to 4 rooms and windows – in the second, a good farm house, or in towns a house in a small street, having from 5 to 9 rooms and windows – and in the first, all houses of a better description than the preceding classes.[32]

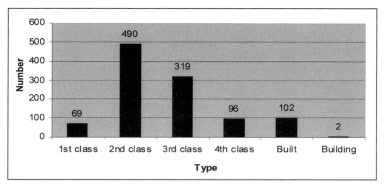

FIG.5: HOUSE TYPE FOR ATHLONE AS RELATED IN THE 1841 CENSUS

30 *Athlone Civic Week 1945* (Athlone, 1945), p.23.
31 Ritchie, Leitch, *Ireland Picturesque and Romantic*, (London, 1838), p.179.
32 *Report 1841*, p.14.

From looking at *Fig.5* (this graph, along with those for 1851 and 1861 shows a total for Athlone town created by adding the returns from both sides of the town together) one can see a low number of 1st class houses, the small majority of which, thirty-six, were located on the Leinster side of the town. The most numerous class of abode, the 2nd class house, was in greater numbers on the Connacht side of the town where 247 had been constructed. The vast majority of 3rd class houses, some 202, were noted east of the Shannon and most 4th class houses were also found there with seventy-one examples recorded. So on the face of it there were almost three times more mud cabins on the east of the town, the supposedly prosperous side, which also had fewer 2nd class houses than the Roscommon side. From looking at this information one could say that by 1841 the trend of poorer habitation on the west bank of the river had actually been reversed. However, what one has to remember is that the population on the Roscommon side of the town was only 247 people less that the Westmeath side but that 130 fewer houses existed there. What this meant was that whilst the houses may have been of a slightly better description, the accommodation they afforded was almost certainly inferior: there were roughly 6.1 people to a house on the east side but almost 7.3 people to a house on the Roscommon side. In total Athlone in 1841 had 974 houses within its boundaries, 552 on the east side and 422 on the west side.[33] These figures exclude the houses that were uninhabited.

By the time of the 1851 census report a number of changes had occurred in the town. Obviously the most important was the Great Famine of 1845–1851. Just before this, Mr. and Mrs. S.C. Hall, who visited the town in 1843, observed that on the west side of the town: '...*the houses run up a hill; they are miserable and dirty.*' The Leinster side of the town they described as '*but a degree better*'; Athlone's dwellings just prior to the Famine were obviously not to their liking.[34]

Another visitor to the town during the Famine, one William Henry Smith, described it as: '...*a wretched looking, irregular, squalid, dirty place, with dingy shops, murky even by daylight and unlit at night.*'[35] What is apparent from *Fig.6* is that the total number of inhabited houses was down by sixty-one from 974 to 913. This can be partially accounted for by the total disappearance of 4th class houses in the town. As a report from the Statistical and Social Inquiry Society of Ireland stated: '*The*

33 *Addenda to the Census of Ireland for the year 1841; showing the number of houses, families and persons in the several townlands and towns of Ireland* (Dublin, 1844), pp. 116-117 (Athlone, Co.Westmeath), pp.406-407 (Athlone, Co.Roscommon).
34 Hall, Mr. & Mrs. S. C., *Ireland: Its Scenery, Character, &c.*, Vol. III (London, 1843), p.325.
35 O'Brien, Brendan, "Some Aspects of Municipal Government in Athlone", in Keaney, M. & O'Brien, G., *Athlone - Bridging the Centuries* (Mullingar, 1991), p.83.

health of our poorer people is lowered in greatest degree by wretchedness of habitation.[36] Indeed, it would have been necessary to destroy the lowest level of housing in the town to help prevent the spread of diseases that would have festered in the unsanitary conditions of mud cabins. Perhaps if the Halls are to be believed some of the poor habitation from 1843 may have been destroyed by the time of the 1851 census, thus leading to an overall improvement in the housing stock of Athlone.

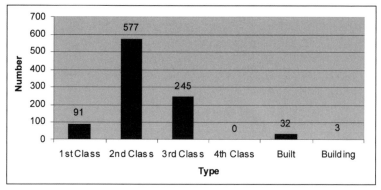

FIG.6: HOUSE TYPE AS RELATED BY THE 1851 CENSUS

There are numerous reports from the Famine period that detail the destruction of houses by fire or demolition and most of the reports, such as one from 17th March 1847, contain observations such as: *'The value of the damage is small owing to the poor quality of the houses.'*[37] The census information also relates that the number of inhabited houses on the Connacht side of Athlone had fallen from 422 in 1841 to 375 in 1851, when during the same period the other side of the town had lost just thirty-three houses, leaving a total of 538. From this it can be assumed that the Roscommon side of the town suffered the greatest house clearances during the Famine. If both sides of Athlone are taken separately the statistics show the Connacht side actually still had a higher proportion of the 1st and 2nd Class houses. 1st Class houses on the Roscommon side of the town were just over 10% of the total there but they accounted for just over 9% of all houses on the Westmeath side. Athlone, Co. Roscommon had a large number of 2nd class houses, 265, which accounted for over 70% of all the inhabited houses on that side of the town. The level of accommodation was still poorer on the Roscommon side with 7.2 people to a house. However, the

36 Wiley, Miriam M., "Housing, Health and Social Welfare", in Kennedy, Kieran A., *From Famine to Feast – Economic and Social Change in Ireland 1847-1997* (Dublin, 1998), p.59.
37 *The Freeman's Journal*, 17 March 1847.

accommodation on the opposite side of town also declined in quality, with 6.5 people to each house.

GRIFFITH'S VALUATION

The survey and *General Valuation of Rateable Property in Ireland*, better know as Griffith's Valuation (after its co-ordinator Richard Griffith) was the most accurate and comprehensive study of dwellings and property in the 19th century. Its aim was to provide the government with a reliable database of property values so that they could receive the correct amount in rate payments from the owners in each Poor Law Union. Because of Athlone's situation, part of the town being in Roscommon and the other in Westmeath, the survey had to be carried out in each of the town's parishes separately. The first completed survey was that of Athlone, Co. Westmeath (St Mary's Parish), published in 1854 with Athlone, Co. Roscommon (St. Peter's Parish) released the following year.

ST. MARY'S PARISH

This parish has traditionally been regarded as the more prosperous of the two Catholic parishes in Athlone. The information related in Griffith's Valuation does nothing to contradict this. On the Leinster side of the town there were roughly 143 immediate lessors of whom 21.6% were women, 74.8% were men, the remainder being business concerns with no single owner. Of all the properties on the Westmeath side of the town, excluding exemptions (these would include the Union Workhouse, Churches, etc.), almost 46% were worth less than £2; roughly 24% were worth less than £5; just less than 14% were valued at between £5 and £10; little over 9% between £10 and £20 and 7% were valued at £20 or more. The obvious conclusion that can be drawn is that most properties were of a low standard and because most of them were dwelling houses the valuation indicates that the majority of people in the Leinster side of town lived in poor-quality accommodation. The most valuable properties on the east bank were the Union Workhouse (£175), Eel Weir (£150) and MGWR Railway line (£79). Only 17 properties were rated at £30 or more and these included the Provincial Bank, two local hotels, an old brewery, Burgess' Department Store and the Church of Ireland parish church. The most highly-rated properties were to be found on Northgate St., Victoria Place and Church St; the main commercial streets. As already noted there were 143 lessors on the east side of the town but a far greater number of properties, roughly 700. This obviously means that some of the lessors had numerous properties that they rented out. Lord Castlemaine, most of whose land lay outside the town boundaries, owned roughly forty-one different properties on the Leinster side of town, which varied between dwellings, the Primitive Wesleyan Church, the parochial school as well as the district dispensary. Surprisingly, he owned nothing on Castlemaine St. and his total annual valuation reached only £297 15s for the east side of Athlone (including non-rateable properties i.e. those that did not have rates levied on them but were still valued).

A number of other lessors dealt mainly in the letting of dwellings, with two, Robert English and Laurence Kelly, owning an entire lane of forty properties between them, twenty each, all of which were valued under £2. The former, Robert English, owned the most properties on the east bank of the Shannon, eighty in total, (his siblings and cousins owned a further forty-eight) only twenty-six of which were worth more than £2; his total valuation was just less than £300. Other buildings he owned included the Baptist Meeting House as well a number of offices and lodgings. The quality of houses on the east side of the town was invariably poor, there were few large structures outside of the churches and workhouse and the majority of houses were rented accommodation some of which did not even have a yard to speak of.[38]

ST PETER'S PARISH

There were fewer property owners on the Connacht side, roughly 100, broken down into 75% male and 23% female. Again the balance of 2% is made up by private concerns. Of all the properties, excluding exemptions, roughly 36% were valued at less than £2; just under 20% were valued at £5 or under; almost 19% rated as worth between £5 and £10; those in the £10 to £20 bracket made up roughly 16% with the remaining group of £20 and over proportionately coming in at just under 9%. One must bear in mind that the Connacht side of the town boasted far fewer properties than the eastern side and this can help account for the proportional differences, which at first glance, would lead one to believe that the Roscommon side of town had a lot more quality properties. A good indication of the social situation of people living on the west side of the town is provided through analysing the number of lodging houses. There were 106 lodging houses in Athlone, Co. Roscommon, mostly grouped together in a ghetto-like arrangement, compared with just four on the opposite side of the river. A large number of those residing on the Roscommon side did not have

38 *General Valuation of Rateable Property in Ireland, Union of Athlone, Valuation of several tenements comprised in that portion of the above-named Union, situate in the County of Westmeath* (Dublin, 1854), pp. 89-113.

the finances to rent a house for themselves, despite the low quality and value of many of the buildings. In total there were only thirteen properties valued at more than £30, the most valuable of which included an old distillery (£90), the castle and its yard (£65), four different houses with a yard and garden (£45, £44, £42 and £40) and the Roman Catholic Chapel and yard (£38). The only concentration of valuable property on the west side of town was Main St., located beside the castle; most of the fourteen properties, generally houses with offices, were worth in excess of £15. Connacht St. also had a number of valuable buildings; it was a thriving commercial street at the time, second only to Church St. on the Leinster side. The person with the greatest number of properties was Denis Kelly (many of his properties were held by his representatives, as he did not live in the town) whose total valuation was £216. Viscount (Lord) Castlemaine had properties with an annual valuation of £73 on the west side, bringing his total to £370 15s for Athlone town. The largest single plot on the Roscommon side of Athlone was the army barracks, which covered thirty-two and a half acres and had a value of £1,220. Needless to say this massive complex severely limited the development potential of Athlone's west bank. The greatest single landowner in the town, with properties on both sides of the river, was the Incorporated Society for the Promotion of Protestant Schools in Ireland; its total valuation, including lands held in tandem with other concerns, was over £1,800.[39]

HOUSING STOCK 1861–1901

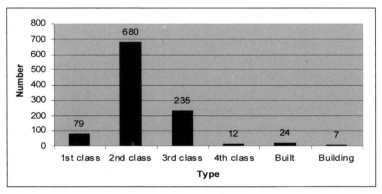

FIG.7: HOUSE TYPE AS RELATED BY THE 1861 CENSUS

For the 1861 census, *Fig. 7*, we are again using the same acreage as the

39 *General Valuation of Rateable Property in Ireland, Union of Athlone, Valuation of several tenements comprised in that portion of the above-named Union, situate in the County of Roscommon* (Dublin, 1855), pp. 26-43.

previous two census though the first thing that is apparent is that the number of inhabited houses in the town had grown to 1,007 in total – 587 on the Leinster side and 420 across the river. The number of 1st class houses had fallen along with the number of 3rd class and the number of 2nd class houses had risen, with 4th class houses again seen on the streetscape of the town. The number of 1st class houses on the west of the town fell by four to thirty-four though the east side had seen a fall of eight, from fifty-three to forty-five. Some of these houses may have fallen into the 2nd class category, which saw a rise of over fifty, to 366 in 1861. Staying with the east side of the Shannon, 3rd class houses had fallen in number and the 4th class category on the Leinster side accounted for eleven of the total twelve houses in that class.

2nd Class houses had grown considerably in number on the Roscommon side of the town, up forty-nine on the census of 1851. The number of 3rd class houses fell by just one and only one 4th class house appeared on that side of Athlone. The changes in the housing stock may be accounted for by the better economic conditions of the late 1850s, which provided some people with the opportunity to erect better quality houses and others with the money to improve existing dwellings. The fall in the number of 1st class houses may have been due to unchecked deterioration over the years.[40] As to the level of accommodation there were only five people to a house on the Leinster side of the town with still just over seven people per dwelling on the west side of the river.

After 1861 the census no longer provides statistics for each town in the county records. Instead all the houses were placed together in what were termed Civic Districts. To qualify as a Civic District a town had to have a population in excess of 2,000 people. In the case of Co. Westmeath this meant that only Athlone and Mullingar qualified. In Co. Roscommon, however, the returns included Athlone, Roscommon and Boyle. Whilst direct comparisons with previous years will not be possible, for this reason charts will not be included, some useful information can be gleaned from these statistics, especially those for 1881 and 1891.

Athlone, Co. Westmeath had 530 inhabited houses in total according to the 1871 census and the Roscommon side of the town had 545 inhabited. The increase in the number of houses on the Roscommon side can be accounted for by the inclusion of the garrison in the figures. Through analysis of the total figures for each county probable trends in

40 *Census 1861, Report*, pp.100-101 (Athlone, Co. Westmeath), pp.420-421 (Athlone, Co. Roscommon).

the housing situation of Athlone can be discerned. However, one has to bear in mind that the commissioners changed some of the criteria under which the classes were categorised for the 1871 census. Many of the houses that would have been in the 3rd class in the 1861 census were moved into the 4th class which in turn was subdivided into two groups, houses built of mud and houses built of brick or stone.[41] This change in classification certainly led to the large increase recorded in the number of the lowest class of house for 1871; the figures show that the numbers of 4th class houses grew by over 100%.[42] For this reason the returns for 1871 cannot be used to show reliable trends: the inclusion of other towns in the statistics changes some of the information quite dramatically and due to constraints of space these effects cannot be analysed in any great detail.

In Westmeath's Civic Districts for 1881 the commissioners reverted to the old pre-1871 census classifications making comparisons and therefore statistical analysis more reliable. There was a fall in the total number of inhabited houses from 1375 in 1871 to 1308 in 1881, despite an increased area. Athlone, Co. Westmeath had 522 inhabited houses in total within its boundaries. The same trend is shown for Co. Roscommon though the fall was smaller. This fall off in the number of inhabited houses may be explained by the poor harvest of 1879/80, which probably saw a number leave their homesteads; there was a large decline in population reported for Athlone in the 1881 census. Athlone, Co. Roscommon had a total of 582 inhabited houses, within the town limits.[43] The information for the Westmeath Civic District in 1881 showed a slight increase in the number of 1st class houses and 2nd class houses. The figures for 3rd and 4th class houses both fell. This fall in the two lesser house classes points towards an improvement in Athlone's east side. The Roscommon figures also showed rises in the numbers of 1st and 2nd class houses. 3rd class houses showed a slight rise though the 4th class houses saw a large fall, bearing in mind classifcation changes, from ninety-eight houses to just eleven in the entire county.[44] It does appear that overall Athlone was seeing an improvement in its housing between the years 1861 and 1881.

The figures for Westmeath in 1891 show that the numbers of 1st class houses had fallen by just two. 2nd class houses rose by over 120, accounting for more than half of all dwellings in the county. 3rd class

41 *Census of Ireland, 1881, Part II, General Report with Illustrative Maps and Diagrams, Tables and Appendix* (Dublin, 1882), p.9.
42 *Census 1871, Vol. 1*, p.866, *Census 1871, Vol. 4*, p.426.
43 *Census 1881, Vol. 1*, p.866, *Census 1881, Vol. 4*, p.426.
44 *Census 1881, Part II*, p.9.

houses accounted for just over one quarter of all houses with almost all 4th class houses gone except one. These figures show that in general the numbers of dwellings of '*a better description*' were growing steadily, though the almost static 1st class house figure shows that these dwellings were still quite exclusive. Athlone, Co. Westmeath had a total 563 inhabited houses in 1891.

A number of houses, probably 4th class, on the Leinster side of the town were in such a bad state in 1886/7 that the Town Commissioners decided to close all of them. Many dangerous hovels were located in Preaching Lane, colloquially known as 'Little Hell'.[45] A description of the area in a later edition of *The Freeman's Journal* from 1891 described the cul de sac as '*squalid*' and '*sweet smelling*'.[46] The move towards eradicating the filthiest and most dangerous dwellings came about as part of Victorian reforms regarding public health and sanitation, which are dealt with at length in a later chapter. Irishtown, also on the Leinster side, was not thought of as the most attractive part of the town either with one account describing it as '*...a long mean street of working class cottages*', with a large number of '*street urchins*' residing there.[47] The images of the town during this period are quite Dickensian and could perhaps be equated with those of Victorian Manchester or Leeds where similar streetscapes were common.

According to the Roscommon figures the number of 1st class houses grew again. Most noticeable about the figures given in the 1891 census returns is that the number of houses in the Roscommon Civic District fell dramatically. This is explained by the fall in the population of Roscommon town, 1,994 people in 1891, thus exempting it from inclusion.[48] This fact makes the rise in 1st class houses all the more surprising; the number was twenty-seven greater in 1891 than in 1881 despite the fact that Roscommon town was excluded. This meant that the Connacht side of Athlone had gained a significant number of these houses. The proportions suggest that Roscommon town was less well developed than either Athlone or Boyle, for with its exclusion the percentage of 3rd class houses fell and 4th class houses disappeared. Athlone, Co. Roscommon had a total of 489 inhabited houses in 1891.[49] It is certain then that by 1891 the west side of Athlone had no mud cabins. One of the archetypal buildings of poor rural Ireland had

45 *FJ.*, 27 Nov 1886, *FJ.*, 5 Nov 1887.
46 *FJ.*, 25 Apr 1891.
47 Langrishe, Rosabel Sara, "Athlone in the 1880s – Being extracts from the journal of Rosabel Sara Langrishe", in *Journal of the Old Athlone Society* Vol. II, No.7 (Athlone, 2004), p.183.
48 Vaughan, Fitzpatrick, p.41.
49 *Census 1891, Vol. 1*, p.866, *Census 1891, Vol. 4*, p.426.

disappeared from the streetscape, the town was modernising and urbanising.

Thom's Directory for 1891 provides more in-depth information for housing in the town as a whole, rating dwellings as to their value. It noted that there were 169 houses worth more than £12; 258 valued at between £4 and £12; 569 worth between £1 and £4 and the remaining 144 houses worth £1 or less. So out of 1140 houses some 62.5% of them were still worth less than £4, highlighting the fact that whilst there had been some improvements since Griffith's Valuation, the majority of the townspeople were still living in low quality houses.[50] However, it must be noted that the directory did not update these figures over the following ten years, thus compromising their reliability. The shops and buildings in Connacht St. on the west side of Athlone had probably not improved much over the years either, with one description stating:

> The houses and the shops, particularly on the Connaught side of the town were small and mean looking, built of grey limestone covered with mortar dashing. They had slated roofs, no pretensions to any kind of architecture, and the whole effect was of a dull greyness depressing in the extreme, especially during the winter.[51]

The author of the above went on to state that the main street on the Roscommon side of the town was one in which almost every second building was: '...*a dirty pub, where the Connaught men got roaring drunk every Saturday night, and the rest were equally dirty little grocer's shops'.*[52]

In the mid-1880s the position of the local Board of Guardians and the Town Commissioners on the provision of labourers' houses was one in which many locals had an interest – schemes had been initiated in other towns such as Sligo with much success. The authorities perhaps saw that the only way to upgrade the conditions that the labourers were faced with was to improve their accommodation themselves. Probably the vast majority of labourers would have wished to move from the houses they were living in to something more modern and comfortable. The procrastination of the board, which was to last for a number of years to come, was lambasted by one member who said of his colleagues:

> Yes there were men who wished to keep the labourer in the filth, in the mud...grovelling in the dirt, if they could, some of these labourers perhaps members of old 'dacency'. Men who have thousands of acres and

50 *Thom's Official Directory of the United Kingdom of Great Britain and Ireland* (Dublin, 1891), p.626.
51 Langrishe, Rosabel, p.178.
52 Ibid., p.179.

palaces and who wallow in riches came here today to deprive the poor labourer of half an acre of land.[53]

The year 1891 again heard mention of the provision of labourers' dwellings in the town. Athlone had a large number of very basic and unsafe dwellings and the new houses were seen as a necessity. In those cases where schemes had been successfully carried off it was considered that the Irish labourer was actually better off than his English counterpart.[54] The scheme had been discussed a number of years previously though the Town Commissioners had never arrived at a plan regarding the project. The meetings held were no more decisive than any held previously with the Commissioners still undecided by the end of the Victorian era.[55] The provision of this class of accommodation was not fully backed in Victorian Britain; some believed that it would create a state of dependency on the part of the labourer and hence be ultimately counterproductive.[56]

By 1901 the census information regarding the class of house under the heading Civic District became even less useful when attempting to chart improvements in Athlone, which, since the changing of the town boundaries in 1899, was included in its entirety in Co. Westmeath. The commissioners decided to put both 2nd and 3rd class houses together under one statistic, leaving 1st and 4th class houses separate. The total number of 1st class houses in Westmeath had grown due to the inclusion of the Roscommon side of Athlone in the figures. The 2nd and 3rd class houses made up the remainder with all but one of the 4th class houses gone from Athlone and Mullingar. The number of inhabited houses in St Mary's Ward, Westmeath, in 1901 was 480. St. Peter's had 588 inhabited houses.[57]

In 1892 the travel writer and artist Mary Banim visited Athlone and was surprisingly complimentary of the town. She believed Athlone, with its '*winding streets*', to be a '*pretty country town*'.[58] The new river bridge had led to modern looking shops opening at its east end, though the ancient nature of the town in this area was not believed to have been lost.[59] Some of the houses just off the main street were described as being '*old, with new faces.*'[60] Church St., the main thoroughfare on the

53 *FJ.*, 22 May 1886.
54 Cullen, Louis M, p.156.
55 *FJ.*, 27 Mar 1886, *FJ.*, 14 Feb 1891, *Athlone Times*, 7 Dec 1901.
56 Daunton, Martin, "Society and Economic life", in Matthew, Colin, *Short Oxford History of the British Isles – The Nineteenth Century* (Oxford, 2000), p.58.
57 *Census 1901, Vol. 1*, p.2.
58 Banim, Mary, *Here and There Through Ireland* (Dublin, 1892), p.186.
59 Ibid., p.187.
60 Ibid., p.188.

Leinster side, was described as '*old and new, quaint and fresh, at the same time,*' with its uneven roofs and attractive chimneys.[61] Some of the houses of the lower classes on the Leinster side of the town were described as being '*…as neat as* [those of] *their higher neighbours and with those delightful institutions of earlier days – half doors.*'[62]

The Connacht side of the town had undergone a number of changes, with some houses taken down to widen the street around the castle.[63] The thoroughfares were noted as being laid out in a maze-like fashion, the shops and houses were older than those on the other side of the town, but '*pretty*' nonetheless.[64] The people were the greatest attraction of this side of the town, where though '*…many of its narrow streets are poor indeed*' they were still genuinely kind, intelligent and mannerly.[65]

Attempting to trace the progress of the housing situation in Athlone during the Victorian period is not an easy task. The changing nature of the information noted by the census commissioners, along with the changes in boundaries and the presentation of information, means that after 1861 only general comments can be made on the quality of housing in Athlone. The first three censuses showed improvements in the classes of houses in the town. All the figures for 1st and 2nd class houses increased, with the exception of the 1861's 1st class total, and all the totals for 3rd and 4th class houses decreased, as should have occurred if the town and its citizens were trying to improve and advance. These returns along with Griffith's Valuation show that the standard of accommodation was lower on the Roscommon side of Athlone and the latter also showed that there were very few property owners in the town; most inhabitants rented.

Griffith's Valuation reveals more useful information about the housing situation in Athlone in the mid-1850s. Most of the properties were of a poor standard; almost 500 were worth less than £2 from a total of just over 1,200. No one person owned the vast majority of land on both sides of the town. Athlone had almost 250 lessors, of which 15 controlled the majority of the property in the town, excluding the army and the Incorporated Society for the Promotion of Protestant Schools in Ireland. The number of lodgers on the west of the town indicates that those living there had less money than their Leinster counterparts, lending credence to the view that the Roscommon side of the town was the poorer part of Athlone.

61 Ibid., p.190.
62 Ibid., p.200.
63 Ibid., p.245.
64 Ibid., p.246.
65 Ibid., p.248.

The remaining four census show that 4th class houses began to disappear from the towns in both Roscommon and Westmeath with, by 1891, only one 4th class house noted in the four towns that were surveyed. Conceivably, Athlone had none in that year. In general the houses were still seen to be improving with 3rd class houses dwindling in numbers and the 1st and 2nd classes growing throughout the period. All of this information suggests that the economic situation of the townspeople was improving slowly, and they could afford to build new houses and upgrade existing structures. The growth of industry in the town, such as the Athlone Woollen Mills and the Athlone Saw Mills (see chapter four) towards the end of the Victorian era provided many people with a secure job and hence with a means to pay for a better quality home. The total eradication of 4th class houses is perhaps the most powerful indicator that progress was being made. The mud or turf huts that had formerly been quite numerous, and necessary to house the poorest of the poor, were no longer in evidence in the town by the end of the Victorian period. This drive towards improvement in living conditions was to be adopted during the 20th century. Schemes such as the Slum Clearances of the 1930s and even the development of high-rise flat complexes more recently illustrate the understanding that for people to prosper they need good quality accommodation in which to raise their families.

CHAPTER 3

Poverty, hunger and deprivation
1830-1851

Athlone's inhabitants, like those in many other towns in 19th century Ireland, had to deal with protracted periods of severe hardship and poverty. At no time was this more obvious than during the Great Famine of 1845-51. However, even before this Ireland was already experiencing severe bouts of penury and deprivation. Gustave de Beaumont, a well-travelled writer, had this to say of the country in 1839:

> I have seen the Indian in his forests and the negro in his irons, and I believed, in pitying their plight, that I saw the lowest ebb of human misery; but I did not then know the degree of poverty to be found in Ireland.[1]

ATHLONE BEFORE THE FAMINE

In Athlone there is evidence of relative good fortune in the decades before the Famine. Rev. Annesley Strean noted that on the west side of the river potatoes and oatmeal were the staples of the diet and that they were in good supply. This diet led to a situation where:

> ...the children are healthy and vigorous, the adults of all ages and both sexes, who seldom use any other species of food, are robust, able-bodied and adequate to every kind of bodily labour and corporeal exertion.[2]

However, it appears that Strean's assessment of food availability, and people's general health, was not indicative of the day-to-day situation in the early 19th century in the town. There were certainly times when the local markets were '...*well supplied with all sorts of provisions, beef, butter, veal, lamb, kid, fowl, fish, and pork, [and] various kinds of vegetables...*' though these prosperous markets must have been infrequent.[3] There is far more

---

1 O'Donoghue, Bernard, *Oxford Irish Quotations* (Oxford, 1999), p.218.
2 Strean, Annesley, p.68.
3 Ibid., p.95.

information detailing poverty than prosperity. As far back as 1817 the levels of food available to the poorest in the town were exceptionally low. Many who had no access to food rioted, ransacking stores and blocking the export of potatoes via the canal system at Athlone.[4] Five years later, a fund was established to cope with the numbers of people applying for assistance.[5] The disease Typhus gripped the town in 1823, brought in by '...*those vagrants and strollers in harvest time exhibiting in their persons the most complicated filth and wretchedness*': it left over 100 dead.[6] An advertisement for a dramatic troupe visiting the town in 1834 mentioned how the performances were intended '...*to help alleviate the distress...they deeply lament is at present too prevalent in this part of the country*'.[7] Another news report dealing with the state of the town after a severe storm in 1839 tells of the base conditions in which some of the townspeople in Connaught St. were forced to reside; '...*every house being more or less deprived of its slating; and for a few dilapidated houses there occupied by wretched beings who were scarcely above the rank of pauper*.'[8] This storm, the major natural disaster of the 19th century in Ireland, was called 'The Big Wind' of 1839. In Athlone the wind caused a fire to spread, leading to over 100 houses burning. A serious humanitarian problem was in the offing:

> The storm...has perhaps, in no other part of Ireland been more severely felt or more destructive to life and property than in this neighbourhood. The town bears the most singular appearance, vast numbers of the houses having been totally unroofed...The artillery barracks and the large storehouses are generally damaged...and hardly a pane of glass remains. The two distilleries suffered severely to the extent of many hundred pounds. The malt house (Mr. Boswell's) was thrown down; houses of worship are in a very sorry plight; and the national school is in a fair way to promise an extension of the school holidays. A large range of cottages, at either extremity of the town took fire and...was (sic) totally consumed, and the unfortunate inmates had hardly time to save the clothes, which cover them. It is a melancholy sight to see the poor people still hovering round the wreck of their former dwellings, trying to recover from the pile something of little property. The few cabins that braved the storm are crowded with the inmates of those destroyed – who but for the charity of one or two gentlemen, would actually die from want.[9]

4   *F.J.*, 28 Feb 1817.
5   *Faulkner's Dublin Journal*, 10 June 1822.
6   *F.D.J.*, 10 Sep 1823, *F.D.J.*, 15 Sep 1823.
7   *The Athlone Sentinel*, 19 Nov 1834.
8   *F.J.*, 14 Jan 1839.
9   *"Kerry Evening Post"*, in Carr, Peter, *The Night of the Big Wind* (Belfast, 1993), p.74.

Numerous other reports exist which mention the poor conditions many found themselves faced with before the onset of famine in 1845, though the scale of that humanitarian disaster was to be far greater than anything previously encountered.[10] Apparently any problems concerning deprivation in Athlone were exacerbated by its geographical location when it came to attracting vagrants and mendicants:

> Athlone being the great pass between Leinster and Connaught, brings thither many settlers of that description, and a number of soldiers' wives (and their children), who are left by their husbands when ordered on foreign service, as well as the widows…serve to render that class of the community still more numerous.[11]

Until the early 1830s the government provided for the most destitute poor in Britain through administering outdoor relief. However, the massive rise in population during the 19th century had precipitated a crisis in the system, which could no longer cope with the numbers of applicants with which it was faced. To deal with the growing problem, outdoor relief was replaced in Britain by the workhouse system under the Poor Law Amendment Act 1834.[12] This system was designed in such a way that only the most desperately needy would even consider entering an institution set up under its provisions. The level of comfort to be experienced by an 'inmate' was to be of a standard so basic that all who entered would be eager to leave if conditions outside improved even marginally.[13] The system was also designed to deter families from entering by separating parents and children upon entry. The policies employed at workhouses were intended to dissuade people from becoming dependent on government relief and to ensure that costs were as low as possible.

As the 1830s progressed it became clear that the poor in Ireland needed some form of help from the government to survive. First the application of the Poor Law system in Ireland was mooted, though this was rejected by the Whately Commission, which found that the level of destitution was too high and that the system would have been destroyed under the pressure of numbers.[14] The same commission advocated a number of different initiatives including an agricultural loan fund, assisted emigration and public works schemes as an alternative to the

10 Weld, Isaac, p.548, Moran, Malachy, *The Moran Manuscripts*, National Library of Ireland, MSS. 1543, pp.337-401, *FJ.*, 11 Jan 1839, *FJ.*, 14 Jan 1839, Venedy, Herr J., *Ireland and the Irish During the Repeal Year, 1843* (Dublin, 1844), p.54, *Gazetteer*, pp.96-99.
11 Strean, Annesley, p.78.
12 O'Tuathaigh, Gearoid, *Ireland before the Famine 1798 – 1848* (Dublin, 1990), p.111.
13 Ibid., p.111.
14 Ibid., p.112.

Poor Law. However, just about all of the suggestions were ignored by the government in London who instead, after a peculiarly short inquiry by a man named George Nicholls recommended it, imposed the Poor Law system on Ireland.[15] The Poor Law (Ireland) Act was passed in 1838 and under its provisions a network of Poor Law Unions was created, each of which was to have a union workhouse.

In 1839, the Athlone Poor Law Union was created. The union was quite vast; it was comprised of almost 200,000 acres and was located in both Co. Roscommon and Co. Westmeath.[16] The union workhouse was built in 1841 at a total cost of £8,801. Tenders for staffing went out in April of that year. The positions to be filled were for a doctor, master, matron and porter.[17] It was originally constructed to accommodate 900 paupers, the first of whom entered on the 22nd November 1841.[18] By Christmas the workhouse accommodated roughly 100 people, many of whom complained about rough treatment and bad food soon after they entered.[19] The history of Athlone workhouse is one dogged by cases of malpractice, abuse, fraud and cold incompetence – all of which are covered in more detail in an existing publication.[20] The situation in Athlone must have been considered more urgent than that of Mullingar, which did not have a workhouse constructed in the town until thirteen months later when it was opened in December 1842.[21]

The establishment of the Poor Law system was part of the government's plan to tackle the growing poverty in Ireland. Economically the country was heavily reliant on farming; in 1841 statistics tell that less than 14% of the population lived in towns of 2,000 or more with 75% of all occupied males working in agriculture.[22] Any agricultural depression and the resultant economic fallout would have caused many farm labourers to consider their options. Many who believed that the trend towards penury was inexorable decided that their best course of action was to emigrate. Nationally, emigration had for some time been a feature of Irish society; large numbers of people had been leaving the country prior to the 1840s. Most historians would agree that the Famine merely '...*solidified an already strong emigrant tradition.*'[23] Many younger Irish men and women must have been

15 O'Connor, John, *The Workhouses of Ireland – The fate of Ireland's poor* (Dublin, 1995), pp. 58-76.
16 *Gazetteer*, p. 98.
17 *A.S.*, 9 Apr 1841.
18 O'Brien, Brendan, *Athlone Workhouse and The Famine* (Athlone, 1995), p.12.
19 Ibid., p.12.
20 O'Brien, *Workhouse*.
21 O'Connor, John, p.262.
22 Hoppen, K. Theodore, *Ireland Since 1800 – Conflict and Conformity* 2nd ed. (London, 1999), p.36.
23 Guinnane, Timothy W., "The Vanishing Irish Ireland's population from the Great Famine to the Great War", in *History Ireland*, Vol.5, No.2, Summer, 1997 (Dublin, 1997), p.36.

enticed away from the country with the promise of employment in America and Britain. Many stories were relayed to them by those travelling towards the ports at Cork and Dublin, tales that certainly reached the ears of some of those living in and around Athlone. *The Athlone Mirror* reported on the numbers travelling through the town in April 1842:

> Nothing can exceed the shoals of persons passing through Athlone particularly on a Monday from all parts of the country on their way to Dublin and America. The tide of emigration that has set in this season is more than anything we have ever witnessed; and should it continue for any length of time the landlords will have plenty of wasteland without the usual agency of the clearing or extermination system.[24]

The remark made in the above quote on the landlords' *'extermination system'* highlights another of the factors that may have caused many to emigrate. The idea that the landlords were to blame in part for the level of emigration in the mid-19th century is one that appears to be, at least in general, true. Comparatively the country landlords in England and Ireland were quite different. The English landlord *'...did much for the countryside and its inhabitants, whereas the rural landlord of Ireland...was a mere exploiter of other people's labour.'*[25] The actions of some, though not all, landlords certainly provided many labourers with no other option but to emigrate. The emigrants going through Athlone during the period 1841/2, would have consisted of a large number of people from the North-Midlands, one of the regions which sent larger proportions of people abroad than western counties. This was due to the fact that more of them could speak English, thus giving them a better chance in their new homes.[26]

Apart from the general economic conditions and the actions of some landlords, the actual scarcity of provisions would also have driven people to emigrate. Athlone had a large number of farms bordering it in the early 19th century, which would have provided vegetables and livestock that would be sold at the local markets and at the town's fleshshambles. The fifty years before the Famine were thought of as *'years of agricultural progress'* in comparison with the late 18th century.[27] The introduction of the Corn Laws in Britain and Ireland in 1815 led to a situation of agricultural protectionism that precluded the importation of corn, which would lower its price at markets. One of the problems with the

24 *The Athlone Mirror*, 19 Apr 1842.
25 Trevelyan, G. M., *Illustrated English Social History: 4* (London, 1964), p.151.
26 Hoppen, K.T., p.46.
27 Ibid., p.43.

laws was that they kept the price of bread artificially high, which in turn led to a greater burden on the poor.[28] The existence of these laws was to exacerbate the agricultural and economic problems in Ireland until their repeal.

A further factor in the massive rise in emigration was the level of unemployment and under-employment in the country. Ireland, unlike Britain, had not had an Industrial Revolution per se (with the exception of Belfast in the northeast); it was a mainly agricultural nation that suffered badly when farming went into decline. The agriculture sector in Connacht alone was to see a 29% fall in employment, 8% more than the national average between the years 1841 and 1851.[29] The farming sector along with the textiles industry was to be the source of most jobs lost nationally in that same decade.[30]

Athlone may not have been in as bad a position as a number of other areas of Ireland. The large-scale investment in the drainage of the River Shannon provided some employment; crowds of people came to the town during the life of the works after hearing of the jobs that were on offer. The large-scale employment on the 'Shannon Improvements', described in chapter four, began in 1842 when the Shannon Commissioners recruited a number of men to work on the river. However, even with this employment the workers were not finding food readily available, such was its price in comparison with their wages. A market held in the town during the works, where provisions were '*abundant*' and prices apparently low, was the scene of some unrest as the buyers who attempted to leave the town with their produce were prevented by the workers.[31] Indeed, this food-related crime was to become quite common in the country during the Famine, along with the sacking of warehouses and ports.[32]

All of the above factors and influences were causing an agricultural and economic depression in Ireland before the Famine. Many people were leaving the country, there was little security in farming, unemployment and under-employment were widespread and even work that was available was underpaid. The eventual failure of the potato crop in successive harvests, beginning in 1845/46, along with the established trend of depression, was to lead to the greatest humanitarian disaster that Ireland and Athlone had ever encountered.

28 Wilson, A. N., *The Victorians* (London, 2002), p.71.
29 Geary, Frank, "Regional industrial structure and labour force decline in Ireland between 1841 and 1851", in *Irish Historical Studies*, Vol. 30, No. 118 (Antrim, 1996), p.177.
30 Ibid., p.118.
31 *F.J.*, 7 June 1842.
32 Lowe, W. J., "The Irish Constabulary in the Great Famine", in *History Ireland*, Vol.5, No.4, Winter, 1997 (Dublin, 1997), p.34.

THE FAMINE

The consensus amongst historians is that the Great Famine began in the autumn of 1845 when the first of the blighted potatoes were reported in the southeast of the country. *Government Distress Reports*, coming from the Irish Constabulary and individual government agents, provide some information on the levels of destitution and on the state of the potato crop both nationally and locally though at times some reports appear to conflict with others. The confusion surrounding the pace of the spread of the blight may have led to these conflicts arising, the disease could progress quickly, devastating crops in just a number of days.

A report from *The Freeman's Journal* commenting on the potato crop around Athlone in August 1845 stated that '...*the growth of the potato plant progresses as favourably as the most sanguine farmer could wish*'.[33] Another report made by the Athlone Constabulary in October 1845 agreed with this assertion and outlined that the crop had not been affected by disease and that the potatoes were ready to be harvested.[34] A subsequent report laid the '*exaggerated*' claims of failure down to the locals' fear of bad weather and frost, stating that '...*a sufficient supply will be found for the people*'.[35] It was not only desirable but necessary that enough potatoes were available for consumption in the country; over three million Irish people ate little else and only certain districts had quantities of other food.[36] Athlone, as already noted was heavily dependant on potatoes and oats, though it may have been lucky in respect to other food sources. Eel, supplied by the River Shannon, was one of the most popular fish and was sold at markets, along with numerous other types of fish, both fresh and salt water, in the town. A visitor to Athlone, who styled himself a 'Cosmopolite', wrote of the prevalence of eels in the town prior to 1840:

> There were, indeed, eels – and in such abundance, exposed at every shop, whiskey-hovel, or lodging window – eels of three, or four or five pounds, which would seem to imply that they constituted the chief food of the people. This turned out to be the fact.[37]

The author interestingly compares the Athlone staple with that of Kerry stating that '*I could never prevail on the people to cook much less eat them – at Athlone, if one may judge, from the abundant display, they are in the highest*

33 *FJ.*, 20 August 1845.
34 *Distress Reports – Z series RLFC2/Z14282*, 10 Oct 1845, NAI.
35 *Distress Reports – Z series RLFC2/Z14362*, 26 Oct 1845, NAI.
36 Wilson, A. N., p.78.
37 Went, Arthur E. J., "Five eel spears from the Shannon basin.", in *Journal of the Old Athlone Society*, Vol. I, No.4 (Athlone, 1974), p.247.

repute.[38] The propensity of the townspeople to eat eel, was even harder to believe for another reporter who thought the locals were spurning a food source that was higher in quality and just as abundant. *The Parliamentary Gazetteer* of Ireland quotes an excerpt from the '*Sportsman in Ireland*', which spoke of the large numbers of fish that were to be found in the river and sold at the market in the 1830s:

> The first thing that aroused my interest at Athlone was the continued exposure for sale of trout of 8, 10, or 15 pounds each, which seemed to excite no admiration among the people. I was almost angry at the sight of such splendid creatures sold for the merest trifle; and apparently regarded with less respect than the eels, which satiated the town.[39]

It would be fair to assume that the river would still have been an important food source for the locals in the 1840s, though a number of factors must be taken into account. The works of the Shannon Commissioners disrupted the flow of the river leading on occasion to disruption in fishing. Perhaps more important, taking the apparent love the locals had for eel, was the destruction of the Elizabethan bridge which had a number of eel weirs attached. Eel fishermen would have had to erect replacements, though there would have been other eel weirs apart from those on the bridge, and due to the fact that the Shannon works at Athlone continued until well into 1849, the opportunity to do this did not perhaps present itself. Indeed, the Shannon Commissioners themselves saw the removal of the weirs along

ILL.1: ATHLONE CASTLE AS A BACKDROP TO MUCH RIVER ACTIVITY

38 Ibid., p.247.
39 *Gazetteer*, p.99.

the bridge as '...*depriving the country of a valuable source of food and useful industry*' though they hoped that another method of catching the '*prolific article*' would be found.[40]

By January 1846 the *Government Distress Reports* began to sketch a different picture with regard to the local potato crop. One stated that over one third of the crop near the town was damaged and that the bad potatoes were being fed to pigs and cattle due to the fact that poor farmers had no other provisions for them. In some cases the poor had to eat the rotten tubers themselves with the devastating situation having, one author believed, '...*exclusively fallen on the most destitute portion of our population...who have no earthly means to procure any substitute for the loss of provision caused*'.[41] In writing the report the author stated his belief that the more affluent farmers had the largest share of the best '*white potatoes*', which were being sold off.[42] This practice of selling the good potatoes regardless of the needs of the poor later led *The Nation* to write an editorial which claimed that most of the potatoes that were being sold were actually being shipped abroad:

> Let us explain to you Irish farmer, Irish landlord, Irish labourer, Irish trader what became of your harvest, which is your only wealth. Early in the winter it was conveyed, by the thousand shiploads, paying freight, it was stored in English stores, paying storage; it was passed from hand to hand among corn-speculators, paying at every remove...some of it was bought by French or Belgian buyers.[43]

During 1846 the government was receiving countrywide reports of the scarcity of potatoes as well as notes on how the prices for provisions had risen, putting them out of reach of subsistence families.[44] The continued export of food from Ireland has been recognised as '...*a triumph of doctrine over humanitarian considerations*'.[45] Disease and starvation were seen to exist parallel to a growing commercial sector in mid-Victorian Ireland.[46] The failure of the potato crop would have been devastating for the townspeople who, like most of Ireland, had adopted the crop as the staple of their diets since the mid-18th century.[47] The lack of positive action on the part of the government in dealing with

40 Went, Arthur E. J., "Eel Fishing at Athlone, Past and Present", in *Journal of the Royal Society of Antiquaries of Ireland*, Vol. 5, lxxx, pt.2, 1950 (Dublin, 1950), p.149–151.
41 *Distress Reports – Z series RLFC2/Z414*, 22 Jan 1846, NAI.
42 Ibid.
43 Kinealy, Christine, "Food Exports from Ireland 1846–47", in *History Ireland*, Vol.5, No.1, Spring 1997 (Dublin, 1997), p.32.
44 Ibid., p.33.
45 Ibid., p.32.
46 Ibid., p.34.
47 Hoppen, K.T., p.37.

the problems in Ireland lends credence to the belief that the attitude of the English to the Irish was that:

> They were poor, dirty, bug-ridden, intemperate, and – above all – Roman Catholic. When, however the British looked outwards to Ireland itself, it was rarely to sympathise with the grievances of that unhappy land, but more often to deplore its lawlessness and its nuisance-value within the general setting of British politics.[48]

By Spring 1846 a plea was sent for a large consignment of Indian Grain to be sent to Athlone to help in the relief of the poor, but the price of the grain was thought of as excessive and if it was sent the cost had to be lowered.[49] Though the Corn Laws were soon to be repealed, at least in part, some evidence suggests that many merchants all around the country were making massive profits during the Famine from the practice of overpricing their foodstuffs.[50] The importation of Indian Grain was one of the schemes designed to deal with the unfolding crisis in Ireland. It was introduced during 1845 under the Conservative Prime Minister Robert Peel. The whole scheme was poorly implemented. Unreliable reports were extant with regard to the amount of grain available and as well as this, though profiteering was supposedly curbed through guidelines brought in by the same government, the reality of the situation was quite different.[51] Price notwithstanding, the quality of the grain was not thought of as very high; one description from a local Poor Law Guardian stated that it was; '...*fit for nothing but for making a sole for a bog road.*'[52] The negative effects of the Famine were not being combated effectively in the town with a Town Commissioners meeting, held in March 1846, hearing evidence from a local Catholic priest as to its progression. He stated that there were over 2,100 people in his parish, St. Mary's on the Leinster side of the town, '...*in a most wretched and destitute state*' and through eating bad potatoes diarrhoea had become rife. He described how, upon entering the house of a local Protestant (starvation was not purely a Catholic concern, and a small number of Protestants entered the union workhouse), the smell of the potatoes that the man was about to eat drove him out, such was its foulness.[53]

As happened on a number of occasions during the Famine, the Athlone Town Commissioners requested that employment be given to

48 Newsome, David, *The Victorian World Picture* (London, 1997), p.128.
49 *Distress Reports – Z series RLFC2/Z5646*, 21 Mar 1846, NAI.
50 Wilson, A. N., p.81.
51 Edwards, R. Dudley & Williams, T. Desmond (eds.) *The Great Famine – Studies in Irish History 1845-52* (Dublin, 1994), pp. 215-219.
52 O'Brien, *Workhouse*, p.19.
53 *A.S.*, 20 Mar 1846.

the poor '*starving and famishing labourers*' who had been unemployed for
four months since the end of the last public works.[54] Actually public
works along with the importation of maize from America were really
the only identifiable government actions in addressing the Famine in
Ireland. Though 140,000 jobs were created nationally because of the
works, the imported corn could not get to the mouths of all those who
needed it – rail and road infrastructure was running behind that of
England, leaving many, especially in the west, in dire straits.[55] Also the
provision of public works was seen by many as being '*disastrous*' – the
low wages meant that the poor could not purchase the food at 'Famine
prices'. Neither were the prices likely to drop in the short term due to
hoarding on behalf of some farmers and dealers who were trying to
drive up the prices.[56] Even during the navigation works at Athlone the
employers exploited the low paid workers to the greatest degree:

> The contractors for the quay and lock at Athlone have made it a practice
> to pay the men in their employment monthly to force them to purchase
> goods in the stores they themselves have established on the ground at a
> great deal a dearer rate than they could purchase them elsewhere.[57]

Public works other than those on the Shannon were also
commissioned at the time. The provision of schemes specifically to deal
with the numerous unemployed people during the Famine was another
initiative brought in under Robert Peel in early 1846. The government
envisaged that the works commissioned would be of great use, with
projects such as harbour construction having obvious positive elements
in improving the economies of coastal towns.[58] The famine was proving
to be more difficult to deal with than the Conservative government first
surmised, though Peel did adapt his approaches to the problem, which
was unusual in a time when *laissez faire* attitudes dominated. A letter sent
to the Lord Lieutenant by the Town Commissioners outlined why the
provision of monies for public works in the town was so necessary:

> We the undersigned Town Commissioners in council assembled, take
> leave to aquaint your Excellency, that at the present moment distress to
> an alarming extent pervades this town and neighbourhood, which is to a
> great degree owing to the want of employment amongst the labouring
> poor as the public works have been stopped for the last four months in
> this town. We further humbly take leave to apply to your Excellency for
> a grant of Five Hundred Pounds for the purpose of carrying on such

54 *Distress Reports – Z series RLFC2/Z5854*, 18 Mar 1846, NAI.
55 Wilson, A. N., pp.76-77.
56 Kinealy, Christine, p.36.
57 *A.S.*, 25 Aug 1843.
58 Edwards, R. Dudley & Williams, T. Desmond, pp. 219-220.

useful works as not only will tend to the health of the town but also give employment to the starving and famishing labourers who are at present in a state of destitution.[59]

Some of the funding required was later awarded, partially as a grant and the remainder as a loan.[60] The funds were soon put to use with public works beginning on the Roscommon side of the town in April 1846.[61] However, the money was quickly spent with the Athlone Relief Committee, headed by Lord Castlemaine – a very wealthy local landowner, requesting more funds from the exchequer just two months later.[62] An article in the local press before the end of the year detailed that the situation in the town was growing increasingly desperate.[63] By December 1846 another injection of funds must have been received for *The Freeman's Journal* reported:

> About 250 people have been employed in the neighbourhood of Athlone breaking stones, cutting down hills and constructing roads. By this employment many people have been saved from starvation. There is still a great demand for work and many are wandering the country in search of food.[64]

The plight of the local people was not completely ignored by the landed gentry with one of the most important local landowners, Lord Castlemaine employing a large number of his own tenants to drain a sizeable area of land on his estate.[65] Though it must be said that his reasons for doing so were not altruistic; through draining he created more farmland on which he grew more crops that he would probably then export.

The lack of employment was a frustrating topic all throughout the Famine in Athlone, with most of the articles and reports written in local newspapers emphasising the willingness of the locals to work. The situation was even more distressing given that, as the Society for the Improvement of Ireland writing in 1846 stated: '...*the labourers migrate annually to England in so great numbers, and it is in evidence that much less remunerative employment at home would detain them in Ireland.*'[66] Ireland was considered the exception in the United Kingdom when it came to maintaining the '*precarious balance*' between the social classes. In England

59 *Distress Reports – Z Series RLFC2/Z5954*, 18 March 1846, NAI.
60 *Distress Reports – Z Series RLFC2/Z5954*, 5 April 1846, NAI.
61 *Distress Reports – Z Series RLFC3/1/1495*, 15 April 1846, NAI.
62 *Distress Reports – Z Series RLFC3/1/3643*, 24 June 1846, NAI.
63 *The Westmeath Independent*, 8 Oct 1846.
64 *FJ*, 7 Dec 1846.
65 *FJ*, 8 August 1851.
66 *Society for the improvement of Ireland* (Dublin, 1846) p.60.

the need to protect the interests of the big farmers and industrialists was of the utmost importance; assisting the poor could not weaken their position. Poor relief supported the poorest people in the south of England and this proved sufficient, for the purposes of the government, due to a better agricultural situation. In Ireland where the potato crop had failed and the relief provided proved inadequate there was: '...*a collapse into famine and disease.*'[67] Part of the problem in Ireland at the time is believed by Martin Daunton to be associated with '*involution*'. This is a process whereby the rural population always rose to '*the limit of available resources*'. In Ireland this essentially meant the population grew in line with potato production leading to the massive fall out when that crop failed.[68] This trend of involution would not necessarily have led to the severe Famine crisis if the potato had not failed, for: '*there is no evidence that pre-famine Ireland was overpopulated in any useful sense of that word.*'[69] The problem was that the population was overdependant on one crop and the interests of commerce limited the availability of other produce for consumption by the lower classes.

As 1846 progressed reporters surmised what the desperate locals would be driven to do in their search for food to save themselves and their families; as one report stated there were '...*evils anticipated from the want of food.*'[70] The necessity of resorting to 'evils' was very real, since many families did not even have enough money to pay for a bowl of soup at the local soup kitchen where it cost just 1d.[71] At this time the new government, which took power in late June 1846, began recommending the opening of soup kitchens to local relief committees. They had witnessed the success the Society of Friends were having and believed that the kitchens could, along with the provision of public works schemes, help alleviate the suffering many Irish were experiencing.[72] The scheme was greatly extended nationally during 1847 and was considered moderately successful.[73] The local authorities continued to maintain, as they had formerly, that the provision of employment was the main solution for the problems being encountered. The Athlone Relief Committee said it could not cater for all those who needed help with its chairman, Lord Castlemaine, stating that more local road improvements would provide employment to many of the impoverished in the locality.[74] Indeed the improvement in

67 Daunton, Martin, p.47.
68 Ibid.
69 Wilson, A. N., p.77
70 *Distress Reports – Z series RLFC2/Z5942*, 22 Mar 1846, NAI.
71 O'Brien, Gearoid, *St Mary's Parish, Athlone – a History* (Longford, 1989), p.149.
72 Edwards, R. Dudley & Williams, T. Desmond, pp. 225-227.
73 Ibid., p.243.
74 *Distress Reports – Z series RLFC3/1/3643*, 24 June 1846, NAI.

the local roads was probably counterproductive from a labourer's point of view; better communication routes meant that food could reach the ports more quickly. Thus they were to some extent facilitating their own deprivation, though they had little choice. A problem that arose from the provision of employment through public works was that the stewards who supervised the works were generally the relations of a member of the committee that solicited the grant. The steward received a wage far greater than that of the labourers, hence shortening the time that the monies received for the works could last. Indeed, some in London believed the entire idea of the scale of the works was not a good idea: '...*the present mode of giving employment to the unemployed of collecting them in masses, by which facility is given to them to form schemes of intimidation and disturbance, is decidedly faulty*'.[75] There was very little sympathy for the Irish situation in many areas of Britain.

Towards the end of 1846 the failure in the local crop was becoming more apparent every day, with the Lord Lieutenant repeatedly petitioned for funding for employment.[76] A correspondent writing from Athlone recounted how in one week he had witnessed the most desperate wretchedness in parts of Co. Roscommon, not far from the town. Hundreds were existing on one meal of 'waxy' potatoes mixed with oatmeal per day, even with the price of oatmeal being quite high at the time, there were few alternatives.[77] An editorial in *The Freeman's Journal* penned soon after this account stated:

> We are now in an alarming state as patience, under the most trying privations, is now exhausted. If employment is not given at once it is frightful to contemplate what the unhappy results will be.[78]

The situation that the impoverished found themselves in eventually did drive them to commit crimes to feed their families. The garrison in Athlone had to send a number of soldiers to Clara in order to thwart attempted thefts from the corn store there, with more on standby, for the threat of a peasant rising outside Athlone was growing.[79] The way that the British saw the Irish peasants as lawbreakers in this type of occurrence shows, according to A. N. Wilson author of *The Victorians*:

> [One of the] ripe examples of British double standards where violence is in question. An Englishman protecting his grossly selfish way of life with a huge apparatus of police and military, prepared to gun down the

75 Wilson, A. N., p.81.
76 *Athlone 1945*, p.23.
77 *F.J.*, 7 Oct 1846.
78 *F.J.*, 8 Oct 1846.
79 *F.J.*, 31 Oct 1846, *W.I.*, 31 Oct 1846.

starving, is maintaining law and order. An Irishman retaliating is a terrorist.[80]

The types of crimes perpetrated during the Famine changed as people's minds turned more towards survival than insurrection. While agrarian crime lessened, others such as burglary, livestock theft and the plundering of provisions all increased in number. The worst year for these types of crimes was 1847 when a 60% increase was reported nationally – it led one contemporary to describe the country as being in '*nearly perfect anarchy*'.[81] To deal with this rise the Irish Constabulary recruited roughly 3,400 extra men in the five years from 1845 to 1850.[82] During this same period less money was being sent into Ireland from England for the provision of relief, which was already badly underfunded. The exchequer was reported as being in the middle of a crisis in the mid-1840s with the Chancellor stating that it was not possible to give Ireland more money: '*Now financially, my course is very easy. I have no more money now and therefore I cannot give it*'. However, as A. N. Wilson points out, the government found over £70 million to deal with the Crimean war, just seven years later.[83] The government that replaced that of Robert Peel was considered less sympathetic to the Irish cause.

Around Athlone there were numerous reports of unemployed people wandering the nearby countryside in search of food with a number of cases of ovine theft.[84] By Christmas 1846 the full extent of the Famine became clear:

> Men maddened with hunger and the starvation cries of their children, resorted to deeds of violence, which became an everyday occurrence, as deaths from starvation increased. Food had to be found and the means to that end were very unimportant.[85]

Reports on the harvest of 1846 told that wheat and barley were good and fair crops respectively, but the mainstay, the potato, was described as '*irrevocably gone*'.[86] In a letter entitled '*Distress in Ireland*' Joseph Crossfield, an English Quaker who was touring Ireland attempting to assess the situation, detailed the deplorable conditions in Athlone Workhouse just prior to Christmas 1846. Just one year earlier the workhouse, which over its short life had a history of financial problems, was said to be in

80 Wilson, A. N., p.82.
81 Lowe, W. J., p.33.
82 Ibid., p.34
83 Wilson, A. N., p.77.
84 *F.J.*, 7 Dec 1846.
85 *W.I.*, 19 Dec 1846.
86 *Athlone 1945*, p.23.

great debt with the master having to go onto the streets in order to collect money for food for the inmates.[87]

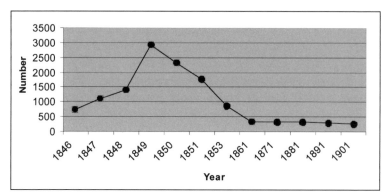

FIG.8: NUMBER OF INMATES AT ATHLONE UNION WORKHOUSE 1846-1901

This situation would only have worsened coming into 1847 as more people applied for relief and Crossfield's letter paints a vivid picture of a poor relief system incapable of coping with Athlone's deprived. He stated that '*...a miserable state of things presented itself*', the inmates had barely any clothes or bedding and the '*oppressive smell*' in the boy's area '*...indicated the want of a proper attention to cleanliness*', whilst the girl's area '*was still more offensive*'. The spread of disease through the town had reached the workhouse around the same time, driving the local Board of Guardians from the building to hold their meetings in a nearby hotel.[88]

The first week of the New Year did not see any improvement in Athlone's situation. If anything the picture that was painted in the local press was one of a town spiralling into severe crisis:

> The streets of our town are rendered almost impassable from the number of miserable, half naked, famishing objects that press upon us and din the ear with supplications for relief. In the Poorhouse hundreds of unfortunate inmates are huddled together – the greater portions on beds of sickness.[89]

A report from the same month describes the first of the four annual Athlone markets, in January, as '*abundantly supplied with grain*' and that the price had come down due to a decree at Parliamentary level – repeal of the Corn Laws.[90] Around this time and more certainly in the spring of

87 O'Brien, *Workhouse*, p.14.
88 Ibid., p.19.
89 *W.I.*, 9 Jan 1847.
90 *F.J.*, 25 Jan 1847.

1847 the importation of grain became more significant though the *'starvation gap'* created by the exports – over 4,000 ships exported food from Ireland to Britain in 1847 alone – and the less than adequate imports meant that the situation would not improve in the short term.[91] The fact that the government was allowing the export of more food than was being imported for the famished masses certainly highlights the inhuman nature of many in the cabinet. In actuality Ireland was possibly the largest exporter of food to England in Europe at that time.[92] The situation with regard to the exportation of corn was summed up by the Lord Lieutenant in Ireland, The Earl of Clarendon: *'No-one could now dispute the fact that Ireland had been sacrificed to the London corn dealers...and that no distress would have occurred if the exportation of Irish grain had been prohibited'*.[93] Though this quote may underestimate the extent and nature of the problem in Ireland, one historian has noted that the British appeared to be reliant on the exports from Ireland to keep themselves supplied.[94] Ireland, '*...drew forth the darkest, most pessimistic, and most repressive aspect of the Victorian character.'*[95] The sacrifice of people to commercial interests was, as it still is, a gross failing of society.

The fall in grain prices did not appear to effect any great improvement locally with a report published soon after detailing the sorry state of some of the local people. One man, who was in the town looking for food, collapsed outside the offices of *The Westmeath Independent* due to starvation. After receiving some soup he garnered a small amount of food, which he brought back to his family. A woman with two small, starving children was described as being found in a *'hopeless state'*; she died soon after being discovered leaving the two orphans to be placed in the workhouse.[96] The hopeless state of the country's poor in 1847 led the government to pass the Poor Relief Extension (Ireland) Act, which allowed for outdoor relief to be provided for those who could not enter the workhouse due to overcrowding.[97] It was part of a drive towards revitalising the Poor Law system, which the government believed could be made far more capable than it had previously been.[98] Previous ideas such as public works, the importation of grain and soup kitchens had not solved the problem and the government now began to explore some other avenues. This extension

91 Kinealy, Christine, p.33.
92 Kinealy, Christine, p.36.
93 Ibid.
94 Ibid., p.34.
95 Wilson, A. N., p.84.
96 *F.J.*, 2 Mar 1847.
97 Roche, Desmond, *Local Government in Ireland* (Dublin, 1982), p.40.
98 Edwards, R. Dudley & Williams, T. Desmond, pp. 245-249.

scheme was the precursor of the home assistance scheme, which ran in a variety of forms until 1977.[99] Also in 1847 the Vagrants (Ireland) Act was passed, aimed at repressing begging, wife desertion and vagrancy.[100]

Public works, consistently seen as a cure for the starvation of the people, appear to have contributed to the poor health of some of the employees rather than to its alleviation. Food provisions on the local works were quite low: on one occasion two labourers collapsed from exhaustion not having tasted food since the morning of the previous day.[101] The level of the wages on the public works in Westmeath can be qualified thus; a family of four to seven people were generally trying to get by on 10d per day. To earn this money many in the county had to walk up to and even over seven miles per day to work, with a small ration of oatmeal served as lunch. As one historian observed: '*No wonder violence broke out when the hungry were able to muster up the energy for it.*'[102] It was during this period that the numbers of people employed on public works schemes nationally reached over 700,000. It was becoming apparent to the government, however, that the schemes were not successful; at times pointless construction took place, and many people actually left whatever little agricultural work they had to enlist on them. By the start of the summer 1847 it was decided to discontinue the works schemes and they were phased out.[103]

The poor of Athlone also had to contend with severe weather conditions, which exacerbated the already terrible conditions. A large fire caused during a storm in March 1847 destroyed twenty-two thatched houses on the east of the town leaving 200 people homeless.[104] The same day saw a smaller fire leave six thatched houses on the west side in ruins, with the homeless '...*left in a most destitute condition*'.[105] The parish priest for St. Mary's on the Leinster side of the town spoke of how more than twice the number of people had died in the six months from November 1846 to April 1847 than in the same period the previous year, when privations were considered extreme. Reports from the workhouse brought news of 405 deaths in the same six-month period, with the sudden death of people in the streets, from starvation and disease, being a regular occurrence. The local public works had been closed almost in their entirety with those financially capable of it emigrating from the town, to England and America, where conditions

99 Wiley, Miriam M., p.50.
100 Ibid.
101 *FJ.*, 16 Mar 1847.
102 Wilson, A. N., p.79.
103 Edwards, R. Dudley & Williams, T. Desmond, p.234.
104 *FJ.*, 17 Mar 1847.
105 Ibid.

were little better, if at all.[106] The prevalence of fever in the town caused the guardians of the workhouse to use government legislation dealing with the construction of fever hospitals; in May 1847 a facility was built with over forty patients already diagnosed as infected.[107] Their continued non-segregation before the hospital was built was a great threat to the other inmates as well as to the visitors to the workhouse who would have been in danger of spreading the disease when they returned to their homes.

The conditions that children in the workhouse were forced to live in were described as deplorable and inhumane. A local newspaper reporter who saw them on their way to mass stated '...*no beggar brats that walk the streets were in such a condition of wretchedness and misery*'.[108] Gruesome tales concerning poor children outside of the workhouse were also reported locally with one detailing how the parents of a seven-year-old boy locked him into his room and left, presumably in search of food. His decaying body was to be found two days later by neighbours who were concerned by the lack of activity in the house.[109] The state of the livestock present at the Athlone May fair was described in derogatory terms; sickly looking animals on view, none of which sold.[110] The Athlone workhouse was catering for numbers far in excess of those for which it was built, precipitating refusals at the door. One family, unable to go any further, collapsed outside it and was eventually given assistance by two locals, a gentleman and a clergyman.[111] The workhouse reported twenty deaths per week from fever, with the burial ground beside it providing a food source for the local dogs, such was the ineffective way in which bodies were interred.[112] The poorest and most badly hit of the townsfolk were becoming so desperate for food and provisions that they resorted to looting well-stocked shops in order to survive.[113]

A retrospective report published in 1892 dealt with the Famine years 1846/7 in the town calling them '...*the most melancholy in the history of Athlone*'.[114] The article described how the years previous to the famine had been good, with a sufficient supply of food, and so many potatoes that at times farmers did not even dig them. When the blight came, the workhouse filled to overflowing, disease was rife and the contractor who had won the tender for the supply of coffins had, during a

106 *FJ.*, 28 Apr 1847.
107 O'Connor, John, p.239.
108 O'Brien, *Workhouse*, p.26.
109 *FJ.*, 12 May 1847.
110 *Athlone 1947*, p.15.
111 *FJ.*, 21st June 1847.
112 *Athlone 1945*, p.23, *Athlone 1947*, pp.12-14.
113 Ibid., p.15.
114 *FJ.*, 16 Apr 1892.

protracted period in 1847, to produce sixty coffins per day. Eventually he had instead to use hinge-bottomed coffins, which were reusable.

The average mortality in the town at the time was around 100 people per week, the dead were transported to the 'Cholera Field', which adjoined the Abbey Graveyard, in a cart and buried there in '*pits*'. Religious fervour caused some to go to the burial ground and pray over the hastily dug graves of the dead, believing the Famine to be '...*evidence of Divine displeasure for our material wickedness*'.[115] This view was also held by a number of prominent Protestants across the Irish Sea; one letter to Robert Peel noted that '...*Famine are the instruments of his [God's] displeasure*.'[116] However, in counterpoint John Mitchel's famous statement, which, whilst noting the actions of God, laid the blame at the feet of mortals: '*The Almighty indeed sent the potato blight, but the English created the Famine*.'[117]

The total crop of potatoes for the year 1847 had been 10% of that harvested in 1844, so with the re-emergence of blight in 1848 the plight of the townspeople and of the Irish in general was yet to see improvement.[118] The union workhouse was over £3,000 in debt by the end of 1847, a situation that was blamed on the guardians who were running the facility.[119] By the start of 1848 a number of the young orphan girls who were in the workhouse were shipped to Australia, such were the numbers there.[120] The plight of the workhouse did little to sway Lord Castlemaine's opinion of the place. He, as head of the local Board of Guardians, stated that he didn't care how the house made ends meet.[121]

An inspection of the workhouse and of its accounts by a Poor Law inspector named Flanagan in January 1848 revealed that the problems there were quite considerable. He found that of all of the rate collectors for Athlone Union none collected the correct amount, in some cases the amount lodged was actually less than half what it should have been, and that their books were unbalanced. The reason for all of the problems, Flanagan stated, was the current Board of Guardians. He believed it an '*absolute necessity*' that they were removed and cited an example as to how poorly the workhouse was managed:

> I have further to report that several hundred unfortunate beings, apparently in the most extreme destitution, pressed for admission to the

115 Ibid.
116 Wilson, A. N., p.76.
117 Ibid., p.80.
118 Newsinger, John, *Fenianism in Mid-Victorian Britain* (London, 1994), p.4.
119 O'Brien, *Workhouse*, p.14.
120 Newsinger, John, p.4.
121 O'Brien, *Workhouse*, p.15.

workhouse yesterday; but from the want of ordinary foresight, and gross neglect of their duties by the Guardians, the greater number were obliged to return unrelieved, there being neither• beds, bedding, nor clothing ready for them.[122]

The Board of Guardians held a meeting at which they voted themselves out of office by a majority of ten to four; their resignations were subsequently accepted by the Poor Law Commissioners due to the level of incompetence reported by Flanagan. Two men were installed as Vice-Guardians – another government policy to deal with situations such as that in Athlone where the incumbents were deemed unwilling or unable to carry out their duties to acceptable standards – who took over the running of the workhouse on a full-time basis for the next twenty-two months. The men, a Captain Drought and a Mr Wall wished to ensure that the facility would not persist as '...*a repository of laziness filth and vice*.'[123] Their initial reports of conditions in January 1848 describe a place that was '...*generally filthy and disgusting, and quite devoid of system and regularity*'.[124] There were not enough beds; in the boys' auxiliary workhouse there were four children to a bed and many had to sleep on the filthy floors with only straw to cushion them. The Vice-Guardians could not accept all of those who petitioned them for help such was the state of the finances in the workhouse. Even though the Roman Catholic clergy's '...*representations on the state of the poor were most horrendous*', nothing could be achieved without a better system of rate collection.[125] The workhouse had also introduced a number of schemes for the inmates in which they created saleable products in an attempt to boost funds. The most unpopular job was the use of the Capstan mill – used for grinding corn, which in Athlone was carried out entirely by girls. It was thought of as cruel and unnecessarily harsh; a later report dealing with education in the workhouses condemned its past use as being extremely harsh, especially in the case of small girls.[126]

Locally the peasantry was thought to be reaching the end of its tether. The army was again on high alert in January 1848 (word of a peasant uprising was spreading) with their orders stating that they were to disarm the poor as well as search for illegal firearms at local houses and farms.[127] The state of the underclass had certainly not improved from the

---

122 *Papers relating to Proceedings for the relief of the distress and State of the Union and Workhouses in Ireland 5th Series 1848* (London, 1848), pp.404–405.
123 O'Brien, *Workhouse*, p.15.
124 *Papers* 1848, pp.407–408.
125 Ibid., p.408.
126 O'Brien, *Workhouse*, p.23.
127 *F.J.*, 17 Jan 1848, *F.J.*, 20 Jan 1848.

previous years, with *The Athlone Sentinel* describing the scene:

> The condition of the poor in the neighbourhood of Athlone is utterly
> lamentable. Without employment and unable to gain admission to the
> workhouse or to get outdoor relief for want of funds they are reduced to
> a state of extreme wretchedness.[128]

The second week in February 1848 saw the appointment of new rate
collectors to the union and the purchase of ninety new beds for the
workhouse, though an illness contracted by Capt. Drought in early
March was to slow progress considerably.[129] It also appears that the Vice
Guardians had personnel problems in the facility for they complained
that '...*we find it very difficult to get our orders carried into effect immediately
or satisfactorily*'.[130] Burial practices at the workhouse were still foul in the
extreme; there were now virtually no coffins and many that were buried
were only interred '...*after long exposure of the body*'. The master of the
workhouse was forced to resign due to his lack of '*energy*' and his
replacement, with a higher wage, was believed to be a marked
improvement. Soon the Vice-Guardians were reporting good progress
on all fronts.[131]

Nationally the Poor Law system was still not working well, many
more people than could be dealt with were applying for relief, in some
quarters the numbers were actually rising. To combat the problem the
Poor Law Commissioners decided to reinstate the Board of Guardians
system and they set about implementing this in March 1849. By
November all of the boards had been put in place, though the Athlone
Board of Guardians did ask that the Vice Guardians they were to replace
be retained due to their excellent record in the provision of relief to the
poor. The request was refused.[132]

The earlier prediction of '*evils*' due to a lack of food was becoming
more of a reality each day with general social order in a state of
meltdown and the entire situation causing many of the town's residents
to live in fear:

> For some time the town of Athlone has been nightly the scene of some
> daring acts of depredation, each succeeding morning bringing news of
> disaster and outrage on the lives and properties of the townsfolk. Houses,
> shops and stores are broken into and pillaged of their contents and even
> in broad daylight it is known that thefts are visited on property
> appropriated by bands of desperadoes.[133]

128 *A.S.*, 27 Jan 1848.
129 *Papers* 1848, p.854.
130 Ibid., p.856.
131 Ibid., p.867.
132 Kinealy, Christine, *This Great Calamity - The Irish Famine 1845-52* (Dublin, 1994), p.269.
133 *F.J.*, 17 Feb 1848.

The local landlords were in the main not disposed to rendering any sort of assistance to their beleaguered tenants, with the wholesale eviction of 104 residents on the Roscommon side of the town in March 1848 illustrating the very harsh situation with which the residents were faced. A report tells that when the people were evicted, with their *'miserable furniture'*, the twenty-one houses were levelled even though most of the residents had paid their rent and those in arrears numbered *'a paltry few'*.[134] As housing statistics have already shown, the Roscommon side of the town witnessed a large drop in the number of 4th class houses between 1841 and 1851. However, whilst one could be certain that the houses were of poor quality their residents would probably have preferred staying there than being rendered homeless and dependent on the poor law. Worryingly, some accounts from the time described how many parents just outside the town on the Roscommon side would sell their right to a holding to their landlord and then emigrate leaving their children behind them; the children invariably ended up in the workhouse.[135] The callous nature of some of the local landowners was incomprehensible for some reporters at the time, and one who penned an article on the evictions by two local landlords showed how unfeeling they could be:

> During the week Athlone presented a melancholy example of the devastating progress of the famine and the number of ragged, wretched and hungry creatures who thronged the workhouse for admission testifying the extent to which evictions are being carried on. The greater part of these unhappy beings were tenants to Mrs. Sarah Kelly of Rockwood and Mr. Newcumben of Dysart. One woman with a sickly infant on her back and a group of emaciated children crawling behind her told the bitter anguish of the story. For more than a century her family lived in the holding from which Mrs. Kelly ejected her and she always paid the rent until the potatoes rotted. She owed one years rent and the children lived on the herbs of the field and must now end their days in the workhouse. Each unfortunate victim had their story to tell and their lamentations in the Irish language over their present condition were painfully touching. There were 500 applications for outdoor relief at the workhouse on Friday and from Dysart alone owing to these evictions there were 210.[136]

Disease was, as before, a major threat, and though typhus fever was still a problem the possible emergence of cholera, one of the *'filth diseases'*, in October 1848 was a far more worrisome occurrence. The

134 *FJ.*, 14 Mar 1848.
135 *Papers 1848*, p.56.
136 *A.S.*, 18 Dec 1848.

last time it was reported in the town was in 1831 and the memory of its effects were certainly known first-hand by many residents.[137] However, it is probable that the diagnosis was premature. The disease was first reported in December 1848 in the northeast and probably did not affect Athlone until the early months of 1849, when it was becoming a national problem.[138] The numbers affected by the disease were substantial though; over 200 local lives were lost by the time it was beaten in June of the same year.[139]

Neither was the garrison immune from the diseases that were ravaging the town. Its facilities also appeared quite incapable of dealing with the problems presented. The toilets were said to be outdated, the hospital wards were '...*overcrowded with sick...the orderlies (having) to sleep among the sick...there (were) no means of lighting except by candles.*'[140] The conditions in the barracks were thought to have made the opthalmia problem (a disease affecting the eye spread by contaminated water) the town was facing far more serious, with water being drawn directly from the Shannon by military prisoners used extensively within its walls. Oscar Wilde's father, William, Surgeon Oculist to the Queen, believed that Athlone's damp was second only to '*India, during the rains*', and this dampness was thought to be a major factor in spreading disease throughout the town with 470 cases treated in one year in the workhouse alone.[141]

If the advent of the railways was to have an effect on the Victorians it was that they were, for the first time, easily capable of witnessing all of the problems caused by the disparity between rich and poor first hand. Indeed, later in the century a greater number of wealthier Victorians set up funds for relief of the poor.[142] The railways also allowed for the dissemination of far more information in newspapers, so that even those who did not have first hand experience of the problems were certainly more likely to be aware of them.

The theft of whatever good potatoes were available and of healthy livestock continued unabated with the local need for food finding no satiation.[143] Whilst there are reports that some employment was available at the works of the Shannon Commissioners, the demand for work far

---

137 Stokes, George T., *Athlone, the Shannon and Lough Ree*, with a local Directory edited by John Burgess (Dublin, 1897). p.41
138 Vaughan, W. E. (Ed.), *A New History of Ireland V – Ireland under the Union 1, 1801 - 70* (Oxford, 1989), p.309.
139 *F.J.*, 28 Oct 1848, Best, Geoffrey, *Mid-Victorian Britain 1851-75* (London, 1979), p.74, *W.I.*, 23 June 1849.
140 O'Farrell, Padraic Col., "Athlone – A Garrison Town" in Keaney, M. & O'Brien, G., Athlone - *Bridging the Centuries* (Mullingar, 1991), p.70.
141 Casey, Patrick, "Epidemic Opthalmia at Athlone" in *Journal of the Old Athlone Society*, Vol. I, No.2 (1970), p.113., O'Brien, *Workhouse*, p.40.
142 Wilson, A. N., p.30.
143 *F.J.*, 28 Oct 1848, *F.J.*, 11 Dec 1848.

outstripped the supply. As well as this the wages received by the workers
were not, as already shown, sufficient to help alleviate the problems in
the quality of life of the townspeople.[144] The year 1849 did see increased
activity on the river as the works finished, though without replacement
public works on a scale similar to those previously seen in the town, the
emigration from Athlone, and coming through it, began to increase,
making the situation even more serious. The staggering numbers
emigrating from Ireland by the end of the Famine led Frederick Engels
to muse if '...there will be Irishmen only in America'.[145]

Reports from the latter part of 1850 tell of the huge tide of farmers
abandoning their holdings around the town due to their fear of the
workhouse, eviction and starvation. The union workhouse was
reporting a number of cases of opthalmia but despite this the large
number of the inmates rendered blind by the disease were still engaged
in the manufacture of baskets, etc., such was the ethic in the
establishment.[146] The local press again warned landlords that refusing to
help their tenants would lead to even more emigration and hence leave
them incapable of farming their lands due to the lack of able hands.[147]
However, not all stories from the time detailed utter deprivation and loss
of hope. One instance recounted how a family evicted by their landlord
went through the town cheering for, on the same day as the eviction, a
sum of money had been wired to them from America and they too
could afford to emigrate.[148] However, this type of story was in the
minority, and most related the hardship and poverty of local families.

Some local tenant farmers were believed to have brought whatever
produce they had harvested to the local market and then used whatever
money it garnered, if sufficient, to leave the town immediately –
returning home would have meant a rent demand from the landlord.[149]
Rev. John Conmee S. J., who later featured in the writings of James
Joyce, believed that even the participants in faction fights would have
laid all their differences aside and '...wept together as they walked on some
sad morning into Luainford [Athlone] on their way to America.'[150] There were
also said to be many stories related back to locals of relatives' success in
America. These stories may have provided the impetus some needed to
make the final decision to emigrate.[151]

144 FJ., 30 June 1849.
145 Daunton, Martin, p.47.
146 O'Brien, Workhouse, p.23.
147 FJ., 19 Aug 1850.
148 A.S., 11 Nov 1850.
149 Athlone Civic Week 1950 (Athlone, 1950), p.33.
150 Conmee, Rev. John S. (S.J)., Old Times in the Barony (Dublin, 1979), p.14.
151 Ibid., p.17.

The situation at the union workhouse degenerated further in 1850 when riots occurred owing to the belief that the food being served to the inmates was of very poor quality. The main body of the riot was made up of the female wing leading them to be described in reports as '*enraged amazons*'.[152] The quality of food on sale in the town for those who could afford it appeared to have been no better, with *The Westmeath Independent* reporting that putrid meat was on display at the shambles on the west side of the town.[153] The lack of regular inspections at slaughterhouses and the shambles meant that this practice persisted over a number of years during the early Victorian era.[154] The reforms in public health that occurred in the 1870s, related in chapter eight, precluded this level of unsanitary practice from persisting.

One historian who noted that roughly 250,000 people left Ireland the following year, 1851, the highest figure ever, has described it as the *annus horribilis*.[155] Evidence of famine and its effects continued locally right into the same year with *The Athlone Sentinel* reporting:

> The migration of the peasantry seems to be setting in, in right earnest. On Monday night a considerable number of country people passed through Athlone accompanied by a number of carts on their way to America. Each day a similar spectacle may be witnessed and the public conveyances are crowded with persons for the same destination.[156]

The town of Athlone suffered horrendously during the Famine. It was the scene of levels of deprivation never previously witnessed, a workhouse badly managed; filthy and overcrowded, an example of what ineffective and badly implemented government policies led to between the years 1845-1851. The lack of useful parliamentary measures in relation to the Famine was indicative of a mindset that saw the Irish Famine as a foreign problem. Towards the end many prominent British parliamentarians actually began describing death from starvation as being of natural causes; they did not sympathise with the human suffering involved. Sydney Smith, a contemporary commentator, may have been correct when he said:

> The moment the very name of Ireland is mentioned, the English seem to bid adieu to common feeling, common prudence and common sense, and to act with the barbarity of tyrants and the fatuity of idiots.[157]

152 *Athlone 1950*, p.35.
153 Ibid.
154 O'Brien, Municipal, p.83.
155 Kennedy, L & Clarkson, L. A., "Birth, Death and Exile: Irish Population History, 1700-1921", in Graham, B. J. & Proudfoot, L. J. (Eds.), *An Historical Geography of Ireland* (London, 1993), p.175.
156 *A.S.*, 14 Mar 1851.
157 Wilson, A. N., p.83.

During the Famine most of the inhabitants of the town were concerned mainly with basic survival. National politics and national issues did not receive much attention in Athlone throughout the years of the tragedy and, indeed it would take some time for these issues to regain importance locally. The disaster probably solidified in people's minds the idea that the government in Britain was not concerned with its Irish citizens, even that it regarded them as inconsequential and dispensable. The poor who applied for jobs on public works schemes must have seen the provision of too few, and the inadequate wage levels, as an insulting gesture on the government's part. For those who could not gain employment and entered the workhouse, the entire regime must have appeared barbaric and destructive. The separation of families, the debased conditions and grossly inadequate levels of food and medical supplies illustrated that if this was the government's best plan of action, it was divorced from humanitarian considerations.

The agrarian conflicts that occurred later in the century certainly had some root in the Famine; hostilities against certain landlords would definitely have been heightened by Famine memories. Landlords who harvested crops and sold them when their tenants were dying must have appeared as evil and inhumane. Local attitudes towards the army would also have changed due to the same disaster. The soldiers, in guarding corn stores, were depriving people of food that was harvested from Irish fields, they were stating through their actions that the people were worth less than the produce. In the enforcement of eviction notices the same soldiers were by their presence again highlighting that the property was of greater importance than the person. The massive emigration that was witnessed in Athlone, be it of those passing through or the departure of fellow townspeople, must have led to a fomenting of anger in people's minds, anger directed at both the British government and the local gentry. These were among the memories that gave rise to the Fenian movement of the 1860s and later struggles, both armed and political.

Perhaps what may have been the hardest thing for people to deal with was their complete inability to help themselves. Parents of families torn apart by the Famine must have felt totally frustrated and sickened by the handicaps they found had been thrust upon them by the government. They had no money to buy food, no land to produce it and perhaps even worse they had to throw themselves at the mercy of the ill-conceived and poorly implemented Poor Law system of those who created the conditions that led to famine in the first instance. A realisation was dawning that the government would never be a friend or ally of the Irish and that Ireland's best interests lay in self-government and providing for her own.

CHAPTER 4

Athlone's Victorian economy: Agriculture, transport, industry and trade

What inhabitant of the town who has passed the meridian of life can fail to notice the painful decline from the numbers of those who in pre-emigration days filled the highway on their weekly pilgrimage to Mass. What an immense throng of moving humanity crowded the roads.[1]

Fr. John Conmee, S.J. (1847–1910)

AGRICULTURE AND POVERTY AFTER THE FAMINE

Ireland after the Famine was a greatly changed country. The disastrous agricultural situation of the 1840s coupled with the actions of many landlords had greatly reduced the population and set in motion a trend of emigration that was to continue for many years. Thousands of people were leaving each month and those that remained, perhaps too old or poor to leave, had to deal with the consequences of Ireland's worst humanitarian disaster in a century. The country was desperately trying to find its balance. This section explores and interprets the agricultural situation of Athlone's population after the Famine, their poverty and their progress. The agricultural situation will be looked at using news on the town's fairs and markets as an indicator of local agricultural prosperity.

In general the situation of rural people is believed to have improved in the early part of the 1850s, as better harvests led to a more satisfactory level of income for both farmers and farm labourers.[2] Populations fell drastically, due to emigration and deaths, as did the rate of marriage, because of the less secure financial situation many found themselves in.[3] Those most affected were members of the Roman Catholic church

1 Conmee, Rev. John S., p.26.
2 Cullen, Louis M., p.137.
3 Kennedy, L & Clarkson, L. A., p.164,

who suffered a larger proportional loss to death and emigration than any other at almost 30% of their total population between the years 1834 and 1861. The two largest of the other denominations, members of the Church of Ireland and Presbyterians saw a fall of less than 20%.[4] Whether Athlone was to see the benefits of the improvement in agriculture is explored next.

The March fair of 1852 appeared to be the first at which a change in the trend of the previous six years was noticed, with a good attendance as well as a brisk trade in cattle and pigs.[5] This apparent upturn did not last, however, with a report from the September fair of the same year indicating the effects of the Famine would not be so easily shrugged off:

> I was grieved to observe the absence of the poor man's stock. They are not one fourth of former years. Death, the landlords and emigration have awfully thinned the small farmers of this once thriving district. The few calves and heifers that were exhibited were but little looked after. Small lots of sheep changed hands at prices rather under Monday's. The demand for horses was disheartening.[6]

The fairs at Athlone during the first two years of the 1850s do not appear to have been well managed; some people purchased much of the produce before it came to market and then re-sold it there at much higher prices. The town had neither a management board for the market or a market house and the method of recording weights of produce was one that was subject to tampering – weights were written on dealers' hats as opposed to dockets.[7] An enquiry was held into the markets held in Irish towns in 1852 and the Athlone market was one of those studied. Most witnesses examined believed that the work of the weights and measures inspector was '*not efficiently carried on*,' leading to the distinct probability of fraudulent practices at the market.[8] The presence of so much livestock in the town during market days was said to generate ill feeling, for they impeded the other commercial interests in the town as well as those travelling thorough Athlone.[9] '*Great inconvenience is occasioned by the fairs and markets in this town being held in the public streets, as it is almost impossible…to get through them.*'[10] A specific act called the Athlone Market Act 1852 was placed before parliament by William Keogh MP, the town's representative at the time. It enabled the Town

4   Proudfoot, L. J., "Regionalism and Localism: Religious Change and Social Protest, c.1700 to c.1900", in Graham, B. J. & Proudfoot, L. J. (Eds.), *An Historical Geography of Ireland* (London, 1993), p.194.
5   *FJ*, 2 Mar 1852.
6   *FJ*, 9 Sep 1852.
7   O'Brien, Municipal, p.83.
8   *Report of the Commissioners appointed to inquire into the State of Fairs and Markets in Ireland* (Dublin, 1855), p.93.
9   Ibid., p.95.
10 Ibid., p.96.

Commissioners to pass bye-laws dealing with the inspection of slaughterhouses, the appointment of a meat inspector to assess the quality of meat sold locally and the appointment of a municipal toll collector.[11] Not all of these provisions were implemented speedily – the appointment of a full time municipal toll collector did not occur until 1860. Indeed, the slow application of this act was repeated in relation to numerous others that the Town Commissioners dealt with, many of which are detailed in chapter seven. One witness at the commission into markets in Ireland wished that the Town Commissioners would use the tolls to clean and pave the streets '...*rather than in paying the parliamentary agents for obtaining their private bill*.'[12]

Over the following number of years the lot of the Athlone people did improve. Reports on theft of livestock and fowl decreased, with the Athlone Fair appearing to have improved to its highest level in over a decade by the time the January Fair was held in 1855.[13] The markets held in the town generally fared reasonably, weather was the main adversary for a number of years, and in 1857 when a fairgreen was opened in the town the fairs were accommodated far more easily.[14] The scenes that were presented of people heading for the fair at Athlone were said to be something to behold:

> What a display of 'dray' and 'kish' and 'crate' – those rustic argosies freighted with the simple merchandise of the homestead and field. Sometimes it would be a farmer seated with praise-worthy self-denial on the narrow shaft of his cart, hard by his horse's tail, who drove along a high crate, which was little less than a menagerie of livestock. Over the top would leer the loutish visage and lolling tongue of a calf – through the bars would peer the bewildered face of a sheep – while a substratum of little pigs – 'bonnuvs' in the local speech – would make their presence known by making protests against the jostlings of the road which huddled them so unceremoniously together.[15]

The effects of the famine and emigration did, however, have a serious effect on Athlone and the surrounding rural population who had apparently lost their fascination with '*going to town*'. Fr. Conmee, author of the above description, believed that whilst emigration had a part to play in this, the '...*glory of the country town in Ireland has almost departed*'. He also believed there to be no more '*painful*' example of this than at Athlone.[16] The numbers that were relying on the workhouses were

11 O'Brien, Municipal, p.84.
12 *Report Fairs*, p.97.
13 *FJ.*, 23 Nov 1853, *FJ.*, 24 Jan 1855.
14 *W.I.*, 3 Jan 1857.
15 Conmee, Rev. John S., p.22.
16 Ibid., p.24.

falling nationally and Athlone also reflected this trend.

The antagonism between tenant and landlord continued unabated, reaching a most serious state when Lord Castlemaine had an attempt made on his life by a tenant wielding a ten-inch knife in the middle of the town.[17] Local attempts to deal with the landlords through political means were initially unsuccessful – the local Tenant Right Society had broken up just four years after its establishment in 1852. The belief of Fr. Conmee that the local landlords were neither numerous, wealthy nor a party in any contentions is certainly untrue, though his close association with a number of the local 'Big House' owners may account for his views.[18] The Westmeath Tenant Right Committee was established in 1863 and did have some level of success in negotiations with the local landlords. The body appears to disappear with the foundation of the National Land League in 1879.[19]

'*If the Widow Malone, och hone, still lives in the town of Athlone, och hone, I do not admire her choice of residence, for its aspect is cold and cheerless.*' The writer of this piece arrived in the town in 1859 on a wet and windy day with '*...the streets looking their narrowest and dingiest and the Castle and the Barracks their greyest and grimmest.*'[20] Still the town did have its luxurious elements also with a local hotel, Rourke's, praised for its standard of accommodation.[21] Another man, an artist, believed Athlone to have attractive features such as the railway bridge and was '*...in itself too interesting, and in the vicinity of objects too remarkable, to justify anyone who deserves the name of a sight-seer passing it.*'[22]

Stories that illustrated the hardship still persisting in and around the town, though less common than during the height of the Famine, showed the deplorable living conditions of some locals. In 1861 *The Freeman's Journal* ran a story depicting the state and trials of a starving local family who entered the town in search of food, after they had exhausted their meagre supply. After abandoning their '*wretched cabin*' the family of five headed into Athlone, the father carried one child, the mother an infant, whilst the third child walked on bleeding feet behind them. Upon reaching the town the mother complained of coldness in her chest and after investigation it was found that the infant had died during the trip. '*It was truly a spectacle of woe to see that emaciated, shivering*

---

17 *FJ.*, 7 June 1858.
18 Conmee, Rev. John S., pp.12–32.
19 Sheehan, Jeremiah, *South Westmeath – Farm and Folk* (Dublin, 1978), p.126.
20 An Oxonian, (Samuel Reynolds Hole), *A Little Tour in Ireland, Being a Visit to Dublin, Galway, Connemara, Athlone, Limerick, Killarney, Glengariff, Cork, etc. etc. etc., By an Oxonian – With Illustrations by John Leech* (London, 1859), pp.113/4.
21 Ibid., p.115.
22 Mahony, Jas., *Hand-Book to Galway, Connemara and the Irish Highlands* (Dublin, 1854), p.26.

group bewailing that little departed creature in the centre of the public street.' The
local relief commissioners were asked for assistance, they refused and
donations from a local priest, some Constabulary members and two
soldiers who had witnessed the scene paid for the burial of the infant as
well as the temporary relief of the *'miserable family'*.[23] The Town
Commissioners set up a relief committee the following week, with the
necessity of the provision of employment again stressed to the
government.[24] This family and many others may have been affected by
the low potato yield of 1861, brought about by bad weather. The levels
of potatoes harvested were the lowest that Ireland had seen since the
Famine.[25] These poor harvests came during one of the worst periods of
'sustained depression' in Ireland, 1859-1864.[26] A travel writer who passed
through the midlands town during 1861 lends credence to this
argument:

> From the information acquired in those localities (Athlone and
> Ballinasloe) from trustworthy sources, I am in a position to state that the
> failure of the potato crop, the deficiency of the harvest generally, and
> above all the want of fuel, are of sufficient extent to justify the prevalent
> opinion, that this winter will be one of severe distress and privation to the
> poorer classes.[27]

The town itself was not thought to be in the worst position however;
there was employment, and the workhouse was not heavily burdened
with paupers, though there were sixty more resident there than at the
same time the previous year.[28] The same author believed that '...*the people
will endeavour to keep out of the workhouse as long as they can, and will endure
the direst suffering rather than enter it, so intense and deep-seated is their dislike
to the system.*' However, the failure of the potato especially in the south of
the barony where the failure was *'universal'* meant that they would
probably have to enter it regardless of their feelings about it.[29] Ironically,
just outside the town in Kiltoom where the soil was considered inferior
to that in the south of the barony the potatoes were supposedly good. At
this time there were also reports of a high porcine mortality rate around
Athlone, which affected the levels on sale at the markets.

The flooding of the River Shannon, still unsolved despite years of
work, was said to have caused a lot of damage to a number of crops,

23 *FJ*, 9 Dec 1861.
24 *FJ*, 17 Dec 1861.
25 Cullen, Louis M., p.137.
26 Turner Michael, *After the Famine, Irish Agriculture 1850-1914* (Cambridge, 1996), p.125.
27 Coulter, Henry, *The West of Ireland: its Existing Condition and Prospects* (Dublin, 1862), p.2.
28 Ibid., p.3.
29 Ibid., p.3.

rendering them '*utterly valueless*.' Rents for the year had been paid, almost in full, but the many problems cast doubt on the ability of many local people to pay the next installment. The high demand for fuel in local houses drove up the price of turf on sale at the Athlone market. Even though the turf on sale was considered very inferior to what had been sold there previously, a lack of supply meant that the price had doubled in twelve months. This was on top of rises earlier in the century brought about by a high demand for turf from the army barracks.[30] However, in general, despite these problems, the town and district of Athlone was said to be improving.

In general the 1860s are thought to have been a decade in which the quality of life of the Irish people improved, living standards rose, more shops were opened and the level of agrarian unrest declined.[31] In Athlone this also appears to be the case to some extent. There were fewer reports of agrarian crimes and more shops were opened in the town, with a massive rise in the numbers of grocers and a more modest increase in the numbers of bakers.[32]

The late 1860s and early 1870s were to see the levels and quality of stock at the fairs in the town rise, with brisk buying reported at the September fair of 1869. The '*best pig fair in years*' was how the January fair of 1870 was described; the April fair the same year was reported on thus:

> Even though the Athlone Fair has been held in April for only two years it has far exceeded expectations. Though at the fair this year the supply of cattle and sheep was very small the sales at the Athlone Fair were very brisk with all the sheep and cattle being sold by 12 noon. One of the reasons that farmers do not bring their livestock to Athlone is that they mistakenly believe the Moate Fair to bring about better prices for their animals. This is untrue however, because of the exposed conditions in Moate – Athlone has a fairgreen in which trading occurs – the animals tend to look less enticing for would-be buyers and their prices fall.
>
> This region is completely free of agrarian outrages and crime, nor does there seem to be the slightest manifestation of any such misguided feeling on the part of the people of this and surrounding districts. Farming operations are progressing with the best results and all the early sown crops about Athlone are now above the ground and doing well for this early season of the year. Ferrier Brothers, Athlone have sold a vast amount of agricultural machinery this year and also seeds of every description.[33]

30 Strean, Annesley, p.68.
31 Cullen, Louis M., p.138.
32 *Slater's National Commercial Directory of Ireland 1856* (London, 1856), pp.5-7, *Slater's* 1870, pp.9-13.
33 *F.J.*, 15 Apr 1870.

Confusingly the writer of the above quote noted that there was very little agrarian crime in and around Athlone and south Westmeath. This is quite untrue; the county had seen a decline but had been proclaimed under the Peace Preservation Act in 1870. It was still considered to be a centre for Ribbonism by the government. This may have been an attempt by the editor of *The Freeman's Journal* to associate good agricultural fortune with a tranquil farming society, the aim being to dissuade further violence.

The optimistic assessments of the fairs and agriculture from 1870 were not repeated the following year. Local farmers had again to contend with the '*Potato Disease*'; between one third and one half of the local crop was wiped out. As well as this a number of cases of '*Mouth-and-Foot Disease*' were reported locally leading to some of the local stock being slaughtered.[34] The lot of paupers in the workhouse improved slightly. On Christmas day 1871, and in subsequent years, the inmates of the workhouse received a *good* meal, of beef and potatoes, donated by Lord Castlemaine.[35]

The fair in the town was again said to be healthy for January 1872 despite the fact that the rail companies were not advertising it, as they were the Moate and Ballinasloe fairs.[36] In the midlands the Athlone fair was considered less successful than the other two, mainly due to its more urban setting and nature, though the methods through which success was measured at each fair were different, making direct comparison difficult.[37] The local autumnal harvest of 1872 was thought to be of very poor quality with *The Westmeath Independent* attempting to place the yield in context:

> The state of the crops in this county generally is rather exceptional when viewed in connection with the reports, which have been published from most other parts of Ireland. Almost every description of crop is light and backward. Turnips are thin, the straw of cereals is short, and in many places yet green and the ear but poorly filled. The potatoes are gone; small in size, ill savoured and taking the rot with usual rapidity.[38]

The paper hoped that the local landlords would take the poor crop yields into account when demanding rents from their already impoverished tenants.[39] The deprivation and penury seen locally caused a benefit concert for the poor to be organised for Christmas 1872 with

34 *W.I.*, 23 Sep 1871.
35 *W.I.*, 30 Dec 1871, *W.I.*, 26 Dec 1874, *W.I.*, 30 Dec 1875, *F.J.*, 24 Jan 1885.
36 *F.J.*, 3 Jan 1872, *W.I.*, 13 Apr 1872.
37 *W.I.*, 28 Jan 1871.
38 *W.I.*, 31 Aug 1872.
39 Ibid.

the proceeds going towards the poor of the town and district.[40] The Athlone fair, though still not entirely successful, continued to grow in 1873. It was extended to one week though, apparently, this only benefited the publicans.[41] The January fair of 1874 was described as '*only second to Ballinasloe*' in importance locally, such was its success.[42] The reports on the fairs vary little throughout the remainder of the 1870s, though problems with '*backwardness*' in the local crops as well as bad weather did cause some problems with levels of produce.[43]

It has been noted that nationally almost all of the harvests in the ten years previous to that in 1877 had been quite good. However, the harvest in that year and the next were said to be very poor and unfortunately only the precursors to the worst harvest the country had seen in many years, that of 1879.[44] The bad weather in that year, around the time of the September fair, caused great distress locally. National figures noted a one third fall in yields, and the local Board of Guardians penned a letter to the Lord Lieutenant detailing the necessity for public works, as well as for the application of the Church Surplus Grant to relieve local rates.[45] The Poor Law Unions all around the country had to deal with large numbers of destitute poor and a massive amount of relief was given.[46] The local fairs at that time and those in early 1880 were described as '*depressed*' by the toll collector with crop levels well down due to the weather.[47]

Nationally, the picture was the same with some areas reporting a two-thirds fall in the value of crops as well as very poorly supplied fairs.[48] The output of potatoes hit their lowest levels for the period 1850-1910 at a time when oats and wheat were not fairing much better.[49] As an indicator of the extreme climate of the time, there were seventeen wet days in August, and twenty-two in both September and October.[50] Distress committees had to be established near Athlone in the townlands of Dysart and Taughboy, where there were thought to be over 500 destitute who would be unable to survive the winter without aid.[51]

40 *F.J.*, 2 Jan 1873.
41 *W.I.*, 22 Mar 1873.
42 *W.I.*, 24 Jan 1874.
43 *W.I.*, 13 May 1876, *F.J.*, 9 Sep 1879, *W.I.*, 1 Sep 1877, *F.J.*, 22 Jan 1878, *W.I.*, 20 Apr 1878.
44 Cullen, Louis M., p.148.
45 *F.J.*, 6 Oct 1879, Cullen, Louis M., p.148
46 Ibid., p.149.
47 *F.J.*, 22 Nov 1879.
48 *The Irish Crisis of 1879 – 80, Proceedings of the Dublin Mansion House Relief Committee 1880*, (Dublin, 1881), p.2.
49 Turner, M., "Rural Economies In Post-Famine Ireland, c.1850-1914", in Graham, B. J. & Proudfoot, L. J. (Eds.), *An Historical Geography of Ireland* (London, 1993), p.299.
50 *Irish Crisis*, p.4.
51 *F.J.*, 15 Jan 1880.

In Athlone a similar committee was established which dealt solely with the Connacht side of the town where the state of the poor was considered far worse than on the Leinster side, another example of the difference between the two halves of Athlone. The committee wanted to petition the Duchess of Marlborough Fund, a charitable committee, for money because it was believed that the measures put in place were inadequate and would result in a number of lives being lost.[52] The committee consisted of both Protestants and Catholics and along with a request to the Marlborough Fund, the usual plea for the establishment of public works was sent to the government.[53] Over the ensuing weeks the Duchess' fund gave the town £300, in £100 lots, for relief and donated a number of blankets.[54] The initial £100 donation helped 4,096 people face the crisis, though there were still 300 destitute in the town after the initial money had been allocated.[55] Another committee that was petitioned for funds was the Dublin Mansion House Relief Committee. The committee did not believe that the problem would reach Famine time proportions due to a lower population, cheaper readily available Indian meal and a lesser dependence on the potato.[56] The report of the committee dealing with the allocation of funds described the national problem in the years 1879–80 thus: '*The condition of Ireland, when the harvest of 1879 lay ruined, was of a character to dismay men of cool and moderate judgement*'.[57]

In relation to Athlone the committee sanctioned nine grants for the destitute in St Peter's ward on the Connacht side of the town and one grant for St. Mary's ward. Again this illustrates that the most vulnerable poor were located on the Connacht side of the town. The grants for St. Peter's were awarded over a six-month period – 20th January to 29th July – and totalled £325, with the grant for St. Mary's awarded in March to the value of £40.[58] The committees that dealt with the Mansion House fund were comprised of Catholic and Protestant clergy, medical officers, poor law guardians and a number of other lay members.[59] The committee admitted that in the case of Athlone: '... [the number of] *applications received...reveal an amount of destitution greater than was anticipated.*'[60] To exacerbate the problem a '*violent downpour*' in July 1880 was thought to have again seriously damaged the crops locally.[61]

---

52 *FJ.*, 19 Jan 1880.
53 Ibid.
54 *FJ.*, 17 Feb 1880, *FJ.*, 21 Feb 1880.
55 Ibid.
56 *Irish Crisis*, p.5.
57 Ibid., p.2.
58 Ibid., p.299.
59 Ibid., p.314.
60 Ibid., p.283.
61 *FJ.*, 16 July 1880.

A visitor to Athlone during the winter of 1880 provided an account of the town, which in general was more positive. Arriving on a Saturday in November 1880 William Sime, a travel writer, was confronted by a market scene on the west side of the town. The Land League was to have a meeting the following day though Sime believed that the motivation of the Athlone people was not one of land for food production for '...*they are definitely out of reach of starving point.*'[62] Lord Castlemaine's tenants were thought to be prospering to an extent with the Leinster side of the town and its market appearing better off that its more westerly counterpart. Generally there was a good stock of winter fuel as well as a good corn crop, which should have ensured a less trying winter for the local populace.

ILL.2: ATHLONE MARKET PLACE, CONNACHT SIDE

More severe weather in January 1881 in the form of a '*great frost*', whilst giving some an opportunity to ice skate and making access to the lake islands easier, caused further problems for the local farmers.[63] This protracted spell of poor weather and low crop yields along with the Land War '...*exposed the tensions at the opposite poles of the social and economic ladder, and finally led to concerted political moves towards Irish Home Rule*'.[64] It was not until July 1882 that news of a good harvest was reported in conjunction with a good Athlone fair.[65] Distress was again expected the following year, however, when local reports stated that bad weather had destroyed as much as two thirds of the local potato crop.[66]

62 Sime, William, *To and Fro, or Views from Sea and Land* (London, 1884), p.136.
63 Ibid., p.136.
64 Turner, Michael, p.216.
65 *F.J.*, 8 July 1882.
66 *F.J.*, 3 Oct 1882, *F.J.*, 28 Nov 1882.

In an attempt to settle disputes with local landlords many tenants resorted, on a number of occasions, to applying for the arbitration of the Land Commission Court, which was set up under the 1883 Land Act. Under its mediation a number of the tenants whose crops had suffered in the bad weather received a lower rent demand from their landlords.[67]

The Athlone fairs appear to show an upturn in the agriculture of the area over the next two years, being well attended with a good supply of livestock present.[68] In what appears to be an example of Victorian commercialism at work some of the traders in the town made a complaint against a number of bakers in the town who were apparently not passing on the savings they were making from lower flour prices to their customers when selling their produce. Locals described the bread as '*weighed like gold*' and of an inferior quality to Dublin bread, which was actually cheaper.[69] At this point in time it must be remembered that many people would still have made their own bread in their homes.

The almost total reliance of the locals on the farmers around the town was seen after the crop of 1885 was harvested. Though the farmers worked during an '*excellent 10 days weather*' the yield was not good, blighted potatoes and '*light*' meadow crops meant that assistance was required locally.[70] The distress that followed led between 200 and 300 of Lord Castlemaine's tenants to lodge 25% less rent when they paid his steward, though his Lordship stated that only true cases of distress would be entertained.[71] This action was taken as part of the countrywide agitation that was growing between the peasantry and landlords as part of the Land War.

The following year the workhouse was still admitting more people than it was discharging, with seventy-seven admitted and sixty-two discharged, leaving a total of 207 inmates.[72] Again the weather hampered agriculture around Athlone and in spring 1886 severe weather conditions such as hail and torrential downpours brought about serious problems.[73] Outdoor relief was provided for a number of families in outlying districts.[74]

During the rest of the 1880s there were virtually no reports of substantial distress locally and the Athlone fair was, in general, well attended though stock levels and prices did fluctuate.[75] In 1889 the press

---

67 Sheehan, Jeremiah, p.136.
68 *FJ.*, 21 Apr 1883, *FJ.*, 22 Mar 1884.
69 *FJ.*, 19 Aug 1884.
70 *FJ.*, 22 Aug 1885.
71 *FJ.*, 28 Nov 1885
72 *FJ.*, 9 Jan 1886.
73 *FJ.*, 1 May 1886, *FJ.*, 15 May 1886.
74 *FJ.*, 17 June 1886.
75 *FJ.*, 1 Sep 1886, *FJ.*, 22 Jan 1887, *FJ.*, 21 Jan 1888, *FJ.*, 8 Sep 1888, *FJ.*, 31 Jan 1889, *FJ.*, 31 Aug 1889.

even reported on the fact that fine potatoes were growing in Irishtown, within the town boundaries.[76]

The transition from the 1880s to the 1890s exhibits still less evidence of agricultural problems with some of the main complaints locally dealing with 'Knockerwrenching' and stormy weather, which affected property in the town.[77] The last decade of the 19th century is thought to have been the point when social and economic good fortunes on a national scale began again.[78] The most impressive rural improvements were said to have occurred in the southwest, west and northwest of the country.[79] The number of fairs in Athlone increased from four to seven per annum with supplies for them more easily sourced due to the upturn in the agricultural sector.[80] Indeed, Athlone's fairs and markets, according to *Thom's Directory* 1891 were '...*growing in importance, owing to the central position of the town, and the extensive railway communications*'.[81]

Mary Banim, a travel writer visited Athlone in 1892 and wrote at considerable length about the town and its environs. She believed that the locals did not regard the fine siting of the town in the way they should have; she believed it to be a very favourable situation indeed. The town was described as having '*great healthfulness*' due to its location; diseases such as cholera had not been seen in the town for many years previous. Emigration was still a feature of the town however, stories were coming back from America as to the prosperity of those who had already travelled, with a number of young men in the town who '...*eagerly and innocently drank in the tales*'. Unfortunately there was '...*no word of the hungry crowds from all nations already too many for the work; of the thousands dying slowly.*[82] Banim appeared to be perturbed by the actions of those who would relay the stories and she had this to say of a returned migrant to the town:

> What is it that prompts so many of our emigrants to brag and boast and lie! Ill-health, unhappiness, overstrain, and but very poor success are indelibly stamped upon this man's face and form.[83]

Some believed that emigration at this time was still to some extent a necessity; as T.P. O'Connor an MP and a native of Athlone noted: '*Who but an Irishman can know the full hopelessness of a youth born into the lower-middle classes of an Irish country town?*'[84]

76 *F.J.*, 25 May 1889.
77 *F.J.*, 21 Sep 1889, *F.J.*, 28 Dec 1889, *The Athlone Times* 4 Jan 1890, *F.J.*, 11 Jan 1890.
78 Cullen, Louis M., p.150.
79 Ibid., p.153.
80 Sheehan, Jeremiah, p.262.
81 *Thom's* (Dublin, 1891), p.255.
82 Banim, Mary, p.195.
83 Ibid., p.195.
84 Foster, R. F., *Paddy and Mr Punch – Connections in Irish and English History* (London, 1995), p.290.

On the Connacht side of the town Banim believed the people were the greatest attraction, and though '...*many of its narrow streets are poor indeed*', the people were still genuinely kind, intelligent and mannerly.[85] The people of the town no longer spoke Irish and though it was only one generation removed on the Connacht side of the town, some still spoke it in nearby rural areas.[87] Banim's assertion is given credence when the earlier notes of Rev. Strean are taken into account. He noted that the only monolingual Irish speakers on the west side of the town were the '*oldest grandmothers*', and that '...*another generation will probably not find an individual ignorant of the English language*.'[88] In general by 1851 25% of the population of the country spoke Irish. English was the language of commerce, of trade (though sources do show that Irish had been predominant at the local markets up until the Famine[89]), more importantly of education and perhaps most effective in the change in language usage, English became '*the language of the pulpit*.'[90] It appears that the Leinster side of the town adopted English more quickly and levels of literacy in that province had always been better than those of Connacht since at least the mid 18th century. The use of Irish was decreasing on the west side of the Shannon though it was still the language of the very poor.[91]

The money that was available for purchasing livestock must have grown considerably in the 1890s when in 1893 reports tell of extraordinarily high pig prices at the Athlone fair and that more surprisingly all the animals were sold.[92] 1895 was the next year in this decade that was to witness hardship on a large scale in the town and, like many years before, the problems were due to bad weather. High levels of snowfall caused the Board of Guardians to give 700 boxes of turf away to the poor along with flour meal and clothes that had been charitably donated by locals. The weather in that year was so cold that Lough Ree had an ice sheet to a depth of 5" in places covering it, and some locals took advantage of this facility. Many attempted to cycle and skate on it in their free time, the amount of which was growing towards the end of the century (*chapter nine*).[93] More weather problems and high

---

85 Banim, Mary, p.248.
87 Ibid., p.253.
88 Strean, Annesley, pp.70/71.
89 Russell, Thomas, "Teanga Thíoramhuil na hÉireann", in Ní Mhuiríosa, Máirín, *Réamhchonraitheoirí – Notaí ar chuid de na daoine a bhí gníomhach I ngluaiseacht na Gaeilge idir 1876 agus 1893* (Baile Átha Cliath, 1968), pp.39/40
90 O'Tuathaigh, Gearoid, p.157/8.
91 Smyth, William J., "The Making of Ireland: Agendas and Perspectives in Cultural Geography", in Graham, B. J. & Proudfoot, L. J. (Eds.), *An Historical Geography of Ireland* (London, 1993), p.427.
92 *FJ*, 21 Jan 1893.
93 *FJ*, 16 Feb 1895.

river levels led to more inconvenience for the locals later in the same year.[94]

Food was still scarce in some quarters, and the means by which one family fed themselves led its members into madness. After consuming meat from dead animals whose cause of death was unknown, they had begun to exhibit evidence of insanity and began attacking one another, leading to one of the sons being fatally wounded. No locals would go to the funeral, believing the family to have been cursed by either the fairies or the devil. The rest of the family was eventually sent to the asylum for the insane, after exhibiting similar homicidal tendencies.[95]

At the end of the 1890s, the levels of poverty and hardship in the town fluctuated but never reached those encountered previously. Advances in local industries such as the Athlone Woollen Mills accounted for some of the prosperity. In October 1896 the price of bread in Athlone, formerly considered high, rose again by 30% due to a shortage of food locally after a bout of bad weather.[96] The situation appears to have righted itself by March 1898 when the Athlone fair was described as the largest ever held such were the levels of livestock and crops on offer.[97] Whilst the situation may not have been as bad as in previous years, a report from April 1899 told of the numbers of '*strapping men and women*' who were departing Athlone and the west in search of new lives abroad.[98] The Athlone fairs in 1901 were unsuccessful from a commercial point of view – the September fair, called a '*big bad fair*', had a surplus of stock that no one wished to buy.[99]

In the half century between the end of the Famine and the end of Victoria's reign Athlone was to encounter a number of difficulties with agriculture and hence, because of widespread dependence on this sector, with poverty. The advent of poor weather conditions and unstable levels of crop production along with their effects showed that the people of the town were still heavily reliant on the farming sector despite some advances in industry and trade. Those people at the lowest levels of society were still suffering to a great extent – many Victorian advances had not really applied to them; they were as an underclass advancing more slowly than the rest. In Athlone there appear to have been different rates of improvement on both sides of the river. Crop failures and the subsequent levels of deprivation always impacted more heavily on the Connacht side of the town than on the Leinster side.

94 *F.J.*, 16 Nov 1895.
95 *F.J.*, 14 Mar 1896, *F.J.*, 11 July 1896, *F.J.*, 13 Mar 1897.
96 *F.J.*, 24 Oct 1896.
97 *F.J.*, 26 Mar 1898.
98 *F.J.*, 15 Apr 1899.
99 *A.T.*, 12 Oct 1901.

When good crop yields were reported along with prosperous local markets, people appeared to readjust quickly to the improved living conditions offered. By the end of the Victorian era, when many people were becoming more economically secure and less dependent on agriculture, reports of deprivation were less prevalent, and though emigration continued, a general sense of improvement was evident locally.

TRANSPORT, INDUSTRY AND TRADE

Nothing in the town impresses you with the idea of beauty, industry or prosperity.[100]

> Athlone singularly combines prime facilities for commerce, military strength, and almost metropolitan command...except in ancient times, for its commanding the passage of the Shannon and in modern times, for its being a central depot for arms and ammunition, its position has been turned into surprisingly little practical account.[101]

In 1837 Louis-August Blanqui used the term 'Industrial Revolution' to describe the social and economic changes that Britain had undergone in the fifty years beforehand. *The Oxford Companion to British History* observes that the use of coal was symbolic of the revolution, people began to use the fuel in larger quantities and by producing more energy through its combustion industry started to grow. The conditions that led to the Industrial Revolution (if indeed there was one, since some modern historians argue that it is a misnomer for the period and the changes that took place) have never been fully decided upon: '...*any argument has to explain the causes of the development of Britain as the first industrial nation*'.[102] Whilst it appears that no agreement has been reached as to the factors that led to the growth of industry on Britain, it is clear that Ireland, with the exception of Belfast, did not experience the same growth. The generalisation of the Victorian economy in Britain and Ireland has been described as meaningless by one academic due to the fact that living conditions in pre-famine Ireland were relatively inferior, unemployment very high and the economy too unstable to make such generalisations useful.[103]

Joseph Lee in his book *The Modernisation of Irish Society, 1848-1918* states that Ireland was a predominantly agricultural country in the early 19th century, and that the changes in the economy were generally

100 "Dublin Penny Journal, 1833", in Woods, James, *Annals of Westmeath* (Dublin 1907, reprinted Ballymore, 1977), pp.338-339.
101 Gazetteer, p.96.
102 Cannon, John, (Ed.), *The Oxford Companion to British History* (Oxford, 1997), p.509.
103 Harrison, J. F. C., *Early Victorian Britain, 1832 – 51* (London, 1971), p.64.

hinged on agricultural fortunes.[104] Obviously just because Ireland was a largely agricultural nation did not mean it could not also industrialise. Formerly, Lee noted, a lack of capital was blamed for the lack of industrialisation in the country. However it appears that money was available and became more so in later 19th century, when some industries started to grow. As stated already coal was one of the main catalysts, which drove industry on Britain, its scarcity along with other raw materials '...*precluded imitation of the English pattern of industrialisation, but not industrialisation itself*'.[105] The 19th century scholar Robert Kane argued that a number of factors were holding Ireland back from industrial development; poor communications, scarcity of common industrial raw materials, poor education and a lack of money.[106] He further claimed that all of the industrial development in Ireland, be it public or private in nature, was an ideal way to improve the country as a whole:

> Above all, with temperate habits, and with the education which the National system will give to every individual of the growing race, there is no danger but that industry may be accompanied by intelligence, intelligence by morality and all by the steadiness of purpose and tranquillity of habits on which the happiness of the family and the peace of the community depend.[107]

Despite the fact that Ireland did not industrialise at a rapid pace, the Victorian era was to see the foundation of a number of industries in Athlone, some of which were quite successful. In this section the industrial and economic development of the town will be explored. In doing this the impact that the Shannon navigation works and the arrival of the railway had on Athlone will be outlined and assessed along with the growth in local industries and changes in trade.

SHANNON NAVIGATION WORKS

Athlone, though commanding a superb geographical location in the centre of Ireland on the banks of the country's largest river, never appears to have developed its potential. In the 18th century, as already noted, it was relatively in decline in comparison with other towns in the country and one of the reasons for this was actually its inaccessibility. Its position in the centre of Ireland meant that arduous road journeys needed to be made to reach it by land from the major ports. The

104 Lee, Joseph, *The Modernisation of Irish Society 1848 – 1918* (Dublin, 1973), pp.9-11.
105 Ibid., pp.12-13.
106 Kane, Robert, M. D., *The Industrial Resources of Ireland*, 2nd Ed. (Dublin, 1845), pp. 387-408.
107 Ibid., p.426.

alternative, using the river to reach the town, had one main problem associated with it. Boats could reach the town, either from Limerick by river or the east coast via the canal system, but due to the shallowness of the natural ford these craft were diminutive and incapable of transporting large quantities of cargo. Recognising this the government set about attempting to improve navigation on the Shannon around the town from the mid-18th century. They constructed a canal on the town's western fringe, which was used by barges to carry goods to Athlone and further north. However, these works were found to be unsatisfactory and deteriorated surprisingly quickly. With the development of large steamboats that could carry vast quantities of cargo, the government realised that the Shannon in its entirety needed to be improved so that these boats could navigate to all of the main centres of commerce. The Victorians saw the advantage of good infrastructure when it came to increasing economic growth and at Athlone prior to the arrival of the railways the river was the only way to transport large quantities of stock to the town.

The major works on the river during the 19th century began in the 1830s with the appointment of the Shannon Commissioners, under the Board of Works, whose job it was to assess the problems being faced and to formulate a strategy to help solve them. The other serious problem identified apart from the problem with transportation was the seasonal flooding of the river. The flooding was detrimental to farmers who worked land on the banks of the river causing the loss of crops and consequently money. To address this the commissioners had to ensure that the works carried out would '...*contribute to the general prosperity, commerce, agriculture and revenue of Ireland*'.[108] The hope was that the returns would far outweigh investment, which was intended to be as small as possible.

> The whole should be executed in the most plain and economical manner; all extra expense for decoration and ornament being rejected, as the magnitude and importance of the work will, in fact, be its most appropriate ornament.[109]

Initially the main concern at Athlone was not the deepening of the Shannon but the replacing of the Elizabethan bridge that straddled the river at the town. The bridge, quite a long structure, was entirely incapable of dealing with the traffic that attempted to cross it each day. Rev. Strean noted how '...*confusion which frequently occur[s] from the*

108 Griffiths, A. R. G., *The Irish Board of Works 1831 – 1878* (London, 1987), pp.49-50.
109 Ibid., pp.49-50.

contrary currents of men, carriages and cattle', led to serious delays on a day-to-day basis.[110] A description of the Elizabethan bridge was given in a Gazetteer for 1844 using the notes made by Isaac Weld in 1832:

> [It] is…the very worst, for both passage and water-way, upon the whole river. It has 9 arches, all narrow in the span, with huge massive intervening piers, and practically operates during freshets as a dam; it is about 300 feet long and not more than 12 feet broad, so that carriages or cars can pass one another only at recesses on the piers…to render its inconveniences complete, it has one flour mill at its west end, another at its east end, and a third over part of its arches, so as to be to some extent a business-street. The mere daily thoroughfare between the two divisions of the town is an overmatch for the bridge's capacities; and on market and fair days.[111]

Maria Edgeworth, the novelist and H. D. Inglis, a travelogue author, were also greatly unimpressed by the bridge with the latter stating that: '[the] *Bridge is extremely ancient and is in a disgracefully ruinous condition…a disgrace to the town and the kingdom.*'[112] Similarly, John O'Donovan of the Ordinance Survey did not hide his true feelings of the structure in a letter he wrote in 1837: '*It's* [Athlone's] *bridge is scandalous. I hope the Shannon will sweep it away and make them build a decent one.*'[113]

The bridge caused most problems on market days; Rev. John Swift Joly, a Protestant clergyman who resided in the town for a number of years retold how:

> …roaring and bellowing as bullocks only can do, with Connaughtmen screeching Irish to them at the tops of their shrill voices, and all the juvenile imps of the town, with mischievous delight, adding to the confusion….on they come, for the terrors behind them, in the shape of bludgeons, oaths and Irish, are far more impressive, and it is quite evident that the passage will be forced.[114]

Joly also mentioned how the small recesses on the bridge were used by many to avoid being trampled – the picture painted by many crossing the Shannon at Athlone when the old bridge was in place was one of rural chaos in an urban setting.[115] John O'Donovan stated that around the area of the bridge on market day there was: '*Such confusion of women, Connaughtmen, horses asses, potatoes, soldiers, peelers would almost make one swear that there is no order in nature. This is market day.*'[116] Joly did mention

---

110 Strean, Annesley, p.54.
111 *Gazetteer*, p.98.
112 Inglis, H. D., p.338.
113 O'Donovan, John.
114 Joly, Rev. John S., *The old Bridge of Athlone* (Dublin, 1881), p.82.
115 Ibid., pp.80-83.
116 O'Donovan, John.

however that he and many other similarly interested Victorians would have liked to have seen the bridge remain: '...*the antiquary...regrets that the Shannon Commissioners did not leave the old bridge for the admiration of posterity*'.[117] Of course retention of the bridge would have defeated the purpose of the works; the bridge was part of the problem.

As early as 1819 plans were being made for the construction of a new bridge across the river and estimates of £9,000 were quoted for total costs.[118] Over the subsequent decades there were various promises made to the townspeople with regard to the provision of a new bridge e.g. '*Hurrah! – A New Bridge*', printed in *The Athlone Sentinel* in 1834 which appeared to confirm that the government had allocated funds for the destruction of the old bridge and construction of a new one, as well as other funds for various improvements along the length of the Shannon.[119] Five years later there was still no movement and the wealthier inhabitants of the town forwarded a petition asking the government to replace the bridge, which was becoming increasingly a hindrance to the good running of the town:

> That the bridge across the river Shannon, which forms the connexion between the provinces of Leinster and Connaught, in the town of Athlone, is now, and has been for many years past, in a most ruinous condition, having its battlements on a complete level with the foot path, thereby endangering the lives and properties of Her Majesty's subjects. The fact that this bridge is the general thoroughfare between the two provinces, renders its present dilapidated state much more alarming, inasmuch, as at a very late date the lives of two persons were in imminent danger, they having fallen over the bridge in consequence of the battlements being completely destroyed; and from the very narrow passage (it being only thirteen feet wide) persons are frequently obliged to cross the river on boats on market and other days.
>
> Your Petitioners therefore humbly hope that your honourable House will take this statement into your serious consideration, and order such means be adopted as will afford your petitioners a speedy remedy for this very great grievance.
> And your Petitioners, as in duty bound shall ever pray.[120]

The letter may have assisted in hastening the commencement of the work, for the drainage of the river at Athlone began in earnest early the next year. The press related that the Shannon Commissioners had erected a temporary '*commodious timber*' footbridge across the river,

117 Ibid., p.84.
118 Strean, Annesley, pp.53/4.
119 *A.S.*, 2 Apr 1834.
120 "Miscellanea", in *Journal of the Old Athlone Society*, Vol. II, No.5 (Athlne, 1985), p.75.

bought all the mills on the old bridge and sold off all the materials from them in preparation for its destruction.[121] Preparatory work on the new bridge commenced in September of 1841, with work on what was to be the submarine portion of the structure reported as *'progressing well'*.[122] Consisting of three seventy-five-foot arches, the new bridge was to be located 150 yards north of the dilapidated Elizabethan structure. The District Engineer laid the first stone of the new structure on Saturday, November 6th 1841 with a small ceremony held to mark the occasion.[123] Luckily, despite a strike in April 1842, the work continued more or less on schedule with the bridge reported as being almost ready to open in September 1844; the old bridge had been blown up using dynamite in January of that year.[124]

ILL.3: ATHLONE TOWN BRIDGE

The work on the town bridge was said to have engaged up to 550 men on a daily basis.[125] The numbers employed on the works in total between middle and upper Shannon averaged between them 644 men in 1841, 2,117 in 1842 and 2,288 in 1843, massive figures for the time.[126] In November 1844 after the bridge had opened, the local press

121 *F.J.*, 1 June 1840.
122 *A.M.*, 25 Sep 1841, *F.J.*, 12 Oct 1841.
123 *F.J.*, 9 Nov 1841.
124 *F.J.*, 27 Sep 1844, *A.S.*, 19 Jan 1844.
125 *A.S.*, 18 Aug 1843.
126 Kane, Robert, p.353.

reported that there was no ceremony involved.[127] The contractor stated that:

> This bridge has been built in a most substantial and satisfactory manner, both as regards the workmanship and the materials used, which were of the best description of their respective kinds.[128]

The other work of the Shannon Commissioners at Athlone involved the construction of a weir wall as well as the removal of impediments to navigation, such as large rocks, from the riverbed. Formerly steamboats found that they could only venture as far as Athlone with a half full cargo hold due to the shallow nature of the river.[129] To effect the necessary changes the bed had to be drained. This was to prove a difficult task again necessitating the employment of large numbers of men. A newspaper article from July 1848 reported that the work was so far advanced that the docks in Athlone were almost completely dry, and that soon large numbers were to be employed in the deepening of the river.[130] It was necessary to have as much of the works as possible completed before the winter flooding season, which if it were bad would have made the job far harder and perhaps impossible to complete on time. A number of local men were hired in the following month to assist in the removal of stones from the riverbed between the new bridge and the woodwork erected for the formation of the docks.[131] Major employment at Athlone in connection with the works of the Shannon Commissioners came in 1849. The local press depicted an animated scene in the town:

> In consequence of a report which had been spread throughout the country, some 1000's of poor creatures crowded into the town during the early part of the day, which towards evening became so numerous, that the interference of the police was found necessary to protect the overseers during their selection of the parties which offered themselves. Towards evening from 600 – 700 men were placed upon the work which consists in deepening the bed of the river, and clearing away the remains of the ancient bridge which formerly connected the provinces of Leinster and Connaught.
>
> A good deal of disappointment was felt by those who had been rejected – many of the starving creatures having travelled a long distance with the hope of being engaged. Yesterday and to-day the number of hands being

---

127 *A.S.*, 9 Nov 1844.
128 Delany, Ruth, "Athlone navigation works, 1757-1849", in Murtagh, H. (Ed.), *Irish Midland Studies*, (Athlone, 1980), p.201.
129 Griffiths, A. R. G., p.48.
130 *W.I.*, 22 July 1848.
131 *W.I.*, 5 May 1848.

considerably increased, and now upwards of 1500 men find employment on these works.[132]

During the period 1841–1851 there was a massive number of jobs lost in Ireland, amounting to roughly 680,000 in total.[133] The jobs that the works at Athlone provided were some of the many offered by the government during the Famine who saw the provision of public works as part of the solution to Ireland's food shortage. Throughout the works:

> Athlone…presents a busy and animated appearance. All is activity and bustle from the number of persons employed in the completion of the Shannon works under the superintendence of the Commissioners. The spectacle of nearly 1000 men engaged in excavating the bed of the river which is completely dry, and which as far as the eye can reach is filled with workmen and horses, miners and engineers, etc., is a novelty not often met with.[134]

However, the massive employment provided by the works was quite short-lived with all the operations officially concluded in September 1849. The river was given a short period during which the Commissioners could judge its flow through the new works, with boats permitted on the river soon after.[135] The estimated total cost of the works around Athlone between 1840 and 1849 was thought to be almost £105,000.[136]

Robert Kane believed that the value of Public Works was not only a monetary one for those employed but:

> The people are not only employed so as to earn a subsistence, but being brought into contact with workmen of a higher class, and of steadier habits, they become themselves gradually improved in character.[137]

Kane's idea that the workers would gain something positive from interacting with the foremen is not supported by the contemporary accounts; the men were treated like slaves and slavery is not a state renowned for 'improving' people: '*According to a correspondent the whips of the gangers were in constant requisition and the view from the bridge would remind you of the manner in which the Negroes of America are kept at work*'.[138] The poor and starving masses were being abused to further the economic lot of the already wealthy; the contrast between the

132 *W.I.*, 30 June 1849.
133 Geary, Frank, p.173.
134 *W.I.*, 14 July 1849.
135 *W.I.*, 1 Sep 1849.
136 Delany, Ruth, p.203.
137 Kane, Robert, p.353.
138 *W.I.*, 30 June 1849.

importance given to the Victorian demand for economic advancement
and the plight of the Irish peasantry was quite stark. It appears that
Engels' and Marx's use of words like slavery and serfdom to describe the
lot of the lower working classes in Britain were true reflections of fact
in Ireland also.[139]

The Victorian hunger for the creation of new technology to make all
facets of life easier was seen on a number of occasions in Athlone.
During the life of the works on the Shannon modern technology was
often used to expedite the process. During the creation of the
foundations for the new bridge two steam engines were put to work
pumping the water out of the holes being excavated by the
commissioners.[140] Reported in the local press with an air of amazement
was the utilisation, during repairs to the weir wall, of sub-aqua diving
equipment, seldom if ever seen in Athlone:

> The stones were restored to their position under the water by workmen
> aided by the diving apparatus, which, in the form of a helmet, encloses
> the head of the wearer and permits him to remain under water for a
> considerable space of time – air in sufficient quantities being admitted
> from above by means of a tube communicating with the workmen
> underneath.'[141]

The introduction of new technologies in the work did not always go
to plan. During the early phase of the drainage of the river one of the
workmen, caught in the workings of an engine that was being used, died
a ferocious death, hacked to pieces by the motor.[142]

As had happened before, these works on the River Shannon were
subsequently found to be inadequate as the river continued to burst its
banks and inundate the surrounding land with large volumes of
floodwater. By 1870 the effect that the floods were having on the local
region caused another round of 'Shannon Improvements' to come into
effect. Initially £93,000 pounds was allocated to cover '*inundations*' on
the river Shannon and its tributary the River Suck, with the
Commissioners of Public Works outlining their intentions in the local
press.[143] The works enacted were not said to be of the highest quality
for in *The Westmeath Independent* a quite unflattering account of the
government's efforts was presented by a correspondent who believed
that posturing was all that was being done, with virtually nothing
attempted to keep '...*the Shannon between its banks. The story of the*

139 O'Farrell, Patrick, *England and Ireland Since 1800* (Oxford, 1975), p.122.
140 *F.J.*, 12 Oct 1841.
141 *W.I.*, 14 July 1849.
142 *W.I.*, 14 June 1842.
143 *W.I.*, 9 July 1870, *W.I.*, 26 Nov 1870.

Government along the banks of the Shannon, is a story of unbroken failure'.[144]
More plans, as part of the Shannon Act 1874, elicited a larger sum than
the most recent works with £300,000 allocated, half as a gift with the
remainder secured against the lands that were to benefit most from the
improvements. The type of work to be carried out was, as before, to be
'the most efficient and inexpensive'.[145] Severe flooding later in the year
caused more bile to be aimed in the direction of the Commissioners for
Public Works:

> For the past fortnight the lands along the river adjacent to Athlone have been
> completely flooded. The water still continues to overflow the banks, and
> judging from the appearances an immense tract of country is still threatened
> with inundation. Thousands upon thousands of acres are thus rendered
> useless, that were counted upon for grazing to the great loss of the occupiers.
>
> The water has risen in some places about 10 feet within the time
> specified. When, may we ask are the provisions of the recent remedial act
> passed, to be brought to bear on this grievance? Echo, answers when!
>
> It is not the way to do it but the way not to do it that unfortunately
> guides the instincts of our public departments.[146]

The works intended for the Shannon were objected to by a number
of landowners who believed that the way in which it was proposed the
land be drained was excessive and ultimately counterproductive.[147] A
board meeting of the Commissioners for Public Works was held in
Athlone for landowners to air their grievances. At this meeting the
actual cost for the works was set down as being £150,000, half of what
was originally allocated – this may have been due to the landowners'
objections.[148] For the remainder of the 1870s the Shannon inundations
issue remained alive. The Town Commissioners in January 1875 believed
that if the same problems were being experienced in England they
'would not last 24 hours'.[149]

The state of the flooding continued to be related through the local
press during the period in which the works were being carried out with
all the usual rhetoric being employed. However, the unrest in relation
to the Shannon works was not reserved for the town's press and
inhabitants alone. The workers, who were carrying out the dredging
etc., decided to go on strike in July of 1882 demanding better wages.[150]
This type of strike action was occurring in Britain at the same time,

144 *W.I.*, 15 Nov 1873.
145 *W.I.*, 27 June 1874.
146 *W.I.*, 17 Oct 1874.
147 *W.I.*, 3 Mar 1875.
148 *F.J.*, 20 Mar 1875.
149 *W.I.*, 6 Jan 1877.
150 *W.I.*, 1 July 1882.

people's minds were modernising, workers began to see that they were essential to the plans of the government and hence had some leverage. Their demands were met just two weeks later with their wages rising from 12/- to 14/-. The works on the Shannon, when completed, again appear to have been ineffective for the number and frequency of complaints in the local press about the issue did not diminish. The best illustration of the ineffective nature of the works was noted in 1897 when it was reported that a boat was able to pass over the weir wall in the town without any difficulty such were the levels of the river. The difference that was meant to exist between the river level and the weir wall was fifteen feet.[151]

With their scheme of Shannon improvements the commissioners had accomplished one of their goals. The river was now open to larger boats allowing for greater ease in transportation of cargo. Achieving their other main goal proved beyond even the considerable capabilities of Victorian engineers. The Shannon continued to overflow and damage thousands of acres of crops. Of course one cannot be too critical of this failure; the same problem is still faced today when the Shannon bursts its banks each year.

RIVER TRANSPORT

Prior to the works to improve navigation on the River Shannon and the spread of the railways, a number of boats plied their trade from Athlone to Limerick, though these were small vessels due to the depth of the river. Steamboats like the 'Gazelle' and the 'Dunally' operated out of the town in the 1840s, though other boats had been in operation since 1827, transporting people as far as Limerick, but a slump in trade caused the 'Gazelle' to be put out of commission.[152] So in keeping with the Victorian economist's aspiration for an improving Ireland it was hoped that the work of the Shannon Commissioners would improve the state of river transport on Ireland's largest artery. When the first set of works were completed, the size of the boats that could travel up the river increased greatly, as evidenced by an account of the arrival of the City of Dublin Steam Company's 'Lady Landsdowne' in Athlone given in the local press:

> The appearance on Thursday evening of…the Lady Lansdowne, on the Upper Shannon was a novelty which came unexpectedly upon the inhabitants of Athlone, as she steamed up our noble river a large number of spectators congregated on the bridge and quays, who by hearty cheers,

151 *FJ.*, 9 Jan 1897.
152 *FJ.*, 28 Nov 1846.

welcomed this, the 1st attempt to open the navigation for vessels of any burden above Shannonbridge, from which the traffic has been heretofore carried on by means of the ordinary canal boats propelled by a small tug-steamer. By the Lady Lansdowne a number of visitors were conveyed from Limerick, who, having inspected our extensive barracks and military outworks, left next morning by the same conveyance for Clonmacnois, to view the ancient ruins of the seven churches and towers. We are happy to learn that in the future the Company's steamers will ply regularly between Limerick and Athlone with passengers and freight.[153]

The vessel made a return trip the next week and attracted a large crowd to the docks when she blew off her steam.[154] After the success of the trips made by the 'Lady Landsdowne' another carrier, the Dublin Steam Packet Company, decided to run their vessels to Athlone.[155]

The two main railway companies that served Athlone, the Midland Great Western Railway (MGWR) and the Great Southern and Western Railway (GSWR) also decided to venture into the steamboat trade in the 1850s. The rail network was not as pervasive as they would have wished, and competition meant that they had to use the rivers and canals to connect people and goods with their rail depots. In July of 1857 the MGWR launched what it hoped would be its first iron steamboat on the river for a test run.[156] Another boat from a different company, called the 'Artisan', was placed on the Athlone/Killaloe route in August of the same year carrying both passengers and freight.[157] By October the MGWR boat the named 'Duchess of Argyle', was ready for service and a launch celebration complete with fireworks was laid on.[158] The boat's Scottish name could be traced back to where it originally plied its trade – upon the River Clyde in Scotland. A number of augmentations were carried out on the vessel to make it suitable for navigating the Shannon.[159] The business experienced by both the 'Artisan' and the 'Duchess of Argyle' was such that both ran daily between Athlone and Killaloe offering rates from 1st to 3rd class. The lack of a direct steamer to Limerick meant that an omnibus had to be provided at Killaloe for travellers who wished to continue further.[160]

Another carrier that came into the Athlone steamboat market was the Grand Canal Company. It arrived in 1861, offering a service on

153 *W.I.*, 8 Sep 1849.
154 *W.I.*, 15 Sep 1849.
155 *W.I.*, 6 Oct 1849.
156 *W.I.*, 13 July 1857.
157 *W.I.*, 15 Aug 1857.
158 *W.I.*, 24 Oct 1857.
159 *F.J.*, 17 Nov 1857.
160 *F.J.*, 15 May 1858.

Monday, Wednesday and Friday from Killaloe.[161] The 'Duchess of
Argyle' ran, possibly in reaction to this new competition, from Athlone
on the same days as above with trips from Killaloe occurring on
Tuesday, Thursday and Saturday.[162] The increased competition between
the two steamboat companies and the railway companies, which were
expanding the network constantly, along with an apparent fall-off in
demand for river travel, caused the passenger conveyances on the
Shannon to fall out of use in 1864.[163]

From the *Reports and evidence relating to Shannon Navigation 1836-65*
a number of reasons for the fall-off in trade were outlined and some
remedies were proposed for the problems being faced. The Grand Canal
Company was singled out for running an unsuitable boat for passengers.
'The Shannon' was according to one witness '...*exclusively a trade steamer
for tugging boats*' and not suited to passengers.[164] The Grand Canal
Company stated, as part of evidence given, that improvements were
being made to the steamer so as to render it more suitable.[165] At the time
of the report in 1865 'The Shannon' was still tugging boats and was the
only boat using the recently built Victoria Lock in Athlone whilst all the
better boats had been abandoned: '*They are a wretched exhibition of the
expenditure of money thrown away; they are rotting in Killaloe...from the want
of passenger trade*'.[166] Many of the boats were sent to other locations
around the United Kingdom where they served out their last days.[167]

The report found that the 'Lady Landsdowne' and the 'Lady Burgoyne'
had both stopped sailing in 1859 whilst the 'Duchess of Argyle' and the
'Artisan' stopped in 1863 but were ready for use. The main reason, other
than a lack of passengers, for the weakening of steamboat business was the
arrival of the railways. The steam companies undercut the freight charges
of the railways by 10% as a matter of policy and were still moving coal
and other freight up the canals and rivers but were facing fierce
competition, mainly due to the speed of rail transport.[168]

The Grand Canal Company decided to purchase the 'Duchess of
Argyle' and set it to work on the river in 1866 for passenger traffic as
far as Killaloe.[169] There is not much evidence of how the steamboat
fared but one can assume that the disruption caused by the Shannon

161 *W.I.*, 9 Feb 1861.
162 *W.I.*, 5 June 1861.
163 *W.I.*, 3 June 1866.
164 *Reports and Evidence Relating to Shannon Navigation 1836-65* (Dublin, 1839-67), p.13.
165 Ibid., p.47.
166 Ibid., p.13.
167 Delany, Ruth, "The River Shannon, Lough Ree and Athlone", in Keaney, M. & O'Brien, G., *Athlone -
     Bridging the Centuries* (Mullingar, 1991), p.31.
168 *Reports and Evidence Relating to Shannon Navigation 1836-65* (Dublin. 1839-67), p.60.
169 *F.J.*, 10 Aug 1866.

improvement works of the late 1860/70s would have been detrimental to the enterprise. It was not until 1878 that more news of a steamer running on the river is mentioned when it was reported in a local newspaper that the two rail companies in Athlone were considering placing one on the Shannon. However, nothing appears to have come of the rumour with no mention of a service over the ensuing months.[170]

The last attempt during the Victorian period for the steamers to run again on the Shannon came in 1897 with the establishment of the Shannon Development Co., which had capital of £20,000.[171] Five steamers were ordered, all of which would serve the usual Athlone to Killaloe route.[172] The first boat to arrive was the 'Fairy Queen', which had room for 200 passengers.[173]

The interest surrounding the river and the use of the boats appeared to grow quite quickly when the number of applications for usage were such as to require a rotation system to be put in place.[174] The Shannon Development Co. had a number of initiatives and viability measures, which they used to encourage tourists to travel the Shannon. The company sponsored yacht races as well as limiting the running of the steamers to the summer months when business was profitable.[175] Complaints were received that the punctuality and speed of the boats was worse than thirty years previously, leading to a review of the systems in place by the Board of Works.[176] The business did not thrive however, the railways had done too much damage and the advent of the motorcar in the early 20th century caused the company to fold in 1914.

ATHLONE AND RAILWAY MANIA

Prior to the arrival of the railways in Athlone the people were limited to transport via steamboats on the river or a choice of a car to Ballinasloe, a caravan to Kilbeggan or a mail car to Mullingar. Other coaches and mail cars also travelled from Dublin to the west, with another 'special car' working between the town and the Royal Canal.[177] The advent of 'Railway Mania' in England during the late 1830s and especially the second phase of the boom in the years 1844-47 soon led to the extension of railway construction in Ireland when the Irish gauge

170 *W.I.*, 25 May 1878.
171 *F.J.*, 13 Feb 1897.
172 *F.J.*, 9 Jan 1897, *F.J.*, 13 Feb 1897.
173 *F.J.*, 1 May 1897.
174 *F.J.*, 15 May 1897.
175 *F.J.*, 31 July 1897, *F.J.*, 28 May 1898.
176 *F.J.*, 5 Mar 1898, *F.J.*, 12 Mar 1898.
177 Griffiths, A. R. G., p.48, *Gazetteer*, p.99.

was standardised at five feet three inches in 1846.[178] In a short period of time the railways were to usurp the Bianconi network of carriages in the country as the main form of land transport. Originally those who wished to construct railways in Ireland had to source half of the capital privately, a situation that changed post 1847 when the government began to offer grants to subsidise work.[179] The process of building railways in the country was made easier by the fact that the cost of construction was almost half what it was in England.[180]

Athlone was always going to be an important railway confluence due to its geographical position. The main line to be brought through the town was that which connected Dublin to Galway. Originally discussed in 1844 it was decided to proceed with the preparatory work due to the belief that the railway line would be positive for all those places that it would connect along its route.[181] The railways were to help Ireland's industry grow greatly during the Victorian period. Formerly only coaches serviced the smaller urban centres, which had only low levels of industry; the penetration of the railways was to give a boost to these areas.[182]

Prior to the line becoming fully extended to Athlone from the west there were three-horse coaches that left the town every morning at 10.30 to connect people with the train to Galway at Ballinasloe. A similar system provided a connection from Ballinasloe to Athlone.[183] In Athlone two railway stations were to be built, one on the each side of the river owned and operated by two separate companies.

Obviously a bridge was required to traverse the Shannon and its construction was described as progressing well by June of 1850 when three of the six pillars that were to be erected were in place.[184] *The Freeman's Journal* reported that it was completed on the 18th of July at 10 o'clock at night and that a number of test runs were attempted to ensure it was in working order.[185] The runs were greeted by, '...*the cordial cheering of the multitude assembled to witness it*'.[186] Initially the contractor G. W. Hemans had eighteen months in which to finish the bridge; it was

---

178 Thomson, David, *England in the Nineteenth Century <1815 – 1914>* (Penguin Books, 1950), p.42, Proudfoot, L. J., "Spatial Transformation an Social Agency: Property, Society and Improvement, c.1700 to c.1900", in Graham, B. J. & Proudfoot, L. J. (Eds.), *An Historical Geography of Ireland* (London, 1993), p.243, Fitzgerald, Garret, "Transport", in Kennedy, Kieran A., *From Famine to Feast – Economic and Social Change in Ireland 1847-1997* (Dublin, 1998), p.88.
179 Cullen, Louis M., p.143.
180 Ibid.
181 *A.S.*, 7 Dec 1844.
182 Nowlan, Kevin B., "Travel", in McDowell, R. B., *Social Life in Ireland 1800-45* (Cork, 1979), p.109.
183 *W.I.*, 2 Feb 1848.
184 *Athlone 1950*, p.41.
185 *F.J.*, 27 July 1851.
186 *W.I.*, 25 July 1851.

ILL.4: ATHLONE RAILWAY BRIDGE

actually finished before this deadline had elapsed, despite a strike by masons in 1850.[187] The use of compressed air to erect the pillars was one of many technological innovations used at Athlone, which was well reviewed in the press.[188] The official opening of the Dublin to Galway line occurred on the 1st of August 1851 though this was, apparently, a low-key affair.[189] The railway bridge at Athlone is still regarded as a fine example of the brilliance of Victorian engineering and along with the town bridge is one of the many important legacies that the era left behind in the town. A 19th century onlooker believed that the bridge had another function along with facilitating transport: it appealed to the sophisticated Victorian aesthetic sense:

> The railway bridge and the other, erected by the Shannon Commissioners, both being stupendous works, add much to the picturesque features of the scenery. The former, due to the genius of Mr. Hemans, may be regarded as a remarkable illustration of the triumph of art over difficulty – massive and grand in all its proportions, it still combines in its ensemble much of the graceful and elegant, and though gigantic in its proportions, it is yet so much in keeping with the mighty Shannon, which it spans, that it appears at a distance to be of no more than ordinary dimensions.[190]

187 Currivan, P. J., "Athlone as a Railway Centre", in *Journal of the Irish Railway Record Society*, Vol. 4, No. 20, Spring, 1957 (Ballyshannon, 1957), pp.209-210.
188 Ibid., p.209.
189 *Athlone 1945*, p.23.
190 Mahony, Jas., p.27.

The effect that the railway had on the town was multifaceted. Large amounts of food and other goods could be moved quickly, a feat that was previously hard to accomplish. This was to prove crucial in the establishment and survival of many new industries both in Athlone and nationally during the 19th century. Important also was the fact that communication with Dublin and the world became far easier – a trip to Dublin took only a few hours instead of an entire day.[191] This ease of transport was to prove crucial to the Irish political movements of the late 19th century, explored in the local context in *chapter seven*.

One of the other side effects that railways had in Ireland was the growth of the local press. Information reached provincial newspapers more quickly with the introduction of telegraph lines, which grew with the spread of the rail network. The newspapers themselves could expand their distribution areas using trains to deliver their product quickly to nearby regions hitherto inaccessible due to protracted journey times. The imminence of a rail link to Athlone was a major influence on the establishment of *The Westmeath Independent* in 1846. The proprietor believed that it was '*...the first medium for advertising...superseding the necessity of advertising in seven other newspapers*', and that the rail network allowed its news to be disseminated further.[192] Conversely though the number of local newspapers increased in Ireland they found that they had to make their news more local; the national press began to use the rail network also, dispensing with the necessity for the local press to report on national and international events.[193]

The Athlone – Mullingar line commenced construction in the winter of 1846 when a grant of £16,340 was secured by the Midland Railway Company from the Brawney Presentment session.[194] The construction of the railway must have been a massive financial undertaking for shortly after the approval for the first grant came through a second grant was sanctioned from a session in the barony of Clonlonan, adding another £15,080 to the total.[195] It appears that the railway had not yet gained a Parliamentary sanction but was confident of receiving one which, when gained, would provide money for the repayment of the grants. The huge expense incurred by the company during construction of the railway caused them to attempt a drop in the rates paid to their workers. The result was to cause 1,500 labourers and 300 tradesmen to call strike

191 Chart, D. A., *An Economic History of Ireland* (Dublin, 1920), pp.104–108.
192 Matthew, Colin, "Public life and politics" in Matthew, Colin, *Short Oxford History of the British Isles – The Nineteenth Century* (Oxford, 2000), p.86.
193 Legg, Mary Louise, *Newspapers and Nationalism, The Irish Provincial Press, 1850-1892* (Dublin, 1999), p.48, Matthew, Colin, p. 86.
194 *F.J.*, 20 Oct 1846.
195 *F.J.*, 26 Oct 1846.

action, a very modern and contemporary move showing the growing consciousness that industrial protest could deliver dividends.[196]

The spread of the railway network from Athlone continued apace with a proposal for a line linking the town with Tullamore mentioned in a local newspaper in the winter of 1856.[197] The continued expansion of the railway network around Athlone was mirrored nationally with over 865 miles of track in place by 1854, considerable increases being made year on year.[198] The Tullamore project was approved and construction began in 1858.[199] Reports on progress in the construction from February 1859 stated that all was going well, the heavy work at Tullamore, Clara and Athlone was almost finished and most other works very far advanced. The numbers working on the project were comparable with those that worked on the Mullingar line, with 1,580 labourers and 183 tradesmen on the books.[200] There were numerous jobs that the men employed in the construction of the railway lines had to deal with, varying from fencing to quarrying to ironwork. In fact the work on the line was going so well that it was predicted that it would open on the 1st October 1859.[201] This aspiration did not come to pass, with a small delay postponing the opening of the line by just two days.[202] Over the following two months the two main rail companies that serviced Athlone – MGWR (established first in the town) and GSWR – posted their timetables for those townspeople who wished to use their services. The two companies were fierce rivals and with the opening of the Tullamore-Athlone line a 'freight war' began between them. Each deliberately undercut the other's prices on certain routes using steamboats to make connections where necessary; eventually an arbitrator had to be called in to broker a deal between the two companies.[203]

A third rail company that also serviced Athlone, but carried fewer customers, was the Great Northern and Western Railway, which tested the line it had laid from Athlone to Roscommon – the track had gained approval in 1857 – on the 28th December 1859.[204] The line was deemed ready to open after the experimental test, though the official opening for traffic was fixed by the Board of Trade for the 6th March 1860 by

196 *F.J.*, 16 Dec 1846.
197 *W.I.*, 15 Nov 1856.
198 Cullen, Louis M., p.143.
199 *W.I.*, 17 Apr 1858.
200 *F.J.*, 8 Feb 1859.
201 *F.J.*, 6 Sep 1859.
202 *W.I.*, 3 Oct 1859.
203 Currivan, P. J., pp.210-11.
204 *F.J.*, 7 Apr 1875, *F.J.*, 30 Dec 1859.

which time it was also connected as far as Castlerea.[205] The national network had grown by this time to 1,909 miles of rail track.[206] The northern line was further extended to Westport in 1866 and later to Foxford (1869) and Ballina (1873).[207] The GNWR, like some of the numerous other rail companies, was in a poor financial state and was leased by the MGWR in 1870, before being purchased by the same company in 1890.[208] The Regulation of Railways Act was passed in 1871 with a view to improving the safety standards of the railways as well as the business practice.[209] Irish railways were not very profitable due to excessive competition. The problem was the number of companies operating in the country, which even after a number of amalgamations stood at twenty-four.[210]

Investment in the railways in Athlone continued during the Victorian period with the MGWR investing in a revamp of their station in order to make it '…*a pretty and accommodating railway station*'.[211] The two main rail companies were still set to do as much as possible '…*to get as much traffic as they could from the other*'. One example cited was that a person travelling from Galway to Waterford had to change trains and companies at Athlone, and with little co-operation between the two the trip took over a day to complete.[212] By the year 1880 the national network had over 2,370 miles of track all over the country.[213] When the government passed the Tramway Acts 1883 – 1896 there was scope for constructing even more railways in Ireland and in the case of Athlone a further proposal for the expansion of the network came towards the end of the 19th century when a line to Ballymahon was mooted in February 1890.[214]

The main impact of the rail expansions, in conjunction with the canals and better roads, was that goods could then be brought to the point of sale far more cheaply (initially at least; later price increases were to become a problem for the rail companies) and quickly. This led to a spread in products from regions that were previously unable to reach the more remote parts of Ireland or even Ireland in the first instance.[215]

205 *W.I.*, 31 Dec 1859, *F.J.*, 11 Feb 1860.
206 Cullen, Louis M., p.144.
207 *F.J.*, 7 Apr 1875
208 Currivan, P. J., p.211
209 Black, Eugene C., (Ed.), *Victorian Culture and Society* (London, 1973), p.28.
210 Fitzgerald, Garret, "Transport", in Kennedy, Kieran A., *From Famine to Feast – Economic and Social Change in Ireland 1847-1997* (Dublin, 1998), p.89.
211 *W.I.*, 4 Oct 1879.
212 Langrishe, Rosabel, p.180.
213 Cullen, Louis M., p.144.
214 *F.J.*, 1 Feb 1890, Cullen, Louis M., p.152.
215 Daunton, Martin, p. 45.

Whilst the safety records for most companies that dealt with heavy machinery in the 19th century were probably far from blemish-free, the occurance of fatal accidents in connection with the railway companies seems to have been prevalent towards the end of the century.[216] There were numerous reports of accidental deaths, most of which involved labourers constructing tracks – in Westmeath alone twelve men died during line construction in just one year.[217] The industrial relations at the railways must not have been amicable either and the trade union, The Amalgamated Railway Society, met in Athlone in 1897, with all workers on the railways urged to join.[218] The local railway servants appear to have joined the 'union' in large numbers, for strike action was threatened a number of months after the meeting in reaction to the Railway Director refusing to receive a deputation from them to discuss the soon to be implemented National Programme for railways.[219] This growth in trade unionism had been occurring in England for a number of decades. The English equivalent of the above-mentioned union was formed in 1872, and the usefulness of unions was beginning to dawn on workers in all sectors.[220] A short report in 1899 detailed the numbers employed permanently at the MGWR in Athlone. There were fifty men in the Traffic Dept., and 150 in the Locomotive Dept., all of whom were supervised by a Resident Engineer whose direct employer was the Superintendent. The total spent on wages at Athlone, a district station, was £14,000 per annum.[221]

ATHLONE WOOLLEN MILLS

During the Victorian period as a result of the Industrial Revolution in Britain coupled with the spread of the railways, the types of private businesses in Athlone changed, with a number of factories being established. The most important manufacturing concern established during the period was the Athlone Woollen Mills. Commenting on the town in 1856 a man called Dr. Edward Gleeson believed that it exhibited '*a lack of employment*' and was '*in a state of decay*'.[222] He thought that a woollen factory would flourish in Athlone upon the banks of the river and set about purchasing the site of a disused brewery to bring this

---

216 *FJ.*, 14 Mar 1891, *FJ.*, 2 Sep 1893, *FJ.*, 4 May 1895, *FJ.*, 28 Aug 1897.
217 Currivan, P. J., p.210.
218 *FJ.*, 13 Feb 1897.
219 *FJ.*, 20 Nov 1897.
220 Pelling, Henry, *Popular Politics and Society in Late Victorian Britain*, 2nd Edition (London, 1979), p.51,
     Thomson, David, *England in the Nineteenth Century <1815 – 1914>* (London, 1950), p.145.
221 *FJ.*, 4 Feb 1899.
222 Fitzgerald, Michael, "Industry and Commerce in Athlone", in Keaney, M. & O'Brien, G., *Athlone - Bridging the Centuries* (Mullingar, 1991), p.38.

about.[223] This was a very brave move to make considering that the textile trade in Ireland had been failing since the 1820s, with the woollen trade going into a *'terminal decline'* as far back as the 1830s.[224] Formally ready for trade in 1859, the business, managed by Gleeson and his brother-in-law, was soon to buy a second premises in Bealnamulla, just outside the town.[225] The optimism for the growth in business was misplaced however, with the partnership between the two men being dissolved in 1864.[226]

After a short diversion into the manufacture of other products such as iron fences, the factory was found to be non-viable and closed. This situation did not last long for Gleeson came into a family inheritance that gave him the funds needed to bring William Smith, a talented woollens manufacturer, on board to restart the business. Smith was said to be a *'grim determined man'* who provided the type of leadership required by a company to ensure its success.[227] The mills soon began to flourish with a newspaper article from 1881 reporting on the mills' situation:'*…from being a little place making up wool from country farmers it has risen to its foremost position employing 200 hands and turning out 600 yards of tweed per week'*.[228]

ILL.5: WILLIAM SMITH (1843-1908)

The company was soon exporting its products to England, Scotland, France and America with demand apparently growing each week. The advent of the telegraph and better oceanic communications meant that as the world was becoming smaller, and Britain and Ireland were no longer as limited by their island status.[229] This massive increase in the speed of communications meant that orders could be received very quickly and speedily dispatched to almost any prospective purchaser.

223 *W.I.*, 27 Jan 1857.
224 Hoppen, K. Theodore, p.44.
225 *W.I.*, 8 Oct 1859.
226 *W.I.*, 24 Feb 1864.
227 *Burgess Papers – Know your Town* (Aidan Heavey Public Library), no.23.
228 *F.J.*, 23 Apr 1881.
229 Thomson, David, p.143.

Even though the mills grew quite steadily, setbacks were encountered. The scarcity of trained employees due to the lack of a technical education caused William Smith to think about establishing a training mill such was his demand for trained hands to put to work.[230] The growth of the company was also hampered by the relationship the management had with the Town Commissioners, and the owners had cause to correspond with them many times on numerous topics. In one instance whilst seeking permission for an expansion programme, the owner, Dr. Gleeson stated that, *'Home Rule in this ancient Borough seems, with some of your members, to be of the historic Saxon type – viz: "Discourage all Irish Industry"'*. The board was reminded that the woollen mills spent between £90 and £100 per week in the borough and over £12 per month on gas.[231] Another setback was encountered in 1882 when a large fire caused the plant to close, but after just four weeks the factory reopened and continued manufacturing.[232]

The company was very progressive and acquired new machinery as soon as it was available. It introduced two new looms in 1884 to aid in the manufacture of its product for which it was *'at its wits end'* to keep production in pace with demand.[233] Its forward thinking approach helped make it the only Athlone firm to be used by the *Select Commission on Industries – Ireland* for its report in 1885.

The Commission was established due to the industrial crisis that the country was facing during the 1870s and 1880s. British manufacturers had flooded the Irish market and overwhelmed local craft-based businesses that could not compete on price or on output.[234] The huge advances made in infrastructure as regarded the railways and the steamships meant that a British invasion of the Irish market was far easier to accomplish than ever before. This crisis had really started with the Industrial Revolution in Britain which saw its gross national income rise from around £340 million in 1831 to £523.3 million twenty years later.[235] To effect this massive gain in wealth there was an intensification of factory-based production which, when the rail network began to spread through Ireland, saw new markets become easily accessible for non-Irish companies. One of the reasons given for British companies not establishing in Ireland and paying the lower wage rates that this would have involved was that the country's grievances with the Union of Great Britain and Ireland, which at times manifested

230 Ibid., p.143.
231 *W.I.*, 17 Feb 1877.
232 *F.J.*, 3 Oct 1882.
233 *F.J.*, 2 Apr 1884, *F.J.*, 3 Oct 1882.
234 Cullen, Louis M., pp.146-148.
235 Harrison, J. F. C., p.23.

themselves as vicious crimes, inhibiting the foundation of businesses in the country.[236] The massive decline in indigenous industry caused some concern at government level and the *Select Commission on Industries – Ireland* was established to inquire as to what the current state of Irish industry was and how it could be improved.

The Athlone Woollen Mills came in for the highest of praise in the report with the manager, William Smith, described by one of the members of the commission as '...*one of the most skilful manufacturers I ever met*'.[237] At the time of the publication of the report the number of workers employed at the factory was 350, with the demand for the product said to be spreading to Canada where a large portion of the police uniforms were made from Athlone-produced materials.[238] One of the recommendations made to the commission by Smith was that a technical education be given to the children of Ireland so as to make them more useful to factories that set up here, for his main problem was still the acquisition of qualified labour.[239] As Kane noted '...*we do not want activity, we are not deficient in mental power, but we want special industrial knowledge.*'[240] Indeed, the lack of provision for a technical education was later outlined as a great deficiency of the Irish workforce, though it was not until much later that it was actually addressed (chapter five). The rates of pay at the plant were not provided in the report; the only mention made of a stipend was that the workers in the Athlone plant were making less than those employed in the same industry in Bradford.[241] Traditionally the rates of pay in Ireland had been far lower than those in Britain. For example, around 1867 the average annual wage in Ireland was £14 in comparison with £32 in England and Wales where higher-skilled jobs were more plentiful.[242]

The prosperity of the woollen mills had a knock-on effect locally with a number of woollen stores being set up in neighbouring towns to maintain the supply needed by the company.[243] At one point the level of exports from the factory to America were so high as to cause the U.S. government to appoint a consular agent to the town to oversee all transactions.[244] Unusually *Thom's Directory* of 1891, whilst recognising that the Athlone Woollen Mills were in existence, believed them to

236 Newsome, David, p.129.
237 *Report of the Select Commission on Industries – Ireland* (London, 1885), p.348.
238 Ibid., p.347.
239 Ibid., App.12, p.750.
240 Kennedy, Kieran A., "Industrial Development", in Kennedy, Kieran A., *From Famine to Feast – Economic and Social Change in Ireland 1847-1997* (Dublin, 1998), p.75.
241 *Report Industries*, p.348.
242 Best, Geoffrey, p.117.
243 *FJ*, 25 May 1889.
244 *FJ*, 25 Aug 1888.

100
Athlone's Victorian economy:
Agriculture, transport, industry and trade

employ less than 100 people. It noted that there were only two mills that employed more than that number, one in Dublin and the other in Cork.[245] However, not all publications misrepresented the plant in that way. The mills were almost always mentioned in travelogues and invariably were singled out for praise. In 1892 Mary Banim during her investigations of Athlone found that the mill employed over 400 people, the vast majority of whom were women. The wages paid were considered higher than those in the north of the country, though the importation of skilled workers from Belfast did cause some problems in the mills the locals believing that all they required was more adequate training. Banim goes on to observe that the Athlone firm was gaining Irish woollens a great reputation internationally; such was its success at exhibitions.[246] In fact the prosperity was said to be assisting Athlone in reversing the national trend of emigration:

> At a time of much agrarian strife, few job opportunities and a long and widespread tradition of emigration, Athlone's population of 7,000 (1880s) was actually on the increase through the employment offered at the local woollen mills.[247]

The company was gaining national acclaim in the press; *The Irish Times* complimented the Athlone Woollen Mills on its quality Cheviot Tweeds that had won a number of awards.[248] The farmers of Meath, Westmeath, Roscommon, Galway, Dublin and Kilkenny were also said to be profiting well from the good fortunes experienced by the factory.[249] Towards the end of the 1890s the company marketed the fact that it used only Irish wool in its products as a guarantee that the customer was purchasing an item of quality.[250] The reports that the company could not keep up with demand continued right into the 20th century (the company folded in 1960, twenty years after a massive fire had delivered a blow from which it never recovered) and it was without doubt the most successful large-scale enterprise that Athlone had seen during the Victorian period.[251]

The prosperity of the Athlone Woollen Mills caused another local entrepreneur to invest in the woollen industry. The founding at 'The Lock Mill' of a small woollen firm by a Mr Sam Heaton, from England, illustrated that Athlone was becoming an even more important centre

245 *Thom's* (Dublin, 1891), p.699.
246 Banim, Mary, p.204.
247 Ledbetter, Gordon T., *The Great Irish Tenor* (London, 1977), p.35.
248 *The W.I., and Midland Counties Advertiser Westmeath Almanac 1890* (Athlone, 1891), np.
249 *F.J.*, 18 May 1895.
250 *F.J.*, 19 July 1898.
251 Burke, John, *Athlone Woollen Mills*, (Unpublished B.A. thesis, GMIT, 2002)

for the woollen trade in Ireland (a fact that has never been alluded to in economic histories of Ireland which mention the woollen industry). A former employee of the Athlone Woollen Mills, Heaton leased the former corn mill in 1893 and set about converting it into a woollen-processing factory.[252] Joined by his two sons he spent over £1,000 on the renovations and opened for business in the same year.[253] By 1896 a newspaper article states that '*his trade is extending greatly*' both nationally and internationally with the small business having a share of the American market.[254] Due to the presence of these woollen mills Athlone was considered by one observer '*...to have few equals in western towns of the country*' by 1905 – the tramp of hundreds of pairs of boots going to work every morning at the factory '*...awakes the slumbering tourist by its novelty*'.[255]

ATHLONE'S OTHER INDUSTRIES

The Athlone Woollen Mills, whilst it may have been the most successful, was by no means the only large-scale industry established in Athlone during the Victorian era. In the 1860s Laurence Wilson bought a premises, a former whiskey distillery, on the west bank of the Shannon with a view to setting up a sawmill on the site. It took some time but Wilson eventually established a mill there in the early 1870s. The business had links to a large firm in England, which probably helped it experience good growth over the succeeding years.[256]

The mill was perhaps to gain more exposure in the local press due to its high accident rate, which saw a number of employees maimed or even killed.[257] A fire in the mill in 1889 showed that the firm was quite an up-to-date one with the '*patent fire extinguisher*' on the roof quenching the blaze before it spread.[258] By the late 1880s the company had employed between 100 and 200 men, suggesting frequent fluctuation in demand for their product. The output at the factory was 7,000 tons annually, making it the largest converter of native wood in the country. The main export market for its product was England where it was used for upholstering work.[259]

The mill was still employing large numbers of people in 1892, though this situation was not to last.[260] The sawmills ceased to be a going

252 *FJ.*, 7 Jan 1893.
253 *FJ.*, 1 Apr 1893.
254 *FJ.*, 29 May 1896.
255 Lang, R. T., (Ed.), *Black's Guide to Galway, Connemara and the West of Ireland 19th ed.* (London, 1905), p.196.
256 *W.I.*, 7 Sep 1872.
257 *W.I.*, 4 Dec 1875, *FJ.*, 10 May 1890, *FJ.*, 31 May 1890.
258 *FJ.*, 31 Jan 1889.
259 *FJ.*, 11 Jan 1890.
260 Banim, Mary, p.204.

102
Athlone's Victorian economy:
Agriculture, transport, industry and trade

concern in March of 1894 and were eventually sold off after twenty-five years in business in the town.[261] All production moved to England with the increase in rail freight charges partially to blame for the closure.[262] The comparison between freight charges is staggering. From Athlone to London the charges were 37s 6d per ton, whilst from America by boat this dropped drastically to 10s 6d per ton to London.[263] A new sawmill was noted in the town in 1897, owned by the Lyster family.[264]

An example of a smaller industry established in the town was Keely and Brennan's mineral water factory, founded in the 1880s.[265] Local mineral water was bottled at the factory in Chapel Street and sold in the town as well as in neighbouring towns. With a staff of nineteen the company gained a contract to supply the military canteens in Athlone, Longford and Birr in 1889.[266] The business did not appear to expand its workforce to any number greater than that already mentioned, with most of the publicity gained in the later 19th century damaging its reputation. In 1899 the company was fined for using foreign water bottles and later summoned twenty two times for using the bottles of other companies for their own product, obscuring their competitors' names with a sticker.[267]

TRADE IN VICTORIAN ATHLONE

The types of shops and the way in which trade was conducted in Britain and Ireland during the Victorian era changed greatly. As tastes developed and new products began to infiltrate previously unreachable markets, the nature of trade began to alter. Athlone was to see many changes during the period with the growth of factories and the decline in cottage industry occurring as in Britain. Strean's notes on St. Peter's parish in 1819 noted masons, carpenters, shoemakers, tailors, smiths, nailers, tinworkers, publicans, butchers, chandlers, glaziers and watchmakers plying their trades in and around the town.[268] In 1837 Samuel Lewis, as already mentioned, noted down a number of industries such as breweries, distilleries and tanneries, though he described others such as the felt hat industry as being in decline. This trend of decline appears to have been changing at least in the commercial sector, as the *The Parliamentary Gazetteer of Ireland 1844* suggests small but numerous

261 *FJ.*, 1 Sep 1894.
262 *FJ.*, 27 Jan 1894.
263 *FJ.*, 19 June 1897.
264 *FJ.*, 31 Dec 1898, Stokes, George T., p.63.
265 *FJ.*, 29 May 1896.
266 *FJ.*, 29 June 1889.
267 *FJ.*, 24 June 1899.
268 Strean, Annesley, p.111.

shops were opening stocking mainly British goods imported via Dublin and the canal system.[269]

The main source used to chart the changes in trade patterns in Athlone is *Slater's National Commercial Directory of Ireland*. The years for which the directory was consulted were 1846, 1856, 1870, 1881 and 1894.[270] Using the information from the directories, a number of the trades in the town will be looked at over these fifty years in order to assess their fortunes. When dealing with this directory one must be aware of the fact that many of the descriptive titles given to businesses changed over the years. Also many businesses, recognising the need to diversify their product and service range, began to expand in various ways towards the end of the century leaving, in some cases, what seems like an unexplained fall in the numbers of certain types of businesses. The best example of this is the case of publicans who numbered forty-three in 1870 but only eleven in 1894. Many of the publicans took on other responsibilities, mainly grocery, and were designated as being of that profession even though they still sold spirits; thus in 1894 sixty-seven grocers also sold spirits.

The presence of certain businesses in the town can help illustrate some of the economic conditions of the time more clearly. For example, the presence of pawnbrokers was indicative of the type of society the townspeople were living in. Their presence made a type of economic slave of the customer, a major fault in Victorian society according to socialists like Karl Marx and Frederick Engels.[271] In Athlone the pawnshops numbered four or five during the times of the worst harvests – the Famine and the crop failure of the late 1870s and early 1880s.[272] Indeed the knowledge that the pawnbrokers had of the local poor led the local Vice Guardians in 1848 to request the figures for loans and sales to them so they could assess local poverty levels. One pawnbroker bemoaned the effect that the famine was having on Athlone: '*small capitalists can do nothing*', he noted unhappily that the starving poor were no longer lining his pockets.[273] The fact that pawnshops were in the town indicates an infrequent supply of wages or money for a number of people. In England it was described as '*a familiar part of working class life in all the large towns*.'[274] H. D. Inglis in his travelogue *A journey through Ireland during the spring, summer, and autumn of 1834* noted:

Pawnbrokers' shops are exceedingly numerous in all the towns; and by the

269 *Gazetteer*, p.99.
270 *Slater's*, pp.4–7, *Slater's* 1856, pp.5–7, *Slater's* 1870, pp.9–13, *Slater's* 1881, pp.329–333, *Slater's* 1894, pp.16–19.
271 Harrison, J. F. C., p.76.
272 Fitzpatrick, Jim, *Three Brass Balls – The Story of the Irish Pawnshop* (Cork, 2001), p.52.
273 *Papers 1848*, p.117.
274 Harrison, J. F. C., p.75.

common practice of pawning articles on Monday morning, and redeeming them on Saturday night, the interest on one shilling lent and received every week throughout the year, with the expense of the duplicate, amounts to 8s. 8d. per annum. The classes who deal with the pawnbrokers are not merely the lowest classes – labourers and artisans – but the small farmers also.[275]

One trade in the town that illustrates how technological advances could have positive as well as negative aspects was that of milling. Athlone had a thriving flour trade in the early 1860s when it was reported that large quantities were sent to various towns around Ireland.[276] This healthy trade in flour was mirrored in other areas that dealt in milling, which saw a prosperous period between 1841 and 1861. Athlone's '*several large millers*' traded extensively with other Irish towns sending '*immense*' amounts of flour to places such as Clonmel and Limerick.[277] Trade was strong up to the 1890s when the number of milling companies in the town fell to just one; there had been eleven in the previous decade. The trade in flour milling as well as in tanning, distilling and some other smaller trades such as tallow chandlers all underwent a decline, eventually leading to a cessation of business in many cases. During the 1880s new technologies were introduced that meant production levels grew massively at factory level, squeezing out small producers.[278]

The Famine and the introduction of public health legislation were to see the number of butchers in the town fall drastically. In 1846 they numbered twenty-three and were all located in the one area, the shambles. However, as already noted in a previous chapter, their hygiene was dubious at best and certainly not in keeping with the Victorian ideal of improvement. By 1870 there were only ten butchers registered for the town, none of which were in the shambles, and this number fell further to eight by 1894. The butchers could no longer trade outside but had to move indoors to comply with regulations. The public health acts also led to a better water supply and to improved sanitary conditions. Plumbers were needed to maintain these services. Up to 1881, none were noted. There were two in 1894.

The growth of the bourgeoisie is also in evidence in Athlone during the Victorian period. Shops and businesses opened that catered for this class of citizen who had more leisure time and disposable income. The number of confectioners in the town by 1894 was three; all the previous

275 Fitzpatrick, Jim, p.39.
276 Coulter, Henry, *The West of Ireland: its Existing Condition and Prospects* (Dublin, 1862), p.3.
277 Ibid.
278 Cullen, Louis M., p.146.

directories noted only two. What were termed 'Fancy Repositories' in the directory were also opening in the town in keeping with the general Victorian emphasis on decorating the home: *'Houses became showplaces of numerous objects, the walls cluttered with pictures and decorations, the furniture elaborately carved, the atmosphere made claustrophobic with the abundance of detail'*.[279]

Furniture shops and cabinetmakers were also present in greater numbers towards the latter part of the century. This demand for greater amounts of furniture apparently led to a fall in the quality of their manufacture: *'New furniture, machine made, was bad...beauty spread her wings and flew away'*.[280]

The arts and crafts movement of the 1860s was having an effect on the aesthetic sense of the wealthier townspeople as it did in Britain.[281] Along with the 'Fancy Repositories', the number of earthenware dealers, which later also sold porcelain and other ornaments, grew quite dramatically, indicating obvious demand for more ornate delph. The need to dress well also led to a rise in the number of dressmakers and milliners in the town, which grew from three in 1846 to fifteen in 1894. The most enduring and largest of these was Burgess' Department Store, founded in 1839; it is still trading today. The presence of a department store was very much in keeping with the trend in Victorian towns all over the United Kingdom.[282] These stores generally catered for those anxious to assert their status, as did hairdressers who first appeared in the directory for Athlone in 1870 and remained in the same numbers in 1894. There were twice as many watchmakers in Athlone in 1894 as there had been in 1846 and demand for their luxury product was also growing. The watchmakers themselves were under no illusions as to who would buy their products; one founded in 1848 mentioned only the *'nobility and gentry'* of the town as being his customers.[283]

In the more basic trades such as blacksmiths and shoe and boot makers there was some fluctuation though generally their numbers remained static. In a more obvious move towards technological advancement one of the blacksmiths in the town in 1894 also described himself as a machinist; a rise in the number of machines needing repair shows that people were purchasing new technologies.

The presence of emigration agents in Athlone in 1870 and 1881 shows that in the 19th century emigration was still quite a force thirty

279 Matthew, Colin, "Introduction: the United Kingdom and the Victorian Century", in Matthew, Colin, *Short Oxford History of the British Isles – The Nineteenth Century* (Oxford, 2000), p. 7.
280 Trevelyan, G. M., p.121.
281 Horn, Pamela, *Pleasures and Pastimes in Victorian Britain* (Sutton, 1999), p.25.
282 Daunton, Martin, p.58.
283 *W.I.*, 13 Jan 1848.

years after the Famine. The spread of the rail network made it far easier for people to reach the main ports of Cork and Dublin. Many manufacturers also had agents based in the town, such as Singer's sewing machines; the spread of their products was certainly due to the improved communications of the 19th century. First amongst these improvements was the railway that changed the commercial face of the town; the ability to use the trains for freight meant that some formerly small businesses could start what was termed *'factory-like'* production.[284] The entry for 'Fire and Office Agents' becomes that of 'Insurance Agents' in 1894. Interestingly there were nineteen of these in the town in 1881; the land agitation may have caused many to be extra cautious about their possessions.

ILL.6: CONNACHT STREET, A BUSY TRADING THOROUGHFARE

The 1870s and 1880s also saw a trend of more general shops opening throughout Ireland. This was also true of Athlone where as the number of grocers grew so did the number of provision dealers. Soaps and cleaners such as *Pears* and *Brasso* were being sold in Irish shops; domestic and personal cleanliness was becoming increasingly important.[285] As well as this there was a rise in the level of tea consumption; it was more readily available in shops with a larger number of people willing and able to purchase it and of course the temperance movement (*chapter nine*) advocated its use in preference to alcohol.[286]

284 Cullen, Louis M., p.144.
285 Daunton, Martin, p.58.
286 Cullen, Louis M., p.151.

The 1890s witnessed a substantial trade carried out around boat building in the town as well as nearby upstream – two boat makers were noted for the town in 1894 and another noted in 1897.[287] The boats were made mainly for working on the Shannon though they were sold for use on other rivers in the country.[288] Also resident in the town were two coachbuilders who were said to be thriving towards the end of the century.[289]

With the growth in businesses came the commercial societies that were another facet of the developing Victorian economy and society. Athlone had a Commercial Society, Grocers and Vintners Society, Vintners and Assistants (Catholic) Society.[290] The movement towards Catholic associations such as that of the Vintners was part of a push, made in part by the Catholic Association, whereby Catholic businesses would help each other to the detriment of Protestants whose '*greedy extremes*' had apparently retarded growth in Catholic businesses.[291] The growth in the number of educated Catholics in the town (*chapter five*) must certainly have translated into a growth in the number of Catholic shop owners, which may have caused some alarm amongst the formerly commercially dominant Church of Ireland congregation.

All of the changes in consumer culture in Britain and Ireland, be it the purchasing of newspapers or groceries, were a factor in helping to define not only personal identities but also national ones. Many items seen as luxuries at the start of the Victorian period were, by the end of it, almost '*common comforts*.[292] Things such as good food and clothing as well as furniture were more widely available with the spread of stock via steamships and railways.

Throughout the Victorian period Athlone saw a massive change in its economic fortunes. Typified by failing businesses in the 1830s, hit by massive unemployment and severe conditions during the Famine, the town's industrial and commercial sectors appeared in terminal decline. The arrival of the railway cannot be underestimated, for its impact was to change the industrial and commercial face of the town forever. Whereas formerly large-scale employment was offered only on public works schemes, the railways helped facilitate the establishment of bigger manufacturers such as the Athlone Woollen Mills and the Shannon Saw Mills. The two railway companies in Athlone were themselves a great

287 Banim, Mary, p.203, Stokes, George T., p.63.
288 Banim, Mary, p.203.
289 Stokes, George T., p.63.
290 *W.I.*, 31 Aug 1872, *F.J.*, 20 Jan 1882, *F.J.*, 10 Mar 1888, *F.J.*, 18 Apr 1891, *F.J.*, 10 Jan 1891, *F.J.*, 21 July 1894.
291 Paseta, Senia, *Before the Revolution – Nationalism, Social Change and Ireland's Catholic Elite, 1879-1922* (Cork, 1999), p.108.
292 Trevelyan, G. M., p.181.

108
Athlone's Victorian economy:
Agriculture, transport, industry and trade

example of business competition. Their tactics would eventually cause the demise of the cargo steamboats which, although heavily invested in by both public and private concerns, could not compete.

Whilst Athlone had some successful businesses, the Athlone Woollen Mills being the most prominent, why didn't many others establish and succeed also? First in the woollen mills there was a powerful driving force in the form of William Smith, a true Victorian entrepreneur. He saw that his company could not compete with larger British-based manufacturers by targeting only the Irish market and set about aggressively marketing the Athlone Woollen Mills products abroad. Businesses needed to modernise constantly, train their staff and remain as up to date as all of their competitors to ensure they could defend and indeed expand their market share. Smith recognised this, as had many businessmen in other parts of the United Kingdom whose tenacity led to the saturation of the Irish market with British goods. Cottage industries were no longer viable in many cases and large-scale manufacture was beginning to dominate many sectors. Many of the local trades such as tanning and distilling were the casualties of this change in production technique. It is certain that the idea of competitiveness between businesses grew during the Victorian era helping to provide shape to the development of industry and trade in the 20th century.

The types of shops that opened in Athlone during the Victorian period also help show how the working class fared over the decades, most notably the pawnshops. Without doubt they also show the growth of à middle class with disposable income, the bourgeoisie. The fashion trends in home décor and personal style were reflected in the goods sold in many Athlone shops, which sold to an increasingly image-conscious public. Though the best decorative products and garments would not have made it into the homes of all Athlone's residents, products such as tea certainly would have been more widely enjoyed.

CHAPTER 5

Faith and education

The 19th century and the Victorian era in particular was a time of great religious change and development. The century has been termed one of religious revival; the Church of Ireland was resurrecting itself from what remained after the 18th century, by which time it was believed to have become ineffectual and weak. The Roman Catholic Church was gaining much strength since the penal laws had been repealed and the Catholic people were beginning to use their numerical superiority to their advantage in many walks of life. In Athlone two religions accounted for the religious beliefs of the vast majority of the population at any one time – the Catholic Church, the largest by far, and the Church of Ireland. Two other bodies, the Presbyterians and Methodists were the largest of the other religions, generally accounting for just less than 5% of the total population between them.

So to help illustrate the changes in Athlone's religious landscape for the Victorian period this chapter will first deal with the proportions of townspeople professing each faith and by this show how another facet of the varied demographic history of 19th century Ireland manifested itself locally. Second, the material progress of some of the religious groups in Athlone will be detailed by assessing how each denomination improved its infrastructure. Finally, some of the contentions that arose between the two main faiths will be looked at with a view to assessing the strength of the religious division in Athlone, which, of course, affected many aspects of people's day-to-day lives.

ATHLONE'S RELIGIOUS PROFILE

To uncover the information relating to the religious denominations in the town the census returns will be used to illustrate changes and help explain them. The religious denomination of individuals was not noted in the 19th century, until the census of 1861. Hence that year is the starting point.

Obviously from looking at *Fig. 9* the Roman Catholic population was by far the largest in Athlone in the year 1861. The numbers of Catholics

Faith and education

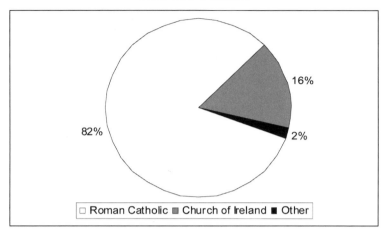

FIG.9: PERCENTAGE OF POPULATION BY RELIGIOUS DENOMINATION
1861

in the town, 5,099 (inc. workhouse inmates) was over five times that of the Church of Ireland with the number of people in other religions, Presbyterians, Methodists, Baptists, Independents and others, accounting for only 2% of the total or just 117 persons. The Roman Catholic and Protestant populations were almost evenly split between the two sides of the town. However, Presbyterians were living on both sides of the Shannon but in greater numbers on the Connacht side, while Methodists were only to be found on the Leinster (east) side of the town. Independents – Unitarians and those of the Christian Brethren – lived only on the Connacht (west) side of the town and the vast majority of Baptists lived east of the Shannon, where their church was located.[1]

Immediately apparent from viewing the 1871 chart, *Fig.10*, is that Roman Catholic numbers had fallen proportionately in comparison with the other four separate religious categories. The actual number of Catholics in the town showed a slight fall to 5,037 people in 1871. On the Leinster side of the town, the number and ratio of the two main religious denominations varied. The number of Roman Catholics fell due to a smaller number in the workhouse, which would have sheltered some people who had lived outside the town boundary. The Church of Ireland members on the same side of the town grew slightly from 505 in 1861 to 517 in 1871. However, the number of Methodists on the east of the Shannon had more than doubled from twenty-one in 1861 to forty-six in 1871 as had the number of Presbyterians from eighteen to forty.

1 *Census 1861, Report*, p.154, p. 443, Murtagh, H., p.10.

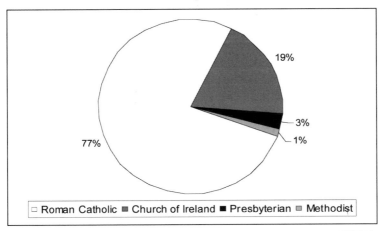

FIG.10: PERCENTAGE OF POPULATION BY RELIGIOUS DENOMINATION
1871

The proportional demographic changes in the town as a whole can be accounted for quite simply: the number of people in the garrison on the Connacht side of Athlone, previously excluded from the town census, were added for the first time in 1871. The actual changes that happened were as follows. On the Roscommon side of the town the number of male members of the Church of Ireland had almost doubled to over 500 with over 130 Presbyterians present on that side of the town whereas previously they numbered just forty-two. Methodists went from having no representation to accounting for forty-three members of the total Athlone, Co. Roscommon population. Roman Catholic numbers also went up on the west side of the town and it is likely that a proportion of that rise can also be accounted for by the inclusion of the garrison in the statistics; there were Catholics in British Army regiments. Independent religions and Baptists had, according to the census, disappeared from Athlone altogether and only seventeen people in total fall into the category 'Other'.[2] This is quite interesting especially when one takes into account that evidence exists of a Baptist church continuing to operate in the town up to 1897 and beyond.[3]

The most striking feature of the 1881 census figures presented in *Fig. 11* is that it again appears that three of the four main Christian religions were growing to the detriment of the Roman Catholic faith. Again, the number of people stationed at the garrison was included in the figures for the 1881 census and this coupled with the political climate of the time can help explain the changes. On the Westmeath

2   *Census 1871, Vol. 1*, p.932, *Census 1871, Vol. 4*, p.474.
3   Stokes, George T., p.71, Murtagh, H., p.10.

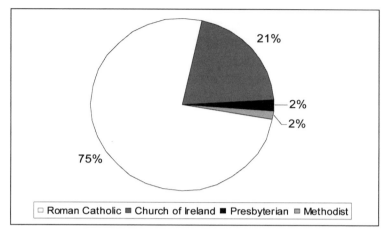

FIG.11: PERCENTAGE OF POPULATION BY RELIGIOUS DENOMINATION
1881

side of the town the Church of Ireland congregation had fallen in numbers to 439, Roman Catholics remained almost static, Presbyterians remained more or less the same with the only real gains occurring amongst Methodists who grew from forty-six members to sixty-two.

The Roscommon side however, presents a more interesting picture. The number of male Church of Ireland members had risen to its highest ever level with almost 800 now resident on the Connacht side of the town – over three times the number in 1861. This can be explained by the drafting in of soldiers to the garrison to deal with any problems that arose locally in connection with the Land War. In total there was almost 1,000 Church of Ireland members living west of the Shannon. The number of Catholics had also grown; the largest gain accounted for by the male side of the population, also possibly due to the need for extra soldiers in the garrison. Presbyterians saw a fall in numbers in both sexes and the Methodists made small gains, again in the male portion of the population. The other religions still showed no Independents or Baptists in the town with the category 'Other' now accounting for just thirteen members of the town's total population.[4]

For the first time in twenty years, as *Fig. 12*, representing the 1891 statistics shows, there was a proportional rise in the number of people of the Roman Catholic faith in the town. Numerically the number of Catholics had grown to 5,231, its highest recorded level since the census returns began noting these figures. The only denomination to witness a substantial fall was the Church of Ireland, with even the 'Other'

4   *Census 1881, Vol. 1*, p.931, *Census 1881, Vol. 4*, p.474.

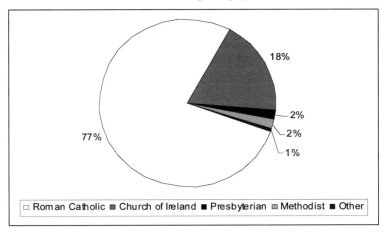

FIG.12: PERCENTAGE OF POPULATION BY RELIGIOUS DENOMINATION
1891

category present in enough numbers as to merit representation on the above chart. On the Westmeath side of the town the number in the Church of Ireland congregation fell again, the number of Roman Catholics rose with the number of both the Presbyterians and Methodists also growing according to the census information.

Data for the Roscommon side of the town shows that the number of Church of Ireland men had fallen to just over 600, Roman Catholic numbers had also seen a slight fall along with Methodists; the Presbyterian congregation remained more or less static with ninety-seven residing on the west side of the town. The number in the garrison was certainly less at this time due to the less violent political climate, which accounts for a large proportion of the decline across the denominations.

Interestingly, the number of those in the 'Other' category for the town showed a massive leap on the Leinster side with twenty-eight accounted for in the category, twenty-one of whom were female. Ten people from the 'Other' category lived on the Roscommon side of the town making a figure of thirty-eight in total.[5] At this time there were a number of occasions on which street preachers were present in the town, which may have brought about a change in the numbers of other faiths. This possibly explains the rise in the figure for the category.

The information presented in the 1901 census for the most part deals with the town of Athlone as a whole. Luckily, to maintain comparative consistency, the returns separate the religions into separate wards – St.

5   *Census 1891, Vol. 1,* p.931, *Census 1891, Vol. 4,* p.474.

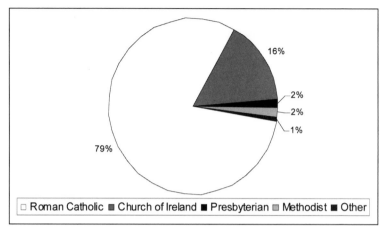

FIG.13: PERCENTAGE OF POPULATION BY RELIGIOUS DENOMINATION
1901

Mary's on the east side and St. Peter's on the west side. The first thing
one may notice is that the proportion of Catholics in the town was the
highest it had been since 1861. The actual number of Catholics had
risen to 5,304. The proportion of the second main religion, the Church
of Ireland, fell by 2% in comparison with 1891 and again this can
probably be explained by a fall in troop numbers at the garrison on the
Roscommon side of the town. Proportionately the other two of the
four main denominations maintained their positions though
Presbyterianism saw a large fall in numbers from 140 to 115 whilst
Methodism saw a small gain. The 'Other' category saw its numbers rise
to fifty – the highest ever. This figure gained the greatest representation
on the Leinster side of the town where there were twenty-six female
and thirteen male members.

The forty years of census returns from 1861 to 1901 show a number
of changes in the religious demography of Athlone. The number of
Roman Catholics generally grew from one census to the next (bearing
in mind that the study began on 1861, after the worst years of
population decline), whilst the remaining three denominations only
grew when the garrison required a large number of troops. Interestingly
the number of Protestants in the town in 1901 was almost equal to the
numbers who were resident in Athlone in 1861; Methodists had a larger
representation by 1901, as did Presbyterians. The Church of Ireland was
the only denomination not to make significant overall gains. The overall
changes in the demographic history of the town have already been
analysed, and consequently whilst it appears that Athlone started to

recover from the effects of Famine and emigration by 1891 and 1901, Catholic numbers had actually started to recover as far back as 1871, though the proportions do not show this evidence clearly. The volatility of the garrison size in the town had a disproportionate effect on the permanently settled population in Athlone, particularly in the Protestant denominations.[6]

RELIGIOUS INFRASTRUCTURE

The religious revival of the mid-nineteenth century was to see unprecedented investment made by many of the denominational groups based in Ireland.[7] Many villages, towns and cities were adorned with new churches along with renovated and modernised existing religious structures. The main investor throughout the 19th century was the Catholic Church, which was beginning to amass considerable wealth. All through the Victorian period in Athlone the levels of investment in new buildings and fixtures by many of the religious denominations in the town was quite high. So to provide a starting point from which to assess the changes in infrastructure, Athlone had, in 1837, two Roman Catholic churches and two Church of Ireland churches, one of each on either side of the river. Also in existence were an Augustinian chapel and friary, two Methodist chapels, a Presbyterian meetinghouse, a Baptist meetinghouse and a Franciscan church.

ROMAN CATHOLIC

The first high-level investment in Roman Catholic infrastructure came with the arrival of the Sisters of Mercy in the 1850s. Their need for premises brought about a drive to collect funds to construct a convent, which was built near St. Peter's Roman Catholic Church. *The Freeman's Journal* reported that the fundraising had gone very well with a very large donation coming from the Archdeacon amounting to £600.[8] A series of special masses and lectures were also given to generate more funding for the project, and the money needed was collected quite quickly. The convent opened in March of 1857, and its facilities were used as a primary school (see section on education) as well as a convent.[9] The Sisters ran numerous bazaars all throughout the Victorian period to raise funds for the convent as well as the sick and the destitute of the town.

---

6 *Census 1901, Vol. 1*, p.101.
7 Connolly, S.J., *Religion and Society in 19th Century Ireland* (Dundalgan, 1987), p.7.
8 *F.J.*, 16 Sep 1856.
9 *Athlone 1945*, p.27.

The largest ecclesiastical construction project during the Victorian period was that of the new Roman Catholic Church of St. Mary's. It appears that the new structure was originally to be constructed on the site of the existing church, which would have greatly restricted its size. The other main Roman Catholic Church in the town was in the parish of St. Peter's and Drum on the Connacht side and it too was quite small. The site where the new St. Mary's church was eventually built had been donated by its proprietor, even though he had only a lease on the land. The passing of The Keogh Act in parliament meant that anybody with a lifetime lease on lands could grant them in perpetuity to the Catholic Church for the construction of new churches and cathedrals. This Act facilitated the local Catholic clergy in their quest, and tenders for the construction of the church went out in February of 1857, with work on the excavation of foundation trenches beginning in May of the same year.[10] A newspaper report that detailed the laying of the foundation stone in July tells why the old church of St. Mary's was no longer suitable:

> On Monday 29th June the foundation stone of St. Mary's Catholic Church in Athlone was laid. The old church is situated in a narrow and inconvenient position and is at present sadly out of repair and by no means commensurate with the requirements of the present vast congregation. The old structure is a relic of the penal times in Ireland when profession of the Catholic faith was a crime punishable by law. It was built 100 years ago. Its site was formerly a portion of the ditch outside the town wall and its erection there was at the time deemed to be a matter of special favour...but owing to the dreadful visitation of the Famine it (the new church) had to be postponed. John Bourke is the architect and John Molloy the builder. In the foundation stone were laid a phial of contemporary coins and a Latin note.[11]

The number of subscriptions for the church was rising all throughout the remainder of the year with the same situation seen in 1858.[12] The church was nearing completion in the summer of 1861 with only the erection of the altars needed for it to come into service. The entire cost of the project was £6,000.[13] The church was consecrated on the 16th June 1861 with its official opening occurring in October of that year.[14] It was located on the periphery of the town, as had happened with many Roman Catholic churches all over the country, but still had an

10 *W.I.*, 14 Feb 1857, *A.S.*, 27 May 1857.
11 *F.J.*, 2 July 1857.
12 *F.J.*, 2 Feb 1858.
13 *F.J.*, 7 May 1861.
14 *W.I.*, 19 Oct 1861, *F.J.*, 17 Oct 1861.

impressive site on the top of a hill, dominating the surrounding streetscape. A lengthy description of the opening ceremony was given in the press, a small portion of which is reproduced here:

> One of the most beautiful churches in Ireland is St. Mary's Athlone, which has just been dedicated to the service of god by the most Rev. D. Kilduff. It is a structure worthy of the faith of the people and illustrative of the undying affection with which they regard the religion of their ancestors. It stands on an exalted site, bearing on the apex of its graceful spire "the cross". The poor who had built it and were gathered round it and the joy and pride which they felt in having contributed such an offering to God was manifest for all seemed to feel that a high and holy duty was to be accomplished. From every part of the surrounding country crowds flocked in and the various costumes of the peasantry as they knelt round the sacred edifice gave it the appearance of a continental church on a great festival. Those who had not seen the church before seemed to be struck with surprise by its graceful and striking proportions and a feeling of joy and pride seemed to fill their hearts.[15]

ILL.7: ST. MARY'S ROMAN CATHOLIC CHURCH

The investment in St. Mary's Roman Catholic Church continued in the late 1860s with the installation of a new organ, which was Irish-built and said to be of the highest and most modern standard.[16] More investment saw a new pulpit erected in September 1878, which was again described as being of the highest quality and form.[17]

Other Catholic investment on a smaller scale in Athlone came from the Franciscan Order. The Franciscan church, which was built between 1812 and 1815 and renovated in 1825, was repaired and upgraded in a 'piecemeal' fashion during further renovations in 1856 and 1861. The Franciscans added to the friary, and improved their living conditions, by

15 *FJ*, 17 Oct 1861.
16 *FJ*, 5 June 1869.
17 *FJ*, 2 Sep 1878.

constructing a new residential extension in 1869 and later partially rebuilt the church in 1884 as part of large-scale renovations.[18]

As well as the Franciscans another Order, already mentioned, were the Augustinians who arrived in Athlone in 1809. They had a small chapel and friary residence on the Connacht side of the town, but never thrived. They appear to have gone out of existence in Athlone around the year 1874, bucking the trend of Roman Catholic Orders locally, when their last remaining member passed away.[19] It appears that the chapel and friary were abandoned. Finally, the arrival of another order of nuns, the Sisters of La Sainte Union des Sacrés Coeurs brought about the construction of a convent on the eastern fringes of the town in 1884, which was also used in education.[20]

CHURCH OF IRELAND

The Church of Ireland had enacted a largescale building campaign nationally at the start of the 19th century, leading to a massive 30% increase in the number of churches under its control.[21] This investment was also to see the facilities for the congregation in Athlone modernise and grow. Initially, the first large-scale investment of the Victorian period in the town was the construction of St Peter's Church of Ireland church. Intended to serve the needs of the congregation on the Roscommon side of Athlone it was built in 1840 and continued to serve all throughout the Victorian period.[22] It replaced an older structure on Excise Street whose site eventually became that of a coach factory.[23]

The other Church of Ireland church, in St Mary's parish, also saw some investment during the Victorian period. The building, which was constructed in 1827, was closed in 1869 for some minor refurbishment that was finished in May 1870.[24] The church grounds however did not appear to have received any updating. A letter written in 1873 outlined the deplorable condition of the entrance to the church and stated that the grounds were uneven and overgrown.[25] The graveyard had been closed officially in January 1872 (an act of parliament had decreed that burials in the centre of towns could no longer be permitted), only four vaults were allowed to remain open, and this may have led to the fall off

18 *F.J.*, 9 Oct 1884, Grannell, Fergal, pp.69-71.
19 Conlan, Patrick, O. F. M., "A note on the Augustinian priory in Athlone", in *Journal of the Old Athlone Society*, Vol. II, No.7 (Athlone, 2004), pp.205-207.
20 Murtagh, H., p.14.
21 Akenson, Donald Harman, *The Church of Ireland – Ecclesiastical Reform and Revolution 1800-1885* (Yale, 1971), pp. 111-121.
22 Inscription Stone on Site.
23 *F.J.*, 20 Jan 1894, Stokes, George T., p.63.
24 *W.I.*, 28 May 1870.
25 *W.I.*, 28 June 1873.

in care.[26] Further renovation took place in the church in 1898 with alterations to the roof, chancel and some other small changes in the general infrastructure which were paid for by prominent locals.[27]

OTHER DENOMINATIONS

Smaller religious groups also built churches in the town during the Victorian period. A Scotch Presbyterian Church began the initial steps towards construction on the western docks in July 1858 when subscriptions were requested.[28] The church was to replace the older meetinghouse noted on the Ordinance Survey map of 1838.[29] Lord Castlemaine, who, for his efforts, received a silver trowel, laid the foundation stone just one month later.[30] The presentation of a silver trowel was a common feature of Victorian commemoration; one of the Shannon Commissioners received a silver trowel when the keystone for the last arch of the town bridge was put in place.[31] The church was open for worship by June 1861.[32]

A new Methodist church was opened in the town in March of 1865 at a site on Northgate Street.[33] It replaced one of the two Methodist chapels in the town that were in use at the start of the Victorian period. The second of the two older chapels was eventually turned into a school in 1891 after periods of use by the Primitive Methodists in 1836, Methodists in 1838 and Wesleyan Methodists in 1874.[34]

RELIGIOUS TENSIONS

Among those loyal to the British connection the contention, at the beginning of the Victorian era so soon after Catholic Emancipation, was that if one were to be a truly loyal subject one was necessarily Protestant. Conversely, those loyal to a free Ireland were traditionally assumed by Roman Catholics to be Roman Catholic. These views, however strongly held, were perhaps one of the main 'sticking points' in the history of the nineteenth century and led to many of the problems encountered during the period.[35] This perceived incompatibility between religious denominations was most vividly represented by the

26 *F.J.*, 16 Jan 1875.
27 *F.J.*, 2 Apr 1898.
28 *W.I.*, 31 July 1858.
29 Murtagh, H., p.10.
30 *F.J.*, 7 Aug 1858.
31 *A.S.*, 26 April 1844.
32 *W.I.*, 9 June 1860.
33 *W.I.*, 4 Mar 1865.
34 Murtagh, H., p.10.
35 Wilson, A. N., *The Victorians* (London, 2002), p.64.

two largest in Athlone, the Roman Catholic Church and the Church of Ireland.

Prior to the Victorian period the Catholics in the town were not considered very devout. Dr. George Plunkett, the Bishop of Meath in the 1820s, remarked that:

> Hundreds of persons had not been to confession for twenty years. Hundreds of couples had been married who had not yet made their first communion. The flock was ignorant of what was necessary to be known *necessitate medii*; attendance at mass on Sundays, not to talk of festivals, was disregarded. …and innumerable couples had lived as man and wife who had never been married, and many others in flagrant and notorious adultery.[36]

The above situation appears, at least in part, to have arrived due to the incompetence of a weak-minded clergyman in the town, who did nothing to entice people to mass or attempt to stop the spread of 'French Principles'.[37] With his removal and subsequent reassertion of the Catholic system of morals, the Roman Catholic townspeople became more religious, as was illustrated by the establishment of a number of religious societies, and high attendance at retreats and confirmations. When the Catholic clergy again found their footing in the town they, along with their Protestant counterparts, engaged in activities that were not necessarily linked to the church. This caused problems when, for example, in June 1835 a warrant for payment of fees from a '*country gentleman*' to a Catholic teacher was strenuously blocked by a parson, who was a magistrate in the case, with no reason provided.[38] However, tensions sometimes abated. There is a story from 1836 to the effect that some Roman Catholics were seen to subscribe to St. Mary's Church of Ireland Church.[39]

A story related in a book dealing with the Grand Juries of County Westmeath detailed a situation encountered in the town in the early 19th century where religious co-operation was agreed to by all, *except* the clergy. One Sunday it was suggested that the entire Athlone Yeomanry Corps, which contained both Protestant and Catholic members, should go to the Catholic church due to the fact that the Protestant church was being repainted. It was agreed with the proviso that the Catholic part of the Corps would go to the Protestant service the following week. This deal was carried off, though, '*As might have been*

36 Keenan, Desmond, *The Catholic Church in Nineteenth Century Ireland – A Sociological Study* (Dublin, 1983), p.103.
37 Ibid., p.104.
38 *A.S.*, 1 June 1835.
39 *A.I.*, 26 Oct 1836.

supposed, the Catholics fell under the severe censure of their Clergymen, who put a heavy penance on them, which was to be performed by each offender within a given period of time.[40] All of the offenders, except one, carried out the penance and despite being threatened with public censure in front of the congregation, the man would not do anything in expiation for his *'offended Church.'* A threat from the man to become a Protestant caused the priest to drop the issue and the soldier later died a *'good Catholic.'*[41]

Many examples of the disagreements and tension between the two main faiths exist during the Victorian period. During the 'Repeal Year' of 1843 one meeting held in Athlone saw the Catholic clergy out in force but, as noted by a local newspaper, the Protestant people and clergy of the town were notable by their absence.[42] The celebration of the Queen Victoria's Jubilee gave the Church of Ireland congregation and clergy cause to congregate and celebrate. On this occasion it was the Roman Catholics who were absent. The occasion of an inter-denominational marriage caused members of both faiths to be present in the same place at the same time, though celebration was not high on the agenda. Apparently the help of the RIC had to be enlisted to protect the Protestant girl from her very angry relatives.[43] The contention of Fr. Conmee, writing retrospectively in 1900 that *'…a delightful characteristic…was the complete absence of any contention between classes or creeds'* is quite untrue, his second-hand information is in this case, in the face of the evidence, unreliable.[44]

The most contentious area in which problems arose between the town's main faiths was in the administration of healthcare in the dispensary and workhouse. When the appointment of a dispensary doctor for a temporary post (the incumbent had applied for a leave of absence) came about in May 1868 there was some hostility to the candidate that the chairman of the guardians of the district wished to appoint, a man named Dr. Langstaff.[45] A letter sent to the local press outlined what the author believed was *'blind bigotry'* and *'partyism'*:

As evidence of this we have in Athlone Union a protestant doctor, a protestant Clerk, a protestant master, a protestant matron of 550 catholic paupers; and now the dispensary Dr. being in failing health they are moving heaven and earth to appoint as his successor a total stranger in

40 Lyons, John Charles, *The Grand Juries of the County of Westmeath from the year 1727 to the year 1853 with an Historical Appendix, 2 Volumes* (John Charles Lyons, 1853), p.107-108, English, N.W., "Athlone's "Ecumenical" Yeomanry Corps", in *The Irish Sword*, Vol. VII, No.28, Summer (Dublin, 1966), p. 262-263.
41 Ibid.40
42 *A.S.*, 23 June 1843.
43 *F.J.*, 1 Feb 1896.
44 Conmee, Rev. John S., p.12.
45 *W.I.*, 16 May 1868.

the neighbourhood, and a protestant. Bear in mind they are trying to do this in spite of 2/3rds of the elected guardians and against the wishes of 9/10 of the people. The opposing candidate to this stranger with nothing to recommend him but his religion, is a distinguished young Dr. a native and resident of this town and who took the Gold Medal a few years since in the Catholic University. It is a crying shame that in a district where the middle and lower classes are exclusively catholic that all the principal public offices should be filled by members of a different and hostile persuasion. If no legislation can reach the root of the evil; if there can be no curb placed on the unbridled power for evil of this (sic) hereditary oppressors of their fellow subjects, then, sir, it is no wonder the people should pronounce 'religious equality' a great sham despite all the triumphs of the Liberal Party this Session. – An Athlone Catholic.[46]

A subsequent vote on the appointment, held due to the candidature of the '*local*' doctor, ended in a tie with ten votes, from '...*the defenders of the Church and State*' including one Catholic, for the '*stranger*' and ten, all from Liberals, for the Catholic doctor, Dr. Lyster. This impasse caused the guardians to appoint a Dr. Hetherington to the position on a temporary basis (he was performing the same role in a neighbouring district and agreed to do both jobs), though this was later blocked by the Poor Law Commissioners.[47] Presumably it was the same Athlone Catholic who had written the letter a number of weeks earlier had this to say on the issue:

> This is one of the many proofs of the corrupt effects of the establishment, which has always conduced to place one section of the community against the other. It is a shame that either a catholic or a protestant resident of this town of Athlone would be found to vote for a stranger against their own townsman who is popular with all classes.[48]

Another vote was held after word of the Poor Law Commissioner's objection came through and on this occasion, with more board members present, Dr. Langstaff was appointed with a slim majority.[49] After the vote was concluded one of those who voted for the eventual winner, the Rev. E.F. Berry, chairman of the board, noted that Langstaff should have been appointed in the first instance. The reverend believed that his recommendation of the doctor should have been more than enough and that no other candidates should have been proposed. Dr. Langstaff's temporary position was made permanent in July; Dr. Poyntz,

46 *F.J.*, 20 May 1868.
47 *W.I.*, 23 May 1868, *W.I.*, 6 June 1868.
48 *F.J.*, 9 June 1868.
49 *W.I.*, 6 June 1868.

the previous dispensary doctor, had passed away soon into his leave of absence.[50]

The most complicated example of the two religions working against one another came with the issue of staffing the hospital in the workhouse. The workhouses had many controversial rules that caused friction between the two main religions. One example was that any foundling abandoned at the workhouse was to be raised in the religion of the state i.e. Church of Ireland. The furore this caused led to an act being passed in 1862 amending the relevant section of the earlier Poor Law Act; the disestablishment of the Church of Ireland in 1869 would have changed it anyway.[51] Another contentious issue was the trend in Ireland during the Victorian period that nuns from the various Roman Catholic orders filled the majority of nursing posts. Lay-professionalism in the area came later.[52] Although the Poor Law Commissioners were wary of the appointment of '*persons bound by religious vows*' as officers in the workhouses, in Athlone nuns from the Catholic Sisters of Mercy were admitted as nurses on a salary of £30 per annum in July of 1888.[53] This Order of nuns was the most commonly instated in the workhouses of Ireland, sixty-four of which had nuns as nurses in 1875, a number which continued to rise until the end of the Victorian period.[54] Nuns were apparently very useful in the workhouses in which they were already employed according to a notice of motion presented at a meeting of the Guardians of Athlone Union, which proposed their appointment.[55] From the moment they took up the post the nuns wanted it made clear that they were running the hospital and that they regulated staff rotation.[56]

The first contention in the hospital came when the nuns demanded the appointment of a dedicated chaplain for both themselves and the Catholic inmates. To speed up the decision of the local Board of Guardians the Rev. Mother refused to fill in all of the forms necessary for the nuns to begin their work, hence the hospital was not staffed.[57] The necessity of a chaplain was soon negated by the offer of a £10 pay increase for the nuns who then decided to make their own arrangements for mass attendance.[58] They also wanted apartments

50 *W.I.*, 18 July 1868.
51 O'Brien, *Workhouse*, p.24.
52 Malcolm, Elizabeth & Jones, Greta, *Medicines and the State in Ireland 1650–1940* (Cork, 1999), p.102.
53 O'Connor, John, p.180, *F.J.*, 21 July 1888.
54 Malcolm, Elizabeth & Jones, Greta, p.103.
55 English, N. W., "Sisters of Mercy and Athlone Workhouse", in *Journal of the Old Athlone Society*, Vol.1, No.3 (Athlone, 1973), p.208.
56 *F.J.*, 28 July 1888.
57 *F.J.*, 25 August 1888.
58 *F.J.*, 15 Sep 1888.

provided for them while they worked at the hospital, but the original estimate for construction and furnishing was too high and an alternative had to be found.[59] Eventually an existing premises was fitted out at a cost of £300.[60]

The length of time between the original idea being mooted and the actual official employment of the nuns was almost two years; the local press informed readers that the Sisters had entered the workhouse to begin their work in April 1890.[61] Soon after this announcement another problem arose when the nuns refused to work the night shift in the hospital. This refusal led to a call for a trained night nurse at a meeting of the local Board of Guardians. The call was not heeded but it did lead to an escalation in tensions.[62] The nuns said they would agree to a nurse being instated but that they wanted one of their members to be instated also to supervise. This was unsatisfactory since it would have left an untrained nun supervising a trained nurse.[63]

Further problems with the running of the workhouse came with the intimation that the appointment of the nuns in the workhouse was anti-Protestant. A complaint came in the form of a letter from the local Church of Ireland, Rector, Dr. Campbell. In the letter he said that the '...*whole atmosphere of the workhouse and especially the infirm wards has become offensively anti-Protestant*'.[64] The erection of Catholic imagery was also deplored in his letter. He described them as '*gross and offensive*' to the Protestant patients. In one case he angrily condemned the erection of a picture of the last rites being performed – he referred to the picture as showing '*some sort of exorcism*' – over the bed of an elderly Protestant.[65] As well as this, the policy that the nuns had apparently adopted of praying and leading devotions violated the Protestants '*deepest religious convictions*'. He also wrote that complaints had been coming to him over time of these problems but that he had ignored them until he received a specific complaint that shocked him deeply.

The Catholic priest for St. Mary's, Dr. Langan had, according to Campbell's evidence, converted a woman of 104 years to Catholicism without ever mentioning it to him as, Campbell believed, was necessary. He believed that the exploitation of the woman in her weakened state was '*scandalous proselytism*' and that a separate ward for Protestants should be set up, excluding all interference by those with different religious

59 *FJ.*, 27 Oct 1888.
60 *FJ.*, 1 Dec 1888.
61 *FJ.*, 5 Apr 1890.
62 *FJ.*, 10 Dec 1892.
63 Malcolm, Elizabeth & Jones, Greta, p.111.
64 *FJ.*, 18 Nov 1893.
65 Ibid.

beliefs.[66] The next meeting of the local Board of Guardians discussed the charges, and even though they criticised Dr. Campbell's method of complaint, a committee was appointed to look into opening a separate ward for the Protestant inmates.[67] The Rev. Dr. wrote a second letter arguing against the criticism he received at the hands of the local Guardians Board, stating that the two religions were different and those differences had to be respected in the provision of facilities to the sick.[68]

Eventually it was decided to open a separate ward for Protestants but the local Guardians wanted to staff it with nuns from the Sisters of Mercy. Needless to say this decision did not go down well with Dr. Campbell who demanded Protestant nurses for the ward.[69] The work of creating a separate ward was finally sanctioned in January 1894, when a letter from the local Board of Guardians gave final permission.[70]

The acrimonious nature of the settlement came to the notice of one of the patients a number of months later who then attempted to use the controversy to his advantage. The man expressed his wish to convert from Protestantism to Catholicism, a call that brought the Rev. Dr. Campbell to the hospital almost immediately. The reverend, upon meeting the man, was told that the conversion would not take place if he (the man) was *'made comfortable'* on the outside. The patient was later discharged into the custody of his brother-in-law.[71] This and other problems prompted Dr. Campbell to suggest at a YMCA meeting the establishment of a *'cottage hospital'* to replace the union one. In one of these hospitals, he believed *'...the poor could obtain modern scientifically trained nursing, and respectable working men and others could be cared for on moderate and equal terms.'*[72]

The number of complaints made by Dr. Campbell led to the establishment of an inquiry. However there was a lack of agreement as to who should conduct it. Eventually the local Board of Guardians decided they would.[73] The nuns and Dr. Shanley, the workhouse physician, had already denied the charges before the inquiry so the burden of proof was on Dr. Campbell.[74]

The first meeting was held in early February 1895 where charges of mistreatment by the nuns against a girl were heard.[75] At the second

66 Ibid.
67 *FJ.*, 25 Nov 1893.
68 *FJ.*, 2 Dec 1893.
69 *FJ.*, 23 Dec 1893.
70 *FJ.*, 13 Jan 1894.
71 *FJ.*, 5 May 1894.
72 *FJ.*, 8 Dec 1894.
73 *FJ.*, 5 Jan 1894, *FJ.*, 12 Jan 1894.
74 *FJ.*, 15 Dec 1894.
75 *FJ.*, 9 Feb 1895.

meeting the charges of proselytising were heard, with a number of witnesses examined and cross-examined.[76] The proselytising charge regarding the 104-year-old inmate was also studied and found to be somewhat dubious. Dr. Campbell had met with the woman who joined the Roman Catholic faith and had, in her own words, stated: '...*nobody asked me, it was of my own free will*'. After this exchange the Reverend said that he took his leave and that he would see her in heaven. Sarcastically, the examining solicitor asked if Dr. Campbell believed he would actually see her in heaven, to which he replied '*I don't know*'.[77]

The inquiry continued over the ensuing months with various other incidents discussed, many of which most probably arose due to personality clashes. The best example of this was Dr. Campbell's idea that his wife was being kept out of the hospital even though the only times she was denied admission was when she arrived outside visiting hours.[78] His wife had levelled an accusation at the nuns that a girl who had died in the hospital had been neglected and was kept in filthy conditions.[79] The sister concerned, Sister de Sales O'Connell refuted the claim, stating that the girl had mental problems that led to difficulties in her care.[80]

Eventually a decision was reached by the local Board of Guardians that a new night-nurse was to be appointed to deal with the workhouse hospital, at an annual salary of £50.[81] Sister de Sales O'Connell applied for the post and was appointed. However, more problems arose when she refused to go to Dublin for training, having received the backing of the Bishop regarding her position on the matter.[82] The Board of Guardians did not want to appoint anyone other than a nun to the position, and decided to adhere to their earlier decision.[83] Later they refused to agree to a motion that the sister was more than qualified as they were insisting that she needed training.[84] The problem continued for a period, with the local Board of Guardians eventually dissolved in September 1895 and replaced by two Vice-Guardians, the reason given being; '...*through default their duties have not been duly and effectively discharged according to the intentions of the Acts for Relief of Distress.*'[85] Evidence suggests that a nurse was appointed under the supervision of

76 *F.J.*, 23 Feb 1895.
77 *F.J.*, 9 Mar 1895.
78 *F.J.*, 18 May 1895.
79 *W.I.*, 25 May 1895.
80 Ibid.
81 *F.J.*, 21 May 1895.
82 *F.J.*, 8 June 1895, *F.J.*, 6 July 1895.
83 *F.J.*, 6 July 1895.
84 *F.J.*, 14 Sep 1895.
85 *F.J.*, 28 Sep 1895.

the nuns, and that the local Board of Guardians were reinstated seven months later, when elections were held.[86]

Athlone during the Victorian period manifested signs of religious development in both the actions of the people and the development of church infrastructure. It could be said that demographically the changes in the religious proportions in Athlone, after 1861, were mainly effected by the changes in the numbers stationed at the garrison on the Roscommon side of the town. The number of people in each religion varied. Catholicism saw a decade on decade increase between 1861 and 1901. Church of Ireland numbers fluctuated but overall remained almost static during the same period. The other denominations, Presbyterianism and Methodism, were relatively small in numbers – neither measured over 200 persons all throughout the period, though both were in a healthier position by the end of the period than they had been at the start.

The investment in the religious infrastructure in the town was massively increased during the Victorian period. The largest projects were undertaken by the Catholic Church, which was then attempting to cater for a large congregation in post-penal law Ireland. The largest church was constructed by the Roman Catholic congregation on the east of the town, a church which was to remain the largest until it was superseded by a new structure on the west of the town in the 1930s. The arrival of two orders of nuns, the Sisters of Mercy in 1856 and the Sisters of La Sainte Union des Sacrés Coeurs in 1884, necessitated the construction of two convents that again altered the streetscape of the town with their modern facades and sizeable proportions. Investment by the Franciscans ensured that their long association with the town was maintained and strengthened.

The Church of Ireland also invested heavily; building a church on the west of the town in 1840 and extensively renovating the parish church on the Leinster side of the town. The other smaller denominations also invested money on infrastructure, though on a smaller scale. The provisions for those people who regularly attended religious services were greatly strengthened throughout the period. One thing that all of the religions had in common during the Victorian period was that they all believed that religious instruction was necessary to improve social order and people's capacity to make proper moral decisions.

Whilst all of the religions may have believed that the Victorian move towards personal improvement included them, they did not cooperate with each other to bring this about in the most desirable manner.

86 *W.I.*, 19 Oct 1895, *F.J.*, 11 Apr 1896.

Evidence of arguments and non-cooperation between the two main religions in the town, Roman Catholic and Church of Ireland, is common and shows that the relationship between the two was almost always tense. The Catholic Church was trying to acquire better representation both locally and nationally; the Church of Ireland was fighting to maintain its representation against the pressure of Roman Catholic numbers.

EDUCATION

Victorians invented the concept of education, as we now understand it; even if we believe ourselves to be more egalitarian than they, it is from them that we derive our axiomatic assumption that learning should be formalised learning, education institutionalised, the imparting of knowledge the duty of society and the state to every citizen.[87]

Victorian society was one which valued education highly. They saw it as essential in the battle to improve people's lives at every level. Education enabled the younger members of society to create more opportunities for themselves and their families; it could help them achieve social and economic advancement. At the start of the Victorian era the state of the education system in Britain and Ireland was very poor. A massive proportion of the population was illiterate. Members of the Roman Catholic faith, which made up the bulk of the Irish population, had very little access to any education at all, and even those for whom an education was a possibility invariably stayed away in large numbers. The challenge for Victorian society was to create an education system that was open to all, had suitable facilities and one that people would use to improve themselves. In Ireland the development of an education system was seen as essential in the fight to advance the country's economic fortunes. If any of the towns in Ireland were to develop they needed to adopt a proper and effective education infrastructure to assist local growth, especially in industry. In Athlone the changes in education will be shown by detailing the types of schools that existed or were opened in the town during the Victorian era, the literacy levels of those who belonged to the different religious congregations as well as the literacy levels of the two sexes in different age groups.

At the start of the 19th century government reports into the education system in Ireland concluded that: '*For nearly the whole [of] last century the government of Ireland laboured to promote Protestant education and tolerated no other.*'[88] Writing in 1862 the author of a book on the history

---

87 Wilson, A. N., p.282.
88 Godkin, James, *Education in Ireland, it's History, Institutions, Systems, Statistics and Progress from the earliest times to the present* (Dublin, 1862), p.22.

of Irish education believed that '...*nowhere has the failure of government, as a sectarian teacher, been more signal and disastrous than in Ireland*'.[89] To address this imbalance a new education system needed to be introduced one that would provide:

> ...a general plan of education for the lower classes, keeping clear of all interference with the particular religious tenets of any, and thereby inducing the whole to receive instruction as one body, under one and the same system and in the same establishment.[90]

During the 1830s one of the most important recommendations in many reports was that children of '*different creeds*' should have been united in the one institution.[91] Whilst this was an admirable intention, problems arose when it came to deciding to what extent religious instruction was to infiltrate the school curriculum.[92] The National Education Board that was established in 1831 with the "inclusive" ideal in mind was unpopular with Protestants and Presbyterians, the latter withdrew from the scheme totally, and only a small number of Catholics co-operated with it initially.[93] Those Catholics who did co-operate invariably turned the school to their own denominational purposes, hence dissuading any children from other faiths attending.[94] Religion was one of the most powerful ingredients of identity in Ireland at the time and its influence in, and perhaps even over, education obviously would have national ramifications. The National School system also encountered problems in the late 1840s when the idea of rigid scheduling of religious instruction was mooted and the prohibition on all religious emblems in schools was attempted. Archbishop Cullen of Dublin, one of the most powerful men in the Catholic Church in Ireland, especially disliked the scheme for he believed that all Catholic children should have had '*A Catholic education, on Catholic principles, Catholic masters and the use of Catholic books*'.[95]

Another important consideration must be noted. A large proportion of the teachers in the country were untrained, despite the fact that a teacher training school had been established in the early 1840s.[96] They were also restricted in what they could teach due to the constraints of

89 Ibid., p.20.
90 Atkinson, Norman, *Irish Education – a history of educational institutions* (Dublin, 1969), p.90.
91 Ibid., pp.95-6.
92 Ibid., p.96.
93 Kennedy, David, "Education and the People", in McDowell, R.B., *Social Life in Ireland 1800-45* (Mercier, 1979), p.62.
94 Garnett, Jane, "Religious and intellectual life", in Matthew, Colin, *Short Oxford History of the British Isles – The Nineteenth Century* (Oxford, 2000), p.211.
95 *F.J.*, 10 Nov 1859.
96 O'Tuathaigh, Gearoid, p.102.

the non-sectarian doctrine.[97] The system was always going to be facing a struggle:

> Because most Victorians saw education as inherently related to religion, they found themselves involved in a constant tug and tussle between the needs of the churches to instil their own varieties of Christian doctrine, the needs of an industrial society for more utilitarian teaching, and the needs of the various classes of society for schools reflecting the values of those classes.[98]

Indeed, in Britain it was believed that parents sent their children to those schools where the education was considered best – the one exception was that non-Catholics were considered '*reluctant*' to send their children to Catholic schools, regardless of the institution's track record.[99] It should also be remembered that the national education system in Ireland predated any similar scheme in Britain '...*by almost a full four decades...[with Britain] a nation well advanced along the path of industrial and urban change.*'[100]

The difficulties that were faced by those wishing to establish a national education system did not dissuade them from believing that learning was indispensable when advancing the lot of an individual. Many believed that Ireland in particular had to see an improvement in its levels of education so that it could pull itself out of the economic doldrums where it languished for most of the 19th century.

Outside of the National School system, improving the education of those who were considered too old to go to school had to be accomplished differently. In many towns and cities, including Athlone, improving the knowledge and education of some of the more mature citizens came with the establishment of reading rooms, generally attached to a society. In Athlone all of the larger societies had a library of sorts, be it the YMCA, CYMS or League of the Cross, all of which are explored in chapter nine. Politics and education were also seen as being inexorably linked; if Ireland had a better educated proletariat the politically motivated actions of the people would be more measured and eventually more successful. In Athlone the Repeal reading room was set up in April 1845, aiming itself at the labourers and lower classes and believing that it was a means of '...*giving the poor mechanic an opportunity of improving his knowledge of men and things and will no doubt have a very*

97 Atkinson, Norman, p.105.
98 Matthew, Introduction, p. 35.
99 Pelling, Henry, p.30.
100 Akenson, D. H., 'Pre-university education, 1782-1870' in W.E. Vaughan, *A New History of Ireland Vol. V, 1801-1870* (London, 1989), p.523.

moral tendency.[101] There is evidence that Ireland's distress was fuelled in part by the uneducated workforce and that: '…*ignorance acted not only as an impediment to practical schemes for the improvement of their condition but also prevented their developing habits of industry and systematic thinking.*'[102] Education in the Victorian period was also noted as having an effect on the unification of thought, if not of actions, in those who attended schools; it would instil proper morals.[103]

Obviously the Victorians believed that the best time to lay down good morals in people was during their youth. In Ireland this meant that the facilities for educating the people at large would have to be improved, otherwise the upper classes would continue to be the sole benefactors of a good education. In Athlone, as elsewhere, the education of the lower classes was supervised mainly by a number of religious orders that established a number of schools in the town during the Victorian era.

EDUCATION INFRASTRUCTURE

Tracing exactly how many schools operated in Athlone during the period is very difficult as the majority were private schools, the establishment and closure of which were not always reported on. Between the late 17th and early 20th centuries roughly seventy-eight schools were opened in the town.[104] Of these the vast majority were established during the 19th century. The types of schools in existence ranged from 'hedge schools' to larger privately run institutions. The problem with attempting to pinpoint how many schools were operating in the town at any one time lies in a lack of evidence regarding the lifetime of the institutions. Many private schools advertised their foundation, but not their cessation, thus creating problems for anyone wishing to analyse the education facilities in the town. For a number of schools that are known to have existed problems arise when one attempts to pinpoint their location; in many cases they cannot be found and this can lead to overestimating the number of institutions in the town.

The Victorian period in Athlone saw roughly thirty-eight schools established of which only around seven survived into the twentieth century – for individual schools, though at times they may have changed premises, the school itself could be described as surviving. In 1837 the

---

101 *FJ.*, 21 Apr 1845.
102 O'Tuathaigh, Gearoid, p.98.
103 Golby, J. M., *Culture and Society in Britain, 1850–1890* (Oxford, 1986), p.297.
104 *Second Report of the commissioners on public instruction, Ireland,* HC 1835, xxxiv, p. 112, Murtagh, H., p.14.

schools that were established and run by individuals, i.e. private schools, numbered fourteen. The religious orders established a number of schools, also accounting for fourteen. The remainder included the workhouse school, the Mechanics' Institute and other educational facilities described as academies.[105]

The non-denominational National School System had a number of establishments in the town during the 19th century. There is evidence dating from 1835 of a national school founded at Anker's Bower on the east of the town with a report into the school from 1880 attesting to its longevity. The report found the male half of the school to be satisfactory but the female side not so. The most damning part of the report was that a number of boys were attending the female part of the school, registered as girls. The school was also the venue for adult education with courses taught there in 1848.[106]

Jacob Venedey, the German travel writer who visited Athlone during the repeal year of 1843, found the fact that there was no public school in the town quite amazing. Whilst he had probably not encountered the establishment at Anker's Bower, there certainly was no national school on the west of the town. He believed that either the children went to private school or none at all and the fact that there were four churches in the town made the lack of a school even more unbelievable in his eyes.[107] He was a believer in the National Education System's non-sectarian schools; '*Tolerance in schools will destroy the intolerance outside them*.'[108] A national school for the Roscommon side of the town was eventually established in 1845 at Deerpark. This school was in operation up to the early 20th century when it was re-sited about a mile away in a new building on the old military batteries, currently the Dean Kelly National School.

The schooling of the poorest of Athlone's children was carried out in the workhouse. Due to disease and malnutrition, attendance at the school was irregular, with the numbers missing school at their highest, unsurprisingly, during the year 1847.[109] Those attracted to the job of schoolmaster in the workhouse were often described as eminently qualified, though it appears that they were not always decent. One teacher was dismissed from the post after he was found to have made a number of the girls resident there pregnant, with others dismissed for

---

105 Ibid.
106 Murtagh, Harman, "Old Athlone", p.20, O'Brien, Gearoid, p.177.
107 Venedy, Herr J, p.54.
108 Bourke, Eoin, "'The Irishman is no lazzarone' German travel writers in Ireland 1828-1850", in *History Ireland*, Vol. 5, No.3, Autumn, 1997 (Dublin, 1997), p.24.
109 O'Brien, (*Workhouse*), p.26.

'*gross inefficiency*' or '*cruelty*'. The children in this school were on the lowest level of society, their health and education were criminally neglected, many who could not attend school had actually died as a result of diseases from which they, the most innocent and helpless members of society, could not protect themselves.[110]

The first large-scale investment by a religious order was that of the Sisters of Mercy who constructed a convent with a school attached on the west side of the town in 1857.[111] The convent school was for young Catholic girls and remained in use throughout the Victorian era – indeed it is still operating today serving families west of the river. Its longevity suggests, along with other evidence, that the education system in that school had its roots first set down in the Victorian era. The next sizeable investment in education came in the same year, with the establishment of a lay and ecclesiastical college outside the town at Summerhill. Formerly an Ursuline convent, the boarding school was set up in the existing buildings on the site with a day school also opened '...*for the convenience of the people of Athlone.*'[112] There were doubts as to the school's long-term viability and these fears proved well founded.[113] The school lasted just 22 years eventually having to close due to falling numbers. It moved to Sligo, where it was hoped that the same high standards could be maintained.[114] The premises were taken over by the De la Salle Order (sic. – the 1881 census returns state it was run by the Novices of the Christian Brothers, though local information contradicts this) as an industrial school for boys and later in the 1890s by the Sisters of Mercy as an industrial school for girls.[115] This may have pleased some of the local Protestants, one of whom wrote in 1873 that an industrial school for Catholics would bring about a situation where: '...*every Protestant in the town will rejoice to see indolence and vice turned into industry and comfortable homes*', moreover '*many sadly neglected children*' would learn something to help them leave behind the lives foisted on them '*owing to the immorality of their parents.*'[116] Opinions such as this may aid one in recognising why the National School System was always going to encounter problems. Whilst poorer Roman Catholic children may have '*improved*' through interaction with those of higher classes and other faiths, it was believed the character of those mixing with Catholics could actually suffer!

110 Ibid., p.25.
111 *Athlone 1945*, p.27.
112 Murtagh, Harman, "Old Athlone", p.20, *F.J.*, 8 July 1857.
113 *F.J.*, 12 July 1878.
114 *F.J.*, 31 July 1880.
115 *Census 1881, Vol. 4*, p.473, *Census 1891, Vol. 4*, p.473, Murtagh, Harman, "Old Athlone", p.20.
116 *W.I.*, 8 Nov 1873.

The Franciscans opened an educational establishment in the town in 1871, St Bonaventure's Academy for Boys, a mathematical and classical school for Catholics only.[117] This seraphic college (intended to finish the education of those boys who were undecided as to whether they would join a religious order) lasted only seven years when it had to close due to a lack of interested pupils.[118]

In 1871 a report of an inquiry into the numbers of pupils attending schools in Athlone on one specific day found that: *'There seems to be a fair supply of schools in this district, and it appears that they are situated in the most populous districts of the country.'*[119] In total on that day the inquiry found that 781 children were attending seven schools, three on the Leinster side and four on the Connacht side. Two of the schools on each side of the river were attached to the National Board, Anker's Bower and the workhouse school on the east side, and Mercy Convent and Deerpark National School on the west side. The remaining schools were St Mary's Erasmus Smith School on the Westmeath side, a Church of Ireland School and the Athlone Grammar School (Ranelagh) on the Roscommon side. Of the total, just 184 attended the three non-national schools. The breakdown of the figures shows clearly that in Athlone the Church of Ireland was steering a course towards maintaining its own school system independent of the National School system.[120] Of the total 597 attending the national schools in Athlone only seven of them were from the Church of Ireland, all the rest being Roman Catholic.[121] Indeed nationally, the Catholic population using the schools put in place under the National School system accounted for 84% of all pupils in those schools by 1860.[122]

The Marist Brothers arrived in the town in 1884 and were initially involved in the education of senior boys.[123] They held a bazaar in January 1885 for the purpose of raising funds for the construction of a purpose-built school.[124] The construction was finished two years later with the official inauguration occurring in January 1887. This school, along with the Our Lady's Bower, caused the closure of the national school at Ankers Bower. However, the construction project had left the brothers over £900 in debt and in order to clear this a meeting was held

117 *W.I.*, 28 June 1871, *W.I.*, 26 Aug 1871.
118 Conlan, Patrick, O.F.M., "St. Bonaventure's Academy, Athlone", in *Journal of the Old Athlone Society*, Vol. II, No.6 (Athlone, 1985), p.155.
119 *Royal commission of inquiry, primary education (Ireland), Vol. VI, Educational Census. Returns showing the number of children actually present in each primary school on 25th June 1868* (Dublin, 1871), p.136
120 O'Tuathaigh, Gearoid, p.103.
121 *Royal commission 1868*, p.79.
122 Atkinson, Norman, p.101.
123 *Athlone 1945* pg.28, O'Brien, Gearoid, p.183.
124 *F.J.*, 10 Jan 1885.

in St Mary's presbytery at which over £200 was subscribed.[125] Further construction at the school was carried out in 1893; with the introduction of the Compulsory Education (Ireland) Act, the facilities needed to grow to deal with the larger number of pupils. The Act required that all children between six and fourteen years of age attended school and only after the age of fourteen were they allowed to take on part-time work.[126] Formerly, attendance in Ireland had been very poor as it had been in Britain where 60% of those children who were of school-going age did not attend regularly partially due to employment committments.[127] The Act of 1893 certainly assisted in increasing the numbers attending schools in the country and that may help account for some of the gains experienced in literacy across the denominations and among Catholics in particular. However, the Athlone School Attendance Committee found that the Act was hard to implement. Generally, before the Act, 75% of children stayed away from school in the mid to late 19th century in Ireland. It was reported locally that every week parents were to be seen at the Petty Sessions being fined for their children's truancy.[128]

A number of fund-raising events were held the following year in an effort to offset the debt the Marists had incurred as a result of the new construction as well as to fund the current school year.[129] The standard of writing taught at the school must have been quite high with twelve pupils winning books at the All Ireland Handwriting Competition.[130] The level of corporal punishment was also high: one man was ordered by the local magistrate to send his son back to school after he had taken him out due to excessive beatings.[131] More improvements to the school were made in 1900 when other premises were added.[132] Like the Sisters of Mercy convent school, it still operates today, albeit at a different location.

The Order of La Sainte Union established a boarding school in Athlone in 1884, Our Lady's Bower, costing them £10,000 from their own funds.[133] The revival of convents and hence of vocations meant that by 1900 a large percentage of all women categorised as working were nuns. There were roughly 8,000 nuns in Ireland, the majority of whom

125 *FJ.*, 29 Jan 1887, *FJ.*, 23 Apr 1887.
126 Atkinson, Norman, p.102.
127 Harrison, J. F. C., p.136.
128 *A.T.*, 25 May 1901.
129 *FJ.*, 7 July 1894, *FJ.*, 29 Sep 1894, *FJ.*, 20 Oct 1894.
130 *FJ.*, 4 Dec 1897.
131 *FJ.*, 8 Oct 1898.
132 *A.T.*, 30 June 1900.
133 *FJ.*, 22 Aug 1884, O'Brien, Gearoid, p.168.

ILL.8: OUR LADY'S BOWER

were actively engaged in welfare and education.[134] Athlone was to have a school for boys up to ten years of age when 'The Bower' opened.[135] The school advertised for the sons of gentlemen from the ages of five to nine.[136] It is also still operating today but as a secondary boarding and day school for girls.

The vast majority of private schools set up in Athlone during the Victorian era were patronised exclusively by non-Catholics. The types of private schools that were established in the town varied from Classical and Scientific schools to seminaries for teaching foreign languages to young girls. The details regarding one such seminary founded in 1837 leave no doubt that it was intended only for wealthier pupils. It was managed by the local Presbyterian Minister, and there were the options of either day or boarding facilities. The fees for entering were prohibitive to any one but the privileged classes; £30 for those under ten years of age and £40 for those over ten.[137] The kind of establishment that the private schools aspired to be can be recognised from an advertisement in *The Westmeath Independent* of October 11th 1851 for a school operating under a Ms. Gilhooly:

> ...who has been educated from childhood in France, in one of the best conventional schools there, [and who] has opened a high-class school in Athlone. It is in Wentworth Street, opposite the Rt. Rev. Dr. Brown's who kindly patronises it. Miss Gillooly promises that no effort shall be spared

134 Howarth, Janet, "Gender, domesticity and sexual politics", in Matthew, Colin, *Short Oxford History of the British Isles – The Nineteenth Century* (Oxford, 2000), p.173.
135 *F.J.*, 22 Aug 1884.
136 *F.J.*, 15 Sep 1884.
137 *Athlone Conservative Advocate*, 1 June 1837.

on her part to form the minds and hearts of her pupils to virtue and knowledge. The course provides a good English education and includes arithmetic and book-keeping (10/- per quarter); music (10/- per month of 20 lessons); drawing, aquarelle and pastel (6/- per month of 20 lessons): French and Italian (15/- per quarter). It is a woman who moulds the youthful mind of both sexes and instils those early principles that are as indelible as they are powerful, for good or evil. She should ever bear in mind that children are better taught by example than by precept. A diploma from a French academical authority attests to Miss Gillooly's aptitude for teaching.[138]

The main private school that persisted all throughout the Victorian Era was Ranelagh Endowed School. Samuel Lewis, writing in 1837, believed the school to be in decline with only about fifteen boys on the books.[139] A report into the school decided that Ranelagh needed a change in how it sourced its pupils, they needed to be more respectable and not '...*sometimes idiotic ...and belonging to ladies maids, and of that class.*'[140] The school did not fail, however, and was sending maths pupils to Trinity to participate in competition in 1864.[141] It was also able to enrol Catholics, after a reinterpretation of a government Act from 1838 saw Catholic pupils admitted into endowed/public schools (basically

ILL.9: RANELAGH ENDOWED SCHOOL

138 *W.I.*, 11 Oct 1851.
139 Lewis, Samuel, pg.33.
140 Quane, Michael, "The Ranelagh Endowed School, Athlone", in *Journal of the Old Athlone Society*, Vol. I, No.1 (1969), p.31.
141 *W.I.*, 13 Feb 1864.

they could be enrolled if they could afford the fees): there were three on
the books at Ranelagh in 1880 and seven in 1888.[142]

The school also appears to have had a thriving sporting curriculum,
all part of the drive towards 'Muscular Christianity' that public schools
in Britain were famed for, with cricket, rugby and soccer played, all
three with some level of success.[143] The number of pupils also rose in
1871 numbering sixty-five in that year, twenty of whom were free. Of
the forty-five who paid fees fourteen were day pupils.[144] The number
dropped to thirty-eight in 1878 but a resurgence occurred in the 1880s
with numbers enrolled in 1885 standing at one hundred and thirteen.[145]
Gas was introduced to the school in 1879, which was earlier than in a
number of local municipal buildings.[146]

The push towards a technical school in the town intensified towards
the end of the 19th century and fundraising events were held in an
attempt to establish one.[147] A Royal Commission from 1884 found that
the lack of facilities for the instruction of children in technical subjects
was a contributing factor in Ireland's poor industrial development.[148]
The Balmoral Commission was established in 1898 to inquire into what
more practical subjects could be taught in schools.[149] Eventually after a
number of recommendations had been made, the Agricultural and
Technical Instruction (Ireland) Act 1899 was passed. Athlone was one of
the first towns in Ireland to adopt a Technical Instruction Scheme under
the Act with the hope that a technical school would soon be established.
William Smith of the Athlone Woollen Mills paid £500 towards the
cause due to his belief in the merits of a technical education and his
need for trained staff.[150] However, the law was not fair according to
Smith. The grant that could be received under the Technical Education
Act was insufficient; town property rates would provide 1d per £1 and
whilst the government would match this 100%, this would only provide
£96 for Athlone – apparently not even enough to hire a teacher.[151]
Fortunately the government matched Smith's donation thus allowing
plans to progress. A technical school for girls staffed by the Sisters of
Mercy opened in 1899, though the one for boys did not open until June
1902.[152]

142 Quane, Michael, p.32.
143 Money, Tony, *Manly and Muscular Diversions: Public Schools and the 19th century Sporting Revival* (London,
      1997), *F.J.*, 19 May 1866, *F.J.*, 16 Mar 1883, *F.J.*, 18 Dec 1888.
144 *F.J.*, 23 Feb 1871.
145 *F.J.*, 2 Jan 1886, *F.J.*, 24 Mar 1888, *F.J.*, 31 Mar 1888.
146 *W.I.*, 8 Feb 1879.
147 *F.J.*, 10 June 1899.
148 Atkinson, Norman, p.108.
149 Ibid., p.103.
150 *F.J.*, 29 July 1899.
151 *A.I.*, 23 Mar 1901, *A.I.*, 1 June 1901.
152 O'Brien, Gearoid, p.187.

It has been noted that in general the National Education System was not particularly successful, as one commentator noted: '*The outward appearance of the National schoolhouse, by the beginning of the twentieth century, scarcely suggested a vigorous and thriving system of education.*[153] Another facet of the system was that Irish culture was still being occulted in the schools, with a view to rendering them and their pupils more British. This Anglicisation had been abandoned in other colonies but never in Ireland, and perhaps this was another reason for a lack of success.[154]

This drive towards educating the masses was believed by some members of British Victorian Society to be counterproductive: '*Overeducation in the middle classes is the curse of this country. The learned professions are crowded; too many doctors and brief-less barristers and nobody able to mend a timepiece or make a good suit of clothes*'.[155] Obviously there was a belief in the necessity of a class system in some quarters in Victorian society when it came to education.

RELIGION AND LITERACY

The main barometer used to gauge the success of educational advances made in the Victorian era in Athlone has been the study of literacy levels in the population. Nationally it should be noted that in 1861 the number of those who were illiterate was quite high – 46% of Catholics over five years of age could not read or write, the Church of Ireland showed a figure of 16% and Presbyterians 11% – overall 92% of all illiterates were Catholic.[156] The literacy levels amongst each of the four main denominations in the town over the period 1861 – 1901 (the literacy levels of all ages of each religious denomination only started to be noted in 1861) are presented and analysed below. It has already been shown that some of the institutions that were established during the Victorian era have survived to the present day, but their longevity is not the only indicator of success. This analysis should provide a better qualification of their achievement in Athlone's educational history.

Table 2 (overleaf) details the literacy of the four main denominations in Athlone during the period 1861-1901. What is immediately apparent from looking at the table is that in 1861 the majority of Catholics were illiterate, whilst the majority of those in the other denominations could read and write. What this meant in reality was that due to the numerical

153 Atkinson, Norman, p.104
154 Porter, Andrew, "The empire and the world", in Matthew, Colin, *Short Oxford History of the British Isles – The Nineteenth Century* (Oxford, 2000), p.145.
155 Paseta, Senia, *Before the Revolution – Nationalism, Social Change and Ireland's Catholic Elite, 1879-1922* (Cork, 1999), pp. 80-81.
156 Connolly, S. J., p.5.

Faith and education

	Year	1861	1871	1881	1891	1901
Roman Catholic	*Read and Write*	35%	45%	53%	64%	71%
	Read Only	13%	13%	12%	9%	5%
	Illiterate	52%	42%	35%	27%	24%
Church of Ireland	*Read and Write*	70%	78%	85%	86%	86%
	Read Only	6%	5%	2%	1%	2%
	Illiterate	24%	17%	13%	13%	12%
Presbyterian	*Read and Write*	68%	76%	82%	91%	91%
	Read Only	10%	3%	2%	0%	0%
	Illiterate	22%	21%	16%	9%	9%
Methodist	*Read and Write*	86%	83%	83%	84%	94%
	Read Only	0%	4%	0%	3%	0%
	Illiterate	14%	13%	17%	13%	6%

TABLE 2: LITERACY LEVELS SUBDIVIDED BY RELIGIOUS
DENOMINATION 1861-1901

dominance of Catholics in the town the majority of Athlone's population was illiterate. The figures show that the Catholics in Athlone did not have an adequate level of access to education: they could not learn because there was nowhere to teach them. The Church of Ireland congregation along with the Presbyterians had relatively high illiteracy levels, though they were less than half the Catholic figure. Methodists had a very high level of literacy, a trend they maintained throughout the period. The Methodist faith, along with the Presbyterian, actively promoted the reading of the bible and this would have had an effect on the level of importance placed on becoming literate as early as possible. Presbyterian literacy levels began to be more or less equal with those of Methodists by 1881.

Table 2 also illustrates that the Roman Catholic group was the greatest benefactor of the Victorian educational reforms. Between 1861 and 1901 the proportion of Catholics who could read and write more than doubled, with a concomitant fall in the proportion of people who were illiterate. The improvement happened over time with the rise being between 11% and 12% every ten years. There were, as already mentioned, new schools opening almost each decade for the education of Catholics in the town, making for easier access. However, even by the end of the Victorian era, Catholic literacy levels were still well below those of the other four denominations. One of the possible reasons for this was inequality between the sexes among the Roman Catholic population.

The Church of Ireland, though it already had a high level of literacy, saw a large improvement in its literacy levels; the proportion of those who were illiterate halved by 1901. What may have been cause for concern in both the Roman Catholic and Church of Ireland congregations was that the illiteracy levels appeared to have reached a plateau in 1891–1901, when only a small reduction was made. This would perhaps indicate that there was a hard core of people in each faith, probably the poorest, for whom education was still inaccessible. Another factor that must be remembered is that the majority of children under five years of age could neither read nor write and their numbers would have inflated the illiteracy levels, perhaps along with the older members of the population for whom educational reform arrived too late.[157]

LITERACY BY AGE AND GENDER

In an attempt to help qualify the results for literacy even further the census returns began to break literacy levels down according to age and gender. In 1861 this was being done for all three levels of literacy but only within two categories, those older than five and those younger than five. In 1871 and 1881 they broke the information into five age categories: 0–7, 7–12, 12–20, 20–40 and 40+. In 1891 the fields 7–9 and 9–12 were added (for the sake of consistency these two fields have been combined in the later analysis) while the returns for 1901 expanded matters even further to include 11 fields: 0–3, 3–5, 5–6, 6–9, 9–11, 11–14, 14–15, 15–18, 18–21, 21–40 and 40+.

The information provided in the 1861 census shows that 27% of the total population was made up by those under five who were considered illiterate for all intents and purposes and therefore will not be considered in this analysis. However, of the remainder the majority were also considered illiterate, mainly Catholic and mainly female. Unfortunately due to the limited information presented in the 1861 census, and the absence of any information in previous years, it is very hard to tell what impact education reforms had on the children, teenagers or adults of Athlone by 1861.[158]

---

157 *Census 1861, Report*, pp.100/1, 154, 155, 165, 420/1, 443, *Census 1871, Vol. 1*, p.932, *Census 1871, Vol. 4*, p.474, *Census 1881, Vol. 1*, p.931, *Census 1881, Vol. 4*, p.473/4, *Census 1891, Vol. 1*, pp. 901, 931, *Census 1891, Vol. 4*, pp. 426, 474, *Census 1901, Vol. 1*, pp. 2, 51, 101.

158 *Census 1861, Report*, pp.100/1, 154, 155, 165, 420/1, 443.

Faith and education

Age Range	0-7		7-12		12-20		20-40		40+	
	M	F	M	F	M	F	M	F	M	F
Read & Write	15	15	169	166	444	374	937	557	469	301
Read Only	25	34	65	60	50	52	68	129	98	151
Illiterate	469	479	102	100	82	88	135	245	237	450

TABLE 3: LITERACY LEVELS DETAILING THE AGES AND SEX OF THE
TOWNSPEOPLE 1871

The above table, *Table 3,* shows the levels of literacy amongst the five
age groups chosen by the commissioners for the 1871 census. What is
obvious is that the highest levels of literacy occurred amongst men in
the 12-20 bracket. By the time children reached the 7-12 age group
over 75% would have been able to read or read and write. The high
numbers of people who could neither read nor write in the 20-40 and
40+ categories were most certainly those who did not have early access
to education; many of them would have grown up during the Famine
when survival rather than education was uppermost in their minds. As
can be seen in *Table 3* the majority of people who were illiterate were
women over twenty years of age. While some of these people could
conceivably learn to read and write late in life it was unlikely that they
would in many cases. Overall there was a striking disparity in the levels
of literacy between men and women. Of the total female population of
Athlone 44% were fully literate, and 43% totally illiterate. When it came
to the men 60% were literate and just 30% were illiterate.[159]

Age Range	0-7		7-12		12-20		20-40		40+	
	M	F	M	F	M	F	M	F	M	F
Read & Write	12	12	195	165	473	427	931	604	469	326
Read Only	28	29	48	76	59	50	59	124	79	162
Illiterate	445	440	89	75	59	76	117	187	246	430

TABLE 4: LITERACY LEVELS DETAILING THE AGES AND SEX OF THE
TOWNSPEOPLE 1881

The statistics for 1881, *Table 4,* show very much the same picture as
those for 1871. The actual numbers of people who were illiterate was
falling, however, proportionally both figures remained more or less the
same in comparison with 1871. The 40+ age group exhibited the
highest levels of illiteracy though those in the 7-12 bracket had an even

159 *Census 1871, Vol. 1,* p.932, *Census 1871, Vol. 4,* p.474.

higher chance of reading and writing than before, almost 80%. This obviously shows that the education system was making an impact on the youngest schoolgoers in the town during the ten years between 1871 and 1881. The numbers of people who could neither read nor write had also fallen in the 12-20 and the 20-40 age brackets, so the effects of education were being felt all along the line. The literacy level among females had improved, with 48% literate compared to illiteracy levels of 38%. The male literacy level had also bettered its previous total; 63% of men were literate and 29% illiterate.[160]

Age Range	0-7		7-12		12-20		20-40		40+	
	M	F	M	F	M	F	M	F	M	F
Read & Write	18	34	250	204	754	467	1164	855	510	403
Read Only	42	45	60	51	18	31	27	65	53	82
Illiterate	427	429	36	39	23	22	63	96	186	292

TABLE 5: LITERACY LEVELS DETAILING THE AGES AND SEX OF THE TOWNSPEOPLE 1891

Table 5 shows that trends that were becoming apparent in 1881 were now more clearly manifested in 1891. Almost all of those older than seven should have become literate to some degree by the age of twelve. The drive towards literacy and the improvements in the education systems and facilities in the town were providing the highest literacy numbers that Athlone had ever seen. Illiteracy levels, as always, showed the highest levels in the oldest category though the numbers were falling in comparison with previous census returns. Again, people were far more likely to be illiterate by the time they reached 40 if they were female; they did not have the same level of access to education as men. A large number of those in the 40+ age bracket for 1891 would have been in the 20-40 bracket in 1871 and some would have availed of earlier educational improvements. It is partially through their inclusion that the literacy figures were the highest they had ever been for the period under study. The benefit of having access to an early education was having easily traced effects on the literacy statistics over time. By 1891 both genders showed improvements in the levels of literacy in comparison with 1881 – females had a 63% literacy rate and a 28% illiteracy level. The men had improved their proportions to 74% literate and just 20% illiterate.[161] Interestingly, looking just at the basic numbers

160 *Census 1881*, Vol. 1, p.931, *Census 1881, Vol. 4*, p.473/4.
161 *Census 1891*, Vol. 1, pp. 901, 931, *Census 1891*, Vol. 4, pp. 426, 474.

of those who were illiterate in each age group between 1881 and 1891 a huge fall is apparent. The foundation of new schools during the 1880s must have had a favourable effect in order for this fall to occur.

The figures for 1901, though not included here due to the reorganisation of the age categories, show the consolidation of the high number of literate people in Athlone by the end of the Victorian period. The 40+ category showed that the education system was most definitely working with fewer than 400 people in total, 230 of whom were female, illiterate by 1901; in 1881 the figure for women was almost twice that number. All of the age brackets exhibited evidence that access to education in Athlone was becoming easier as the decades progressed. Female literacy was still lagging behind that of men though it made up considerable ground by 1901 reaching levels of 73% literate and 22% illiterate. The same year saw slight gains for the men's percentages, which reached 77% literate and 20% illiterate. Illiteracy in females above 40 was still the highest number outside infants and small children and had been for the entire period, though the total numbers had fallen sharply in comparison with two decades before.[162]

In general it is fair to say that the education drive of the Victorian era was delivering dividends for the townspeople in Athlone. Towards the end of the 19th century a number of new schools had opened in the town and these brought about a higher literacy rate amongst the younger members of the population, and this is reflected in the 1901 census. The arrival of religious orders such as the Marist Brothers and the foundation of schools such as the Bower were instrumental in creating access to education. This access afforded Catholics the opportunity to make great gains in their levels of literacy though they still appeared to have a hard-core sector who either had no access to education or perhaps were too young to avail of it. The other three denominations all showed relatively high levels of literacy throughout the period, for they had access to private education from an earlier period, with Presbyterians and Methodists appearing to be the best educated. The Church of Ireland, like the Roman Catholic Church, had halved the rate of illiteracy amongst its members, though it still appeared to have a similar unreachable proportion that remained illiterate.

Interestingly the levels of literacy amongst women did not grow at quite the rate it did for men though the percentages for each of the sexes in the individual religious denominations were levelling quickly. However, whilst the numbers of illiterate townspeople from both sexes was falling decade on decade, proportionately there were always more women who could neither read nor write than men.

Education in the Victorian Age was without doubt the precursor to our present day system. Some of the national schools established during that period still survive in Athlone; some even operate out of the same buildings. Educating the people of the time was a struggle, truancy levels were high and certainly in some cases people must have been cynical about the advantages of attending certain schools. In the main however, it was a time when the necessity for education was recognised by not just the already well educated but obviously also by those who saw that more could be achieved for both Athlone and Ireland if its people gained useful and useable knowledge. Of the many systems put in place during the Victorian era it would be fair to say that education has been the most successful, the most enduring and perhaps the most positive.

CHAPTER 6

Victoria's Barracks

Athlone was said by Samuel Lewis, writing in 1837, to have '...*retained much of its character as a military station*'.[1] For many years the presence of the barracks in Athlone was one of the main factors in the town's development topographically, with the men stationed there helping to influence the evolution of Athlone society. Indeed, British army posts were prevalent throughout Ireland with towns such as Galway, Sligo, Newbridge, Mullingar and Longford very much influenced, as Athlone was, by their presence. In this chapter the effect that the garrison had on the town of Athlone during the Victorian period will be assessed. In doing this the interaction between the soldiers and the townspeople, the cultural influences the garrison infused into the town, as well as the evolution of the relationship between the town and the garrison will be analysed.

THE GARRISON AS A SYMBOL OF EMPIRE

When one studies the British army in Ireland during the Victorian period what becomes apparent is the fact that many, if not most, Irish people saw it as an occupying force. Though at times there may have been a large number of Irish-born soldiers stationed in regiments at the barracks in Athlone, the role of the army remained generally consistent – it was to protect the Crown's interests in Ireland. Evidence shows that the numbers of soldiers in the country increased many times during the Victorian era, usually when economic or political tensions were apparent. This was especially evident during the Famine and throughout the Land League period when the number of men stationed in Ireland reached their highest levels for the period.[2] Ireland has been described by Andrew Porter as '...*strangely anomalous among Britain's possessions*' when the military was involved; the stationing of the army in Ireland was not seen as being a move designed to protect the nation from

---

1 Lewis, Samuel, pg.32.
2 Porter, Andrew, "The empire and the world", in Matthew, Colin, *Short Oxford History of the British Isles - The Nineteenth Century* (Oxford, 2000), p.145.

external forces but rather to protect the British from subversive Irish ones.[3] The garrison and the men stationed there were first and foremost in the service of the sovereign ruler of the United Kingdom – it was essentially a very potent reminder of the fact that Ireland was under British rule.

However, it did not require a military engagement for the townspeople to be reminded of the British influence that the army could exert. Prior to the coronation of Queen Victoria in 1837 the army had most years, on the King's birthday, fired a *'feu de joie'* to celebrate. This method of marking the event would certainly have been noticed by all the townspeople, and though only the local gentry were invited to join in the official celebrations, the pomp and colourful nature of the affair would have had an effect on all who witnessed any part of it.[4] The celebration of the monarch's birthday aside, other celebrations were held by the army in honour of visiting royal dignitaries. Again on these occasions gun salutes were fired, the army bands played and decorations were used to light up the barracks. Many Athlone people, perhaps not aware of who the visitor was would still recognise the celebrations as something different and exciting. The army added colour to the lives of the townspeople on many occasions.

At the time of Queen Victoria's coronation in 1837 the Athlone barrack was renamed Victoria Barracks in her honour. From an official point of view the naming ceremony would have been useful in reminding the inhabitants of the town that a new monarch had been crowned as well as in highlighting the fact that the monarch was *their* sovereign served by a large garrison situated in the heart of the town. The party was a loyalist occasion. The inhabitants of Athlone were provided with an unusually vivid display to mark the coronation of Queen Victoria in 1837; the quarters of the officers and soldiers within the garrison were described as having an *'amazing effect when lighted'*.[5] As well as visual stimulation the army band was on hand to play to a large *'respectable'* audience with the celebrations continuing into the night.

It appears that as the years went by celebrations for the Queen's birthday were held less frequently; during times of strife the celebrations were possibly seen as a dangerous diversion whose loyalist overtones would only foment nationalist feelings and resentment. Though the profession of loyalism was an intrinsic part of celebrating the Queen's birthday, it was at times celebrated for ulterior motives. In 1850, the *'feu de joie'* was discharged with the hope that the public display of affection

3 Ibid.
4 *A.S.*, 28 Sep 1834.
5 *F.J.*, 3 July 1838.

and loyalty to the Queen, during the visit of Prince George of Cambridge, would help to have a recently reassigned general, whose move led to the barracks being downgraded in the military command sturcture, reinstated.[6] It appears that these celebrations were less a matter of military policy, than a discretionary act on behalf of the commander of the garrison.

However, the army continued to deal with visiting dignitaries in much the same way as they had formerly. The Lord Lieutenant, the Earl of Eglinton, upon his arrival in the town in 1852, was greeted by an artillery salute and the road adjacent to the garrison was renamed in his honour.[7] Again the decorations and ceremonies held for the Earl must have had some effect on the people of the town whichever social class they belonged to.

ILL.10: VIEW OF VICTORIA BARRACKS FROM THE NORTH

During the 1870s the tradition of celebrating the Queen's birthday appears to recur on a more frequent basis. Perhaps a more staunchly loyalist commander was in place who believed that the local population needed to be reminded that their loyalty should lie with the Queen whose army was well-equipped and strategically positioned. In the main however, the celebrations were all held within the garrison walls. The evolution in attitudes towards the monarchy in Athlone can be more easily illustrated with an example from 1887, the year of the Queen's golden jubilee. Within the garrison walls the army played 'God Save the Queen', cannons were fired and the Union Jack was hoisted as part of the ceremonies. Though the Church of Ireland congregation did have special jubilee services, the actions of the majority of townsfolk were

6   *Athlone 1950*, p.47.
7   *A.S.*, 28 Aug 1852.

summed up thus in *The Freeman's Journal*: '*They did not jubilate. Why? They don't care a thrannen for Her Most Gracious Majesty.*'[8] Whilst one must be aware of the Nationalist tendencies of the newspaper, the momentum being gathered by the Land League at the time in the town, viewed as a strongly nationalist heartland (*chapter seven*), must also have played a part in the reaction of some of the townspeople to the occasion.

The army's efforts for the diamond jubilee in 1897 were less substantial due to the fact that most of the servicemen were at training, however, fireworks were ignited, a spectacle that amazed many of the townspeople, who would have seldom witnessed such pyrotechnics. A number of Athlone people, members of a bicycle club, attempted to cycle through the town with Chinese Lanterns but they were jostled by others and greeted with cries of '*Remember Allen, Larkin and O'Brien*'.[9] Perhaps in an attempt to compensate for the army's celebration of the jubilee, songs such as '*God Save Ireland*' and '*The Boys of Wexford*' were sung by crowds, and at any house where decorative illuminations were present the crowd halted for a more personal rendition.[10] These two anniversaries point towards another effect that military celebrations had on the townspeople. Recent political occurrences may have solidified nationalist opinion in the minds of many of Athlone's inhabitants. Any celebration of the monarchy ran contrary to this sentiment and the people reacted accordingly with 'Irish' songs and anti-British behaviour.

Upon the death of Queen Victoria in 1901 the army marched through the town to a Church of Ireland service in St. Peter's Church where the band played the dirges. The account of the day, reproduced in *The Athlone Times* reports that '*Mourning was extensively worn by the townspeople.*'[11] Initially one may be led to believe that on past evidence this mourning may have been restricted to the loyalist members of the community. However, it must be borne in mind that in 1901 Home Rule had lost much of its former potency, the 'Great Man', Charles Stewart Parnell had died, and generally the times exhibited less evidence of radicalism. A lack of reporting on anti-British feeling at this time could also be accounted for by the change seen in values over the Victorian period. People and newspapers may have seen any gloating over the death of Queen Victoria as offensive and distasteful and therefore would not report it. It is possible though, that most nationalists in Athlone were not saddened by the passing of Victoria; it is doubtful that their nationalist ideals had been so quickly dispelled.

8 *FJ.*, 2 July 1887.
9 *FJ.*, 26 June 1897.
10 Ibid.
11 *A.T.*, 10 March 1901.

REDCOATS AND FRIEZECOATS

When the effect of the army on the people of the town is analysed one must be cognisant of the fact that the military had two very different classes of recruit, the officer and the soldier. In general the officer class was viewed as a positive influence on all those people with whom they came into contact, as one lady put it: '...*the close association of the officer class with the civilians of like mind created and encouraged a Loyalist standpoint which no other influence could have created.*'[12] So contemporaries saw the officer as integral in the process of maintaining strong Unionist influence, be it in the army itself or through mixing with loyal civilians. Eventually prolonged exposure to men of such standing was believed by a modern historian to lead to a situation where:

> It might be argued equally well that the very substantial Irish element in the rank and file of the British army and navy...necessitated – in terms of retaining confidence in the forces so composed – the assumption that under the authority and discipline of an English-officered situation, the Irish were transformed.[13]

The point of the above claim when viewed in context is that the British themselves believed that exposure to certain types of Loyalist influence, culture or education was a good way to instil more traditionally British sentiment in the Irish, to metamorphose them. In Athlone this kind of interaction between officers and locals *was* believed by Isaac Weld, writing in 1832, to have effected positive social change in the town:

> In no part of Ireland, as far as my own observation extends, have I seen more urbanity, or more civility and attention to customers, than in the shops of Athlone: perhaps this may be in some measure attributable to the frequent intercourse with the officers of a numerous garrison; but I pretend not to announce that it is so.[14]

Many ladies viewed the officers with great affection, and regularly courted them with a view to marriage. One lady spoke of the officers in the army as being of great interest to ladies in Ireland '...*only a confirmed anti-Britisher...could hold off his daughters from associating with these fascinating creatures*', who were '...*well turned out and so ready to enjoy themselves.*'[15] The life of an officer in garrison towns was seen as being one to be envied for it was: '...*spent in dining, drinking, dancing, riding,*

---

12 Spiers, E. M., "Army Organisation and Society in the nineteenth century", in Bartlett, Thomas & Jeffrey, Keith, (Eds.), *A Military History of Ireland* (Cambridge, 1997), p.342.
13 O'Farrell, Patrick, pp.68–69.
14 Gazetteer, pg. 96.
15 Paseta, Senia, p.86.

steeple-chasing, pigeon shooting, tandem driving, garrison balls and garrison plays.[16]

Evidence from Athlone would appear to support this view to some extent. There are numerous reports dealing with soirées involving the army officers to which acceptable local families were invited. One man noted that anyone wishing to become an officer in the army should really have attended public school and have a love for *'outdoor games'* so as to keep the reputation of the officer as high as possible.[17]

When dealing with the interaction of the officers and the townspeople, it must be noted that in general it was only the élite of Athlone that socialised with this level of the military. Perhaps the most frequent venue in which the mixing of the officers and gentry occurred was the theatre. Indeed, in Athlone it appears that the barracks was the first place in the town to have a purpose-built theatre. A decade before the Famine and many years before Athlone appeared to have any privately or municipally sponsored theatre, a regiment stationed at the garrison in the town had: *'...fitted out a theatre exclusively at its own expense and spared no cost to render it commodious and agreeable.'*[18] Although there is evidence for the presence of theatrical performances in the town in the late 18th century in the form of playbills, the garrison theatre was almost certainly the first purpose-built theatre in the town.[19] Prior to the setting up of the facility in the barracks Athlone's gentry would have mainly relied on the post-race theatrical performances at the local Garrycastle or Athlone Races.[20] Larger towns such as Limerick and Galway had constructed theatres with finance from wealthy citizens, yet it is probably the case that many smaller towns, such as Athlone and Mullingar, received their first dedicated theatrical buildings through the presence of a garrison.[21] During the Victorian period the garrison theatre was used regularly, and all the plays were viewed by select members of the local gentry as well as the officers stationed in the barracks.[22] In general the army and the gentry mingled happily, though on one occasion a pedantic soldier refused to admit any civilians into the barracks for security reasons:

> Many were debarred the pleasure they anticipated owing to the refusal of the Lieutenant in charge of the guard to permit civilians to pass into the

---

16 McDowell, R. B., "The army", in McDowell, R. B., *Social Life in Ireland 1800-45* (Cork, 1979), p.79.
17 Paseta, Senia, p.86.
18 *A.I.*, 9 Mar 1836.
19 Morash, Christopher, *A History of Irish Theatre - 1601-2000*, (Cambridge, 2002), p.68.
20 O'Brien, Brendan, "They once Trod the Boards in Athlone", in *Journal of the Old Athlone Society,* Vol. II, No.5 (Athlone, 1978), p.6.
21 Morash, Christopher, p.70.
22 *A.S.*, 12 Apr 1839, *A.S.*, 19 July 1839, *W.I.*, 3 Nov 1849.

barracks. This exercise of a little brief authority while it was anything but complimentary to the noble patron of the evening was a sad disappointment to those who were discourteously dismissed from the gate.[23]

The quality of the acting in the garrison, though it did fluctuate, was at times said to be of a very high standard, with a play in 1849 coming in for praise from a local reporter who was delighted '...*to observe the display of dramatic talent which would do credit to more distinguished boards*'.[24] One must remember that at this time the Famine was still ongoing within the town, diseases such as cholera were still a danger and the workhouse was overcrowded with extremely poor people living in its cramped and filthy conditions. The fact that the officers in the garrison could afford to lay on a play for the gentry of the town exhibits a distressing lack of sympathy on their behalf, which possibly led to angry feelings being directed at them by the local population. In Britain the army, perhaps in particular the officer class, was viewed with distaste and due to its reputation as an aristocratic institution it: '...*became increasingly unpopular with the rising democracy both of the middle and the working classes*.'[25]

The theatre was used mainly for dramatic performances, as in December 1877 when two plays were put on for the Christmas period.[26] However, it was occasionally used for more charitable reasons as in May 1888 when amateur theatricals were staged for the benefit of the family of a recently drowned army man.[27] Towards the end of the Victorian era the military theatricals had become extremely popular with certain locals whose love for them caused a second night's performance to be staged in the garrison theatre in May 1889.[28] The presence of the theatre in the garrison also provided dedicated theatrical facilities for travelling companies in Athlone. When the J. C. Cussons English Opera Co. visited Athlone in the early 1890s they performed for a short season in the military theatre.[29]

Another officer-related event staged at the garrison, the soiree, was to prove very popular with the elite of the town. As far back as May of 1839 the C. O. of the 99th Regiment ordered that the band that constituted part of it was to play '...*for the amusement of the respectable inhabitants of Athlone...every Wednesday evening in the lines*.'[30] Outside of

23 *W.I.*, 3 Nov 1849.
24 *A.S.*, 10 Oct 1949.
25 Trevelyan, G. M., p.72.
26 *W.I.*, 15 Dec 1877.
27 *E.J.*, 19 May 1888.
28 *E.J.*, 4 May 1889.
29 *E.J.*, 28 Feb 1891.
30 *E.J.*, 27 May 1839.

the theatre the garrison was to play host to the local gentry on numerous occasions right throughout the Victorian period, providing them with the kind of splendour that they may not have had in a town without a garrison. This class of entertainment was very much in keeping with the trends developing in Victorian England. The garrison was providing British entertainment for the loyalist population, which must have made its members feel closer to their English counterparts.

The severe differences noted by Karl Marx in the *'fundamental social cleavage'* of Victorian Britain were illustrated when a massive party was held during October 1846.[31] The 75th Regiment had their military ball at which they entertained the *'fashionable and elite of the neighbourhood'* with music and dance and also served them a meal that was *'on a large and significant scale.'* The quality of the furnishings, weaponry, flower arrangements and the bar gave a definite feeling of largess and grandeur.[32] As already noted in regard to the staging of a play in the garrison, the flagrant use of money to pamper the upper classes must have been deeply galling for many within the town who knew of the event and could neither feed nor clothe themselves. Such soirées continued to be held by those in the garrison during the worst years of the Famine. *The Athlone Sentinel* related that a number of officers from the garrison met their friends on Carberry Island in Lough Ree for a picnic in the summer of what became know as 'Black '47'.[33] Perhaps the officers were attempting to escape having to witness the effects of Famine in the town.

An account penned later in the century stated that social life in the barracks was very good, with the facilities on offer of the highest standard: *'More agreeable quarters for military could not be found. Its social qualities were of the highest order. Boating parties, picnics, and balls followed each other in rapid succession.'*[34] The feeling one gets from much of the information about the officers in Victoria Barracks is that they had a considerable amount of free time to kill. The fact that the Victorian era was considered to be one of international calm may have contributed to this availability; the officers spent less time on duty abroad or on a state of high alert.

Social events did indeed continue to be staged with dancing to *'agreeable music'* and performances by regimental bands common occurrences in the barracks.[35] Other exhibitions held in the garrison for

31 Thomson, David, p.114.
32 *W.I.*, 20 Oct 1846.
33 *A.S.*, 3 July 1847.
34 *'Leaves from my notebook: being a collection of tales, all positive facts portraying Irish life and character'* (Aidan Heavey Public Library, nd.)
35 *F.J.*, 7 Jan 1863, *W.I.*, 6 May 1871, *F.J.*, 13 Aug 1883.

the entertainment of the local upper class were the 'Grand Assault at Arms' displays that were held in the barracks's gymnasium.[36]

The interaction between the officers and gentry of the town did not always occur inside the garrison with at least one party for both the respectable citizens and officers held in the Town Hall just after Christmas 1886.[37] The garrison also played host to social occasions for the younger members of good families. The following account of 'The Flappers' Dance' (flapper referring here to a young teenager) from c.1886 gives and idea of the facilities and entertainment on offer:

> There was nowhere to 'sit-out' in the gym itself so round the outside they had put up a lean-to canvas, along the gym wall, with a passage next to the wall and the rest converted into cubicles for 'sitting-out' with two chairs in each. The only lighting was a hurricane lamp in the passage so the cubicles were too dark to see who was inside. As the regiment was just back from India the 'sitting-out' places were introduced to us as "khala jaggahs" otherwise black places. I may say after I grew up I was never at another dance with "khala jaggahs" and we flappers found it all very exciting.[38]

The officers' previously mentioned love of '*outdoor games*' also manifested itself in Athlone during the Victorian era. A number of sports currently played in Ireland such as cricket and rugby are often referred to as 'garrison games' due to the fact that their spread was attributed to the British army. At Athlone one of the more popular games in the army was cricket, though due to the expense of the equipment used and the origin of the game in public schools in Britain few opponents for the garrison teams were to be found locally, at least not until the 1860s when a local club was founded. Perhaps their most frequent adversaries were the pupils from Ranelagh Endowed School, with evidence of a number of matches taking place between the two in the early 1890s.[39]

Another event held by the officers was the annual regatta, which, dependent on the weather, could draw quite a substantial crowd from all levels of Athlone society.[40] Towards the end of the 19th century sports were becoming ever more important for soldiers as well as officers. The army in general was very much involved with the locals and teams turned out for hockey and football. The foundation of Athlone Town Football Club in 1887 provided the garrison with formidable opponents against whom they played repeatedly with varying degrees of

36 *FJ.*, 22 Mar 1876.
37 *FJ.*, 1 Jan 1887.
38 Langrishe, Rosabel, p.183.
39 *FJ.*, 14 June 1890, *FJ.*, 23 May 1891.
40 *FJ.*, 29 Sep 1888, *FJ.*, 29 July 1889.

success.[41] Impromptu games of hockey were also a common occurrence in the town when the army team would play a number of hastily chosen civilians.[42] Army sports days also occurred but the level of interaction between the military and civilians is unclear.[43] All of these occurrences show the growth of organised sport as one of the important legacies of the Victorian era. Indeed, it is fair to say that the garrison in Athlone was instrumental in developing many sports in the town during the period.

The officers in some regiments also took an interest in hunting, with a former garden in the barracks used for housing '*a pack of harriers*' for a period during the 1870s. Apart from foxes, hares, etc. the main target for the hunters was snipe, which had a significant population on boglands adjacent to the town.[44] The army also brought the game of golf to the town for the first time in the 1890s when the batteries raised at the time of the Napoleonic wars were dismantled and replaced by pastureland and a golf course.[45]

As to the effect the officers had on the lower classes it was possibly restricted to those occasions such as celebrations, etc. when the full pomp and ceremony of the army was on show.

> The large number of cavalry and artillery, as well as of infantry, contributed in no small degree to the local colour of the streets and the general attractiveness of the town. But it was the parade in the barrack square that afforded the most unfailing delight to rural visitors.[46]

Such brightly coloured musical events must certainly have entertained many in the town to some extent – it was a distraction from the habitual and banal lives that many in Athlone, and other provincial garrison towns, were living.

SOLDIERS - THE RANK AND FILE

The life of 'the common' soldier in the rank and file army was considerably less geared towards sophisticated social interaction with the more privileged citizens of Athlone. In general, recruits to the army joined because of a lack of alternative employment. As R. B. McDowell has succinctly remarked '…*most soldiers belonged to the British army because of poverty*'. So it would certainly have been the case that the least

41 *EJ.*, 21 Jan 1888, *EJ.*, 3 Nov 1888.
42 *EJ.*, 21 Feb 1891, *EJ.*, 14 Nov 1891.
43 *EJ.*, 6 Aug 1883.
44 O'Farrell, Padraic Col., p.70.
45 Collins, Tom, *Athlone Golf Club 1892 – 1992* (Athlone, 1992), p.5.
46 Conmee, Rev. John S., p.25.

educated or qualified were signing up.[47] A. N. Wilson has noted that even though many joined due to a lack of income, the wages they earned would never have afforded them a comfortable life.[48] It must be remembered that whilst the army wage was higher than the average agricultural wage of the time, all the recruits had to pay for their own food and clothes, for they could produce neither.[49] G. M. Trevelyan, in his *English Social History* noted that many in 19th century British society saw enlistment in the army as evidence of failure in life.[50] Apparently if one wished to defend the Crown's interests the navy was considered a far better career choice.[51]

The life of a soldier was considered hard; wages as already stated were in relative terms low, barrack conditions were generally poor though they did improve in the latter part of the Victorian era.[52] At Victoria Barracks an officer's mess was added in 1840, new gates were added in 1851 and 1852, new quarters were built in 1862 and a gymnasium was opened in 1875.[53] By 1900 the Garrison had accommodation for 1,500 men, 15,000 stand of arms, a hospital and '...*all the necessary adjuncts to a garrison town*.'[54] The considerable size of the barracks affected the growth of Athlone's west side, covering as it did an area of thirty-two acres. As already noted the scope for both commercial and housing developments on the Connacht side was severely impeded, making the Leinster side more attractive for new businesses to set up.

Despite the hard life of soldiers in the British army, their behaviour was generally considered satisfactory during the first part of the 19th century.[55] However, in Ireland especially from the mid–1840s on, the soldiers had to deal with situations that differed from those in other parts of the United Kingdom. The political climate was unique, as were social conditions. Stresses on the Irish recruits and on British soldiers stationed in the country would have caused them to respond differently when stationed in Ireland. As with many working–class civilians who felt emotional strain arising from their circumstances, the soldiers turned to alcohol in an attempt to cope with the stress. This dependence on drink led to many drunken brawls between army men and Athlone people. The history of the army in the town in the mid to late 19th

47 McDowell, R. B., p.73.
48 Wilson, A. N., p.357.
49 Ibid., p.78.
50 Trevelyan, G.M., p.71.
51 Ibid.
52 McDowell, R. B., p.74.
53 Hanley, Lt. Col. M. K., *The Story of Custume Barracks Athlone* (Athlone, 1974), pp.7-14.
54 Cooke, John, (Ed.), *Handbook for Travellers in Ireland* (London, 1902), p.217.
55 McDowell, R. B., p.76.

century is peppered by accounts of drunkenness, lewd behaviour and generally disorderly conduct.

It appears from reading many of the accounts written in local newspapers that the interaction between the soldiers and townspeople did not, for the most part, lead to the latter being improved as was supposed to happen when civilians interacted with those of the officer class. A survey from as far back as 1819 stated that Athlone had a very high number of '*common prostitutes*' in its streets, whose clients were mainly the soldiers stationed in the garrison. Desmond Keenan in his book *The Catholic Church in the Nineteenth Century* noted that a 19th century observer believed that the presence of the garrison '*...may account for much of the immorality in Athlone.*'[56] Rev. Strean noted that '*houses of industry*' should have been established that would free Athlone '*...of a multitude of common prostitutes, who, in the face of the sun, infest the streets, as well as the hedges and the ditches about the town.*'[57] Isaac Weld mentioned the same problem. Dealing with the more debased elements of army life, be it prostitution, excess drinking or violent conduct Weld remarked that:

> Evils of this description are, however, more or less prevalent in all garrison towns, and where the troops are numerous and frequently changed, may unhappily be considered as almost irremediable.[58]

There is evidence of prostitution in the town for much of the Victorian era though the nature of their trade made its practitioners, by necessity, secretive. The period when most reports on prostitution are to be found date from the 1840s, 50s and 60s, when many single women were noted attempting to gain admittance to the workhouse. Though many euphemisms were employed to describe the women's social standing there was no doubt as to their trade.[59] It is probably true that with the high turnover of soldiers in the garrison, the fact that many had to leave their wives and girlfriends at home (not the case with officers whose families were accommodated) along with many younger recruits with no such connections, demand for female company was high. One of the solutions proposed for preserving the virtue of the town's women came about when a number of ladies were observed flirting with some army men. Members of the local population, disgusted by such casual behaviour, called for the establishment of a night school for girls.[60]

56 Keenan, Desmond, p.104.
57 Strean, Annesley, p.80.
58 O'Brien, *Workhouse*, p.31.
59 Ibid., pp.31-33.
60 *F.J.*, 17 Nov 1888.

In the case of drink-related incidents reports in the local press are numerous and varied pointing towards a serious problem, within the general army ranks. Elizabeth Malcolm in her book *Ireland Sober, Ireland Free* stated that heavy drinking was an anxiety-based reaction in an attempt to alleviate the pressures felt under '*intolerable socio-economic circumstances*.'[61] Those recruits who joined the army were poorly paid and many were very young and perhaps found the training or the career very hard to deal with. Of course the fact that so many drunken incidences occurred must cause one to wonder where the army men found the time to visit local public houses. The assumption that a soldier's day was filled by army-related duties is dispelled by an account from Victoria Barracks in 1846, which details the regime of an average day:

> I rose at 5 o'clock in the morning and made up my bed which occupied at least a quarter of an hour and was rather a troublesome job. I then made my toilet and at 6 turned out for drill from which we were dismissed at a quarter to eight when we breakfasted. From 10 until 12 we were again at drill, had dinner at one in the shape of potatoes and meat, both usually of the most wretched quality, and at two fell in for another drill which terminated at four, after which hour my time was at my own disposal until Tattoo, provided I was not ordered on piquet or other such duty. During this period of leisure I generally amused myself by strolling in the vicinity of the garrison (no soldier being permitted to go to a greater distance than one mile) or by reading in prevention of going to the Beer Shop.[62]

The fact that the soldiers had so much free time on their hands, even in 1846 during the Famine, and, unlike the officers, had few organised social events to attend, probably meant that they tried to alleviate their resulting boredom by visiting the local hostelries.

The army as an institution did recognise the fact that drinking was a massive problem within the ranks. The *Report from His Majesty's Commissioners for Inquiring into the system of Military Punishments in the Army* from 1836 presented evidence gathered concerning excess drinking with a view to determining its root causes and proposing solutions. A large number of officers were asked if they would correspond with the commission, sending their views on how the problem could have been dealt with. The most common answers offered for dealing with the prevention of drunkenness were the establishment

61 Malcolm, Elizabeth, *Ireland Sober, Ireland Free – Drink and Temperance in Nineteenth Century Ireland* (New York, 1986), p.327.
62 *W.I.*, 10 Oct 1846.

of temperance societies and prohibition on the sale of alcohol in the military canteens. The replies presented in relation to dealing with the effects of drunkenness were all intended as deterrents to future would-be drunks and included docked pay, lashes and imprisonment. Interestingly as has been noted of 19th century working class society in Ireland when it came to temperance (*chapter nine*), a number of the respondents believed the alcohol culture within the army to be an intrinsic part of what it meant to be a soldier, rendering it an incurable problem.[63]

Transgressions perpetrated by drunken soldiers in Athlone varied widely though many tended to be quite serious. In one case from 1842 a young soldier decided that the army was not for him and sold his uniform to finance a drinking session. Upon discovery of his actions he was arrested and sentenced to six months imprisonment. In the same week another soldier received seventy-eight lashes (no obvious reason as to why such a specific number) for drunkenness. Indeed, at this time the situation was becoming so serious in Victoria Barracks that a high-ranking officer attended the garrison with the express purpose of inspecting the troops.[64]

At times the effect that alcohol had on a soldier could have fatal consequences. One example from July 1845 details how one soldier throttled another to death after being accused of not being a credit to the army.[65] In that same month a man received 100 lashes for being drunk at the Lecarrow Pattern, whilst a second received a lesser number on account of his usually '*excellent*' character.[66] The fact that excess drinking was being witnessed in those soldiers who usually displayed exemplary behaviour showed that the drink culture in the army was capable of spreading.

During the Famine years the army had the extra responsibility of policing a populace being ravaged by disease and starvation. Furthermore, the barracks itself was not immune from the diseases of the time, soldiers must have feared for their own health on top of everything else. It was a time when the army was present in the greatest numbers seen during the 19th century; over 27,000 soldiers were on duty.[67] Army responsibilities included dealing with unrest among the peasantry in nearby regions or perhaps protecting stores of grain from

63 *Report from His Majesty's Commissioners for Inquiring into the system of Military Punishments in the Army, with Appendices* (London, 1836), pp. 92-98.
64 *F.J.*, 21 Dec 1842.
65 *F.J.*, 1 July 1845.
66 *F.J.*, 2 July 1845.
67 Kennedy, David, p.62.

pillaging as well as assisting in evictions.[68] These duties would probably
have put a strain on all the soldiers, perhaps more so on Irish recruits
who would have to deploy against their fellow countrymen. The duties
would also have had the effect of fostering feelings of hatred against the
army who would probably become more recognisable as the occupying
force, many already thought they were. Towards the end of the Famine
there were even reports of murder attempts against soldiers.[69] Many high
ranking officers in the army realised that the duties during this crisis
must prove too much for Irish men in the forces, conceivably leading to
defections. In Athlone officers issued a decree that there was to be no
fraternising between '*redcoats and friezecoats*', hoping to keep interaction
to a minimum. One effect that this order had was seen when the largely
Irish 31st Regiment of Foot arrived in 1848; the distance they kept
from the local population caused them to be very unpopular.[70]

In the cases outlined above it would seem that the problem with
drinking and generally violent behaviour in the army was an internal
one with little effect on others outside the barracks. This was not always
the case however. In one instance during 1855 members of the local
constabulary had to retreat into their station when a large group of men
from the 60th Rifles and Mayo Militia threw stones at them and broke
all the windows in the barracks. It took the arrival of a large force of
other soldiers to halt the attack, with a number staying behind to protect
the police.[71]

At times during the Crimean War the military barracks at Athlone
was said to be almost empty. *The Westmeath Independent* stated that
'*...there is not a Red-Coat left in the Athlone Garrison.*'[72] There can be no
doubt that when Britain was at war the economies of garrison towns
suffered greatly for the want of business from the absent soldiers and
officers. Indeed for the next ten years the population at the barracks was
said to be so low that an order to close and send all remaining troops to
Mullingar was given but later countermanded.[73] The garrison was later
reported as being '*at its full strength*' by May of 1871.[74]

In the wider context the reputation of the regular soldier was to be
boosted by the conduct of those who fought in the Crimean War and
the soldier's reputation as an '*...idle, drunken, hard-swearing fighting man*'

68 *W.I.*, 24 Oct 1846, *F.J.*, 31 Oct 1846.
69 *F.J.*, 28 Mar 1850, *F.J.*, 1 Apr 1850.
70 O'Brien, Brendan, "Early Days of Garrison Theatre in Athlone", in *Journal of the Old Athlone Society*, Vol. I,
   No.4 (Athlone, 1974), p.280.
71 *F.J.*, 10 Oct 1855.
72 *W.I.*, 30 June 1855.
73 Aidan Heavey Public Library, Garrison File.
74 *W.I.*, 6 May 1871.

underwent change thanks in part to the testimony of Florence Nightingale.[75] Whilst this may have been true of the British army in general, the new, more respectable reputation did not appear to effect any noticeable positive change in the behaviour of the soldiers stationed in Athlone.

At Victoria Barracks, as part of ongoing investment, a military canteen complete with a full menu of alcoholic beverages was introduced. Obviously the chances of the military controlling any drunken fracas became far higher if the venue was within the walls. However, the soldiers must also have recognised the fact that their behaviour would have been more easily monitored if they were on site, possibly deterring them from using the facility. In the town publicans must have been dismayed when the news reached them, since a number of establishments were heavily dependant on army patronage - some had even gone so far as to section off part of their premises to make an officers' lounge.[76]

One of the main causes for concern amongst soldiers was the army drafts. In Athlone towards the latter end of the 19th century the main destination for those drafted was India. Almost without fail when these situations arose a number of men would decide that it would be safer if they avoided overseas duty. A report in the local press details one such occasion from 1874. Several soldiers, having left the barracks without permission, proceeded to a local public house followed by a corporal, who, when he caught up with them, ordered them to return. The men refused and promptly assaulted him. When he had been subdued they began to vandalise the public house and it was not until more soldiers arrived from the barracks that the incident was brought to an end. Eventually they were returned to the garrison, fined £1 for drunkenness, sentenced to forty-two days hard labour and made liable for all the damages to the establishment in which the incident occurred.[77] Over a decade later, in 1888, a number of soldiers acted in a similar fashion when the call to protect Her Majesty's interests in India was again issued. During December of that year when the regiments were leaving for Dublin port several soldiers looted a number of public houses and became drunk, while other intoxicated army men were arrested for attempting to steal a keg of Guinness from the storehouse on the docks.[78]

75 Newsome, David, p.106.
76 *W.I.*, 18 June 1870.
77 *W.I.*, 17 Oct 1874.
78 *F.J.*, 8 Dec 1888, *F.J.*, 29 Dec 1888.

Apart from disorderly conduct precipitated by an aversion to certain duties and excess alcohol consumption, soldiers at times engaged in criminal activity to finance drinking sessions. In June 1878 four soldiers mugged a local man relieving him of between £10 and £20, apparently deciding that it was a good way to finance a day's drinking. A complaint was made to the constabulary and the men were arrested a short time later in a local pub.[79] Activities such as these must have caused consternation amongst the local population who probably came to hate not only the duties carried out by soldiers but also their general behaviour.

In the late 1870s with the start of the Land War this hatred may have been magnified as the duties became more repressive and, in nationalist regions, anti-Irish.[80] Aware of this growing local sentiment the army in the town was on high alert during the period of Land League meetings – the soldiers who overlooked the market crowd one Saturday in November 1880 were described as having '*no local ties*'.[81] The fear of Irish recruits being unduly influenced by nationalist emotions was considered very real by the commanders in the army.

The most serious incident involving members of the garrison occurred in June of 1887, when a riot occurred in the town. The account of the lead-up to the main incident relates that four '*civilian blackguards*' were arguing with a like number of soldiers over a local girl on a Thursday night (after an evening spent in a local public house) in the centre of the town. Eventually a fight broke out leaving one of the soldiers very badly beaten. The following day a large number of his colleagues – who it seems were misinformed about the fight – went to Connacht Street in search of the four civilian perpetrators, to exact revenge. After engaging them, one of the army men was stabbed in the stomach, though luckily for him a number of other soldiers, who were coincidentally passing that way, saw the situation and joined the fracas. The RIC was called and after their intervention the fight broke up.

Obviously annoyed at the incident, a mob of 150 soldiers, from the Royal Berkshire Brigade, (members of which had intervened the night before) raced up Church Street on the following Saturday and positioned themselves in Mardyke Street on the east of the town. The appearance of the soldiers led many locals, believing their intentions were hostile, to close window shutters and flee the area in fear of their safety. The RIC was alerted to the gathering, though upon arrival, took

79 *FJ*, 12 June 1878.
80 *FJ*, 20 Feb 1882.
81 Sime, William, p.135.

no immediate action even though the army men '*seemed disposed*' to attack them. Around the police a number of civilians gathered, it seemed with the intention of backing the RIC in their face-off, or more probably just to join in a fight against some British soldiers. The army men moved west towards Victoria Place jeering and shouting at the locals with some of them removing their belts and rushing the crowd that had gathered to watch. The constabulary, armed with their batons, spread out across the road and even though they numbered only six succeeded in deflecting the attack. The soldiers then turned towards Northgate Street where they attacked the Town Hall after noticing a number of civilians rush there to protect themselves. A further attack on the hall seemed imminent when a military piquet arrived thwarting any such action.

Later, after the rioters had been sent back to barracks, a dozen soldiers were heard singing and chanting whilst walking up Irishtown much to the annoyance of the locals. The police were called on again to silence the men for it was believed that the civilians were about to take matters into their own hands. This appeared to be the correct interpretation of the mood, for a short time later an army sergeant had a lucky escape from a severe beating at the hands of a local mob. The situation calmed later in the evening but that was not to be the end of the strife.

The next day, Sunday, over 200 soldiers rushed up Church Street shouting in a '*frenzied manner*'. Women and children ran for cover in any building to which they could gain access, with the soldiers described as being '*like demons*'. The army men got their hands on three young boys, two of whom escaped but the third was kicked '*senseless*' and left in the middle of the road. The newspaper account stated that there were '*...100 of these ruffians around this one poor boy.*' They then proceeded to Ashes's Corner in Irishtown on the town's eastern fringe where they began vandalising houses before marching along the street, hitting civilians with their belts. One man named Lyons, who was the unlucky victim of a blow, grabbed his attacker, dragged him into his house and thrust his head onto the fire '*...with as little ceremony as if he were a sod of turf.*' Another soldier rushed to his compatriot's aid attacking Lyons and his eighty-year-old mother. Eventually other locals intervened to stop the assault. Outside on the street the civilians had armed themselves and organised a mob to deal with the soldiers, who were soundly beaten and driven back into the barracks. The locals then began to sing 'God Save Ireland' in such a way that the mostly English regiment could have no problem hearing. In an attempt to calm the locals, the soldiers were confined to barracks by their Commanding Officer.

However, some of the men were not satisfied with their loss to the locals. Almost 100 disregarded his orders, overpowered the guard on duty and fled into the town. They rushed up to the RIC Station on the west of Athlone and proceeded to smash the windows. Eventually they were secured by a military piquet. In the interim, however, another 100 soldiers had escaped and were fighting with civilians who had just avoided running into the first group from the garrison. One boy was viciously attacked and '…*beaten in a brutal manner so that his life was in danger*'. The soldiers proceeded to the bridge where they were set upon by a large number of civilians. Soldiers stationed in the Castle threw stones at the local crowd and a vicious fight ensued. The RIC arrived to attempt to separate the two groups but it was not until the arrival of an extra military piquet that the soldiers were driven back to the barracks.

Word of the riot had spread to the outlying region of Coosan where up to 1,000 men were said to be armed and en-route to render assistance to the townspeople. Their arrival in the town did not precipitate any further violence for the situation had been calmed. The reason for the escalation in the riots was said to be not only the assaults perpetrated by local men on a number of soldiers but also hissing noted by the soldiers on their way from church. All those soldiers involved in the riot were confined to the barracks, but to ensure civility a large number of police was drafted into the town on the following Monday. It appears that the officer in charge of the garrison over the weekend had invited guests, including a number of ladies, to the town and it is possible that he devoted most of his time to that engagement as opposed to the running of the garrison.[82]

Whilst one must be conscious that this report was related nationally in a Catholic Nationalist newspaper, *The Freeman's Journal*, the fact still remains that the incident occurred. Leaving aside the probably inflated estimates of those involved (100 men around one boy seems rather unlikely) the actual occurrence of this riot speaks volumes about army life in the period. In this instance the low wages, slowly improving conditions of the garrison, along with operating in a predominantly nationalist town during the Land War, may have led to poor discipline and high levels of anxiety in many of the soldiers. Perhaps the incident could be viewed as a catharsis of sorts for the frustrated men.

Of all of the soldiers who were involved in the riots only five of those charged with assault were sentenced at the assizes held almost one

82 *FJ*, 4 June 1887.

month later.[83] Subsequent to this the Lord Lieutenant decreed that all those that were jailed for assault were to be unconditionally discharged from service.[84] The '...*troublesome, riotous Royal Berkshire Brigade has been removed from Athlone*' was the opening line of an article written in *The Freeman's Journal* for August 6th, which said that the locals exhibited no ill will against the regiment for the two days of riots![85]

One should not reach hasty conclusions about what was behind such a fracas. This class of military rowdyism was not limited to Ireland. An issue of *The Westmeath Independent* from January 1879 related a similar incident in Falmouth, England where a large number of soldiers decided to '*spring*' a member of their regiment from the jail in which he was interred for fighting with a local man.[86] Another report from November 1893 detailed how 60 Munster Fusiliers '*ran amok*' on a train, indicating that this class of large-scale army disturbance was not that uncommon.[87]

The riots in Athlone over that June weekend may have created the sense that the townspeople could not have another English regiment stationed there in the near future. Perhaps the incident contributed to the Wiltshire Regiment cheering for the Irish Home Rule politician Charles Stewart Parnell whilst on their way to the town from Boyle in an attempt to appease the inhabitants. The cheer apparently created a sensation in certain quarters in England for the regiment was believed to be a thoroughly loyal and intrinsically English one.[88]

The drink-related disturbances in the town continued unabated however. Problems with the effective implementation of army conduct regulations appear to have been the serious deficiency in this regard. This can be seen soon after the riot occurred with an example from June 1888 describing how one army man assaulted another leaving him for dead after a few drinks in the town on a Friday night.[89] Later in the summer of 1889 double piquets were sent out to a disturbance in Irishtown where a number of army men were remonstrating with a local man over his interference earlier in the day. The problem was linked to a number of girls that were in the soldiers' company, who had departed the scene subsequent to the interference. Eventually the incident led to the arrest of sixteen drunken soldiers.[90] At this time the

83 *F.J.*, 2 July 1887.
84 *F.J.*, 23 July 1887.
85 *F.J.*, 6 Aug 1887.
86 *W.I.*, 18 Jan 1879.
87 Spiers, E. M., p.348.
88 *F.J.*, 19 May 1888.
89 *F.J.*, 2 June 1888.
90 *F.J.*, 15 Jun 1889.

Home Rule movement was gaining momentum with the effect of heightening political tensions at both national and local level. The soldiers may have felt that they were more unwelcome and under more stress during this period when British-Irish inequalities were being regularly highlighted.

Interestingly the British Secretary of State speaking at this time, noted that though the Irish members of the armed forces were *'probably disposed to be loyal'* a rise in the wage earned would *'...make it worth their while to remain so'*.[91] Obviously the tensions between Irish nationalist civilians and the British Army, including its Irish contingent, were seen at cabinet level to be detrimental to the good running of the army. However, upon the departure of the Wiltshire Regiment from Athlone they appeared to be quite popular as a large crowd had gathered to see them off.[92] Even the Town Commissioners, when first informed that the regiment would be leaving, let it be known that they were unhappy to see them go.[93]

The Royal Irish Fusiliers were their replacements and upon arrival they marched through the town playing 'Come Back to Erin'. Of the 646 in the regiment roughly 500 were Catholics and their Fife and Drum band had played the Catholics of the town to mass.[94] Though the Fusiliers, were by all accounts, viewed favourably by the town's inhabitants simply because of their composition, they too were guilty of a number of crimes similar to those perpetrated by their predecessors. The reports in the press detailed no decrease in the number of incidents after they arrived, although one must be aware of the fact that not all soldiers at the garrison belonged to one particular regiment at any given time.

The army regiments also fought against each other. When a fight broke out between members of the Lancashire regiment and members of the Royal Artillery, piquets had to be called to the scene. The harassment of the local ladies continued: one girl complained to the Officer in Command of the barracks of the *'molestations'* she suffered at the hands of army men every time she walked through the town.[95] It reached a point in the 1890s when almost every week an army related transgression was being reported in the local newspapers. In a week where a break-in by nine soldiers at a local residence was reported, a man, believed to be from *The Westmeath Independent*, which had reported

91 Spiers, E. M., p.348.
92 *FJ.*, 24 May 1890.
93 *FJ.*, 10 May 1890.
94 *FJ.*, 24 May 1890.
95 *FJ.*, 21 Sep 1895.

extensively on army-related law breaking, was badly beaten.[96] Possibly the soldiers felt that they were the victims of unfair press reports.

Further evidence that a regiment's place of origin did not appear to have affected the numbers of crimes perpetrated in Athlone came with the arrival of the Connaught Rangers. This popular regiment, which had an Irish contingent traditionally over 65%, arrived in the town in 1898 after a twenty-year absence but appeared to engage in the same behaviour as most of the other regiments that were stationed at Victoria Barracks.[97] Pressures felt by Irish recruits may have been even more pronounced than those affecting English or Welsh soldiers. Irish men in the army had to work against their fellow countrymen, some may have seen them as traitors, and accordingly they may have been reviled to an even greater degree in some quarters.

It was during this last decade of the Victorian period that the Commander-in-Chief of the forces in Ireland thought: '*It would be well to get all the Irish Regts. out of Ireland as soon as possible & not to send any more until Mr Gladstone dies or is turned out of office. I would not trust them in a riot here.*'[98] However, in general it was believed that Irish regiments and soldiers were still not disposed towards dissension when in service in the British Army. They '*...sustained their military reputation by an immense range and diversity of service*' and '*...if properly drilled, equipped and organised, they regularly served with distinction*'.[99] The political tension noted in the earlier years of Home Rule was again highlighted at cabinet level. It appears that the government perceived a fall off in loyalty of Irish soldiers and thought of them as even less reliable when dealing with Irish problems. Towards the end of the Victorian era the issue of trust declined in importance. Irish recruits were not enlisting as much as they had, due in part, to the actions of Maud Gonne and her anti-Boer War drive as well as a general disillusionment with the force and the prospects it offered.[100]

The development of Athlone during the Victorian era was greatly affected by the fact that the British army had a sizeable barracks on the town's west side. Symbolically the facility was a potent reminder of Ireland's colonial status and that their head of state was the Queen of England. The celebrations held at the garrison for marking the Queen's coronation, birthdays as well as the visits of royal dignitaries would all have lent an extra degree of splendour to the town; more than this

96 *FJ.*, 28 Sep 1895.
97 Spiers, E. M., p.339, *FJ.*, 14 May 1898.
98 Spiers, E. M., p.348.
99 Ibid., p.357.
100 Ibid., p.341.

however they served to remind the townspeople of their place in the Empire. Later in the century when the Land War and Home Rule were gaining momentum, the local population appear to have achieved a more militant sense of their Irishness. They would thwart celebrations of royal occasions outside the garrison; perhaps its constant presence also provided them with a focus for their opposition to British rule.

The officers at Victoria Barracks were, like their colleagues in Britain, believed by contemporaries to have an improving, civilising influence on all those, of lesser standing, they came into contact with. They were depicted as very sociable, sporting and affluent people whose duties appeared, in the calmer international military climate of the Victorian era, to extend more to entertaining both themselves and the local gentry at plays, soirees and picnics than to defending the realm. Without doubt their love of the arts introduced Athlone to far more plays and concerts than would have happened had they not been present. The officers were also responsible for bringing many new sports into Ireland. Cricket, rugby and golf were all introduced into Athlone via the garrison. However, their recreational pursuits must have angered many of the people of Athlone, especially during the Famine when the juxtaposition of their excesses and the suffering being experienced all around them was a major source of scandal. The officers of the garrison operated in a vacuum, almost as if no outside occurrences appeared to concern them.

The social cleavage greatly apparent in the Victorian era in general was also seen in microcosm in the army. Comparisons between the gentlemanly lifestyle of the officers and that of the regular soldiers highlight great divisions within the institution itself. Whilst the association of young ladies and officers was encouraged a similar association involving regular soldiers was deemed iniquitous: the presence of prostitutes in Athlone was attributed almost entirely to the presence of the garrison. Being an army recruit appears to have been a last resort for many who joined, and in many cases the relief of poverty was the compelling motive. They perhaps had more in common with the working classes who lived outside the barrack walls, than with their superiors. The daily regime of the soldiers appears to have provided them with an excess of free time, with a large proportion of this spent in the local pubs. Unfortunately the effect alcohol had on certain soldiers led to illegal acts such as theft, assault and even murder. The reliance on alcohol was probably derived from the recruits' dislike for some aspects of their occupation. Without doubt certain duties, like the Indian drafts, raised the levels of anxiety the men were feeling and they turned to drink for solace. Many officers quoted in a commission report believed that disassociating being in the army from drinking alcohol was impossible. Even when drink wasn't involved, reprehensible behaviour could not be ruled out. In June 1887 Athlone was the site of a serious army riot, which lasted for an entire weekend. At this point in Ireland's history the Home Rule movement was quite vocal and well supported and the soldiers in the garrison may have felt under great pressure. They were despised by locals for what they stood for and for their association with the laws they helped enforce. It was not merely the case that the townspeople were hostile to the actions of 'British' regiments; those regiments with a significant Irish membership were at times no more popular nor less rowdy than those consisting mainly of Englishmen.

Overall the army influenced Athlone and its people greatly. Its presence helped shape the evolution of the town in the Victorian era and its legacy is enduring. The same extensive facility is still an important military command for the Irish army, dominating the western riverbank.

CHAPTER 7

National and local politics

NATIONAL POLITICS

The historiography of Ireland during the 19th century invariably centres on the political developments of the time. Each of the key political movements such as Catholic Emancipation and Home Rule is always given great weight in many accounts for they, perhaps more than any other events, provided the change necessary for Ireland to develop a greater national consciousness. In Athlone, a large provincial Irish town, the national politics of the Victorian era had great influence over how it developed, how the locals saw themselves and indeed how the town was managed on a local level. To outline the political history of Athlone during the Victorian era three subsections have been created under the heading National Politics. In the first section Daniel O'Connell's Repeal movement will be looked at, along with this the borough elections during the Victorian era will be explored, how they were carried off and the candidates that participated. In this section William Keogh's career will be given prominence due to his position among first, the members who represented Athlone and second, in the judiciary of Ireland. The third section will cover the growth of agrarian crime and the strengthening of Ribbonism in the Athlone area. It will also outline the situation in Westmeath as a whole with a view to establishing the situation before the advent of the Land War, Parnell and Home Rule, which will be covered in the concluding section.

O'CONNELL, KEOGH AND ATHLONE BOROUGH ELECTIONS

For a number of years previous to the Victorian period the Liberal Club in Athlone had been highlighting what it saw as the absolute misrepresentation of the inhabitants of the town at parliamentary level.[1] Under the Corporation there were only thirty-six people in the town who were entitled to vote even though the population of the borough

---

1 *FJ*, 30 Apr 1830.

during the 1830s was believed to be over 11,000.[2] Though this lack of representation did change significantly with the introduction of Victorian reforms, the number of people not entitled to vote formed the overwhelming majority of the townspeople. With such a small number of people actually voting, corruption in elections was rather easy to accomplish, though in later years as the franchise grew it became slightly more difficult as greater time and investment were required in 'persuading' larger numbers of voters. Throughout the Victorian era the political manoeuvring in Athlone relied on the venality of voters, as opposed to their ideals, and the corruption of the invigilators. Over the decades the methods for securing votes did not vary all that much, bribery and intimidation being the most common tools.

At the start of the Victorian era in 1837 Athlone's representative was Daniel O'Connell's son John. He was elected unopposed in that year but decided to run in another borough in the subsequent 1841 election. It is that election, the first of the 1840s, which provides a good example of how bribery and corruption could greatly influence an Athlone Borough election.

In the run up to polling day, the 9th July 1841, a local newspaper led with a story about how the hopes of the Tories in Athlone had been shattered due to a change in the Liberal camp. Initially there were two Liberal candidates running, which would have spilt the vote, leaving the Tories with a probable majority. Eventually the Liberal Party called a meeting, the end result of which was just one candidate running in the election, which apparently meant certain victory.[3] This was not to be the case however; nearly three-quarters of the Liberal votes were disregarded due to supposed '*improper description on the certificate*'.[4] The interpretation of the act that dealt with borough elections by the Athlone Election Committee was such that no scrutinising of the vote or certificates was to be allowed, and the Conservative nominee, George de la Poer Beresford, won the seat by thirty votes to seventeen. The number who turned up for the vote on the Liberal side was 110, with those on the Conservative side, including freemen, numbering only fifty.

A newspaper article printed after the election described the consternation in the town when news of a similar dubious count was delivered in Dublin.[5] The losing Athlone Liberal, Daniel Henry Farrell,

---

2 *Athlone 1945*, p.39.
3 *FJ*, 9 June 1841.
4 *FJ*, 13 July 1841.
5 Ibid.

went to Westminster to plead his case and after the establishment of a committee to inquire into the election a decree was read stating that the committee found the Liberal candidate to be duly elected. This decree was delivered much to the delight of some Athlone voters.[6] Needless to say the Conservative Party petitioned against the installation of the new MP citing intimidation of Tory voters on polling day amongst other reasons.[7] Farrell, the Liberal, was unseated, and Beresford, the Tory, again assumed the position.[8] The subsequent by-election of 1843 was no less corrupt with those individuals put forward as candidates presenting weak mandates, which showed they were uncommitted to any particular ideals. The lack of privacy at the polls in all elections was a contributing factor to their contentious nature; intimidation, bribery and general commotion were the hallmarks of canvassing on both sides of the political divide.

Perhaps due to this type of corruption in the parliamentary election the fervour that locals displayed in the cause of Daniel O'Connell's Repeal movement was quite strong. O'Connell had one main goal, the repeal of the 1800 Act of Union. Irish Catholics wished to have better representation at parliamentary level and the problems caused by this were to lead to very strained Anglo-Irish relations for the entire Victorian era and beyond.[9] Support for Repeal had re-emerged after the achievement of Catholic Emancipation in 1829 and headed by O'Connell it was to gain over three million supporters and garner large funding through the 'repeal rents' collected by Catholic priests.[10] It appears that Athlone's populace supported the Repeal Association early in the Victorian era, with a £10 donation received from the men on the Roscommon side of the town in 1839 and another donation made by those on the Leinster side soon after.[11] A meeting was held to discuss repeal in September 1842 and 3,000 people attended – apparently the number would have been larger but for some confusion over cancellation. All of those who heard the speeches cheered for the speaker, The Queen, O'Connell and repeal. O'Connell was not attempting a complete break in the British connection, hence no condemnation of the Queen at the meeting; that type of rhetoric was characteristic of political discourse only after the Famine. The same meeting was also attended by a number of local clergymen; O'Connell actively attempted to draw the clergy into the movement, recognising

6   *FJ.*, 16 June 1842.
7   *FJ.*, 21 June 1842.
8   Lenehan, Jim, *Politics and Society in Athlone 1830-1885 – A Rotten Borough* (Dublin, 1999), p.28.
9   Thomson, David, p.62.
10   Cannon, John, (Ed.), *The Oxford Companion to British History* (Oxford, 1997), p.799.
11   *FJ.*, 19 Jan 1839.

the assistance they could render.[12] The crowds, though probably disillusioned with their local representatives, still had great faith in O'Connell and the movement in general; they hoped that something positive would come out of it. The arrival of O'Connell himself in the town in June 1843 saw the largest crowds that ever assembled in Athlone for the entire 19th century. As part of his efforts to build support for the movement O'Connell staged a number of 'Monster Meetings' around Ireland where he would declare the intentions of the repeal movement to truly massive crowds; an estimate for the meeting at Tara puts the figure for attendance at 800,000. Athlone was chosen as the site for one of the midlands meeting.

Upon his arrival in Athlone on the third Saturday in June, O'Connell travelled to Summerhill on the west of the town where he stayed the night. The following day after attending mass, he led a parade through the town to Scotch Parade on the Leinster side, which was said to be:

> ...crowded to excess, not merely with townspeople and tradespeople but also with thousands who flocked into the town at the earliest hour from the remotest districts of Meath, Westmeath, King's County, Roscommon. All the adjoining hills and eminences of every kind were literally black from the denseness of the crowds.[13]

After this meeting concluded a massive parade over three miles in length marched in the direction of Summerhill to the music of the temperance bands from Athlone, Clara and a number of other towns. The police and the military, though present in great numbers for the meeting, were said to be redundant such was the exemplary conduct of the massive crowd. To ensure that none of the middle class ladies were disturbed by other locals they were accommodated in a separate grandstand at the site.[14] The calculation of the crowd that accumulated at Summerhill for the meeting made by a *Freeman's Journal* reporter who attended, though only a '*moderate*' one in his own estimation, was 150,000 people.[15] Another figure that was quoted for the level of attendance at the Athlone meeting was 200,000.[16] The visitor who furnished this estimate, a German named Venedy, was shocked by the power that O'Connell had over the crowd. When asked by O'Connell to '*stand still*' Venedy says that all went silent and that; '...*in England they*

12 *FJ.*, 27 Sep 1842.
13 *FJ.*, 20 June 1843.
14 Owens, Gary, "Nationalism without Words, Symbolism and Ritual Behaviour in the Repeal 'Monster Meetings' of 1843-5", in Donnelly, J. S. Jr & Miller, Kerby A. (Eds.), *Irish Popular Culture 1650-1850* (Dublin, 1998), p.258.
15 Ibid.
16 Venedy, Herr J., p.53.

neither know the power of the man himself nor the character of the movement in which he is engaged.[17]

Unsurprisingly, whilst the subsequent meetings of the repeal movement in 1844 and 1845 were heavily attended by locals the votes of the towns' electorate did not support the repeal candidate who was put forward for election in 1847. Instead they went for the Peelite William Keogh.[18] One of the reasons provided for the failure of the repeal movement in Ireland by one modern scholar is that the middle-class Catholics were less enthused about it than they were about O'Connell's emancipation drive, with very few Protestants interested at all.[19] The electorate in Athlone would have consisted to a large extent of men from these classes, hence ensuring its failure at the local level. Also it must be remembered that the fervour of the locals for the movement would have been greatly affected by the onset of the Famine.

The election of William Nicholas Keogh, described as: '...*the best known and most controversial figure to represent the borough of Athlone in the nineteenth century*' in 1847, though apparently as corrupt as the previous election (Keogh won by just six votes), was most remembered for the man rather than his methods.[20] Born in Galway in 1817, educated at Mountjoy School Dublin and Trinity College Dublin, where he was called to the bar, Keogh won the Athlone seat riding on the words he gave at the public address before polling:

> I can sincerely pledge myself that there is no sacrifice which I will not freely make; no professional advancement or personal case, which I will not unhesitatingly forego to win the reputation of an earnest and useful advocate (for) ...an independent party in parliament is the only hope of the country.[21]

Keogh also believed that with '*little exertion*' the town could be made into something great, though it appears that the priorities stated in his speech were not those he actually wished to pursue. However, this would not become apparent until later. As was typical of the system in Britain at the time, Keogh did not live in Athlone; instead he had a Dublin address as well as another in Bray.[22]

One of his greatest attributes as a politician, which during the 19th century could apparently help one win or lose an election, was his capacity for alcohol. Some of his success at elections was said to stem

---

17 Ibid., p.54.
18 *FJ.*, 19 June 1844, *FJ.*, 28 July 1845, *FJ.*, 6 Aug 1847.
19 Hoppen, K. Theodore, *Elections Politics and Society in Ireland 1832-1885* (Oxford, 1984), p.31.
20 Lenehan, Jim, p.35, *FJ.*, 6 Aug 1847.
21 *FJ.*, 22 July 1847.
22 *Dublin Almanac and General Registry 1847* (Dublin, 1847), p.331.

from the fact that he was said to be at: '...*the bedside of the companions of his debauch the next morning with a brandy and soda in his hand and the Christian name of a scarcely recovered inebriate in his mouth.*' His tolerance for alcohol led to one of his opponents, who joined him in a public house in the town for a debate, being carried off: '*in a violent fit of delirium tremens.*'[23]

After the 1847 election Keogh was the sole Irish Catholic at Westminster. The local and national press reports of the time suggest that the MP, who supported a number of important causes such as the Catholic Defence Association, of which he was a founder, and the Tenant Rights Movement, was popular. In his early career he appeared to have an instinct for associating himself with powerful popular movements. The Tenant Rights Movement held '...*one of the largest and most imposing demonstrations*' in the town where 10,000 people gathered and were addressed by Keogh. The meeting dealt with the liberty of the Catholic Church and for Keogh

ILL.11: WILLIAM KEOGH, MP (1817-1878)

to be seen supporting this meant that he probably won the support of the Catholic clergy in the town.[24] Though Keogh advocated supporting what a local priest deemed an '*exterminating landlord*' at the same meeting for the coming Westmeath elections, he did not appear to lose popularity amongst the electorate and he won the next parliamentary election in 1852, this time as an Independent Liberal, by 70 votes.[25] Incidentally his recommendation for the aforementioned landlord, a Mr Mangan, proved useful with the County result going in Mangan's favour.[26]

A visitor to the town, interested in 'Election Warfare' believed that fair play was not evident in Athlone whose 1852 results, along with those of Cashel, Ennis, Mallow and New Ross meant that five MPs were elected by only 356 electors in total.[27] What occurred at Athlone was that of an

23 Hoppen, K. Theodore, p.80.
24 *FJ.*, 29 June 1852.
25 *FJ.*, 1 July 1852, *FJ.*, 21 July 1852.
26 *FJ.*, 21 July 1852.
27 Neave, Sir Digby Bart, *Four Days in Connemara* (London, 1852), p.10.

electorate of 181 only ninety-seven votes in total were deemed acceptable, eighty-seven of which went to Keogh. This same type of situation was reflected at the four other boroughs. These figures illustrate that a select few in the town had a say in its representation: 181 people out of over 6,100.

Keogh, though having stated that as policy he would remain independent of the government, accepted the position of Solicitor General for Ireland in the same year as the election, a move that led to him being heavily censured.[28] A meeting was held in Athlone at which he was to explain his actions and the crowd that gathered was apparently satisfied by his motives for accepting the position.[29] Just one week after this, news from a ward meeting in Dublin, where the Athlone voters were described as venal and corrupt, was received angrily in the town where it was denied that £2,000 exchanged hands at the last election in 1847.[30] This reaction served to reinforce the view of some commentators who believed that the people at the meeting saw Keogh in his new position as someone who could give jobs to constituents, for there were no civil service examinations at the time, and through this rationale they readily accepted his explanation and would accept no word of fraud.[31] *The Freeman's Journal* reported that a committee was established to examine these claims, at which Keogh QC was questioned, though obviously his answers were all denials of any wrongdoing. However, interestingly he did admit to spending £2,000 of his own money on the 1847 election, though he did not mention the ways in which the money was used.[32] Keogh's appointment to the government position meant that he had to re-seek his seat in 1853, and needless to say his methods allowed him to prevail over his Liberal opponent, Thomas Norton.

Shortly after his third election victory took place Keogh had accepted the position of Attorney General, a move that made him hugely unpopular in Athlone. His name was deliberately excluded from toasts at Town Commissioners meeting in Athlone due to his 'shirking' of responsibility when it came to the Land Question. Many believed that he was adopting the views of those he worked with as opposed to those of the people he was supposed to be working for.[33] Despite this fall in popularity, the fourth election that Keogh contested in 1855 was

28 Lenehan, Jim, p.36.
29 *FJ*, 11 Jan 1853.
30 *FJ*, 18 Jan 1853.
31 Lenehan, Jim, p.36.
32 *FJ*, 30 Mar 1854.
33 *FJ*, 5 Mar 1855.

something of a non-event. He faced no opponent, for it appears that after the backing of the Bishop of Elphin, Dr. Browne, opposition dried up.

Soon after this Keogh's true self, one dominated by self-interest rather selflessness, was beginning to surface publicly. Just one year after the election he was appointed as a judge in the Court of Common Pleas in Ireland, where he tried many prominent Fenians.[34] His judicial career caused Athlone-born and future MP, T. P. O'Connor, to state: '*Of all the men and forces that created Fenianism, Judge Keogh was the most potent.*'[35] William Keogh is believed to have died after slashing his own throat (though this is disputed, there is apparently no documentary evidence in Germany to support this claim) in 1878 at Bingen-am-Rhein, Germany.[36] One historian believes that '*the mecca of Irish corruption was probably Athlone*'; evidence from the 19th century states that in one of Keogh's elections a single bribe may have cost up to £100.[37]

A Conservative, Capt. Henry Handcock, of the Castlemaine family, surprisingly won the bye-election of 1856, at which Keogh's replacement was to be found. The Catholic vote far outweighed that of the Protestant by fifty-six so there was a large-scale defection from the traditionally Liberal vote to that of the Conservative.[38] Of the loser, John Ennis, one commentator noted that he:

> ...was defeated by that most unfair, extraordinary, and unworthy combination of clerical intimidation and brute force for which the Irish elections of last year were so generally and notoriously famous.[39]

This defection was probably the result of well-placed bribes. Handcock, MP, did not retain his seat long. His rival, a wealthy landowner and Independent candidate, whom he had faced in the previous election, regained the Catholic vote and took the Athlone seat in 1857. Apparently Handcock had backed a number of government initiatives his electors disagreed with, which along with Ennis' 'canvassing' lost him the seat.[40]

John Ennis, however, was not considered a popular man locally. His occupation as a landlord worked against him in attempting to gain popular acclaim and it appears he used his large wealth to place stealthy bribes in the hands of voters, which had caveats attached should his

34 Lenehan, Jim, p.38.
35 Ibid., p.34.
36 *FJ*., 2 Oct 1878.
37 Hoppen, K. Theodore, p.78.
38 *FJ*., 11 Apr 1856.
39 Lyons, John Charles, p.71.
40 *FJ*., 4 Apr 1857, Hoppen, K. Theodore, p.82.

attempt to be elected not succeed.[41] A copy of his notebook found a number of years later detailed those who 'helped' him retain his seat in the 1859 election and did nothing to improve the memory of his legacy to the political history for the town.[42] '*Mr Bayley offered £35 to each voter and Sir John gave £40 and was returned*' was the reason supplied by one of his agents for his eventual victory.[43] The inquiry, conducted in 1874, unearthed a lot of evidence regarding how pervasive and protracted the culture of bribery was in the Athlone Borough, which is visited in more depth in another publication.[44]

Soon after Ennis' second successful election in 1859 the Fenian cause was beginning to build momentum in and around Athlone, as it was nationally. The country was experiencing a phase of good agricultural growth and this meant that people could turn their minds to matters other than survival. One of the first cases taken in the country against a man for being a suspected Fenian had occurred in Athlone in November 1864 after he attempted to: '*…seduce several members of the 25th regiment from their duty and allegiance to her majesty*'. The man, an Irish-American called Patrick 'Pagan' O'Leary said he had space for ninety names, all of whom would then join with the American Army in the liberation of the country. The jury assembled to try him could not come to a verdict and he was acquitted.[45] This case falls into the period 1863 to 1864 when the Fenian movement had '*…launched determined recruiting drives within the army*', which garnered the names of up to 15,000 men, mainly Irish Catholics, for the cause.[46]

Athlone was prominent in Fenian plans, with the legislature for the government of a free Ireland intended to be located there, with the executive in Limerick. Dublin was considered too British to be suitable.[47] The local clergy's dislike for the movement caused them to attempt to unseat John Ennis, who had used a prominent local member of the Fenians in his election campaign, and install someone more to their liking. Their candidate for the 1865 election, though not overtly stated as such, was an Englishman, Denis Reardon, who eventually defeated Ennis after some '*…subtle deployment of Episcopal power behind the scenes*' ensured that he appeared more attractive to the voters.[48] This result was all the more surprising when one takes the church's public

41 Lenehan, Jim, p.40.
42 *FJ.*, 14 Nov 1885.
43 *FJ.*, 1 July 1874.
44 Lenehan, Jim.
45 Comerford, R.V., *The Fenians in Context – Irish Politics & Society 1848-82* (Dublin, 1998), p.125, *FJ.*, 8 Mar 1865.
46 Spiers, E. M., p.346.
47 Garvin, Tom, *Nationalist revolutionaries in Ireland 1858-1928*, (Oxford, 1987), p.119.
48 Lenehan, Jim, p.43.

stance on corruption into account: a report from the year Athlone lost its MP, 1885, claimed that the election in 1865 '*was remarkable for its dishonesty.*'[49] T. P. O' Connor noted that the way that the elections in Athlone were carried off sent a '*thrill*' through the town, their corrupt and unpredictable nature generating great excitement.[50]

This growth in Fenianism in the early 1860s caused great concern in the British Parliament compelling the passage of a bill, suspending *Habeas Corpus*, in February 1866 to protect the country from the '*fenian scourge*'.[51] *The Freeman's Journal* reported in its issue dated 20th February 1866 that ten people had been arrested in Athlone directly resulting from the new law.[52] However, despite the creation of some considerable momentum the subsequent Fenian rising in 1867 failed due to a shortage of weaponry and bad planning.[53]

The Ennis family was again to send an MP to parliament in 1868 with John James Ennis, the former MPs son, securing the election through the usual means, though this time bribery was apparently of a less overt nature.[54] Events in this and previous local elections had caused a witness at a trial to name Athlone as the '*...most rotten and corrupt borough in Ireland*'.[55] The scourge of rotten boroughs in England was thought to have been eradicated in the year 1832 as part of the political reforms that came with the Great Reform Bill. This political reform, which for some historians marked the start of the Victorian era, was part of the overall drive towards improvement during the period which also saw the Municipal Reform Act 1835 passed in England and Wales as well as the Municipal Corporations Act passed in Ireland in 1840.[56]

The next election, in 1874, was groundbreaking for two main reasons; it was to have a secret ballot (which many in parliament had opposed over the years) and secondly the question of Home Rule was a topic that all the candidates had to have at the centre of their campaigns.[57] The Home Rule candidate, Edward Shiel, with the backing of the local Catholic clergy, won the contest against J.J. Ennis and after a court inquiry the final margin was just five votes from 301 valid declarations.[58] This win occurred despite Ennis again providing large amounts of money for a number of the electorate.[59]

49 *FJ*, 10 Oct 1885.
50 O'Connor, T. P., *The Parnell movement – with a sketch of Irish parties from 1843*, 2nd ed. (London, 1886), p.126.
51 Comerford, R.V., p.133.
52 *FJ*, 20 Feb 1866.
53 Newsinger, John, pp.55-59.
54 *FJ*, 20 Nov 1868.
55 *FJ*, 4 Feb 1868.
56 Trevelyan, G. M., p.123.
57 Thomson, David, p.130, Lenehan, Jim, p.45.
58 *FJ*, 26 Apr 1874.
59 Hoppen, K. Theodore, p.63.

The next election between the two same candidates took place in 1880, which, as already noted in chapter four was a time of great distress around Athlone, with Ennis winning by one vote. Shiel, who had the financial backing of the Land League, sent a petition to Parliament to investigate the close result.[60] Bribery and coercion were said to have reached new heights during this election with people drafted into the town to vote with the promise of well-paid employment.[61] Ennis was an extremely wealthy man with 8,774 acres in his name providing a large income that he used to coerce those voting in the elections.[62] Even the presence of Charles Stewart Parnell, who called Ennis '*a miserable West British whig*', at an election rally in the town could not help Shiel, and Ennis was eventually confirmed as the local representative.[63] Ennis' actions after his election to the position of MP show, to good effect, the disregard he had for the townspeople. He ignored the wishes of the majority of the town's electorate in his voting patterns when he was in Westminster, which led to some local anger.[64] It appears he was later called on to resign his seat at a meeting held in the town though there is some confusion about whether the meeting ever took place.[65]

Ennis' death in 1884 left an opening for the last time in the Borough of Athlone and the winner of the election, without opposition due to a lack of interested Liberals, a Home Ruler, J.H. McCarthy, served just one year in office when Athlone had its right to send a member to parliament rescinded.[66]

RIBBONISM AND AGRARIAN CRIME

During the Famine in Ireland there had been a severe drop in the number of cases of agrarian crime in the country. Those transgressions that were committed were more often linked to the struggle to survive than to the struggle for land. In the early 1850s agrarian crimes were increasing again as people began to focus their attention on the landlords as perhaps the main contributors to the devastating progress of famine.

A government report from 1852 detailed what was seen as the cause of Ribbonism in Ireland, which was thought to have originated in the 18th century. The name came from the practice of members of 'Ribbon

60 *FJ.*, 5 Apr 1880, *FJ.*, 20 Apr 1880.
61 Lenehan, Jim, p.46
62 *Land Owners in Ireland - Return of owners of land of one acre and upwards in the several counties, counties of cities, counties of towns in Ireland in 1876* (Baltimore, 1988), p.83.
63 *FJ.*, 25 Mar 1880.
64 *FJ.*, 30 Mar 1882, *FJ.*, 11 Apr 1882.
65 *FJ.*, 12 Apr 1882.
66 *FJ.*, 3 Oct 1885.

Societies' wearing a white ribbon in their hats so they could be distinguished at nighttime. Believed to have stemmed from '...*more a sectarian and religious system at first*' the practices of Ribbon Societies were seen as '...*aimed at the rights of property, without distinction of creed*.'[67] The report believed that the organisation of the local societies was an exclusively Catholic occupation that generally occurred in public houses.[68] It also contended that the members of the groups were not averse to attacking other Catholics in an attempt to achieve their goals.[69] The report stated that whilst the clergy were making an effort to stop Ribbonism they were not being heeded.[70]

Westmeath was thought to be one the worst affected areas of the country when it came to Ribbonism and agrarian outrages in the post-Famine period.[71] Though L. J. Proudfoot believes that the movement died out in the county in 1869 there does appear to be evidence to refute this claim.[72] The entire county of Westmeath was proclaimed under the Peace Preservation Act 1870, such were the level of outrages there.[73] The town had previously seen three Ribbonmen hanged for their part in crimes, though the story related to Mary Banim in 1892 by an old local did mention that it was easy to get hung in those times![74]

A number of British newspapers detailed the state of Ribbonism in the county in January 1871. *The Manchester Guardian* declared the Ribbon Societies in Westmeath, as '*omnipotent*' with many people paying protection money to them as they lacked faith in the police. *The Daily Express* outlined a case of attempted assassination near Athlone and believed that the '*Government have made no provision to meet the danger which is every day increasing and spreading more alarm*'. *The Morning Mail* detailed that a number of prominent landholders in the county expected to be shot by an assassin at every minute of every day such was their lack of faith in the local constabulary. It went further to state that the inhabitants of Westmeath should be assured that they would not be left under '*Ribbon Jurisdiction*'.[75] Showing that this situation was not as bad elsewhere in Ireland the report of an *Observer* journalist visiting Cork cited a local magistrate who believed that the Land Act was working there. The journalist even went as far as to state that the

---

67 *Report of the Select Committee on Outrages* (Ireland) (London, 1852), p.674.
68 Ibid., pp. 675, 671, 46.
69 Ibid., p.46.
70 *Report on Outrages*, p.677.
71 Proudfoot, L. J., p.213.
72 Ibid., p.213.
73 *F.J.*, 27 Apr 1870.
74 Banim, Mary, p.207.
75 *W.I.*, 28 Jan 1871.

political influence of the Catholic clergy, whom he obviously believed
were tied into the Ribbon Societies, was weakening and somewhat
optimistically that '*their day of secular dictation has passed*'.[76]

This was not the case in Westmeath when it was again cited in
February 1871, along with those parts of King's County and Meath that
bordered it, by the Marquis of Huntingdon as one of the only places in
Ireland that did not have a diminution in agrarian crimes.[77] The
Marquis said that the county was the '*centre of a strangle hold of conspiracy*'.
The initiation of a report into the crime in the county caused a question
to be asked in the House of Commons if there was a secret society in
Westmeath that went around massacring Protestants and destroying
their property.[78] The result of the inquiry was that the Westmeath
Coercion Bill was passed in May 1871, for it was believed that the
chronic Ribbonism in the country was '*principally confined to Westmeath*'
and that it was causing interference with the operation of railways and
canals.[79] It is certainly possible that the county might not have been so
well targeted by the government if not for its important midland
position along some of the main transport arteries. It was one of only a
few places in the country that had an especial extension of the Peace
Preservation Act 1870, which was originally designed to deal with
Ribbonism and other outrages nationwide.[80] The only other counties
included were Meath and Mayo.

The application of the workings of the Act had secured a number of
arrests and caused the closure of a number of public houses in Athlone
and around the county in general.[81] The lack of convictions in cases
where Ribbonism was suspected were accounted for by the fear jurors
had of reprisals. In fact during the period 1850–1870 in the case of the
forty murders linked to the movement there were only two
convictions.[82] The percentage of young people involved in Ribbonism
in the county in the late 1860s and early 1870s was considerable;
estimated at 25%, this level of involvement meant that any.threat against
jurors could certainly be delivered on.[83] It is interesting to note that
there had been '...*no marked difference in nature or frequency, between
emergency legislation in Ireland and Britain*' until the 1820s. Subsequently
much of the legislation passed was of a nature that appeared '*to create an
air of continuing crisis*'.[84]

76 *W.I.*, 11 Feb 1871.
77 *F.J.*, 28 Feb 1871.
78 *F.J.*, 28 Feb 1871, *F.J.*, 10 Mar 1871.
79 *F.J.*, 3 May 1871.
80 *W.I.*, 6 May 1871.
81 *W.I.*, 27 May 1871.
82 Sheehan, Jeremiah, p.123.
83 Ibid., p.122.
84 Hoppen, K. Theodore, p.49.

The introduction of the Home Rule movement into Irish Politics in the 1870s appears to have lessened the frequency of reports on Ribbonism and violent agrarian crime. The advent of the Tenant Rights movement in the late 1860s was perhaps the first attempt to move away from violence since O'Connell's Repeal Association but it did not espouse ideas that were agreed with by all. The government's attempts to 'pacify' the Irish with the disestablishment of the Church of Ireland in 1869 and the Land Act 1870 did not have the desired effect.[85] Tensions remained high locally; even when the appointment of the borough's first Home Rule candidate occurred the political solution still caused unrest in some circles.[86]

The Westmeath magistrates did not recommend the withdrawal of the Peace Preservation Act in February 1875, since they believed the county still had a number of subversives at work within its borders.[87] The application of the Coercion Act in the same year after an inquiry into the state of the county was seen as oppressive and unnecessary by the priests of Westmeath: '...*of all the witnesses summoned, there was only one who could have the smallest sympathy with the people whose liberty was about to be immolated.*'[88] They went further and made a clear statement on the matter:

> That we, the priests of Westmeath, as the friends of civil liberty, and in vindication of the character of our flocks, hearby express our entire dissent from the resolutions of the magistrates of this county, calling on the government for measures of coercion, believing as we do, such exceptional and irritating enactments unnecessary and unjustifiable under existing circumstances.[89]

This enforcement of the act, along with local agricultural distress and The Land League movement appears to have quelled the Ribbon Society in and around Athlone and Westmeath in the late 1870s and early 1880s, for at this time the reports coming in describe nationalist meetings as opposed to politically motivated crimes. Some historians believe that the 'Irish Question' began to dominate the British parliamentary scene in 1875, a situation that was to last for the remainder of the Victorian period, such was the energy that was building behind the issue and its wider implications.[90] Perhaps this shift

85 Matthew, Colin, p.102.
86 *W.I.*, 7 Feb 1874.
87 *F.J.*, 9 Feb 1875, *F.J.*, 20 Feb 1875.
88 *The Westmeath Coercion Act - Letter addressed by Rev. Dr. Nulty, Bishop of Meath to Right Hon. Benjamin Disraeli* (Dublin, 1875).
89 Ibid., App II.
90 Thomson, David, p.180.

in political focus helped ease tensions within the county's nationalist areas, which, seeing some movement on the issue, may have decided to try political avenues instead.

THE LAND WAR AND PARNELL

According to A. C. Murray the Land War of 1879-82 was not high on the agenda for many people residing in Westmeath:

> In Westmeath, a county of comfortable, conservative shopkeepers and graziers, the Land War had been late starting and had lacked any spontaneity; its people had garnered little national credit from the agitation.[91]

The above comment is taken from a study of politics in Westmeath that dealt almost exclusively with Mullingar and the surrounding area of northeast Westmeath. However, it does appear that Westmeath as a whole did become quieter during this time. Perhaps the people in and around Athlone, though formerly militant, were now moving away from violence and towards politics. Despite this move away from violence the fight against the '*moral ugliness*' of the circumstances of the Irish peasantry in Ireland with regard to their landlords was one that was to rage in political circles for many years.[92]

The spread of the railways, and with them the spread of better communications, ensured that the message of the political movements of the late nineteenth century was disseminated far more quickly. Men such as Charles Stewart Parnell were capable of attending more meetings in many distant areas of the country and through this build up a far more effective grass roots support for their cause. The distress brought on by the failure of crops in 1879 and 1880 coupled with growing nationalist sentiment gave the Land League the energy of what some historians have termed '*a quasi-revolutionary moment*'. Indeed the actions of many involved with the organisation led to the imprisonment of a number of its leaders.[93] The first great demonstration held in Athlone in support of the land movement came in November 1880, with a vivid description provided by the press:

> The town presented a gala appearance. Triumphal arches spanned the principal streets; banners hung from windows and everywhere there was a profuse display of green favour, and the people wore ivy and laurel in their hats. Parnell arrived by train and was greeted by a large crowd.

---

91 Murray, A. C., "Nationality and local politics in late nineteenth-century Ireland: the case of County Westmeath", in *Irish Historical Studies*, Vol. 25, No. 98 (Antrim, 1986), p.145.
92 Wilson, A. N., p.460.
93 Matthew, Colin, p.117.

Outside the Prince of Wales Hotel where he was staying banners were arranged with slogans such as 'Athlone Welcomes Parnell', 'Down with the Land Sharks', 'Shannon Sawmills men warmly sympathetic with the Land League.' A banner in the centre of the town bridge proclaimed that Leinster and Connaught were united.[94]

William Sime, a travel writer in town for the occasion noted that the army had been increased in strength along with the RIC whose 150 extra men were *'served with charges of buckshot'* in case of disturbances. Sime was surprised by how the political movement appeared to affect the people, describing how it *'...sits upon them in the most prosperous style'*, such was their well-to-do appearance.[95] Indeed, he believed of the farmers who were at the market that day *'...that politics are fully as much in their minds as merchandise.'*[96] The thoughts of Athlone's citizens were obviously modernising with regard to how they could achieve their goals; it had been a struggle but the evidence for it was in plain view according to Sime.

The morning of the meeting in Athlone was described as unnaturally quiet, the church bells were ringing and the RIC were conspicuous on the streets of the town. The soldiers in the garrison were ordered not to show themselves in case of inciting bad feeling and so the barrack wall was deserted. The meeting had created great excitement among the younger members of the townsfolk, hundreds of medals of the Home Rule Leader Charles Stewart Parnell were in evidence along with green sashes which became more numerous as the time for the meeting neared. Many of those assembled in the town were said to have made trips of up to 40 miles to see Parnell. The town's brass bands provided entertainment until a 'waggonette' made its way to the address platform.

However, not all went smoothly when it came to the time for making speeches. Those against Parnell and Home Rule had sabotaged the address platform and it collapsed under the weight of the dignitaries. While Parnell inspected the structure himself sections of the crowd called out *'treachery'*. It was found that part of the structure supporting the platform was almost wholly sawn through.[97] A number of farmers gathered at the meeting found the spectacle quite funny, only to be criticised by others around them.[98] Luckily, no one was injured and a lengthy address followed. In his speech Parnell condemned what were later to be known as The State Trials as well as government inaction

94 *FJ*, 8 Nov 1880.
95 Sime, William, p.136.
96 Ibid., p.135.
97 *FJ*, 8 Nov 1880.
98 Sime, William, pp.137-138.

when it came to the land question. A reporter also noted down some of the local commentary on Parnell himself with statements like '*he's a grand man*' and '*the best in the world*' being commonplace.[99] The cheers given to Parnell bore '*...much the same stamp as a body of shareholders might give to a chairman of a company moving a successful dividend.*' Many at the meeting called out that Parnell, or as he was called in the town '*Parnle*', was a greater leader than O'Connell.[100]

The crowd, in their fervour were accused by an English journalist of assaulting him for no more reason than his nationality, which he thought the Athlone crowd decided must make him '*of necessity ...an enemy to Irish aspirations.*'[101] The Land League meeting in Athlone made the pages of *The Daily Express* newspaper in England, where it was referred to as a gathering of Communists, a charge strongly denied in a letter of reply from the chairman of the meeting.[102] The meeting was one of the first in many years staged in Westmeath that employed strong nationalist rhetoric, the 1860s and 1870s having been relatively quiet in this regard.[103] The defeat of the Home Rule candidate in the parliamentary elections of 1880, unsurprising in the face of the corruption and bribery already mentioned, may seem to indicate a lack of genuine motivation amongst the voters of Athlone to back Parnell. The general populace in Athlone, and a number of the surrounding villages, however, left no impression of a lack of support when the results of The State Trials were released in January 1881. Large-scale celebrations were held, with those not supportive of the result singled out for special treatment:

> Every house was lighted, tar barrels blazed and huge bonfires capped the snow covered Anker's Bower Hill. A torch light procession took place through the town. Stones were thrown at some windows not illuminated – 2 arrests were made.[104]

The town of Athlone also had a branch of the Ladies Land League that met to deliberate in the Prince of Wales Hotel in the centre of the town soon after the celebrations.[105] The establishment of the League was a cause for concern to the Bishop of Ardagh and Clonmacnoise who, in his Lenten Pastoral, discouraged women from taking part in public meetings as well as saying that all those who joined '*secret societies*' would

99 *FJ*, 8 Nov 1880.
100 Sime, William, p.138.
101 *FJ*, 9 Nov 1880.
102 *FJ*, 13 Nov 1880.
103 Murray, A. C., p.144.
104 *FJ*, 28 Jan 1881.
105 *FJ*, 12 Feb 1881.

be denied the rites of the Church.[106] However, the ladies were not discouraged and forwarded money to the central Land League fund just two weeks later.[107]

Perhaps due in part to the number of Land League meetings in and around Athlone and south Westmeath generally – there were five large-scale meetings in less than three months – the county found itself proclaimed under the 'Arms Act' or 'Peace Preservation Act' in April 1881. The Athlone branch of the Land League remained resolute with a strongly worded statement regarding the imprisonment of John Dillon MP, who had protested against the Land Bill being reviewed at government level.[108] The Parnell-backed idea of impeding the progress of evictions taking place in the country was implemented in the hinterland of Athlone with one crowd gathering near Moate in such numbers that the army were called in to keep the sheriff safe.[109]

The intense feeling surrounding the Athlone Land League increased when the solicitor they used received a death threat in September 1881.[110] Local tension escalated even further after the arrest of Parnell, described at a meeting in the town as '...*an act of despotism worthy of the Autocrat of all the Russias*'. Parnell did not support the Land Act of 1881 and encouraged others to disregard it, leading to his arrest.[111] At the same meeting a strong statement was issued concerning the arrest and the continued practice of Parnell's tactics by the local League. The calls were heeded; just two weeks later the branch secretary was imprisoned after actively promoting the avoidance of rent payments.[112] His Dysart counterpart was also arrested by the Athlone RIC and imprisoned on the same grounds shortly afterward.[113]

The heightened tensions around the country at this time led the government to enlist the assistance of the army. In Athlone the soldiers from Victoria Barracks were on alert, ready to disperse any and all Land League meetings that were thought to have been planned. A more serious decree was that the soldiers were to have skirmishing parties and a flying column ready at an hour's notice.[114] This was obviously an attempt to intimidate those organising any other meetings.

The Town Commissioners passed a resolution in December 1881 stating their belief that all those arrested under the Coercion Act should

106 *FJ*, 7 Mar 1881.
107 *FJ*, 21 Mar 1881.
108 *FJ*, 7 May 1881.
109 *FJ*, 10 June 1881.
110 *FJ*, 20 Sep 1881.
111 Wilson, A. N., p.455.
112 *FJ*, 15 Oct 1881, *FJ*, 28 Oct 1881.
113 *FJ*, 4 Nov 1881.
114 *FJ*, 1 Nov 1881.

have been released for Christmas.[115] In an attempt to achieve this, or at least work towards the permanent release of those imprisoned, the Political Prisoners Aid Society held a meeting in the town in the week prior to December 25th.[116] The attempts by the police and army to halt any Land League-centred activities was again seen three days after Christmas when 250 police and 100 soldiers left Athlone for neighbouring estates to catch members who were supposedly there poaching game for prisoners. All that was discovered, much to the annoyance of the assembled forces, was a small number of children playing.[117]

The attempted suppression of the Land League continued into the New Year with a meeting disbanded by a large number of police and army as well as the arrest of the Honorary Secretary of the Athlone Land League, one James O'Connor, in February.[118] The Ladies Land League was still holding meetings which appeared to be undisturbed by the authorities.[119]   However, nationally the Ladies Land League did not last much longer and the local branch probably soon disbanded.[120]

The army was continuously kept on high alert in the early months of 1882, and the garrison placed double sentries on the entrance gate with additional parties sent out scouring the country with the hope of detecting subversives.[121] All of the activity around the town and the deployment of the police and army would appear to show that the Land League had a considerable level of support around the southern part of Westmeath and Roscommon. A. C. Murray's assertion that '...*there had been little enthusiasm for the Land League*' in Westmeath, though possibly true in relation to the north of the county, was not so in and around Athlone.[122]

In an escalation of judicial attempts to thwart the land movement a local lady was sent to jail for airing her views on how rent should remain unpaid. Miss O'Connor, a sister of the MP T. P. O'Connor refused to comply with the conditions of her bail and hence was imprisoned in Mullingar.[123] She was released just nine weeks into her six-month sentence. Presumably her brother and Michael Davitt, whom it appears she knew, had a part to play.[124]

115 *W.I.*, 17 Dec 1881.
116 *W.I.*, 24 Dec 1881.
117 *F.J.*, 28 Dec 1881.
118 *F.J.*, 7 Jan 1882, *F.J.*, 4 Feb 1882.
119 *F.J.*, 7 Feb 1882, *F.J.*, 8 Mar 1882.
120 Howarth, Janet, p.178.
121 *F.J.*, 20 Feb 1882.
122 Murray, A.C., p.145.
123 *F.J.*, 3 Apr 1882.
124 *F.J.*, 8 June 1882.

The release of Parnell from jail in April 1882 was intended to be a cause of huge celebration in Athlone. However, a death in Parnell's family caused the townspeople to review their plans and no parade was staged.[125] The jubilation was not long postponed for only four weeks later the town played host to a procession at which the liberated prisoners Parnell, Dillon and O'Kelly were cheered as well as those still interned. The military and police did not interfere with the parade due to its good-natured disposition.[126]

The Phoenix Park murders, where the viceroy Lord Cavendish and his undersecretary, T.H. Burke, were murdered by the 'Invincibles', were condemned by a large crowd that assembled at the Town Hall a week after the parade. As well as this a suspect was arrested in Athlone in connection with the assassinations.[127] The clergy in the town used the murders to illustrate why they exhibited such opposition to secret societies.[128]   Michael Davitt passed through the town in June 1882 on the way to Galway and though the notice given of his arrival was short a large crowd greeted him. He took the opportunity to ask if the people of Athlone would entrust their borough to John Ennis again. He was assured they would not but that they would entrust themselves to him if he would stand for them. Davitt declared that he was not interested in parliament at that point but just asked that Athlone did its duty and he left the town on the train with cheers of 'Home Rule' and 'Davitt' ringing around him.[129]

Eviction meetings continued apace and boycotting started appearing on estates outside Athlone.[130] Whilst the labourers were attempting to place landowners and workers in a '*moral Coventry*' the new Coercion Bill was criticised at a meeting of the Town Commissioners who believed that an increase in agrarian crime was more likely than a decrease.[131] They also condemned the strictures within which the Irish press had to work after the arrest of E. Dwyer Gray, a journalist and editor, in August 1882.[132]

The actions of locals against the gentry were said to be placing the latter in a precarious situation. Fowl belonging to the Langrishe family, who lived in 'Shamrock Lodge' on the western fringes of the town, were killed and their cows were milked dry. The diary of Rosabel Langrishe

125 *F.J.*, 12 Apr 1882.
126 *F.J.*, 4 May 1882.
127 Wilson, A. N., p.453, *W.I.*, 13 May 1882, *F.J.*, 13 May 1882.
128 *F.J.*, 15 May 1882.
129 *W.I.*, 3 June 1882.
130 *F.J.*, 22 June 1882.
131 O'Donoghue, Bernard, p.72, *W.I.*, 24 June 1882.
132 *F.J.*, 25 Aug 1882.

related that some of the gentry were on the point of starvation and had to resort to baking their own bread and sending away to Dublin for supplies![133] Her attitude is indicative of the problems in the social makeup of the Victorian era in the town. Just two years earlier dozens had died due to not having any food or money to purchase it. Ms Langrishe was annoyed that her family, who could easily purchase what provisions they need, had to send away for food.

After the agitation of the Land League Parnell established the Irish National League. It was a more political and regulated manifestation of the Land League and it had numerous branches around the country. The Athlone branch of the Irish National League (INL) was set up in September 1884 and all those who joined at the meeting held in the Town Hall were advised of the necessity of following the rules that the League had laid down.[134] The first meeting of the Athlone branch was held in October with the town bands present for the occasion. The topics discussed were centred on the right to self-government, religious tolerance and the necessity of keeping Orangemen from representing the town.[135] The League later asked for a public meeting to refute the claims of the English press that the Irish were content with the rule of a foreigner due to the reception the Prince of Wales gained during a recent visit to the country.[136] The meeting was not well attended however, with only seven people showing up and the matter was dropped.[137] This meeting, along with many held in Mullingar, which were also poorly supported, led many to believe that the new movement was weak in the county, though of this one cannot be certain.[138]

The National League, recognising the local apathy, decided that moves had to be made to set up a number of branches in districts surrounding Athlone.[139] In September 1885 a meeting held outside the town was told that one of the local bishops Rev. Gilhooly, of Elphin, would not allow any of the clergy to take a place on the national platform, a fact that was found regrettable by those assembled, for the clergy's support would have been a great boost for the cause in the Roscommon area.[140] A report from Mullingar RIC would appear to show that the clergy were supportive of the cause however; '*Roman Catholic clergy as a body are now beginning to give their countenance and*

133 Langrishe, Rosabel, p.181.
134 *FJ*, 16 Sep 1884.
135 *FJ*, 6 Oct 1884.
136 *FJ*, 4 Apr 1885.
137 *FJ*, 25 Apr 1885.
138 Murray, A. C., p.146.
139 *FJ*, 12 Sep 1885.
140 *FJ*, 19 Sep 1885.

support to the movement.[141] Furthermore the clergy in the county were said to have been very active in establishing branches of the INL in north Westmeath, and in many cases they maintained a senior role in all branches.[142] A meeting held on the 27th September in Athlone dealt with confidence in Parnell, lamented the loss of the MP for the borough and described the Gladstone government as '...*the worst government that ever misgoverned and insulted Ireland*'.[143] Gladstone's government did not last the year, having fallen apart over the future governance of Ireland (in fact one of the last votes that Athlone's final MP had a say in was that which brought down the Gladstone government). Its Tory replacement under Lord Salisbury appeared to consider Home Rule an option. However, the subsequent re-election of Gladstone meant that Parnell had to deal with the party he had actively campaigned against in the election.[144]

The fact that Athlone had lost its own MP in 1885 meant that the interests of the townspeople, certainly those on the east side, lay in the election of a nationalist to one of the Westmeath County seats. Four candidates for Athlone (South Westmeath constituency) were decided upon at a meeting in Mullingar in October 1885.[145]

Locally the INL continued the practice of assisting those subject to eviction notices or property seizure as well as taking the unusual step of welcoming a Protestant into their ranks in December 1885.[146] Of course Parnell was himself a Protestant and his political aspirations were not designed to damage Protestant interests but this was not clear to all or even most nationalists. Protestants owned the vast majority of the country's land and this in the minds of many labourers made them the enemy. The actions of the local INL against evictors were a step up from that which was witnessed a number of years earlier. Negotiations were entered into in a case involving Lord Castlemaine's land but whilst the offer of paying 75% of the rent due was rejected the INL footed the bill for a tenant who was allowed to remain.[147] The action taken by the INL caused Lord Castlemaine to state that he would look into the individual case of each tenant and award them what he thought was a fair reduction in rent. The landowner probably had a massive number of tenants on his land around the town; a report on the landowners of Ireland from 1876 gave his property in Westmeath to be 11,444 acres,

---

141 Murray, A. C., p.146.
142 Ibid., p.146-148.
143 *FJ*, 3 Oct 1885.
144 Matthew, Colin, p.118.
145 *FJ*, 17 Oct 1885.
146 *FJ*, 14 Nov 1885, *FJ*, 12 Dec 1885.
147 *FJ*, 2 Jan 1886.

making him the third largest landowner in the county.[148] The proposals he eventually presented to the INL were rejected by Andrew Moore, the local branch treasurer, due to the vague way in which they were structured.[149]

The power that the INL had locally was recognised by the local sheriff who decided not to seize any of the property of a tenant who was in arrears to Lord Castlemaine after it was explained to him that negotiations were ongoing. A large crowd had gathered for an eviction to jeer the sheriff but when he took no action against the tenant he was cheered by those assembled.[150] The INL had, on occasion, to censure some of their own members who would not follow the party line. The chairman of the Clonown branch was removed from his position after he paid his rent despite the INL asking locals not to do so.[151] The Grand Jury for Co. Westmeath, perhaps sensing that the authorities in England would view a reaffirmation of the Jury's loyalism favourably penned a letter stating their position:

> We, the Grand Jury of Co. Westmeath assembled at the Assizes of 1886, desire to express our attachment to the Throne and Person of our most Gracious Sovereign the Queen.
>
> We declare our opinion that any measure giving to Ireland separate legislative powers, or even tending to weaken the Union at present existing between Great Britain and Ireland, would be productive of consequences disastrous to the well being and safety of the country.
>
> We regret that respect for the law and for the rights and security of property has been lessened in many parts of Ireland, and we earnestly hope that any future land legislation may be founded on justice, believing that injustice has never produced and never can produce good results.
>
> R.J. Handcock, Foreman.[152]

In 1886 the INL fielded two candidates for a position on a local Board of Guardians. Unfortunately, the canvassing took the form of each man highlighting the others faults – a fact that must have confused the electorate, for both men's principles should have been similar.[153] Factions amongst nationalists themselves may have been the greatest impediment towards achieving the greater goals all throughout the 19th century. Similar contradictions in policy and infighting were witnessed at an INL meeting in May 1886, where a resolution passed by the Clara

---

148 *Land Owners in Ireland*, p.82.
149 *FJ.*, 13 Dec 1886.
150 Ibid.
151 Ibid.
152 *FJ.*, 19 Mar 1886.
153 *FJ.*, 27 Mar 1886.

branch was condemned.[154]In Mullingar the lack of agreement between the clergy and some laymen led to two separate branches being established in the town leading to a massive fall off in support for the league there.[155] The conflict in Mullingar became very bitter and eventually tenant concerns were secondary to the fight between the factions.[156] This type of infighting led William O'Brien to write that '*Wretched local squabbles should not become obstacles on the path towards independence.*'[157] The fractiousness and indecisiveness that characterised the INL in Athlone, and Westmeath generally, was to impede its work throughout its history, with a number of other examples evident for the remainder of the party's existence. Interestingly, the INL has been described as '*a highly efficient political machine*' by J.J. Lee, though this was not apparent in the Westmeath branches.[158]

Despite some problems in the INL locally, the issue of Home Rule did unite many local politicians on occasion. One such occasion was the censuring of a local landlord, The O'Donoghue, who had stated, in March 1886, that the Irish had enough legislation in their favour and needed no more.[159] A meeting was organised and over 8,000 people attended, and though it seems that O'Donoghue was not in attendance he did apparently state beforehand that if O'Connell was alive he would have been happy with the legislation in place. The large crowd backed the speakers in their condemnation of the man and his rhetoric.[160] Perhaps the most obvious attempt by the Church of Ireland in the town to put forth their views on Home Rule came when a vestry meeting was asked to vote on a resolution basically backing O'Donoghue's stance. Sensibly many of those present abstained, whilst many more stayed away. Yet the eventual passing of the condemnation of Home Rule, whilst farcical because of the small numbers, was still controversial locally.[161]

It was during 1886 that the practice of reinstalling evictees as caretakers first appears to have occurred locally.[162] The actions of the INL also contributed to a local landlord decreasing his tenants rent by 15%, with another decreasing rent by 20%.[163] The main local landlord in south Westmeath, Lord Castlemaine, also eventually acquiesced in a proposal from tenants that meant they paid half a year's rent in

154 *FJ.*, 22 May 1886.
155 Murray, A. C., p.148.
156 Ibid., p.150.
157 Ibid., p.149.
158 Lee, Joseph, p.110.
159 *FJ*, 20 Mar 1886.
160 *FJ.*, 3 Apr 1886.
161 Ibid.
162 *FJ*, 22 May 1886, *FJ*, 19 Sep 1886, *FJ*, 25 Sep 1886, *FJ*, 2 April 1887.
163 *FJ*, 26 Mar 1887, *FJ*, 28 May 1887.

December/January and another in March.[164] As already noted one of the main problems affecting the INL was their inability to agree, even when it came down to less important jobs such as town rate collector.[165] The INL was also forced to pass a resolution regarding the supply of cars by certain Athlone residents to the police for evictions, apparently the practice was becoming well known in other districts:

> In consequence of the bad reputation that Athlone has got for supplying vehicles to Police for evictions it is the opinion of this meeting that car owners of the town should recognise their unpatriotic action in the matter complained of.[166]

The tradition of holding large rallies did not diminish with over 7,000 people attending a national demonstration in Athlone in November 1887. The town was decorated with banners and the members of the INL addressed the crowd.[167] The local clergy joined nationalists in the Town Hall in supporting William O'Brien MP who had recently been imprisoned for inciting tenants to resist landlords and boycott new tenants.[168]

Even though INL meetings were frequent locally it took an inordinate amount of time for the Athlone branch to realise that Moate did not have a branch of its own, over three years after the establishment of the Athlone INL.[169] Perhaps due to this inefficiency, waning support and the introduction of laws such as the Criminal Law and Procedures Act 1887, which carried harsh penalties for boycotting and intimidation, the town branch of the INL appears to have lost its focus and had to be reorganised in March 1889.[170]

The political manoeuvring along with religious motivations in the town also played a role in the appointment of a dispensary doctor, as they had previously, to St. Mary's ward with the press coverage of the event coming in for criticism. A Dr. Shanley had been given the job temporarily in April 1889 after the death of his father.[171] When the time came for the appointment of a permanent replacement the two main contenders were Shanley, a supposed Tory, and Dr. Fitzgibbon, a Nationalist. *The Westmeath Independent* was accused of bias in stating that a preliminary meeting of the Guardians was unnecessary, and of

164 *FJ.*, 24 Dec 1887.
165 *FJ.*, 26 Mar 1887.
166 *FJ.*, 10 Sep 1887.
167 *FJ.*, 12 Nov 1887.
168 Wilson, A. N., p.532, *FJ.*, 9 Feb 1889.
169 *FJ.*, 10 Dec 1887.
170 Wilson, A. N., p.530, *FJ.*, 9 Mar 1889.
171 *FJ.*, 6 Apr 1889.

inferring the formulation of a pre-determined outcome.[172] A meeting was held, however, and due to the attendance of many townspeople each with their own idea on the subject, it was reported as being unruly. The subject was of some ideological importance with a letter, from William O'Brien MP asking that Dr. Fitzgibbon be supported, read at the gathering. Abuse was exchanged between some of those assembled as to their allegiances to the nation with some attempting to assert their love for Ireland in an attempt to discredit others. Eventually the room was cleared of all but the Guardians and press and the job was given to Shanley by thirty-four votes to fourteen.[173]

The final important political meeting of the 1880s was the arrival of the English Home Rule Party in September 1889, which attracted a crowd of 5,000 supporters.[174] The support for the INL and Parnell's Home Rule movement appears to have maintained a high level amongst the working class throughout the decade, though the greatest test for Parnell and Home Rule in Athlone was yet to come.

Early in the year 1890 when it was discovered that Parnell had had an indiscreet affair with a married woman named Kitty O'Shea there was a mixed reaction locally. The local Board of Guardians passed a vote of confidence in him, stating that they had '...*confidence in the purity of our beloved leader's character, morally as well as politically.*'[175] The INL passed a similar resolution, sending it to the two MPs for the county James Tuite and Donal Sullivan, both of whom had condemned Parnell.[176] A rally for the Home Rule Party in September 1890 was said to be '...[one of the] *largest, most orderly and enthusiastic demonstrations held in Athlone for many years.*'[177] It appeared that the citizens of Athlone were also still supportive of Parnell and the cause.

Apparently, the Athlone Town Commissioners were generally supportive of Parnell though, after he had married O'Shea in July and been confirmed an adulterer, in the eyes of some, in November, one member later condemned Parnell for seizing the concept of 'United Ireland', a condemnation in which many fellow members took no part.[178] Apart from political statements made by local politicians the Parnell controversy was to bring about the break up of perhaps the largest society in Athlone, the League of the Cross.

172 *FJ.*, 18 May 1889.
173 *FJ.*, 8 June 1889.
174 *FJ.*, 14 Sep 1889.
175 *FJ.*, 11 Jan 1890.
176 *FJ.*, 29 Nov 1890.
177 *The W.I.*, np.
178 Wilson, A. N., , p.533-5, *FJ.*, 20 Dec 1890.

Dissention arose in the society when a demonstration for Parnell was held soon after the news of his affair came to light. It was to push the idea of temperance, the League's central theme, very much to the back of member's minds for the two years of the debacle.[179] At the rally in December 1890 a resolution was passed and sent to Parnell telling him of the League's faith in him as a politician. A meeting of the League was held a number of days later at which there was a heated discussion. The President condemned the resolution, because it was a political statement, which the League was not meant to make, and as well as this it had been passed without the consent of the President or Vice President. Dr. Langan, President and administrator of St. Mary's, barred the dissenting members from the League's hall, as it was church property. The disenfranchised members then decided to use separate premises and renamed themselves the 'Suppressed Branch of the League of the Cross'.[180] After the split in the League had raged into the spring of 1891 information on the organisation becomes scarce. It is certain that the differences were not reconciled by late 1891 when it was proposed that the band attached to the League, still described as '*dispossessed of their hall*' should, along with new recruits from other local bands, form '*one good band*' for the town.[181]

In Westmeath generally the clergy were seriously campaigning against Parnell, a man: '*...stamped with the double (sic) crime, that of treachery, injustice and adultery*.'[182] In the north of the county the priests apparently started to sway the people's opinions when they asked if their allegiance to Parnell was greater than to their clergy; a Home Rule meeting held soon after the affair became public was poorly attended.[183] In Athlone Rev. Dr. Langan, who was involved in the problem with the League of the Cross, applied pressure to the local Board of Guardians in an attempt to make them reverse their stance on Parnell. A motion was later tabled at a meeting of that body in which a member called him a '*convicted adulterer*' and also stated that they supported the Church and the majority of the Irish Parliamentary Party in condemning him. The meeting condemned *The Freeman's Journal* for misleading the people and *The Westmeath Independent* for not supporting the national cause of Ireland. The members passed the motion, without the condemnation of *The Westmeath Independent*, though the fact that the previous resolution of faith in Parnell was not rescinded compromised its validity.[184]

179 Malcolm, Elizabeth, "The catholic church and the Irish temperance movement, 1838-1901", in *Irish Historical Studies*, Vol. 23, No. 89 (Antrim, 1982), p.12
180 *FJ.*, 27 Dec 1890.
181 *FJ.*, 31 Oct 1891.
182 Murray, A. C., p.151.
183 Ibid., p.152.
184 *FJ.*, 4 Dec 1890.

The INL and the Athlone National Band both passed more votes of confidence in Parnell with the latter burning a copy of Davitt's paper 'Labour World.'[185] The new political climate locally caused the establishment of a Parnell Leadership Committee whose first resolution was a condemnation of Dr. Langan for his attempts to influence the Board of Guardians in relation to their resolution in support of Parnell.[186] The clergy's attempts to sway the Guardians were again in evidence when Langan, along with another clergyman, was present to see the condemnation resolution he asked for wiped from the books as it was illegal, due to the lack of notice with regard to the previous supportive motion.[187]

The influence of the clergy was not to be enough to sway either the Guardians or the townspeople. Posters went up around the town asking the locals not to allow the local Board of Guardians to '...*condemn the Great Man nor betray Ireland's Best Friend*', and these along with the inclination of a number of the Guardians, ensured that the subsequent condemnation motion was not passed by the body.[188]

Parnell himself travelled to the town for a day in the same week as the motion and was accorded a massive reception at which over 10,000 people were present along with two town bands and a number of dignitaries from the local Board of Guardians, INL and the Roscommon Town Commissioners.[189] Parnell's other visits to the town, which came in quick succession, could have left no one in doubt as to the affection Athlone people held for him, with large crowds greeting him no matter what the length or purpose of the visit.[190] The local Board of Guardians elections saw Parnellites take the three top positions of Chairman, Vice Chairman and Deputy Vice Chairman. A hoax letter ascribed to a local Canon supporting Parnell, which may have led some to believe he was gaining clergy support, was fiercely denied as being authentic by the actual Canon after it was published in the press.[191]

In opposition to the Parnellites a branch of the Irish National Federation was established in Athlone in May 1891 with Dr. Langan as its chairman.[192] Whilst the party did meet with John Dillon (later accused by *The Freeman's Journal* as being a member of the group that '*drove Parnell to his grave*'[193]) and William O'Brien, it would not entertain

185 *FJ.*, 4 Dec 1890, *FJ.*, 27 Dec 1890.
186 *FJ.*, 2 Jan 1891.
187 *FJ.*, 10 Jan 1891.
188 *FJ.*, 17 Jan 1891, *FJ.*, 24 Jan 1891.
189 *FJ.*, 17 Jan 1891, *FJ.*, 24 Jan 1891.
190 *FJ.*, 7 Feb 1891, *FJ.*, 21 Mar 1891, *FJ.*, 25 Apr 1891, *FJ.*, 12 Sep 1891.
191 *FJ.*, 11 Apr 1891, *FJ.*, 28 Mar 1891.
192 *FJ.*, 2 May 1891, *FJ.*, 16 May 1891.
193 *FJ.*, 16 Apr 1892.

anyone it perceived as not being in agreement with its policies. This led to a reporter from *The Westmeath Independent* being disallowed entry to one of its meetings.[194]

The defining political moment in the latter half of the Victorian era in Ireland was the death of Charles Stewart Parnell. One of his last engagements was in Athlone in the autumn of 1891. He had arrived in the town by train and while he did speak, his frail health meant that he could not shake anyone's hand. Parnell's many visits to the town, including some which were very short, inevitably helped strengthen the local ambitions for Home Rule. Unfortunately, as his train was leaving, an elderly Parnellite fell under the wheels and was killed. The incident was said to have distressed Parnell, who had a phobia regarding train safety. Timothy Michael Healy, one of Parnell's fiercest critics, used the incident to highlight Parnell's lack of religious faith – Healy claimed Parnell had not even cared about the accident – and as well as this he noted that Parnell had a '*peculiar*' fear of death. Parnell, who had been looking '*wretchedly ill*' before he reached Athlone, died less than two weeks later.[195]

When the news of Parnell's passing reached the offices of *The Westmeath Independent* they placed a notice in the window. The shocked locals who saw it wired London requesting confirmation of the news, which, to their dismay, they received. The reaction of the people was such that the press stated that '*…never was Athlone moved in such a manner*', and when the news reached the factory workers in the woollen mills '*…it was remarkable to see the dismay depicted on their countenances*'.[196] The death of Parnell may have spurred those voting in the Town Commissioners elections one week later, for all but one of the seats were filled by declared Parnellites, though one has to be aware of possible opportunistic changes in affiliation. The Town Commissioners sent letters of condolence to all of the Parnell family and over 1,000 people paraded to the tune of the 'Dead March' on the day of his funeral.[197] An editorial from *The Freeman's Journal* spoke of the love that Athlone had for 'The Chief' observing that: '*…to him it was loyal, great and true when other places proved false to the man who had done so much for Ireland*'.[198] T.P. O'Connor noted:

> What the Irish saw in Parnell was a man who was proud, scornful of English indignation…The strong nation was humbled by the weak, in the

194   *FJ.*, 1 Aug 1891, *FJ.*, 10 Oct 1891.
195   Callanan, Frank, *The Parnell Split 1890-91* (Cork, 1992), pp.179-180
196   *FJ.*, 10 Oct 1891.
197   *FJ.*, 17 Oct 1891.
198   *FJ.*, 16 Jan 1892.

person of Parnell; the proud conqueror baffled; the scorn of the dominant race met with a scorn prouder, more daring and more deep....[199]

The ensuing years were to see political sentiment in Athlone remain quite similar to that which had gone before. There were still the usual tensions between the clergy and the INL who condemned the Bishop of Meath for stating that no Parnellite or Protestant should be appointed coroner to Westmeath.[200] The successful candidate, a solicitor, John Gaynor, had the backing of the voters of Athlone and Moate, who accounted for all but 310 of his 1,407 total. It appeared that the voters were, as in times past, not entirely principled when they cast their ballots; many were asked who they were voting for and changed their votes to ensure that there were no repercussions.[201]

Athlone was still very much a Parnellite town when the convention for proposing candidates for the South Westmeath constituency was held there in April 1892.[202] The candidate who was chosen, The O'Donoghue, probably won the nomination due to the fact that he may have been the only runner who could afford the election expenses. However, he proved unpopular (his earlier ideas on Home Rule were not forgotten locally), and some local farmers called for him to step down soon after he was chosen.[203] The Irish National Federation held its meeting in Mullingar and the candidate they chose to run against O'Donoghue was Donal Sullivan. The latter won the contest with a split in the Parnellite vote, due to O'Donoghue's candidacy, meaning that he gained only 30% of the total number of votes cast.[204] One man who had featured prominently in the political struggle in Mullingar noted that the people appeared to have voted for the priests as opposed to the actual candidates.[205] Despite this loss, the memory of Parnell and the Home Rule Question was still highlighted, even to small children in the town who could purchase 'Home Rule Sweets', in a packet stamped with a harp, in some of the shops in the town.[206] T. P. O'Connor remarked that '*Devolution is Latin for Home Rule...*' and that '*...Home Rule was Irish for independence.*'[207] The anniversary of the death of Parnell was remembered each October for a number of years and the town sent representatives to the main service in Dublin on each occasion.[208]

199 Murphy, William Michael, *The Parnell Myth and Irish Politics 1891-1956* (New York, 1986), pp.72-73.
200 *FJ*, 6 Feb 1892.
201 *FJ*, 27 Feb 1892.
202 Murray, A. C., p.154.
203 Ibid.
204 Ibid., p.155.
205 Ibid.
206 Banim, Mary, p.202.
207 Boyce, D. George, *Nationalism in Ireland* (London, 1982), p.279.
208 *FJ*, 14 Oct 1893, *FJ*, 13 Oct 1894, *FJ*, 12 Oct 1895, *FJ*, 17 Oct 1896.

The candidates for parliament during the 1890s were generally popular with the constituents of Athlone, whose interests lay in the South Roscommon and South Westmeath constituencies, but the nomination of Anti-Parnellite Nationalist John Dillon for South Roscommon in 1895 caused a number of problems. At two meetings held in Athlone at which Dillon was a speaker, a local priest decided to attempt to keep order by use of a blackthorn stick, making one protestor bleed profusely.[209] The support of the clergy did not ensure election for Dillon who was soundly defeated at the polls.[210] In contrast the South Westmeath Anti-Parnellite Nationalist candidate Donal Sullivan was elected unopposed.[211] One historian has noted that again it was the power of the clergy that affected the return of Sullivan in Westmeath.[212]

The final election of the Victorian era saw two nationalists returned for South Westmeath and South Roscommon. The former constituency was again won by Donal Sullivan who, on this occasion, declared himself as simply a Nationalist candidate. The redefining of Athlone's boundaries in 1899, which placed it entirely in Westmeath, basically meant that he was Athlone's representative in parliament. The South Roscommon winner was John Patrick Hayden, a nationalist, whose father Luke Patrick had won the previous election standing as a Parnellite Nationalist. The electorate for South Roscommon appeared to support Parnell's ideals well after his death. The west side of Athlone and the areas bordering it, always the poorer, appears to have been more nationalist than the settlement across the river.

Locally the idea of refusing to pay rent was still practiced successfully in the late 1890s with a case from one of the islands of Lough Ree highlighting this.[213] The evicted tenant's fund received a £25 donation from the townspeople of Athlone in 1898. It appears that they were in favour of maintaining a body to help evictees.[214] Nationalist sentiment was also strong in the town at the time of the Queen's Diamond Jubilee. As already noted an attempt by the Athlone Bicycle Club to have a cycle parade for the Queen was blocked by a large number of unsupportive locals. Any houses that were illuminated for the occasion received the special attention of the crowd with Nationalist songs sung all night, the final song being the 'Dead March' in memory of Parnell.[215]

Athlone, in common with many other parts of Ireland had to contend with the changing nature of politics in Britain as a whole as

209 *FJ.*, 20 July 1895.
210 *FJ.*, 27 July 1895.
211 *FJ.*, 20 July 1895.
212 Murray, A. C., p.157.
213 *FJ.*, 3 Oct 1896.
214 *FJ.*, 26 Oct 1898.
215 *FJ.*, 26 June 1897.

well as dealing with those aspects of politics that were peculiarly Irish. The introduction of the secret ballot in 1872, the Representation of People Act (1884) and the Redistribution Act (1885) were all designed to improve the local political systems in place in Ireland at the time. In relation to changes in processes and procedures perhaps the town's greatest change came about in the loss of its MP franchise in 1885. The parliamentary elections in Athlone — described as a 'rotten borough' — in their execution and management illustrated serious levels of corruption and highlighted the unrepresentative nature of the political system in Ireland during the greater part of the Victorian era. The machinations of men such as William Keogh and J. J. Ennis show to good effect how the most important asset a candidate could have was money. The levels of bribery that almost all of the candidates engaged in was nothing less than criminal and even after a member had been elected he invariably did not represent the wishes of the townspeople at parliament. The loss of the MP franchise for the town, though decried locally was part of a process through which the Victorian government believed it was improving the character of national politics. Corruption was rife in many of the boroughs in Ireland, places like Ennis, Cashel and Clonmel all exhibited similar behaviour at election time. Athlone was more indicative of a system of corruption rather than the nucleus of it. The rotten boroughs of England and Wales had been dealt with half a century previously in the 1830s and it was only a matter of time before the focus would turn towards remedying similar problems in Ireland.

When it came to the larger issue of Ireland's place in the Union the vast majority of the townspeople were without doubt nationalist in their opinions. The first major example of this came with O'Connell's Repeal movement which led to the largest crowd ever assembling in the town in 1843, though the coming of the Famine was to dampen the fervour of many in the local population for a number of years to come. After the Famine, Athlone and south Westmeath were seen as a centre for agrarian crime and Ribbonism. The lack of any powerful political movement in the late 1840s and 1850s meant that the people decided to take it upon themselves to achieve their goals and their modus operandi usually involved violence.

The move from agrarian violence to nationalist politics in the late 1870s and early 1880s was, for the most part, well received in Athlone and its environs. Though the Land Movement and the Home Rule question were not enthusiastically received in north Westmeath, the numbers who turned out for important meetings in Athlone were generally high, signifying a good level of support. Parnell himself was always well received by the vast majority of the townspeople, though his indiscretions did illustrate how people could be divided over the important issues arising from the moral standards of public figures. Perhaps people's sense of right and wrong changed, and the moralistic traits of the Victorian era were filtering down through society. Towards the turn of the century a nationalist consciousness was without doubt growing in the town. As more of the local Catholic population was enfranchised, the friction between them and the formerly dominant Conservative Protestants became clear with numerous examples of sectarian divisions in elections and politics. By 1901, Athlone was a town more obviously anti-Union than in 1837, the formerly underrepresented had found their voice to be strong; times had changed and the people with them.

LOCAL POLITICS

The Victorian period was one in which the administration of towns went through a number of changes at local authority level. In theory all those changes that were made were intended to improve the processes and effectiveness of municipal bodies. Prior to the commencement of the period many of the bodies in charge of the management of local authority funding were antiquated, non-representative and incapable. In a more progressive society these features could not persist.

ATHLONE CORPORATION

At the start of the Victorian Period the municipal authority in Athlone was the Corporation. It consisted of:

- Sovereign
- Vice-Sovereign
- Two Bailiffs
- Thirteen Burgesses – including a Constable of the Castle
- Recorder
- Deputy Recorder – also acted as Town Clark
- Sergeant at Mace
- Billetmaster

Also attached to the Corporation was a select body called the Common Council, which consisted of men elected by the burgesses and freemen of the town.[216] The Sovereign was elected each year on June 29th – he took up his post in September – and after his appointment he

216 *Athlone 1945*, p.38.

would choose a vice-sovereign. The bailiffs were elected by the freemen of the Common Council and were all ex-officio members of the same council. The freemen, who in turn were elected for life by the Common Council, elected the burgesses, also for life. The council could hold elections as often as they wished provided there were twelve members present. The Common Council also chose the Recorder and Town Clark whilst the Sovereign chose the Sergeant at Mace and the Billetmaster. The Common Council consisted of around twenty men including the Sovereign, Vice Sovereign and the two bailiffs; the burgesses and freemen filled any vacancies. The members of Athlone Corporation could have increased their number on any occasion if they so wished.[217] In general, the *Report of the Commissioners appointed to inquire into the Municipal Corporations in Ireland* found that: '*There is in fact no general, uniform and absolute right to admission into Municipal Corporations*'.[218]

The Sovereign had a number of duties including those of returning officer in the parliamentary elections, coroner, escheator, and clerk of the market as well as justice of the peace along with the Vice Sovereign and the Recorder.[219] He was also able decide on monetary disputes in the Corporation court, usually held every three weeks, and if the amount was less that 5s he could decide '*summarily*' on the settlement. Any disputes arising from commercial transactions on fair days were ruled on in the Corporation's Pie Pondre Court.[220] The Sovereign in Athlone (as in five other corporation towns), in his role as justice of the peace had complete jurisdiction over cases exclusive of the county magistrates and as one report put it: '*The uncertainties and difficulties of this state of things must be prejudicial to the administration of justice.*'[221] In practice the Sovereign could have sent whomever he wished to Athlone Gaol, which was described as '*unwholesome in the extreme.*'[222] During the life of the Corporation the number of people entitled to vote in elections to parliament was thirty-six, which meant that manipulation of the vote was quite easy. An historical account described bribery as '*open and unashamed*'.[223] The method by which the Corporation was selected ensured that its members could quite easily retain their seats if they so wished. Indeed, during the 1830s it was believed: '*The Corporations have long become unpopular and objects of suspicion. As at present constituted they*

217 *Report of the Commissioners appointed to inquire into the Municipal Corporations in Ireland* (London, 1835), p.12.
218 Ibid., p.13
219 Lewis, Samuel, p.87.
220 Strean, Annesley, p.98.
221 *Report into the Municipal*, p.26.
222 Ibid., p.48.
223 *Athlone 1945*, p.39.

are in many instances of no service to the community; in others, injurious; and in all insufficient and inadequate.[224]　From studying the history of 19th century Corporations it is obvious that:

> Irish Corporations had long ceased to pay any attention to the interests and welfare of the inhabitants of Irish towns and cities but devoted their energies to protecting the position of the narrow political and sectarian class.[225]

Athlone was a good example of this during the early part of the nineteenth century as the Handcock family, who were given the title Castlemaine, had full control over the town Corporation and its administration was nothing less than self-serving and biased.[226] The same situation was mirrored all over the United Kingdom during the early 19th century where the Corporations have been described as *'self-electing, unaccountable and corrupt.'*[227] The *Reports of Commissioners on the State of the Municipal Corporations in Ireland* stated: '*To the prosperity of Athlone the corporation have at no time contributed, nor is it likely, that as present constituted, they ever will.*'[228] Under the Corporation its insignia of office, the silver mace, was sold off to a Dublin jeweller for £29 9s, the town clock and bell were given away to the rector of St. Mary's church and, a number of years before its destruction in the autumn of 1845, the gates of the North Gate were detached and sold off, despite the Corporation having no claim over them.[229]

Athlone, along with a large number of other Irish towns, did not function well under this type of municipal authority and in 1840 the Municipal Corporations Act abolished 58 of the 68 Corporations in Irish towns and cities.[230] The ten that remained were altered in nature so as to remain consistent with the provisions of the act. This legislation was a follow-on from the Reform Act (Ireland) 1832 and the Municipal Reform Act of 1835 in Britain, which as already stated had similar problems associated with its local government.[231] Not unexpectedly the members of the Athlone Corporation sent a letter of protest to government regarding the move.[232] Their protests came to nothing and in 1840 the Athlone Town Commissioners superseded them.

224　*Report into the Municipal*, p.39.
225　Crossman, Virginia, *Local Government in 19th Century Ireland* (Belfast, 1994), p.75.
226　O'Brien, Workhouse, p.7, *Athlone Common Council Minute Book 1804-1816* (Aidan Heavey Public Library).
227　Daunton, Martin, p.63.
228　*Report into the Municipal*, p.136.
229　O'Brien, Municipal, p.81, Ireland, Aideen, M., "The North Gate, Athlone", in Condit, Tom & Corlett, Christiaan (Eds.), *Above and Beyond – Essays in memory of Leo Swan* (Bray, 2005), p.465.
230　Roche, Desmond, p.34.
231　Trevelyan, G. M., p.123, Proudfoot, L. J., p.204.
232　*Athlone 1945*, p.38.

ATHLONE TOWN COMMISSIONERS

The Town Commissioners were, as a body, designed to be more representative, progressive and capable than their predecessors. They were however just a step along the path of local political reforms, an increment in the struggle to modernise local government. Those elected as Town Commissioner included businessmen and members of the local clergy; the eligibility for voting ensuring that only the more affluent would have a say in the process. For example in 1847 the Athlone Town Commissioners had a local Roman Catholic parish priest and a medical doctor as well as many prominent local businessmen among their number.[233] They usually met once a week, on a Thursday, with one extra meeting on the first Monday of every month.[234] Initially their responsibilities were in keeping with the act for paving and cleaning towns from 1828.[235] The body was in power for the vast majority of the Victorian period with various new responsibilities being granted to them over the years as part of Victorian political reforms. The successive acts and reforms were Irish examples of how the successive Victorian governments '...*groped their way towards more efficient and flexible methods of administration*'.[236] This move towards better methods came about as part of a drive during a period that saw itself as '*reforming*'.[237]

However, putting many of the reforms and laws into practice proved difficult for them. As part of their brief, they had to modernise the town's infrastructure in line with laws passed, as well as maintain the town on a day-to-day basis. With the advent of gas lighting the municipal bodies around Ireland had to meet to decide if they would adopt the new energy source, and regulate and maintain the related infrastructure. The Lighting of Towns (Ireland) Act 1828 gave local authorities the power to deal with providing a municipal lighting scheme in towns but it was very restricted, due in part to the reluctance of the government to provide too many powers to the Corporations which were still in power at that time.

It was not until 1850 that the Athlone Town Commissioners convened a public meeting to decide if they could extend their powers to '*lighting and watching*'. The locals that had gathered were not in favour of the new schemes as they believed that the levels of taxation, which were already considered high, would rise even further. All during the proposal speech there were shouts of '*overtaxed*', '*humbug*', '*want no light*'

---

233 *Thom's 1847*, p.800.
234 *W.I.*, 8 Oct 1870.
235 *Thom's 1847*, p.800.
236 Thomson, David, p.115.
237 Matthew, Colin, p.128.

and '*scheme job*'.[238] It appeared that implementing any modernisation in Athlone was going to be a struggle. The meeting resulted in a decree that houses valued under £5 would not be taxed for the scheme, but neither could their occupants vote on it.[239] Bringing about this lighting required finance and the Town Commissioners were forced to levy a Town Rate of one shilling in the pound in 1853 – they had previously relied on revenues from fines, cranage, tolls and customs.[240]

The government was aware that the acts they had passed were inadequate for the purposes of improving Ireland's communication, sanitation and municipal infrastructure and they set about pulling together all the relevant acts dealing with lighting, sewerage etc. and created the Towns Improvement Clauses (Ireland) Act 1850.[241] This act along with the 1828 Act formed the foundation for the Towns Improvement (Ireland) Act 1854. After this act was passed by parliament the chairman of the Town Commissioners spearheaded a movement, consisting of all those with houses worth in excess of £8, to have Athlone proclaimed under it, a drive which was successful.[242]

Athlone was one of the first towns in Ireland to adopt the act; many others decided to stay with the less expansive act of 1828.[243] The fact that towns were allowed to operate under inferior legislation was deemed to be one of the more '*anomalous*' aspects of local government in the 19th century.[244] However, the superiority of the 1854 act in comparison with what had gone before, did cause many other towns to adopt it and by 1878 fifty-five towns that operated under the 1828 act had adopted the more recent one.[245] The Towns Improvement Act allowed local authorities to operate in a similar way to their Welsh and English counterparts who had been provided with more powers a number of years previously. They could bring about the construction of new sewers at the districts' expense as opposed to the ratepayers, using loans to finance the infrastructure. The water supply could also be improved with new pumps added and filterbeds installed; this was subject to a rate levy of 6d in the pound.[246] The Athlone commissioners did not wish initially to impose the part of the legislation that dealt with the water supply; they believed that the pumps already in existence were sufficient. The number of commissioners allowed under the act was

238 *F.J.*, 27 Dec 1850.
239 *F.J.*, 27 Dec 1850.
240 O'Brien, *Municipal*, p.83.
241 Roche, *Desmond*, p.35.
242 *W.I.*, 14 Oct 1854, *W.I.*, 20 Jan 1855.
243 Crossman, *Virginia*, p.80.
244 Ibid., p.74.
245 Ibid., p.67.
246 Ibid., p.67.

eighteen – though this figure was not always reached –, nine from each ward, St Mary's on the east side and St Peter's on the west side.[247] Previously up to twenty-one commissioners had been on the board.[248]

As with all legislation, the Towns Improvement Act was effective only if it was properly implemented. As already noted in chapter four, with the Athlone Market Act 1852, this was generally not the case in Athlone, as the provisions of numerous acts were introduced slowly and, even then, poorly. For example when the Town Commissioners eventually added extra water pumps, which the Town Improvements Act provided for, the lack of professionalism when it came to repairs and maintenance rendered them unusable at times.[249] The act also provided for the provision of public baths, washhouses and places of public recreation, none of which the Athlone commissioners implemented.[250] It was not until 1890 that the commissioners provided the town with the amenity of the promenade on the western bank of the river with very little else done to improve the social facilities in the town.[251] The main areas to which funds secured under the act were allocated were street cleaning, lighting, sewerage, sanitary expenses, salaries, printing and stationery.[252] It is obvious that in some cases the Town Commissioners appeared to work against the grain of Victorian modernisation when it came to improving the town's facilities and thus, according to Victorian thought, against the townspeople. They refused to implement the provisions of a later act that provided for a museum, gymnasium or library for the town, deeming each of them to be unnecessary in Athlone.[253] The provision of municipal libraries had begun in England in the 1850s, where they were seen as essential for personal growth and modernising the mind, though unfortunately this decree by the Athlone Town Commissioners meant that Athlone people would have to rely on private societies for reading material.[254]

Another act which was adopted by the Town Commissioners but poorly implemented was the Local Government Act 1872, which expanded the remit of the local authorities, in conjunction with the Towns Improvement Act, to effect positive changes in Irish towns. The problem with a town such as Athlone when it came to local government was that it had four authorities in charge of its affairs; the

247 *Thom's 1858*, p.824.
248 *Thom's 1849*, p.824.
249 O'Brien, Municipal, p.86.
250 Crossman, Virginia, p.67.
251 O'Brien, Municipal, p.84.
252 Saint, Andrew, "Cities, architecture and art" in Matthew, Colin, *Short Oxford History of the British Isles – The Nineteenth Century* (Oxford, 2000), p.285.
253 O'Brien, Municipal, p.88.
254 Saint, Andrew, p.285.

Town Commission, the local Board of Guardians and two Grand Juries. The difficulties encountered locally with the lack of co-operation between these bodies led to a large number of infrastructure problems persisting longer than necessary. Each separate authority was liable to have a singular interpretation of each act leading to an unworkable overlap in duties and responsibilities between mainly, in the case of Athlone, the Town Commissioners and the Grand Juries. In 1873 the Wexford Town Commissioners had used the 1872 act to gain jurisdiction from the Grand Jury in that county, though the act did stipulate that the latter's consent was necessary for that provision of the act to work.[255] The Grand Juries with jurisdiction over Athlone were less willing to co-operate (*chapter eight*); in fact the Town Commissioners in Athlone did not gain control over Athlone's streets until 1894.[256]

The implementation of a number of the acts passed that had a bearing on the town was, as stated, haphazard at times, though never more so than in relation to public health, which is explored in *chapter eight*. Neither, as mentioned in *chapter two*, was their handling of the Working Classes Housing (Ireland) Act 1890 any better; a scheme was not begun until the early years of the 20th century by which time the Town Commissioners had been replaced by the Urban District Council.

Apart from the poor implementation of the provisions of various acts (*see chapter eight for additional examples*) the Town Commissioners had to cope with the changes in franchise that occurred at various times throughout the Victorian period. The Towns Improvement Act expanded the pool of eligible voters in municipal affairs to include householders valued at £4 or over, up from the previous cut off level of £5, as well as local lessors valued at £50 or over. The eligibility for people who could run for the post of Town Commissioner changed, with only those rated at £12 or more entitled to put their names forward.[257] It was not until the year 1880 that all voters became eligible to run for posts on the Town Commission. This must have made gaining a seat harder, for it is possible that the local elections were contested in a similar way to those for parliament; candidates who won their seats usually did so through corrupt means.[258] Those who fulfilled the criteria for voting and running for election all throughout the period were few in number, ensuring a situation – while not as bad as that under the Corporation – in which a small minority managed the town's affairs.

255 Crossman, Virginia, p.73.
256 *FJ.*, 16 Nov 1894.
257 Saint, Andrew, p.285.
258 Crossman, Virginia, p.70.

Apart from a duty to improve the town's infrastructure the Town Commissioners also found time to improve their own facilities. Early in their existence they met in local hotels, the courthouse and even their own homes on a number of occasions. The cost of meeting in the courthouse was the main deterrent to their convening there though after they came to an arrangement with the sheriff they used it frequently until 1855. However, at times they did not meet at all. The *Athlone Town Commissioners Minute Book 1846-1847* details how on numerous occasions hardly any members showed up for meetings and indeed how on two consecutive occasions nobody showed up at all, despite the Famine crisis surely requiring action on their behalf.[259] In 1855 the town rate had garnered enough funds for the conversion of a room in a disused Presbyterian Church to a boardroom.[260] In 1864 a decision was reached to construct a new Town Hall – improvements in municipal buildings appeared to take precedence over more important matters such as sewers, which at the time were, in places, either very basic or non-existent. The construction of the hall was promptly completed and the commissioners moved into the new building in December of that year.[261] Not all municipal buildings received the same prompt treatment – the necessity of having a new courthouse appears not to have been high on the agenda with a period of thirty-three years elapsing from the date when the old courthouse was deemed unsuitable, 1868, and when the new courthouse opened, 1901.[262] The Town Commissioners could also vote for member's pay rises; one received by the Town Clerk in 1870 caused a number of local ratepayers to converge on the Town Hall to ensure that taxes would not rise as a result.[263]

The political affiliations of the Town Commissioners can be seen from looking at their stance on a number of national issues. They attended the 'Monster Meeting' in the town in 1843 when Daniel O'Connell spoke of repeal, and offered their support to him.[264] They stated their unwavering support for the Athlone Borough MP William Keogh when he called for religious and civil liberty in Ireland, holding a banquet in his honour.[265] They supported the idea of Sunday closing for all public houses in 1873 and issued a directive to the MP for Athlone to let their thoughts be known at parliamentary level on one of the many occasions when the topic arose.[266] They blamed the

259 *Athlone Town Commissioners Minute Book 1846-1847* (Aidan Heavey Public Library).
260 O'Brien, Municipal, p.81.
261 *W.I.*, 5 Nov 1864, *W.I.*, 12 Nov 1864.
262 *A.T.*, 17 Aug 1901.
263 *W.I.*, 19 Mar 1870.
264 *F.J.*, 20 June 1843.
265 *F.J.*, 22 Sep 1851.
266 *W.I.*, 5 July 1873.

subsequent defeat of the Bill at that level on the English, who had the vast majority of seats in the House of Commons.[267] The Commissioners protested about the result and passed a resolution that the bill was of no political significance and that the Irish point of view should not be disregarded in the way it had.[268] The Town Commissioners also made known their agreement with the resolution passed by the Cork Corporation regarding the unfair treatment of political prisoners in 1871.[269] On the very contentious issue of a Catholic University the Town Commissioners also pledged their support stating that: '...*the Catholic people of Ireland are entitled from their numbers, wealth, and influence, to be placed in a position of perfect educational equality with their Protestant fellow-countrymen*'.[270] It is interesting to note that an observation has been made that the Town Commissioners exhibited very little evidence of religious bigotry during their existence, finding that differences over how the two sides of the town should be equally treated were enough to cause friction.[271]

There were also a number of occasions when the Town Commissioners supported the Land League and Home Rule. The discussion of national and international issues was not the purpose of the board however, with a local pointing this out to them in a letter printed in the local press.

> How much more beneficial to the interests of the town would it be if the watering and cleansing of the streets, whitewashing of the houses of the poor, and giving additional water by means of a few more pumps, could receive as much public attention as the political purification of public notabilities. The watering cart is idle, whilst the dust is destroying the goods of the ratepayers. The Sanitary Inspector has, I dare say, a nose, but it does not take offence at trifles. The streets are unswept; the fairs badly managed. But all those matters are only secondary, and political manoeuvring of primary consideration.[272]

At some meetings the behaviour of the Town Commissioners could at times degenerate into something that at best can be described as immature. In one instance a debate on who should attend the anniversary commemoration of Daniel O'Connell in 1875 ended up with two of the commissioners detailing the faults and sins of the other; eventually each declared that they would rather travel alone.[273] Some

267 *W.I.*, 5 Dec 1874.
268 *W.I.*, 5 Dec 1874.
269 *W.I.*, 11 Feb 1871.
270 *W.I.*, 29 July 1871.
271 O'Brien, Municipal, p.81.
272 *W.I.*, 24 May 1873.
273 *W.I.*, 31 July 1875.

members also had quite high opinions of themselves. One such person, a Mr. Bergin, half of the former controversy, believed himself not unlike Daniel O'Connell, such were the powers of oratory at his disposal. When he stated this at a meeting of the Town Commissioners it was recorded in a local newspaper, one to which Bergin had great hostility, as causing '*...some amusement and considerable pain to the other members of the board*'.[274] The same man appeared to carry out all of his duties with a petulant air, even going as far as non-participation in a board meeting in March 1876 due to his belief that other members conspired against him in the recent Poor Law Guardian elections.[275]

Sometimes, the Town Commissioners came in for criticism from local people though, as they stated on one occasion after a series of complaints had been made, they were as capable as their counterparts in Scotland or England.[276] In what was perhaps the most humorous waste of time seen at a Town Commissioners meeting, all the assembled members spent most of one session comparing times on their watches to see if any agreed with the time as observed in the military barracks, which apparently ran six minutes ahead of that at the railway station.[277] The childlike temperament of some of the commissioners again came to the fore in June 1886 when the minute book was used as a projectile in an attempt to decapitate a member of the body who was disagreeing with another on a point of procedure.[278] As regards the municipal finances, they were over £1,000 in deficit by 1896, which was actually a small improvement over previous years, though their poor management was not to be allowed to last much longer.[279]

LOCAL GOVERNMENT ACT 1898

During the year 1898 the government decided to pass another act that dealt with the local administration of Ireland. Called the Local Government (Ireland) Act, it was to be the '*...last major change in local government before it came under the control of an Irish government*'.[280] There had been a previous Local Government Bill in 1892 though its provisions were believed too hard to implement and it was never passed. Home Rule was considered to be '*sleeping very soundly*' by the late 1890s and some politicians in Britain believed that an act of '*conciliatory*

274 *W.I.*, 8 Apr 1876.
275 *W.I.*, 1 Apr 1876.
276 *W.I.*, 15 Sep 1877.
277 *W.I.*, 7 Jan 1882.
278 *F.J.*, 19 June 1886.
279 *F.J.*, 3 Oct 1896.
280 Roche, Desmond, p.47.

unionism' was appropriate, hence the 1898 act.[281] Throughout the 1880s
some members of the government had begun to believe that the Irish
would be content if they had more power on a local level and the fact
that local government reform had '...*always been the classic unionist
alternative to Home Rule'* made the law easier to pass.[282] This school of
thought gave rise to the idea that if local administration were in the
hands of the Irish, they would lose interest in the national Home Rule
movement, hence as one politician suggested the move would '*Kill
Home Rule with Kindness'*.

The act, attempted to deal with the '*jumble of authorities'* that were
governing the counties, cities, towns and villages of Ireland.[283] Its
primary purpose was to '...*put county government on a representative basis'*.
In practice this meant the creation of County Councils, who took over
the Grand Juries, and Urban District Councils who took over from the
urban sanitary authorities (Town Commissioners), with the final new
body being the Rural District Councils.[284] Many believed it to be:
'...*nothing short of a revolution in local power'* such were its caveats on
voting rights – all occupiers could vote irrespective of sex (with age
limits), religion or wealth.[285] In 1898, *Thom's Directory* gave the number
entitled to vote in Athlone as 476.[286] After the act was passed that
number increased to 1,008 people.[287]

On January 1st 1899 the Urban District Council (UDC) replaced the
Town Commissioners, though a large number of those seeking election
to the new body were members of the former.[288] What this actually
meant when the votes were counted was that twelve of the former
Town Commissioners were then Urban District Councillors.[289] This
lack of new blood may explain why *Thom's Directory* did not change
Athlone's municipal details until 1901 when it eventually noted the
UDC as being in power. The administrative functions of the new body
were not intrinsically different from those of the Town Commissioners;
the more serious local authority changes occurred at county level.[290]
Nationally the new bodies furthered '*a moderately progressive spirit'*, with
water and sewerage schemes being completed, as well as labourers'

281 Gailey, Andrew, "Unionist Rhetoric and Irish local government reform, 1895-9", in *Irish Historical Studies*,
Vol. 24, No. 93 (1984), pp.56-58.
282 Ibid., p.59.
283 Roche, Desmond, p.45.
284 Ibid., p.46.
285 Gailey, Andrew, p.58.
286 *Thom's 1898*, p.1196.
287 *Thom's 1899*, p.1196, *Thom's 1900*, p.1196, *Thom's 1901*, p.1195.
288 *F.J.*, 14 Jan 1899.
289 *Thom's 1900*, p.1196.
290 Crossman, Virginia, p.90.

housing schemes and technical institutes being founded.[291]

The main political statements made by the Urban District Council came around the time of Queen Victoria's death in 1901. At a meeting, a resolution was passed to send condolences to the King. At least one member believed '...*that the Queen was an excellent woman, and although we cannot say our little country was prosperous within the reign we did not go back, and politically we gained something.*'[292] Though all those present did not echo this sentiment the resolution was passed. It was believed that since the Dublin Corporation had sent a letter of sympathy Athlone would have been unwise not to follow suit. The next national political item dealt with by the UDC was the removal of the British Coronation Oath, for they believed it to have '*objectionable*' references to Catholics in it. They sent a letter to this effect to the relevant authorities.[293]

Outside the larger political forum, the UDC could still be as lax about their duties as the Town Commissioners. The lethargic proceedings at a meeting dealing with the sewer problem in the town were noted in the local press:

> For two mortal hours the Urban Council discussed sewers on Wednesday evening. The British Cabinet might have been formed in the time, and the Urban Councillors are getting worse and worse – slower and slower in getting through their business.[294]

Perhaps the most telling example of the councillors lack of interest in the work they were elected to do was the occasion on which not enough members showed up to a weekly meeting to create the quorum necessary to deliberate.[295]

After the changing of the Athlone Town boundaries in 1899 the town in its entirety was placed in County Westmeath, much to the annoyance of a number of Connacht-side residents. To deal with the affairs of Westmeath as a whole, the County Council was brought into being, which, for all intents and purposes, replaced the Grand Jury. The Grand Jury was a long-established body that was not deemed fair or successful in its workings, with nepotism and monopolisation seen in its work and makeup.[296] It was considered an outdated system of local government that '...*had little to recommend it*'.[297] One British politician described the juries as '*antiquated*' and '...*no longer in harmony with the spirit of the age*',

291 Roche, Desmond, pp.47-48.
292 *A.T.*, 2 Feb 1901.
293 *A.T.*, 2 Mar 1901.
294 *A.T.*, 17 Nov 1901.
295 *A.T.*, 3 Aug 1901.
296 Crossman, Virginia, pp. 30-41.
297 Roche, Desmond, p.44.

an age which saw itself as progressive and right thinking.[298] In fact over a number of years '...*a succession of Government-appointed committees made their enquiries and found the system in many instances unjust and at all points inefficient.*'[299] County Councils had been in existence in England since 1888 and the government believed that it was a good system for reforming the local authority problems in Ireland caused by the Grand Juries.[300] The County Council was the most powerful body in the county with responsibility for county institutions and all the major roads and bridges – the minor repairs and public works were left to the Urban District Councils and their rural counterparts.[301] The new century saw virtually all landlords disappear from these local bodies hence rendering them more representative of society in general.[302]

At a meeting prior to the election for the Westmeath County Council in April 1899 it was decided that: Home Rule, a Catholic University, Compulsory Land sales, release of political prisoners, readjustment of labour grievances, reinstatement of evicted tenants and fair settlement of financial relations would all be embraced by the body.[303] Similar resolutions were passed in a large number of other county councils around the country.[304] This sort of decree showed the shift in power that had occurred in local authorities in Ireland with the national figures showing that Nationalists took roughly 75% of all county council seats with only some parts of Ulster showing a strong Unionist influence.[305] The Westmeath County Council, in another distinctly nationalist and unique move, replaced the Union Jack, which had flown above the courthouse for many years and instead erected a flag with a harp on a green background.[306] Some politicians in England lamented the nationalist trend of the councils, though Arthur Balfour, Prime Minister of the time, remarked that unionist majorities in the councils generally '...[were] *not to be expected*'.[307]

Throughout the Victorian period obvious efforts were being made to improve the administration of towns and cities at local level. At the start of the period those bodies that were in place were unrepresentative, inefficient and non-progressive. Their members were against change, for in Ireland when a body had to become more representative it, in

298 Gailey, Andrew, p.58.
299 O'Tuathaigh, Gearoid, p.84.
300 Matthew, Colin, p.128.
301 Crossman, Virginia, p.93.
302 Roche, Desmond, p.47.
303 *FJ*, 18 Feb 1899.
304 Gailey, Andrew, p.55.
305 Crossman, Virginia, p.96.
306 *FJ*, 16 Sep 1899.
307 Gailey, Andrew, p.60.

essence, had to have fewer Protestants and more Catholics. The landed gentry of the Grand Juries and the Municipal Corporations must have sensed the shift in power and were certainly alarmed by it.

In an era that saw minds turn towards modernisation and efficiency, it was only a matter of time before replacements were found. The loss of the Corporation in Athlone was the first positive step towards creating the municipal authorities that operate today. Though the replacement body, the Town Commission, was still inefficient, and to some extent impotent, the trend towards municipal improvement can be seen through the provisions of acts such as the Town Improvement (Ireland) Act 1854. This act, along with numerous others, though poorly implemented in Athlone, was certainly far superior to that which had gone before. Through learning from past mistakes local authorities and the legislation that governed them were evolving.

The lack of success that greeted some of the changes in local government may be accounted for by a lack of planning when it came to local matters. One commentator believed that the government '...*had adopted expedients to meet difficulties as they arose or as the political complexion of parliament changed.*'[308] This kind of administration was thought to have led to a situation where '*local administration was still in a chaotic condition*' by the end of the 19th century.[309]

The eventual passing of the 1898 Local Government Act was to herald a new era in local politics in Ireland. At the start of the Victorian era local government had been in the hands of the wealthy landed gentry; by the end few of this class were represented on the boards of local authorities such as the County Councils. Clearer roles and responsibilities had been defined for the local bodies so that work could be carried out more efficiently. Indeed, the success of some of the reforms can be seen in the longevity of the bodies associated with them. Athlone's UDC was still in existence up to the first year of the 21st century and the County Councils we have today are all based on the Victorian model. The groundwork had been laid for the democratic changes that were to occur during the 20th century.

308 Roche, Desmond, p.44.
309 Ibid., p.44.

CHAPTER 8

Health, sanitation and local utilities

PUBLIC HEALTH

It has been said that the English viewed Irish people, during the 19th century much as they didi the Italians; '*…a people of dirty habits, offensive to those who came from a nation that valued cleanliness.*'[1] This judgement, whilst perhaps not exactly enlightened, does mention one of the dominant Victorian obsessions: cleanliness. Be it personal or urban, the Victorians actively tried to improve the levels of hygiene through a number of initiatives. During the era more acts and schemes were put in place than ever before in an attempt to combat problems in public health. Starting in the early years of the 19th century, a number of sources will be used to construct a detailed account of how the town fared in the battle to improve public health standards, and to see if the situation had improved by the end of the Victorian era.

In Athlone in the early part of the 19th century the levels of hygiene were not considered adequate by any means. The Rev. Strean noted that while there were no epidemic diseases in the town in 1819 there was a tendency for typhus to emerge in the summer due to, in his estimation, poor personal hygiene:

> '…a charge which is too justly made against the peasantry of Ireland in general, and those of the western side of the Shannon do not afford any grounds for making an exception in their favour.'[2]

Describing the town in their own words, before resorting to the *Statistical Survey of County Roscommon* by Isaac Weld, the authors of *The Parliamentary Gazetteer of Ireland 1844* had this to say of Athlone:

> The town, especially when viewed in connection with its size and importance, not only disappoints all travellers, but disgusts some and astonishes others. To describe it with fidelity, yet without apparent

1 Newsome, David, p.96.
2 Strean, Annesley, pp69/70.

invidiousness or prejudice, is so nearly impossible that we gladly allow the chief part of the task to be performed by Mr. Weld...[3]

Thirteen years after Strean's comments on the locals' personal hygiene Weld criticises the state of Athlone's public health using the strongest terms: '*The dirt and filth of these places* [houses] *are disgusting in the highest degree, and can scarcely fail to be injurious to the general salubrity of the town.*'[4] In the year 1832, that of Weld's visit, the country was undergoing a cholera crisis that without doubt manifested itself in the town due to the unsanitary conditions.[5]

Neither was the local press ignorant of the problems with hygiene in the town and an editorial from *The Athlone Independent* set out what was believed to be the general sentiment locally:

> With shame we are obliged to state that our town has become a proverb to our neighbours; for it is no unusual thing to hear them, in speaking of an ill-regulated or dirty place, say "Oh it is just as bad as the sweet town of Athlone."[6]

Another article that predates the Victorian era stated that the town was in a deplorable sanitary condition. The piece requested that the residents of the town be '*up and doing*' in relation to cleanliness, citing the example of other smaller towns in which a voluntary subscription was given for the cleansing of the streets. An act from 1828 did make provisions for the upgrading of some of the infrastructure in towns though the Corporation never appears to have applied it to Athlone. They believed it to be flawed, citing its failure in other towns as evidence enough.[7]

A letter dated 23rd November 1833 a concerned local requested that the current Corporation reinstate the old practice of selling, in lots, the sweeping of the town's streets. The letter writer believed that:

> [It would be] no difficult matter to get an ostensible person, who would undertake to keep the streets and lanes swept, and the manure at once carted away, solely for its emolument, provided that the undertaker was supported by the proper authorities.[8]

In what is probably a satirical piece some of the problems that could be encountered by someone in the job of scavenger were laid out in the

---

3 *Gazetteer*, p.96.
4 Ibid.
5 Houston, C. J., "The Irish Diaspora: Emigration to the New World, 1720-1920", in Graham, B. J. & Proudfoot, L. J. (Eds.), *An Historical Geography of Ireland* (London, 1993), p.344.
6 *A.I.*, 20 Nov 1833.
7 Ibid.
8 *A.I.*, 27 Nov 1833.

same paper in the following week:

> On the subject of cleansing the filthy streets of Athlone, and your proposing to give the manure to whosoever should undertake the Herculean task little inferior to that of the stable of Augeas – I had the boldness to offer myself to the Sovereign as Scavenger in Chief and had the honour of being graciously accepted, and was immediately installed into that office with free and uninterrupted privilege to sweep, clean, take, convey, and carry away, all dung, dirt, filth and manure, from the Queen's Arms on the Bridge, down to, and through Irishtown, as far as I pleased and back again, on the one side; then up Connaught-street and so on in a westerly direction and back again on the other side.
>
> Duly impressed with the importance of this grant, I forthwith commenced and swept, and swept, and swept, with the diligence of a house-maid who had lost a penny, and neatly collected at convenient distances my little heaps of mud ready for shovelling into my carts on this blessed morning. But at dawn of day I had the mortification of finding that the choicest and richest of my little heaps had been feloniously carried away, conveyed, taken, or otherwise surreptitiously disposed of, during the night; and several men, women and children, without any fear of their Sovereign before their eyes, audaciously opposed my carting away any portion of what I conscientiously believed to be my own sole right and property. I remonstrated in terms as strong and expressive as the nature of a case of such earthly importance very naturally wanted, but, all in vain! In vain I assured my clamorous opponents that I was "Scavenger in Chief of the town of Athlone." "The Devil scavenger you!" said one, "for coming here to take the widow's morsel." – "Bad luck to the one spoonful of my dung shall ever you taste," said another "silence, you thieves you!" said I. "I am Scavenger in Chief of the town of Athlone! And that dung is all my own, and if you prevent me from taking it I'll call out the Police." "I don't care one fart-hing (farthing, I suppose) for all the Poleesh in Connaught, was the indecent and rebellious reply, "neither you nor they shall ever take my dung from before my face and again my will, and if you attempt to take one pound of it, we'll make you ate it on the spot".Not feeling inclined to stomach these threats I withdrew my men and carts.[9]

The letter from the 'scavenger' purports to outline the opposition of the locals to seeing 'their' dung carted away by a man who had paid for the privilege, mainly due, one could assume, to the fact that they had received no payment themselves for the materials. By 1838 the situation still had not improved when the travel writer Leitch Ritchie described the state of the town's streets in less than glowing terms:

> You cannot walk in the streets of Athlone: you must wade. So

9 *A.I.*, 11 Dec 1833.

inconceivably dirty a place does not exist in Europe, and the broad streets are as filthy as the narrow ones…I understand that the actual governor of the town is very generously, though by no means justly, rewarded for his negligence or incapacity.[10]

The following decade did not see an overall improvement in either the town's cleanliness or people's perception of it. The only time during the 1840s where the streets were described as swept or clean was the arrival of Daniel O'Connell in 1843 when the inhabitants made special efforts to improve Athlone's appearance.[11] *The Parliamentary Gazetteer of Ireland 1844* stated that the Leinster side of the town had a number of features that saved the town from outright denunciation but that the Connacht side was lost to the mire.[12] It appears that in many facets of Victorian life the Connacht side of the town was not to develop as quickly as the Leinster side.

The hygiene problem in public areas could not be alleviated during the second half of the decade, with the onset of famine causing even more problems than had been previously encountered. In August 1846 the Town Commissioners had their attention drawn to the fact that the filth on some of the less frequented lanes had rendered them almost impassable, with householders dumping their waste in ever-growing mounds.[13] In the months that followed, reports came in detailing the deplorable condition not only of the streets but also of the Abbey graveyard, which was situated beside the union workhouse:

> The lanes of which (Athlone) are choked up either with dung heaps or stagnant cesspools, together with the crowded state of the burial grounds, in which the dead are so promiscuously thrown with scarcely a covering of earth that the famished dogs are gragging the bodies hardly decomposed from the resting place.[14]

Following this report a watch was placed at the graveyard and in the first week two dogs were shot, one of which had a man's leg in his mouth.[15]

The severe health crisis brought about by the spread of cholera and other diseases in England caused the government to pass a number of acts in an attempt to combat them. Those that were relevant to Ireland, which was in the middle of the Famine and experiencing similar problems with the spread of disease, were published together in 1848 and outlined a number of laws that had to be administered locally.

10 Ritchie, Leitch, p.181.
11 *FJ.*, 20 June 1843.
12 *Gazetteer*, p.96.
13 *A.S.*, 8 Aug 1846.
14 *Athlone 1947*, p.14.
15 Ibid.

Indeed, the cholera outbreak in England had been the catalyst needed to force Victorian society to be: '...*scared...into the tardy beginnings of sanitary self-defence.*'[16] There were a number of problems associated with these early Victorian health acts however. For example in the case of 'The Nuisances Removal and Disease Prevention Act 1848' fines were to be issued to offenders, with the money garnered used in the cleanup. In practice those 'offenders' were for the most part the sick, the starving and the impoverished, who most probably had no money to pay the fines or if they did had far more important expenditure to consider. Other parts of the act required that all new houses i.e. those built after 1848 were not permitted to '*issue forth nuisances*'. One can assume that it was envisaged that a municipal sewerage scheme was to be drawn up to deal with the waste from these dwellings.[17] Standards were seen to improve slowly in Britain in response to the Public Health Acts of 1848, though substantial improvements would not be seen until the after the Public Health Act of 1874.[18] The Famine in Ireland slowed the efficacy of the 1848 act here and it was not until the 1870s that noticeable improvements were made nationally. These acts were all intended to assist in '...*promoting the public health, better working conditions, and general welfare of the working classes.*'[19] The Victorians saw the problems with public health as a challenge that could be tackled with the application of the proper legislation and throughout the era the evidence shows that this was exactly what they attempted to do.[20]

During the Famine the public health situation in Athlone was in its most dire state. It was only a matter of time before disease and sickness began to spread through the town. Fever and food poisoning were rife; however, the most serious outbreak of disease during the Famine was the cholera outbreak of 1848. The local press reported that in October of that year two committees had to be formed to deal with an epidemic that was sweeping the town. Each member of the committees was given one or two streets to inspect and to report on the progress of the disease.[21] It took almost eight months for the disease to subside. Just one week after the declaration that the epidemic was at an end the temporary cholera hospital was closed and the staff disbanded.[22] During the epidemic, initial figures put the number of infected at 175, and of those 120 cases proved fatal, though these figures were later increased.[23]

16 Trevelyan, G. M., p.127.
17 Moore, Arthur S., *Sanitary Acts for Ireland* (Dublin, 1848), p.33.
18 Saint, Andrew, p.259.
19 Thomson, David, p.127.
20 Ibid., p.134.
21 *W.I.*, 28 Oct 1848.
22 *W.I.*, 16 June 1849.
23 *W.I.*, 9 June 1849.

After making the additions later in the year *The Westmeath Independent* stated that the outbreak actually affected 330 people of whom 150 recovered. The 180 deaths were exclusive of those from the higher societal class and the military. Those in the more privileged sections of society and behind the garrison walls had a total of roughly forty cases.[24] The fact that diseases such as cholera were affecting the respectable classes would certainly have spurred the government on in deciding the necessity for disease legislation. The area of disease was one in which all members of society were in danger of being affected; the cleanliness of the town was not just an aspiration but a necessity. Similar problems were reported in Britain for the years 1848-49 when a large number of people were killed by cholera. It took substantial investment over a long period of time to bring about the improvements in public health needed to wipe out the disease in urban environments.[25]

In 1851 the administration of the Nuisances Removal and Disease Prevention Acts was placed under the jurisdiction of the Poor Law Commissioners.[26] In the same year it was thought that towns in Britain, mainly those places directly affected by the Industrial Revolution, were '...*poisoning themselves with their own human, animal and industrial wastes.*'[27] In fact in England a child born in 1851 in Liverpool had almost half the life expectancy of another born in the same year in a rural village.[28] This type of statistic was another reminder to the government that it had to bring in useful legislation to combat urban public health problems. The progress of the Victorian era was not always wholly positive.

Probably the most important legislation for urban centres that was enacted by the government for Ireland was the Town Improvement Act 1854. It was intended to '...*make better provision for the paving, lighting, draining, cleansing, supply with water and regulation of towns in Ireland.*'[29] As noted in the previous chapter Athlone's Town Commissioners had the town proclaimed under the act soon after it was passed.[30] However, the act's potential was not to be fully realised, and of all those improvements that could have been carried out only a percentage actually were. Of course an existing impediment to the increase in funding to alleviate public health problems and upgrade infrastructure was the fact that the Town Commissioners had amassed debts of over £2,000 by 1853 when

24 *W.I.*, 23 June 1849.
25 Matthew, Introduction, p.8.
26 Roche, Desmond, p.41.
27 Daunton, Martin, p.62.
28 Ibid., p.63.
29 Vanston, George T. B., *The Law relating to Municipal Towns under the Towns Improvement (Ireland) Act 1854* (Dublin, 1900), p.24.
30 *W.I.*, 20 Jan 1855.

the town rates were introduced.[31] So the Town Commissioners were restricted by a number of factors when it came to implementing the provisions of the act. The fact that Athlone wanted to use the act may show that it was intent on being progressive. Many towns did not adopt the act at all until they were forced to so by the 1898 Local Government Act and by 1900 ninety-eight Irish towns operated under the legislation.[32]

Some of the problems with the cleansing of the town's streets lay in the work ethic of those employed by the Town Commissioners. The methods used by the scavengers when collecting the waste on the town's streets was not appreciated by the local press who described the work as '...*leaving noxious heaps, redolent of disease, oozing their unsavoury juices far into the Shannon.*'[33] Indeed, the scavengers in Britain appeared to be equally work-shy and were satirised on many occasions along with crossing sweepers in the pages of *Punch* magazine.[34] As part of the overall Victorian picture the streets in Ireland were not developing as favourably as those in Britain where the streets of the major cities and towns were said to be '*more tidy, business-like and consciously impressive.*'[35]

By the 1860s the Town Commissioners had begun to pave certain parts of the town, since the stone was far more easily maintained than the rough mix of gravel and earth that was already in place. By the mid-nineteenth century most English towns had been paved, but the process appears to have taken far longer in Ireland.[36] A footpath was laid outside St. Mary's Church of Ireland parish church in January 1861 with a flight of stone steps put in place at Scotch Parade on the outskirts of the Leinster side of the town in 1864.[37] Again the planning and allocation of paving was not in any way comprehensive with the vast majority of the town's thoroughfares left untouched by these improvements. Athlone was not the only midland town that was encountering these problems. Mullingar was to have similar problems in the 1860s when it came to sanitation with the Poor Law Guardians and Town Commissioners unable to decide upon an approach to the provision of sanitation facilities in the town.[38]

In 1862 an article in *The Dublin Builder* highlighted how the poor public health facilities in Athlone and Mullingar were leading to a

31 O'Brien, Municipal, p.83.
32 Vanston, George T. B., p.24.
33 *W.I.*, 27 Apr 1853.
34 Wohl, Anthony S., *Endangered Lives – Public Health in Victorian Britain* (London, 1983), p.81.
35 Best, Geoffrey, p.83.
36 Wohl, Anthony S., p.85.
37 *W.I.*, 19 Jan 1861, *W.I.*, 8 Oct 1864.
38 Murray, A. C., p.147.

higher than expected mortality rate in the Westmeath towns. The article relates how the mortality rate in 1851 was over 22% higher than it should have been when compared with the mortality rate of London.

> We can well understand why in a densely populated city such as London, there should be a less healthful state of things than in small country towns, but the converse must surprise and alarm.[39]

The article went on to detail how the '*bad sanitary arrangements*' namely, cess pools, poor drainage, poor ventilation in houses, poisoned drinking water, etc. were to blame for the most part: '...*the murderer actually harboured by his victims, surely but slowly and openly doing his deadly work.*'[40] The author lays most of the blame squarely at the feet of the municipal authorities: '*When will the Town Commissioners and others morally responsible...become sufficiently impressed with a conviction of the paramount importance of their duties?*'[41] Indeed the geographical situation of the towns, allied with other factors should have ensured a healthier environment for the inhabitants:

> Indeed there is nothing else to justify it. [The population decline in the census returns, after emigration was taken into account] either in the geographical position of the towns, which are in the midst of a great agricultural district, diversified by hills, valleys and lakes, and where rude health ought to hold dominion, nor in the occupations pursued by the inhabitants themselves, which unlike those in numerous manufacturing towns throughout England, are rather conducive to longevity than otherwise.[42]

The article ended by concluding that the areas of the towns where the impoverished resided must have been in a very poor condition and that the sanitary '*evil must be superlatively dominant.*'[43]

At the start of the 1870s the matter of expanding the municipal sewerage system came up for discussion on a number of occasions. Described as one of '*the prime essentials of mid-Victorian sanitary improvement*' a modern sewerage system in the town was considered fundamental to the improvement of the town's sanitary state.[44] The main reason for so many discussions appears to have been that there was no overall plan for the building of the sewerage system. The contractor who was carrying out the work returned to the Town Commissioners repeatedly to clarify where they wished the sewers to begin and

39 *The Dublin Builder*, Vol. IV, June 1, 1862, no.59, (Dublin, 1862).
40 Ibid.
41 Ibid.
42 Ibid.
43 Ibid.
44 Best, Geoffrey, *Mid-Victorian Britain 1851-75* (London, 1979), p.68.

terminate. In July of 1870 a ruling made at a meeting of the Commissioners stated that the job of building the new sewers would go out to tender. At the same meeting it was decided that the sewers that already existed in the region of St. Peter's Port and Excise Street, on the west side of the town, were to be repaired.[45] Two months later at another meeting of the Commissioners, the chairman told the contractor upon his enquiry regarding the positioning of the sewer, that he should '*run*' it as far as a local yard for he had seen '*...drainage from the yard coming out on the footpath.*'[46]

The haphazard way in which the Town Commissioners and their predecessors approached the issue of the town's public hygiene problems can be seen to persist all through the Victorian period. There are numerous examples of repairs not being carried out, with unsatisfactory explanations being given in most cases. For example the residents of Strand Street, which led to the river, had petitioned the Town Commissioners on a number of occasions to repair the sewer outside their houses. The explanation as to why the work was not carried out was that the member of the commissioners whose job it was to pass on this information to the contractor had been unable to meet him, and thus the job was left undone.[47]

Twenty years after the Famine, when times were considered far better, the condition of the streets in Athlone had apparently not improved. '*Insufficient cleansing*' of the streets was highlighted at a meeting of the Town Commissioners where the purchase of a second scavenger cart was proposed. One member stated that the streets were in a scandalous state the previous Sunday after the market on the Saturday. The transport of animals through the town to the fair green was responsible for most of the deposits. That the streets should be cleaned on Sundays in the future was mooted, an idea that was rejected at a later meeting.[48] The footpaths in the town were said to be '*...so dirty and greasy that it was with difficulty a pedestrian could keep his feet*'.[49] The Sanitary Inspector had been informed of the problem, as it was his job to enforce the bye-laws that dealt with the cleansing of streets.[50] The main communication routes again became the subject of an editorial in a local paper, which descried the lack of action and the current position in which people coming through the town found themselves:

We feel compelled to again call attention to the dilapidated state into

45 *W.I.*, 9 July 1870.
46 *W.I.*, 17 Sep 1870.
47 *W.I.*, 8 Oct 1870.
48 *W.I.*, 10 Dec 1870.
49 *W.I.*, 19 Nov 1870.
50 Ibid.

which the roadway of this bridge has been allowed to lapse by the neglect of those (county officials, grand jurors or contractors, we cannot tell which) to whom it has been entrusted. During the past week upwards of thirty yards of the roadway has been covered by a sheet of water of from 2 to 6 inches in depth; the centre of the road being several inches below the level of the channels constructed to carry off the water. Several of the roadways in the vicinity appear to be equally neglected. In one instance, upwards of one hundred yards of a footway was ripped up some four months since, so as to render it impassable, and has been allowed to remain in that state ever since. Considering the large amount of county cess levied off the town, we think we are deserving of a little more consideration at the hands of the county.[51]

Within the garrison on the west of the town a Sanitary Board had been established to deal with the health and safety of the troops stationed there and the board offered its assistance to the Town Commissioners if they required it.[52] They were never taken up on their offer. The problem of flooding on the bridge was brought to the attention of the Town Commissioners at a meeting in February of 1871, with the explanation given that the run–offs were too high and the water could not drain away. The Town Clerk pointed out that it was the duty of the Grand Juries of both Westmeath and Roscommon to deal with any such problems.[53] The blurring of the lines between the responsibilities of Town Commissioners and the Grand Juries is very confusing during this period and very much a subjective issue. It appears that the Town Commissioners could resurface roads but not repair them by digging them up, though this is not certain. The lack of planning when it came to the sewerage infrastructure was again shown to cause serious problems when it was revealed that the sewage from the workhouse was flowing directly into the river at too northerly a point.[54] When it flowed south it met the proposed outlet for sewage from Church Street, all of which then flowed towards the area where bakers extracted water for their steam ovens.[55]

The bureaucratic problems, highlighted by the Town Clerk, that appeared to be preventing any effective action being taken in relation to cleansing the town's streets was made clear by a letter from the Grand Jury. The jurors stated that the Town Commissioners were not to sanction any upgrading work on the streets without the Jury's approval, which could be received by holding a presentment meeting. In reaction

51 *W.I.*, 21 Jan 1871.
52 *W.I.*, 4 Feb 1871.
53 Ibid.
54 *W.I.*, 11 Feb 1871.
55 *W.I.*, 25 Feb 1871.

to the letter the Town Commissioners stated that the Grand Jury was neglecting the most seriously affected parts of the town, and even when the Commissioners would finance the work themselves the Jury would not allow it.[56] The aggravation caused in local authority circles by the state of the streets led to a visit by the County Surveyor to Athlone in April 1871. He was shocked by the state in which he found the town and wanted furnished, for his perusal, all the plans that had been drawn up with regard to sewer construction. He stated that he would revisit the town in the near future. In another example of tension, a member of the Town Commissioners wondered if the County Surveyor had a right to interfere with the running of the works, whilst another condemned him for only visiting the town once throughout his tenure.[57]

A sanitary report carried out by a number of individuals independent of the Town Commissioners was read at a subsequent meeting with the town, especially the Connacht side, being described in less than glowing terms: '...*several of the lanes and alleys on the Connaught side of the town particularly...were in a filthy state, manure, mire, and night soil lying in heaps upon the street*.'[58] The town's Sanitary Inspector contradicted the evidence in the report, stating that the streets mentioned were in the best condition he had seen them in, in quite some time, though this was not necessarily a statement of good progress. He was directed to again explore all of the relevant streets and report back to the commissioners.[59] In his subsequent report, he stated that the lanes were revisited and found to be '*in a fair state*'. The chairman however, did not appear convinced and recommended that a member of the board accompany the inspector on his next rounds.[60] The lack of a positive work ethic on the part of the Sanitary Inspector seems at this point in Athlone's history, to be the most criticised aspect of the town's sanitation problems, though one must be aware of the possibility that he was being used as a scapegoat. This could be true, for when a Poor Law inspector visited Athlone he recommended that an inspector be installed independently of the Town Commissioners, who, he believed, may not have been providing the necessary backup needed by the Sanitary Inspector.[61] The problems that had been encountered with the Municipal Corporations in Ireland, certainly made many in government wary of local authorities, which were seen as requiring monitoring. In

56 *W.I.*, 11 Mar 1871.
57 *W.I.*, 1 Apr 1871.
58 *W.I.*, 8 Apr 1871.
59 Ibid.
60 *W.I.*, 15 Apr 1871.
61 *W.I.*, 29 Apr 1871.

a full-length report issued by the inspector, one Dr. Brodie, it was stated that:

> No improvement had been made since his last visit – that the making of main sewers had been discontinued, and that in no case had proceedings been taken under the Sanitary Act to compel the occupiers of houses to connect their premises with the main sewers – that several of the back lanes were still in a filthy and disgraceful state.[62]

He went further to recommend that the current Sanitary Inspector be dismissed due to the fact that the man was a full-time publican who obviously was unable to attend to the tasks that the job required. Surprisingly, Brodie told the Commissioners that generally the town was in the cleanest state he had ever seen it in (this may be a relative statement) and that if the sewer system were extended in a correct way the situation would improve to an even greater degree.[63] Subsequent to Dr. Brodie's inspection, a number of '*nuisances*' were rectified – he had sent letters to the owners of certain buildings threatening legal action if they did not comply with the local bye-laws. Connections from a number of residences to the main system were put in place and one man received a fine for throwing filthy water out onto the street. Also the body of a dead pig was removed from the front of a school and buried.[64]

Again it should be pointed out that the situation in Athlone was not unique. An article on Mullingar stated that the thoroughfares of that town were in '*a most unfavourable state*'.[65] There was even a threat that the army men stationed there would be removed, such was the level of filth present. The Town Commissioners for Mullingar were heavily criticised for their inaction, though, as already stated, they only had authority for the cleansing of the streets and limited responsibility for resurfacing them. It must also be noted, however, that they had but one Grand Jury to deal with whereas Athlone had two. The article goes on to state that the town should have been one of the healthiest places in the country due to its geographical location but that the condition of the town was one that was capable and predisposed to '*...harbour and develop the germs of infection*.'[66]

At a meeting of Athlone's Town Commissioners, it was decided that an experiment was to be attempted: the area in front of the municipal gasworks and Town Hall (ensuring their own comfort of course) was to be asphalted with a view to extending the measure to the rest of the

62 *W.I.*, 13 May 1871.
63 Ibid.
64 *W.I.*, 27 May 1871.
65 *W.I.*, 30 Sep 1871.
66 Ibid.

town.[67] Towards the end of 1871, the Sanitary Inspector appeared to have either been replaced or become more work-conscious, as he stated that the contractor with responsibility for removing filth had to keep the quantities being removed high or face a summons. A scavenger was also reprimanded for sweeping filth into the offshoot channels of the streets instead of removing it completely.[68] The Town Commissioners however did not appear to be entirely in favour of continued investment in the streets and withdrew funds for a new walkway in Castlemaine Street after their experiment had concluded.[69]

The Local Government Act 1872 was intended to assist local authorities in sanitation and infrastructure in towns and cities. Supplementary to all related existing acts, the most useful element of the legislation was that the Town Commissioners could: '...*transfer to themselves the powers of the Grand Jury as regards roads, bridges, footpaths or public works; or to increase the rates for the purpose of defraying the expense of such transfer.*'[70] However, it was not applied to Athlone for one main reason – it required the co-operation of the Grand Juries in passing their powers to the Town Commissioners, something they were unwilling to do. So even after another piece of legislation had been approved, the situation remained the same.

The state of the streets did not improve by the next year, with numerous complaints coming into the Town Commissioners who, one ratepayer believed, as already noted in a previous chapter, had their attention turned to national issues that were not really their concern.[71] It is possible that ratepayers had, due to improved communications and transport, quite a good idea of the standards in England and elsewhere, and this changed their notion of acceptable standards in sanitation.[72] Another account from November 1873, when the dire state of the town was mentioned yet again, dealt with the contractor who was censured for neglecting his duty.[73] This complaint led to the Town Commissioners in turn complaining to the County Surveyor about the contractor. The almost constant friction between all the local authority figures and bodies worsened when the report they received exonerated the contractor.[74] *The Westmeath Independent*, incredulous at the state of the streets and in the actions of the contractor set forth their views that

67 *W.I.*, 18 Nov 1871.
68 *W.I.*, 23 Dec 1871.
69 *W.I.*, 30 Dec 1871.
70 *W.I.*, 14 Oct 1871.
71 *W.I.*, 24 May 1873.
72 Kennedy, L & Clarkson, L. A., p.166.
73 *W.I.*, 8 Nov 1873.
74 Ibid.

the surveyor had found:

> What no other person could...that the streets were perfect. He would
> need Mr Weller's "fourteen hundred power pair of spectacles" to be able
> to see anything but the most ill-constructed, woe-begone, worn out,
> neglected set of streets that ever disgraced the meanest country village.
> We state emphatically that the streets of Athlone are worn out to the very
> sole, and now, as we write, the foundation layers are visible through the
> leading streets of Athlone, on the Westmeath side of the town...The
> ratepayers...are deserving of more than curt, unsatisfactory epistles from
> county officials.[75]

The paper went on to say that it would champion the cause but that it
had faith in the Town Commissioners to do the job properly! The next
meeting of the Commissioners may have dampened the trust that the
paper seemed to have in them, as one member believed that the streets
were in no need of immediate improvement, whilst another believed
the lanes of the town to be in such a state as to be unfit for human
habitation.[76] The inability of the Town Commissioners to agree led to
more delays in improvements with the differences in opinion appearing
irreconcilable. Interestingly, the opinion of the County Surveyor did not
remain the same regarding the problem of sanitation and cleanliness in
Athlone – the information he gave at a Grand Jury meeting in
Mullingar contradicted that which he had imparted to the
Commissioners. He said that a contract for the improvement of the
streets had been much delayed and that was the reason for the current
state of the streets, which he did not describe as satisfactory.[77] The
editorial in *The Westmeath Independent* from October 3rd, 1874 again
outlined the status of the town's sewers as well as its opinion on the
people in charge:

> The inhabitants of Athlone breathe as pure an atmosphere as can be
> found in any midland town in the country; but we see by a statement
> made by the Chairman of the Town Commissioners at one of their
> deliberations, that the water of the Shannon is polluted by a sewer
> running from the workhouse, that it is of the most poisonous
> decomposition, and slowly enters the river above the point at which the
> water is taken for domestic use by the poor inhabitants of the town.
>
> We regret to say that there are a few who obstruct the legitimate
> business by indulging in the pastime of questing in search of those
> imaginary nurseries, commonly called 'mares nests' and who, like all
> hobby-horse riders are little good for any other occupation.[78]

75 Ibid.
76 *W.I.*, 10 Jan 1874.
77 *W.I.*, 28 Feb 1874.
78 *W.I.*, 3 Oct 1874.

The Public Health Act (Ireland) 1874 was another attempt to legislate for the tendencies of the population to befoul their own towns and villages. This act was the precursor of the legislation that is in place in Ireland today, and reinforces the idea that modern Irish society was influenced by Victorian practices and values. One historian has noted that the 1870s and onwards are *'in touch with our world'*: the modernisation, plans, reforms and changes all have a resonance in the twentieth century.[79]

The Secretary of the Local Government Board, who would ensure the introduction of the act at local level, said that its main objectives were to make it possible for all inhabitants of the island to *'...enjoy the privilege of drinking pure water and...of breathing pure air.'*[80] Under the act a nation-wide network of sanitary authorities was created, those towns with a population over 6,000 were given an Urban Sanitary Authority and those with less than 6,000 received the title Rural Sanitary Authority.[81] Athlone, with a population of over 6,000, was eligible to have the powers of the former and these were vested in the Town Commissioners. In the act the appointment of more Sanitary Officers and Sub-Officers was deemed necessary to deal with the problems being faced by Irish urban centres. As well this, the provisions of earlier legislation such as the Towns Improvement Act were built upon.

Even with the new act in place the streets of the town showed no improvement. There were numerous articles and meetings dealing with the deplorable state in which they were perpetually to be found. A letter from a *'Suffering Ratepayer'* outlined what they saw as the failings of the Commissioners when it came to the implementation of the Public Health Act. They believed that none of the provisions in the act had been put in place, be it the steps for water purification or the regulations as regards the keeping of animals. The author says that *'If our municipal body did its duty there would be few deaths by measles, scarlatina, small pox and typhus fever.'*[82] The local press believed that the Town Commissioners needed to install more water pumps in the town to ensure that its inhabitants were not forced to drink from a polluted river.[83]

Apart from the problems with drinking water, those associated with simply walking around the town were still extant. The installation of *'footways'* in Connacht Street was mentioned at a meeting of the Town Commissioners in January 1876 and a mason was employed to do the

79 Wilson, A. N., p.352.
80 *W.I.*, 3 Oct 1874.
81 Roche, Desmond, p.36.
82 *W.I.*, 20 Feb 1874.
83 *W.I.*, 3 Oct 1874.

work.[84] As with many of the jobs commissioned by the local authority, it was not fully and professionally implemented, and only three weeks later it was believed that having a path on one side of the street was sufficient.[85]

A commission of inquiry mainly dealing with taxation and sanitation was held in the town in November 1876 and received evidence as to the sanitary state of Athlone. Apparently there were only five cases of fever in the previous three years, the water supply was good and the streets clean and well kept.[86] The evidence given may not have been reliable and was certainly not impartial – a copy of the minutes of the meeting in a local newspaper showed that the chief informant was the Town Clerk who, one can assume, would not paint a picture of incompetence on behalf of either himself or his colleagues.[87]

It was perhaps out of desperation or possibly in an attempt to shirk responsibility that the Town Commissioners sent a deputation to meet a member of the Shannon Commissioners in September 1877. They wished to convince the latter Commissioners that it was their responsibility to mend the footpaths of the town that bordered the river and their offices.[88] It is unlikely they succeeded. The year 1878 was to be a better financial one for the Town Commissioners. They received a grant of £1,314 for sewerage works in the town – the period of repayment was thirty years at 5% interest.[89] The last sewerage works prior to this were carried out in 1873.[90]

The government, perhaps recognising that the Public Health 1874 Act was not accomplishing all that they had hoped, enacted an updated version in 1878, which provided a more contemporary approach to sanitation in the country.[91] Bad food could be destroyed, slaughterhouses subjected to inspections and those people who were obviously affected by diseases such as cholera could be quarantined.[92] The Irish public health acts, as in the case of many acts passed in Ireland, were based on previously enacted legislation from Britain. In general many of the acts were the same with certain aspects tailored to be more easily applicable in Ireland.

In March of 1879 a meeting of the Town Commissioners was almost wholly dedicated to the question of the town's roads. Apparently '*many*

84 *W.I.*, 29 Jan 1876.
85 *W.I.*, 19 Feb 1876.
86 *F.J.*, 17 Nov 1876.
87 *W.I.*, 18 Nov 1876.
88 *W.I.*, 29 Sep 1877.
89 *W.I.*, 7 May 1878.
90 *W.I.*, 18 Nov 1876.
91 Roche, Desmond, p.36.
92 Wiley, Miriam M., p.54.

heaps of manure' were to be seen on a number of streets, with the usefulness of the scavenger's horse being analysed.[93] Many other Victorian towns in England appeared to have had the same problems as Athlone when it came to animal waste: '*Strangers coming from the country frequently described the streets as smelling of dung like a stable yard.*'[94] Later in the same year the town bridge was still reported as holding water, eight years after a similar complaint had been lodged, and many commented that the ratepayers were not getting value for their money from their local authorities.[95] The fact that the public health situation did not appear to be improving to any great extent must be seen as an indictment of the local government systems that were in place. Constant wrangling between the Grand Jury, whose elite members probably resented having to deal with other 'lesser' local bodies, and the Town Commissioners retarded the development of Athlone's infrastructure. Despite legislation there appeared in the case of Athlone to be a genuine lack of initiative when it came to implementing improvements in the town's infrastructure.

Improvements in public health in urban areas were realised in the United Kingdom as a whole in the later 19th century because of the investment in infrastructure; the Victorians aspired to achieving '*a healthy and civilised urban society.*'[96] Between 1850 and 1900 investment in utilities rose by a factor of ten and eventually Irish towns did see the benefit of this.[97]

By the 1880s however, it appears that the investment in sanitary maintenance was, according to the returns for Athlone Union, quite insubstantial, with just £400 loaned for the year to August in 1880. Conversely the amount of money loaned to landlords was £15,880 for improvements to, and the upgrading of, their properties.[98] The lack of funding caused the level of complaints made about the state of the town to remain constant during the following year, with bad drainage and nuisance build-up at Connacht Street mentioned, as well as the filthy approaches to a number of the town's churches, decried.[99] The issue of responsibility for the cleansing of the streets was discussed at a Christmas session of the Town Commissioners in 1881. The County Surveyor, who answered to the Grand Jury, believed that before he could repair the streets they had to be cleaned, with the commissioners

93 *W.I.*, 1 Mar 1879.
94 Wohl, Anthony S., p.81.
95 *W.I.*, 28 June 1879.
96 Daunton, Martin, p.64.
97 Ibid.
98 *F.J.*, 16 Aug 1880.
99 *W.I.*, 10 Dec 1881, *W.I.*, 24 Dec 1881.

believing the cleaning to be part of the fixing process i.e. his responsibility.[100] Writing retrospectively of Athlone in the 1880s, Rosabel Sara Langrishe believed:

> Athlone always seemed to be muddy. The paths were a degree better than the roads as they had only about half an inch of mud, compared with at least two inches on the latter. The result was that on Sunday afternoons everyone went for a walk on the railway, quite as a matter of course. Even that was muddy at the sides, and then one had to walk on the track itself.[101]

Ms. Langrishe noted that the only place where one could have a 'mudless' walk near the town was at the fortifications on the west side known as the Batteries, which later became the venue for Athlone's first golf course.[102] It was not until the 1890s that a promenade was created between the river and the barracks and Athlone's inhabitants had an animal-free area on which to stroll.[103]

In Athlone towards the end of 1881 the Town Commissioners continued to complain about the County Surveyor. They believed that he never visited the town at all and that the knowledge of the town that he had must have been acquired through '*inspiration*'.[104] The work ethic of the town scavengers was questioned again at a meeting in July of 1882, when they were apparently not visiting, at any time, a number of streets in the town where the filth was '*ankle deep*'. The lack of movement on contracted works to improve the sewerage system was also mentioned, with the surveyor asked why the work had not commenced.[105]

During the summer and autumn of 1883 it appeared that contagious diseases were again present in Athlone, and when a Court of Law Commission deemed the town too unhealthy to stage appeal hearings, they instead moved to Roscommon.[106] Later in the year the first prosecution of a man who waked his dead child was carried out – the child had died of an infectious disease and the proper precautions against its spread had not been taken.[107] The portion of the rates that was to be spent on the sanitation of the town for 1885 was 10d from every £1. The money was to be put to use by the new Sub-Sanitary Officer who was appointed in February of that year, under a provision in the

100 *W.I.*, 24 Dec 1881.
101 Langrishe, Rosabel, p.177.
102 Ibid., p.179.
103 Horn, Pamela, p.12.
104 *W.I.*, 31 Dec 1881.
105 *W.I.*, 22 July 1882.
106 *F.J.*, 23 May 1883.
107 *F.J.*, 3 Sep 1883.

Public Health Act 1878.[108] The berating of the town scavengers
continued unabated and one, who was presumably fed up with being
criticised, foully cursed his critics at a Town Commissioners meeting
and was subsequently removed from his post.[109] In actuality the general
sentiment when dealing with the scavengers was invariably the same,
with the condition of one street blamed almost entirely on the
scavengers' indolence:

> The condition of the street is a scandal and it would require a cart - whip
> to get those employed on the streets to do the work properly. It ought
> not be necessary to have a ganger over these men to do their so-called
> work properly. The names of High Street and Queen Street are given as
> the worst and most neglected streets.[110]

The importation of Chinese labourers to do the job of cleaning the
streets was suggested at the meeting where the above sentiments were
voiced, for it was believed that the Chinese were famous for doing their
work properly.[111] Though this may have been tongue in cheek no doubt
news of the progression of the rail network in America at the time
provided some information on the aptitude of the Chinese for labour-
intensive work. The lack of progress in the cleansing of the streets was
again highlighted in December 1887 when a member of the
Commissioners stated:

> Only fancy once you pass the house of Mr John Walsh you must either
> go back a distance or go to the end of the street before you can cross to
> the opposite side without sinking to your ankles in the gutter…High St.,
> we presume has been given up by the scavengers as hopeless.[112]

The inefficient way in which the commissioners handled the
problems with the streets was the basis of a prank where a local
advertised on the commissioners' behalf for twelve strong boys to clean
the streets. A large number arrived at the Town Hall seeking
employment; they were turned away.[113] The outbreak of Typhus Fever
in the town during the year 1888 caused the fever hospital nurse to state
that she was overworked. In addition to this, the quarantine was also
quite ineffective, for a number of people were climbing over the walls
of the building to visit relatives.[114] This type of outbreak coupled with
an earlier one in 1883 shows that the provisions of the Public Health

108 *F.J.*, 7 Feb 1885.
109 *F.J.*, 5 Nov 1887.
110 *F.J.*, 19 Nov 1887.
111 Ibid.
112 *F.J.*, 17 Dec 1887.
113 *F.J.*, 26 May 1888.
114 *F.J.*, 14 July 1888.

Acts were not being implemented in the town; again a lack of motivation in local authority circles appears to be to blame.

A letter dated January 4th, 1890 characterised Athlone's current reputation, which appeared to be unchanged from that of sixty years previously:

> Athlone has become ill-famed for its filthy and neglected streets, and the travellers who pass through the town, forced to walk through our characteristically mucky thoroughfares and involuntarily sniff the unpleasant (sometimes disgusting) odours from our stagnant sewers and channels, can hardly be blamed for spreading still wider our unenviable public reputation.

The author clainmed that a standard encyclopaedia described Athlone as '…*a small dirty town on the banks of the Shannon.*'[115]

The contentions between the contractors and the Town Commissioners continued unabated. The latter attempted to lay all of the blame for the problems with the roads in the town at the feet of the contractor and made a statement to that effect:

> We believe there is no town in Ireland more 'humbugged' by the road contractors than Athlone. All the parties concerned should be brought to a sense of their duties to the heavily-taxed inhabitants of the town.[116]

The state of the streets and infrastructure was even ridiculed at the first public showing of 'Edison's Wonderful Talking Machine' or Phonograph, which took place in Athlone in November 1891. A local priest who was asked to speak into the machine said, '…*we are going to have the streets properly cleaned and then the waterworks*' much to the amusement of a portion of the crowd.[117] After being discussed at a number of meetings during the previous two decades, a second watering cart for the town was eventually purchased in May 1892, costing £33.[118]

In early 1893 the Town Commissioners started a process through which they would acquire the total control of street maintenance from the Grand Jury. The matter was left in the hands of the Local Government Board whose decision required the establishment of another enquiry, which the Victorians appeared to love just as much as statistical compilations.[119] In the summer of 1894 it was reported that the Town Commissioners had, after years of struggle, gained control

---

115 "Miscellanea", in *Journal of the Old Athlone Society*, Vol. II, No.5 (Athlone, 1985), p.75.
116 *FJ.*, 2 Feb 1889.
117 *FJ.*, 28 Nov 1891.
118 *FJ.*, 14 May 1892.
119 *FJ.*, 14 Jan 1893.

over the streets of Athlone.[120] Now they had the opportunity to improve the town's infrastructure as they saw fit.

As was happening elsewhere in the United Kingdom, the need for the public to inform themselves of their duties in regard to health and hygiene was recognised in the town; a meeting dealing with hygiene was held in Longworth Hall and was well attended.[121]

Despite obvious local support for serious improvements in the cleanliness of the town, the addition of the second water cart did not see a marked improvement in the roads. Again the scavengers were blamed and a member of the Commissioners reasoned that if they did not do their jobs their wages should be reduced. Luckily for the scavengers, a vote on the topic saw the resolution defeated.[122]

The year 1895 witnessed the completion of the sewerage and waterworks system, which it was hoped would solve a number of the town's problems. Completed by a local contractor, the job had taken over two years to finish, and was the last major investment by the Town Commissioners in local infrastructure prior to their dissolution.[123] Typhus fever re-emerged near Athlone during the summer of 1897 though it does not seem to have entered the town; perhaps the improvements in local sanitation guarded against this.[124] In late 1897, new bye-laws were adopted by the Town Commissioners dealing with drainage of buildings, scavenging and cleaning, keeping of animals, common lodging houses and slaughterhouses.[125] Yet, as seen previously, the adoption of new laws was not always followed by the enforcement of them.

In 1899, when the Urban District Council (UDC) replaced the Town Commissioners, the problems that had persisted previously still arose. In October of that year, the UDC decided that the cleaning contractors for the town were to be prosecuted for their bad work.[126] The scavengers were causing problems in the poorer parts of the town by not emptying ash pits and privies. They were obliged to do this for the UDC tenants but not for anyone else – the council was split as to whether a fee was to be charged to non-tenants or whether they should just empty their own privies.[127] The bye-laws that were adopted by the Town Commissioners a few years previously were not being enforced. A councillor complained that pigs were being raised beside his house

120 *F.J.*, 16 Nov 1894.
121 *F.J.*, 26 Jan 1895.
122 *F.J.*, 31 Aug 1895.
123 O'Brien, Municipal, p.86.
124 *F.J.*, 29 May 1897.
125 *F.J.*, 20 Oct 1897.
126 *F.J.*, 28 Oct 1899.
127 *A.I.*, 14 Apr 1900.

when no animals were allowed to be within fifty feet of a dwelling.[128] It was certain that any reforms would take time before they were fully adopted by locals.

With the gradual shift from rural to urban life came an adjustment period in which people became accustomed to the differences between their former lives in the country and their new lives in towns and cities. Athlone was a town that was bounded on all sides by agricultural lands with many farmers taking advantage of the rich alluvial soil that was deposited by the River Shannon. Many former country people would bring their animals with them when they moved into towns creating an impression that:

> The Victorian town would strike us as an incongruous mixture of urbanity and barnyard setting, with townhouses interspersed with stables, pigsties and slaughterhouses, and where sheep and cows jostled with horse traffic, and pigs and chickens dwelt in close proximity with human inhabitants.[129]

The same type of sentiment was expressed by Mary Banim who believed that the Athlone Market was a place where the mixture of '*town and country*' could be witnessed.[130] This mix could have slowed down the implementation of sanitary reforms. The people who moved into Athlone may have seen little wrong with the 'barnyard setting' that was a Victorian town. They were used to the mixing of people and livestock, and if it was not a problem for them why would they try to remedy it?

A sanitary report from November 1901 confirms that almost all of the problems that handicapped the town throughout the Victorian era were still present by the end of it, though perhaps not on the same scale. The report stated that the entire sewerage system needed to be improved and that slaughterhouses in the town were filthy, with heaps of manure in the yards beside the animals being prepared for slaughter. The fluids from the same slaughterhouses were entering the main sewer system. The streets were said to be in satisfactory condition given the weather, though in a separate article in the paper a member of the UDC reported that a lane in the town was '*in awful condition*' due to people dumping their rubbish there at night time.[131] In keeping with the state of towns all over the United Kingdom, Athlone did not see a considerable reduction in the levels of manure on the streets until the spread of the motorised car which reduced the need to use animals to transport people and stock.[132]

128 *A.I.*, 5 May 1900.
129 Wohl, Anthony S., p.82.
130 Banim, Mary, p.244.
131 *A.I.*, 23 Nov 1901.
132 Wohl, Anthony S., p.85.

INTRODUCTION OF GAS

One of the most important advances during the Victorian era was the introduction of gas. Municipal improvements were of course a very important ingredient of the Victorian era, and the advances in illumination would certainly have been welcomed by the inhabitants as an obvious improvement. In England and Wales the illumination of towns using gas became widespread during the 1830s and 1840s, though this level was not reached in Ireland until later.[133]

The initial phase of lighting in Athlone was, as was the norm of the time, the establishment of a committee in 1851. The members were to meet to decide on how to light the town in the most efficient way, i.e. which streets were to have gas lighting.[134] Their deliberations must have taken well over two years as the contractor who was hired to design and draw up specifications for the proposed Gasworks did not start work until November 1853.[135] Gas power was one of the most important innovations of the Victorian era. The lamps powered by gas lit up towns and houses, a beacon for progress that Athlone would need if it were to improve. When the works were finished the price that was fixed for the provision of gas to houses was to be 10/- per thousand cubic feet.[136] The Gasworks were later to house the Town Commissioners meetings and the site manager's dwelling in 1864 at a cost of £520; the meetings were held on one floor and the manager lived on the other.[137]

The job of maintaining and lighting the lamps was given, by appointment from the Town Commissioners, to a man entitled 'The Lamplighter'. The work ethic of successive lamplighters, like that of the scavengers, did not appear to be the best, since a number of examples of their dereliction of duty were noted at numerous Town Commissioners meetings, the most common problem being the non–lighting of certain lamps.[138]

The extension of lighting to various parts of the town did continue throughout the Victorian period though local reports suggested that the reasons for erecting some lamps were based more on the route taken by certain Commissioners on their way to meetings rather than the convenience of the town's inhabitants.[139] Gas was also extended, soon after its introduction, to the religious houses with St Mary's Church of

133 Murphy, Brian, *A History of the British Economy 1740-1970* (London, 1973), p.593.
134 *W.I.*, 11 Jan 1851.
135 *W.I.*, 19 Nov 1853.
136 *W.I.*, 5 Aug 1854.
137 *W.I.*, 12 Nov 1864.
138 *W.I.*, 18 Nov 1871.
139 *W.I.*, 16 Dec 1871, *W.I.*, 2 May 1874.

Ireland church being the first to receive it.[140] Ranelagh School received gas in 1879, but the supply did not reach the local courthouse until 1901.[141] Houses in Britain, including those of the working classes, had the option of gas by the 1890s when the slot meter was installed in many homes, although Ireland and Athlone were lagging behind somewhat.[142] The barracks had it own gas supply; they apparently made it more cheaply than the Town Commissioners.[143]

Maintenance of the town supply and of the lamps, along with many other municipal utilities, was not approached in a professional manner, either by the gas works manager or the Town Commissioners. During the summer of 1874, a report stated that thirteen lamps were useless, fifteen required repair, the gas-works had to be updated and a coal supplier had to be found due to the low levels of fuel remaining.[144] The cavalier attitude of those managing the gas supply was well illustrated by a decision, in January 1877, not to fix a lamp on the town bridge due to bad weather; instead the repairs would be carried out in the summer.[145]

The problems with the management of the gasworks had not been set right by the end of the 19th century for, in 1896, they again ran out of coal and hence produced no gas, a state which persisted, on and off, for over a week.[146] The lack of reliability of gas supply nationally was one of the reasons behind the formation of the Shannon Electrical Power Syndicate in 1898 which inquired into the possibility of utilising the river as a source of power generation.[147]

William Smith of the Athlone Woollen Mills commented on the poor supply of gas in Athlone in November 1900. He was seeking compensation for losses from the Urban District Council for the '...*inferior description of the gas and limitation of the supply.*'[148] The Gasworks were considered very dated by 1901 when an explosion helped ensure that updating took place sooner rather than later.[149] Upgrading work carried out during the tenure of the Town Commissioners was deemed an unnecessary waste of money according to a report commissioned by their successor the UDC. Their report recommended that the entire facility needed to be upgraded, at a cost of £3,800.[150]

140 *W.I.*, 11 Feb 1860.
141 *W.I.*, 8 Feb 1879, *A.T.*, 17 Aug 1901.
142 Daunton, Martin, p.58.
143 *W.I.*, 24 June 1882.
144 *W.I.*, 6 June 1874.
145 *W.I.*, 13 Jan 1877.
146 *F.J.*, 11 Jan 1896, *F.J.*, 18 Jan 1896.
147 *F.J.*, 8 Oct 1898.
148 *A.T.*, 3 Nov 1900.
149 *A.T.*, 22 June 1901.
150 O'Brien, Municipal, p.87.

Generally towns in the United Kingdom were seen to be improving by the end of the Victorian period for they were '…*a source of civic pride, the centre of new patterns of consumption and a symbol of modernity, of fractured identities and endless possibilities*'.[151] From the 1870s onwards death rates had begun to fall though it was not until the end of the century that '…*sanitation in English cities was at all what it should have been*.'[152] By 1901 the government's urban health strategy had led to a far higher life expectancy for people living in urban areas in England and Wales, indeed it was equal to that of country people.[153] Diseases such as cholera were no longer seen in Britain's major cities due to the investment in sewerage systems.[154] Ireland, however, did not witness the same decline in mortality rates that were witnessed in Britain; between 1891 and 1901 the death rate fell by 25% in Britain and only by 4% in Ireland. The older population that had to remain in Ireland when younger people emigrated was one factor in this, but so too were the poor conditions in which many lived, especially in urban areas to which many had migrated during the Victorian period.[155]

Despite excessively protracted implementation periods Victorian public health reforms appeared to be showing dividends four years after the end of the era. Even though *Black's Guide to Galway, Connemara and the West of Ireland* may have seen Athlone as '*dull and unpicturesque in appearance*' it noted how recent local efforts had really improved the town's state of cleanliness.[156]

> The neatness and cleanliness of this, compared with many other Irish towns, will appeal to visitors as much as the smoothness of the streets will give the cyclist pleasure. In one respect Athlone has few equals in western towns of the country.[157]

There is no doubt that the implementation of new schemes for improvement in public health in Athlone was haphazard at best. The condition of the streets was never spoken of in glowing terms and only on very few occasions were they described as satisfactory. The wrangling between the different local authorities was without doubt to blame in part for the condition, although even if there had not been a perceived overlap in jurisdiction success in implementation would not have been

---

151 Daunton, Martin, p.65.
152 Trevelyan, G.M., p.129.
153 Ibid.
154 Ibid.
155 Kennedy, L & Clarkson, L. A., p.171.
156 Lang, R. T., (Ed.), *Black's Guide to Galway, Connemara and the West of Ireland 19th ed.* (London, 1905), p.195.
157 Ibid., p.196.

certain. Modernising the town's infrastructure was an almost constant struggle. On the positive side Athlone did gain more modern and useful infrastructure during the Victorian period. A sewerage system was built, roads were improved in parts of the town and the water supply was also modernised. The town was certainly a healthier place in 1901 than in 1837. Necessity and experience had taught people to become more aware of the need for better hygiene and to implement better safeguards against the spread of disease.

The arrival of municipal lighting schemes during the Victorian era was an inescapable indicator of change in both Britain and Ireland. Illuminated streets, houses and public buildings showed to good effect the advantages of modernising and improving existing facilities and infrastructure. The creation of the gasworks and a gas supply was, along with other public utilities, dealt with poorly by the local authorities. However, perhaps the residents would have been able to appreciate in the spread of gas across the town a tangible effect of the modernisation for which the Victorian era was famed.

CHAPTER 9

Leisure, entertainment and temperance in Victorian Athlone

As the Victorian era progressed the economic and social changes that were experienced began to reshape how people spent their time. New machinery meant that jobs became less labour-intensive and took less time to accomplish. More and more people were becoming part of a regulated workforce that worked only for a set number of hours in the day; cottage industries and farming, which were full-time jobs in every sense, were gradually employing fewer people. The better economic security offered by full-time employment meant that people could actually spend time and money developing their hobbies without worrying about more basic concerns such as providing food for their families.

It has been noted that during the Victorian era there was '...*in every town and city of any size...the crystallising of a cultural apparatus providing for every level of community*.'[1] Leisure time was a void that had to be filled, and the Victorian mind visualised a number of activities that would allow them to do just that. Indeed, *'ready-made leisure'* was to account for a rise in the popularity of the arts, sports and even shopping towards the end of the Victorian period.[2] The growth in the levels of disposable income amongst the Victorian bourgeois meant that they could create new facilities and purchase all the paraphernalia needed to participate in the new pursuits. The development of different pastimes was to permeate all levels of Victorian society; all classes recognised, at least subconsciously, the positive affect that creating clubs and societies could have in the effort to introduce positive societal changes.

RELIGIOUS AND SECULAR SOCIETIES

While many societies established in the Victorian period were secular in nature numerous others could trace their roots back to an affiliation

1 Best, Geoffrey, p.219.
2 Wilson, A. N., p.410.

with a religious denomination. The clergy of the various faiths usually saw societies as a good way to regulate the free time of the laity and with the right guidance, to ensure their maintenance of moral virtue. In some cases the societies were deemed attractive to the less frequent churchgoers and through membership one maintained a link with the church.[3]

The first major society set up in Athlone on the basis of religious affiliation was the Young Men's Christian Association or YMCA. Though the association was established earlier in other towns, plans for its foundation in Athlone had fallen by the wayside until 1852 when it was officially inaugurated in the Methodist Church.[4] The association wished to divert the attention of members away from iniquitous activities, offering a safe haven where the pressures to give into vice would not be so great. A non-Catholic organisation, the Athlone YMCA held lectures throughout the 1850s and eventually established a library at their premises in Northgate St. on the east of the town in 1860.[5] The state of the association in 1870 was said to be good when its 15th annual report was delivered. By 1871 there were almost 100 members, and the policy of '...*including men of every calling, from the humblest artisan to the aspiring statesman, from the simple ferryman to the profound philosopher*' – excluding non-Protestant denominations of course – was to ensure the continued success of the YMCA.[6]

Throughout its existence the society invited a number of speakers to its meetings to deliver lectures on various topics. It was on the issue of politics that the lectures appeared to demonstrate the polarised nature of the opinions within the YMCA. For example in the month of November 1887 the society appears to have been Loyalist and elitist. At one meeting a speaker used '*fanatical expressions*' of loyalty to the Queen, a local clergyman castigated Gladstone and the Irish party, while another, the concluding speaker, stated that the British Constitution would weather the political storm of Home Rule.[7] Later in the month a lecture entitled 'Classes and Masses' was based on the proposition that life was better when the classes made the laws instead of the masses.[8] In opposition to these views a meeting held in 1888 was told that the gap between the classes and the masses had to be bridged for the good of all people.[9] Another later in the same year also appears to contradict some

3   Horn, Pamela, p.243.
4   *A.S.*, 15 Sep 1852.
5   *W.I.*, 18 Aug 1860.
6   *W.I.*, 22 Oct 1870.
7   *F.J.*, 12 Nov 1887.
8   *F.J.*, 19 Nov 1887.
9   *F.J.*, 27 Oct 1888.

of what was said in November 1887, with the meeting espousing Home Rule as being in the interests of equality. The meeting also heard condemnation of the Orange Order in the north whose only prayer was apparently '*To Hell with the Pope*'.[10]

The construction of a YMCA hall was discussed at a meeting in 1889 with over £450 of the necessary £800 raised there and then.[11] This ability to raise considerable finances quickly shows that the members were affluent. After more fundraising efforts Longworth Hall was opened in Northgate Street in 1891.[12] Towards the end of the century the thinking of the YMCA was changing, and some very progressive ideas as regards the role of women and young men were presented at lectures.[13] The establishment of a bicycle club attached to the association occurred in 1894 due, in part, to the success of the already established Athlone Bicycle Club.[14] The tone of the YMCA could be judged as more Nationalist than Unionist by the end of the 19th century. The reaction of a crowd to a pro-union lecture given in 1895 was described as '*hostile*' particularly when it was suggested that there would be a time when Ireland would proudly take her place in the heart of the Empire.[15] By 1897 there were just eighty-nine men on the books and due to this a suggestion was made to merge the men's association with the women's, the YWCA. Even though the lectures on the role of women had been liberal, the men were not happy to put the theory into practice and the suggestion was strongly rejected.[16] The association was still in existence and flourishing to the end of the Victorian era.[17]

The first Catholic society set up with the backing of the Church was the Catholic Young Men's Association or CYMA (sometimes referred to as the Catholic Young Men's Society[18]). Originally mooted at a lecture in 1857 (probably in reaction to the YMCA), the interest was so strong that by the end of the presentation over 250 men had joined.[19] The progress made by the society was rapid with a premises in Excise Street on the west side of the town secured one month later and plans for the establishment of a reading room and library put in place.[20] By the time the annual mass was held in 1858 the numbers had swelled to 500, and

10 *FJ.*, 1 Dec 1888.
11 *FJ.*, 26 Oct 1889.
12 *FJ.*, 2 Aug 1890, *FJ.*, 10 Jan 1891.
13 *FJ.*, 31 Dec 1892.
14 *FJ.*, 4 Apr 1894.
15 *FJ.*, 2 Feb 1895.
16 *FJ.*, 6 Nov 1897.
17 *FJ.*, 31 Dec 1898, *A.T.*, 23 Mar 1901.
18 *FJ.*, 2 Sep 1858.
19 *FJ.*, 9 Sep 1857.
20 *FJ.*, 17 Oct 1857.

a band had also been established. The society promoted social events for its members, with dances held at various times under the watchful eyes of the Catholic clergy from both parishes in the town.[21] Excursions, which grew in popularity in the Victorian era, also took place, with the steamer 'Artisan' ferrying 150 members up the river to Lanesboro in the summer of 1859.[22]

The advent of the railways, as well as steamships, in Ireland was to provide for '*the great novelty*' of the Victorian era – excursions.[23] The ability to transport large numbers of people quickly and comfortably to a wide variety of destinations around Ireland was always going to be a popular idea with societies wishing to create a type of social cohesion. The trips would take people away from the familiar and banal town they lived in and show them new and exciting places.

The CYMA had a large number of lectures during the 19th century with speakers such as John Ennis MP delivering talks on diverse subjects such as 'The duty and rights of Christian Parents' and 'Historical recollections of Athlone'. The lectures were held in the rooms in Excise St. that were '*beautifully decorated*' from money garnered through fundraising initiatives.[24] The society also branched out into the field of theatre with a report in *The Freeman's Journal* detailing how they enacted Sir Walter Scott's 'Lady of the Lake' and comedy 'As Cool as a Cucumber' to a full house in June 1862.[25] The fact that the association was exclusively Catholic did not stop toasts being raised to the Queen, as occurred at the annual soirée of 1863. Other toasts included one to the Pope and another to the 'Irish Hierarchy'. The makeup of the members seemed to be those of a higher social standing, with the '*respectability*' of all those at the party commented on in a press report. The presence of a number of soldiers was also mentioned.[26] Curiously the association seems to have ceased to function in the 1860s. The next time a similar club were mentioned was in 1894, when the Catholic Young Men's Society was established. It seems likely that the League of the Cross acted as a replacement for the society from the mid 1880s until it was re-established under a slightly different name. Surprisingly there was no allusion to the prior existence of the CYMA/S. Again, subscriptions were collected and lectures were given on topics similar to those already mentioned.[27]

21 *F.J.*, 26 June 1858.
22 *The Lamp*, 17 Sep 1859.
23 Best, Geoffrey, p.222.
24 *The Lamp*, 24 Nov 1860.
25 *F.J.*, 17 June 1862.
26 *F.J.*, 4 Feb 1863.
27 *F.J.*, 17 Feb 1894.

The League of the Cross was founded in January 1885 by the curate of St Mary's parish, Fr. McGoey. Originally established in England by Archbishop Manning in the late 1860s as a Catholic proselytising total abstinence society, the League was to have many of the same characteristics as the Salvation Army; including open-air meetings accompanied by banners and processions.[28] The first meeting of the Athlone branch saw £50 collected with the view of establishing a band for the members.[29] The band was quickly formed under the administration of Fr. McGoey, who early in the League's history had to defuse heated discussions between members.[30] The League had gained a large membership by April 1885 with a report stating that the meetings had a regular attendance of 200.[31] The society, through promoting total abstinence, had at its heart the provision of alternative forms of entertainment – the band being the main outlet. Annual trips to Galway and Dublin were examples of their efforts to distract people from the public houses, with the first trip to Galway occurring in August 1885.[32] The League may have been seen as even more necessary in Athlone due to the presence of the garrison on the town's west bank. The soldiers in the garrison were typically believed to be hard drinking, fighting men; the League was a counter-weight to this type of behaviour.

When the Confraternity of the Holy Family held a mission in Athlone the number of members of the League of the Cross swelled with many apparently becoming convinced of the virtues of abstinence.[33] The League, as with all of the other religious societies, had a number of soirées, at which the partygoers enjoyed minerals and other non-alcoholic beverages.[34] The first annual Christmas Banquet, held on St Stephen's Day, in 1885 was said to be '*substantial*' with a large attendance.[35] The League members also had their own hall in which they laid on what was described as a '*dramatic*' night of entertainment for St. Patrick's Day 1890.[36] With the assistance of the League St Patrick's Day 1890 was '*quietly and becomingly celebrated*'.[37] From its inception the band played concerts every year on the evening of St. Patrick's Day. One account of St Patrick's Day celebrations in 1887 noted a procession of

28 Newsome, David, p.218.
29 *F.J.*, 31 Jan 1885.
30 *F.J.*, 2 May 1885.
31 *F.J.*, 4 April 1885.
32 *F.J.*, 15 August 1885.
33 *F.J.*, 19 Sep 1885.
34 *A.T.*, 4 Sep 1885.
35 *F.J.*, 2 Jan 1886.
36 *F.J.*, 22 Mar 1890.
37 *The W.I.*, np.

600 members marching through the town with the Fife and Drum band.[38] A similar number took the annual excursion to Dublin the same year.[39] Anniversaries celebrated by the League included that of Fr. Mathew, the driving force behind the earlier temperance movement, and that of their foundation.[40] The Athlone branch also had a library for its members, and received donations towards the facility from members.[41] A number of bazaars were held throughout the lifetime of the society with all the funds put into the library and running costs of the League.[42] The official number of members for 1889 was 200 adults and 350 juveniles.[43] The Society also organised excursions for its bands, as in May 1890, when the Fife and Drum Band went on a trip to Clara where they played some '*national airs*' for the locals.[44]

The League also espoused the positive effects of exercise in their excursion choice – the visit to Hodson Bay outside Athlone took the form of a sports day featuring boat racing, tug of war, and weight lifting.[45] The lectures given to the members of the League were generally concerned with the evils of drink and the virtues of abstinence.[46] The members also branched into drama with the League of the Cross Dramatic Society being an integral part of the whole. Examples of the plays enacted from December 1890 were 'That Rascal Pat' and 'The Irish Tutor'.[47] As already related, the League dissolved in the early 1890s over the Parnell affair.

In the case of more secular clubs, associations and societies there were a number in Athlone in the Victorian period. The town had a Masonic Lodge – Lodge 101, originally founded in 1739. It had been abandoned in 1838 and an attempted revival six years later came about mainly because lodges in other towns were flourishing.[48] Citing unanimity and brotherly love as its main objectives, it actually reopened in 1849 and a number of years later set about raising funds for a Masonic hall.[49] The masons established a Royal Arch Chapter in 1850 with twenty members attached.[50] Named the Shamrock Lodge in 1855 it met in January of most years during the 50s, 60s and 70s to celebrate the feast of St. John.[51]

38 *F.J.*, 19 Mar 1887.
39 *F.J.*, 2 July 1887.
40 *F.J.*, 15 Aug 1887, *F.J.*, 11 Feb 1888.
41 *F.J.*, 24 Dec 1887.
42 *F.J.*, 7 Apr 1888.
43 *F.J.*, 28 July 1889.
44 *F.J.*, 17 May 1890.
45 *F.J.*, 2 Aug 1890.
46 *F.J.*, 9 Aug 1890.
47 *F.J.*, 13 Dec 1890.
48 *A.S.*, 26 Apr 1844.
49 *W.I.*, 30 June 1849, *W.I.*, 11 Jan 1857.
50 *Royal Arch Chapter 101 Athlone 1850-1950* (Athlone, 1951), p.4.
51 *A.S.*, 1 Jan 1853, *W.I.*, 9 Jan 1858, *W.I.*, 8 Jan 1859, *W.I.*, 7 Jan 1871, *W.I.*, 11 Jan 1873.

The members acquired a hall in 1867 where they remained for twenty years – the lodge is still active in Athlone today.[52] A second Masonic lodge called the 'Princess Victorias' was inaugurated in the town in 1890. This lodge may have seen an opening in Athlone since Lodge 101 appears not to have been very active for a number of years prior to 1890.[53] However, there was no other mention of this lodge, which claimed to have non-sectarian, non-political philanthropists as members.

The Ancient Order of Foresters – Court of Good Intent was a similar organisation to the Masonic lodge and re-established in the town in 1888 after a twenty year absence.[54] Initially thirty members were initiated with another five enrolled by the end of the year.[55] The foresters had fortnightly and annual meetings yet, though reports conflict, were struggling to survive up to 1893.[56] The annual report from 1895 tells of the success of the branch, which had fifty members as well as a credit balance of £90. The members went on excursions and had annual banquets with a report from 1898 recording that the club was a great success, a situation that remained into the late 20th century.[57]

Social clubs were also to be found during the period, with the Catholic, Protestant and Methodist temperance societies being the largest amongst the denominations.[58] Other societies included the Literary and Harmonic Society, the Musical Society, the Reading and Recreation Society and the Workingmen's Association – which had a temperance association attached.[59] The Athlone Musical Society founded around 1874 is still in existence making it one of the oldest in the country. In Britain workingmen's clubs had become popular in the 1850s with the temperance affiliation becoming widespread during the 1860s.[60] The Reading and Recreation Society, along with the YMCA and CYMS, and their provision of reading rooms were indicative of the Victorian move toward a greater intellectual vitality in society. Public libraries had become very popular in England in the 1840s and 1850s, which, along with the spread of societies, provided the possibility of a better education than had previously been on offer.[61] Public lectures were also seen as a popular form of entertainment, not only for strictly

52 *1739 – 1939 Bicentenary of Shamrock Lodge 101, Athlone* (Athlone, 1940), p.6.
53 *F.J.*, 21 June 1890.
54 *F.J.*, 21 Aug 1888.
55 Ibid., *F.J.*, 19 Jan 1889.
56 *F.J.*, 15 June 1889, *F.J.*, 9 Jan 1892, *F.J.*, 23 Dec 1893, *F.J.*, 13 Jan 1894, *F.J.*, 12 Jan 1895.
57 *F.J.*, 3 Aug 1895, *F.J.*, 15 Feb 1896, *A.T.*, 28 June 1900.
58 *W.I.*, 11 Mar 1871, *F.J.*, 12 Dec 1885, *F.J.*, 20 Mar 1886.
59 Forbes, John, M. D., F. R. S., *Memorandum made in Ireland in the Autumn of 1852* (London, 1853), pp. 206-210, *W.I.*, 23 Oct 1875, *W.I.*, 2 Mar 1878, *F.J.*, 2 Nov 1889, *F.J.*, 12 Dec 1891.
60 Horn, Pamela, p.254.
61 Best, Geoffrey, p.234.

educational purposes and they began to occur frequently.[62] Later legislation for museums and libraries created further opportunities for cultural and educational development, though Athlone's Town Commissioners did not believe that the town required either when the opportunity arose to create them.

BANDS

Generally the Victorian period saw a proliferation of bands both in Ireland and in Britain. The emergence of free time and disposable income meant that those interested in creating a band now had the money and time in which to do so. Bands, along with choirs, provided an outlet for people from different levels of society, with the growth in the number of bands leading to the creation of a new form of social and sometimes competitive recreation.[63] As bands in Ireland proliferated and developed they frequently played at rallies and demonstrations, helping the Irish cause in '*political advancement*'.[64] During the Victorian period in Athlone many bands were formed, sometimes as part of a society or as stand-alone bands. In an article '*Some Calm Observations on Irish Affairs*', John Grey Porter advised that all large towns form a good band to help people channel their free time more effectively.[65] In a garrison town such as Athlone numerous regimental bands would have influenced how the civilian bands were created, their form and appearance.

Evidence suggests the existence of 'The Athlone Band', which may have also constituted the choir, in 1845 though it appears to have faded quickly.[66] A brass band appeared in the town around 1850, though little was written of it and it was described as having a '*brief but ephemeral existence*'.[67] The growth of brass bands was encouraged in the United Kingdom for it was seen as an '*improving*' pastime, and the number of bands attached to various organisations grew massively during the later decades of the Victorian era.[68] The myriad temperance organisations in both Ireland and Britain, if large enough, invariably had a band as part of their makeup. The Mechanics Institute on Queen Street had a band attached to it from 1857, which was said to be the first new band since the time of Daniel O'Connell and the monster meeting, though this is uncertain.[69] In Athlone the band scene was quiet until the formation of

62 Newsome, David, p.144, Best, Geoffrey, p.233.
63 Daunton, Martin, p.57.
64 White, Harry, *The Keeper's Recital – Music and Cultural History in Ireland, 1770 - 1970* (Cork, 1998), p.8
65 Porter, John Grey, *Some Calm Observations on Irish Affairs* (Dublin, 1846), Letter C.
66 *FJ.*, 30 Apr 1887.
67 *FJ.*, 26 Feb 1887.
68 Horn, Pamela, p.187.
69 *FJ.*, 3 Dec 1887.

larger societies such as the CYMA, which had a band by 1858.[70]

'The Athlone Band' was probably reformed in 1863. Though initially its members used whatever instruments they could get, some being of the lowest quality.[71] Again, as with other associations, excursions were held for the two years of its existence.[72] A brass band was also noted as being formed in 1865 and was said to have made remarkable progress in its short career.[73] One historian has described the brass bands as being '...*soccer's musical counterpart in every respect*' such were their popularity with the working and lower-middle classes.[74] 'The Athlone Amateur Band' was noted as in the process of being reformed in 1871, possibly the same outfit that must have disbanded five or six years earlier.[75] Evidence suggests that this attempt at revival was unsuccessful since an editorial from 1874 decries the lack of a band in the town:

> We are forced to ask ourselves – why has the town been so long without one? And we are unable to find a satisfactory answer. There are very few small towns in Ireland without a Trades or Temperance Band; and it may be well to remind our readers that Athlone scarcely ranks among the small towns of the country as there are not certainly, in round numbers, more than, say two dozen cities and towns in the island having a larger population.[76]

After the publication of this editorial, a letter was sent to the newspaper asking if the townspeople could form two sections of the one band. On the west of the town a brass band could be formed, whilst on the east side a fife and drum band would operate.[77] One was subsequently formed which played classical music but again it appears to have disappeared from the scene soon after its inception.[78] Another 'Athlone Band' was noted in November 1885, at the height of the Land War, when it was attacked just outside the town, but a lack of evidence makes it hard to pin down its establishment date.[79] From records it appears that the formation of a long-lived band did not come about until the establishment of the League of the Cross in 1885 which had a fife and drum band.[80] This band was to be perhaps the most important

70 *F.J.*, 26 June 1858.
71 *F.J.*, 3 Dec 1887.
72 *F.J.*, 28 July 1864, *F.J.*, 5 Jan 1865.
73 *F.J.*, 20 Apr 1887.
74 Best, Geoffrey, p.233.
75 *W.I.*, 31 June 1871.
76 *W.I.*, 30 May 1874.
77 *W.I.*, 6 June 1874.
78 *F.J.*, 20 Apr 1887.
79 *F.J.*, 14 Nov 1885.
80 *F.J.*, 31 Jan 1885.

in Athlone during the late 19th century and played regularly throughout the years.[81]

Athlone certainly had a brass band in 1886 when an article on infighting reported the seizure of the band's instruments by their president who believed members were operating over his head and outside their remit.[82] The problem must have been solved by St. Patrick's Day when the Brass Band joined the League of the Cross Fife and Drum Band in celebrations.[83] This Brass Band may have been recently founded, and though it does appear to have had a dedicated band room, it was only in February 1887 that the funds were available for the introduction of a band uniform. It was to be a tight fitting '*parole jacket*' trimmed with lace in front and back and coloured dark green; the influence of the army on band attire is obvious here.[84] The town appeared to go from one extreme to the other for by the end of February 1887 the local press reports the presence of three bands in the town:

> Not in any other provincial town in Ireland is there such a passion displayed for instrumental music among the working classes as in Athlone. There is the Brass Band, The Fife and Drum and the Workingman's Brass Band.[85]

Reports from St Patrick's Day 1887 noted the presence of a Brass Band attached to the League of the Cross, which played with the Drum Fife and Drum band which was based just outside the town.[86] All three local bands mentioned above played at the Regatta in August 1887 after an argument about whether they or the army band should provide entertainment.[87] The Athlone National Band (Brass Band) appeared to be garnering some level of success when a report tells that they came third in a competition held in Dublin in 1887.[88] (This type of competitive participation was growing all over the United Kingdom at the time, all organised and regimented in accordance with Victorian tradition.) Soon after this achievement they moved from their band room in Main Street to a new premises in Queen Street.[89] Perhaps the award drove the band to practise too often, for they, along with the League of the Cross band, had to issue an apology to the Protestant

81 *FJ.*, 21 Mar 1885, *FJ.*, 20 Mar 1886, *FJ.*, 19 Mar 1887, *FJ.*, 23 Mar 1889, *FJ.*, 22 Mar 1890, *FJ.*, 21 Mar 1891.
82 *FJ.*, 20 Feb 1886.
83 *FJ.*, 20 Mar 1886.
84 *FJ.*, 5 Feb 1887, *FJ.*, 26 Mar 1887.
85 *FJ.*, 26 Feb 1887.
86 *FJ.*, 19 Mar 1887.
87 *FJ.*, 20 Aug 1887.
88 *FJ.*, 8 Oct 1887.
89 *FJ.*, 3 Dec 1887.

minister in the town for playing music during the funeral of a member of the local clergy.[90] All three bands were still in existence in 1889 when they jointly welcomed in the New Year.[91] The League of the Cross was again reported as having two bands in 1889 when both played at a funeral of a former member.[92] Both the League bands and the National Band appeared to be flourishing into the 1890s when trips and premises expansions were noted.[93]

News of Parnell's affair with Kitty O'Shea was to change not only the face of national and local politics but also, at least in Athlone, the number of bands. The National Band saw the necessity of coming out on one side of the adultery argument – they passed a vote of confidence in Parnell.[94] Both the League bands and the National Band greeted Parnell at Athlone station in February 1891 and at his two subsequent visits that year.[95] The town's two Brass Bands, that of the League of the Cross and of the National Band were to be amalgamated in October 1891 due to the former band being dispossessed of their hall, after the League split over the Parnell affair.[96] This formation appears to have gone ahead when it was reported that the new band went on a trip to Clara in April 1892 and leased a premises in Glass Lane in October 1893 for practising.[97] The Athlone Fife and Drum Band also appears to have been formed around this time from the remnants of the League Band.[98]

Both bands had fundraisers and trips – for enjoyment and to remember Parnell – during the early 1890s with the Fife and Drum Band appearing more successful due to a larger number of reports pertaining to it.[99] Indeed, news of the need to reorganise the National Band came in November 1894, with a meeting in January 1895 in the Workingmen's Club attempting to move the issue on.[100] A band working under the name 'Independent Fife and Drum Band' had a meeting early in 1895. It appeared to be attached to the Workingmen's Club, for a resolution passed at the meeting was forwarded to that organisation.[101] Evidence suggests that the Independent Fife and Drum Band had disbanded in late 1897, after roughly ten years in existence, for members had to decide what to do with their instruments in January

90 *FJ*, 10 Dec 1887.
91 *FJ*, 5 Jan 1889.
92 *FJ*, 22 June 1889.
93 *FJ*, 17 May 1890, *FJ*, 30 Aug 1890.
94 *FJ*, 27 Dec 1890.
95 *FJ*, 28 Feb 1891, *FJ*, 21 Mar 1891, *FJ*, 12 Sep 1891.
96 *FJ*, 31 Oct 1891.
97 *FJ*, 23 Apr 1892, *FJ*, 28 Oct 1893.
98 *FJ*, 5 Aug 1893, *FJ*, 23 Sep 1893.
99 *FJ*, 25 Nov 1893, *FJ*, 27 Jan 1894, *FJ*, 28 July 1894, *FJ*, 13 Oct 1894, *FJ*, 12 Oct 1895, *FJ*, 17 Oct 1896.
100 *FJ*, 10 Nov 1894, *FJ*, 26 Jan 1895.
101 *FJ*, 12 Jan 1895.

1898.[102] It appears that the Brass Band and the Fife and Drum Band survived for the remainder of the Victorian Period.

RIVER TOURISM

In Britain during the Victorian period tourism flourished. Huge numbers of people were taking advantage of the spread of the railway system and venturing to beaches, historic sites and tranquil river settings away from the increasingly busy towns and cities.[103] The spread of tourism in Ireland did not occur as soon as it had in Britain, due mainly to the Famine. However after the Famine had ended many Irish people took to the idea of discovering new places and the tourism industry developed quickly.[104]

Athlone was lucky in comparison with other midland towns for it had the River Shannon to attract tourists to it. It also had Clonmacnoise, or the Seven Churches as it was known, just a few miles to the south and these factors along with a good rail network serving the town meant that Athlone was easy to reach and provided enough sites of interest to attract tourists in some numbers. Not unreasonably it was believed that if Athlone were to be developed as a tourist destination it had to make as much use of the river as possible. The development of river tourism was haphazard initially. As already mentioned in chapter four many of the boats were unsuitable, and the spread of the railways made investment in river transport extremely risky.

The establishment of the Shannon Development Company in 1897 was to see the first organised and concerted push to increase tourist numbers on the river. The business did appear to be developing well towards the end of the 19th century with a number of trips laid on such as one in the summer of 1898 when 340 people travelled up the river on the 'Lady Betty Balfour'.[105] Aware of the potential for profit, the MGWR put on special trains from Dublin to Athlone to coincide with the steamer trips, which began to run to a timetable, such were the numbers of people who wished to use the boats.[106]

However the initial enthusiasm waned and by the first years of the new century it appears that the steam trade in the town was failing as it had before. Day trips were advertised as commencing in May of 1901

102 *FJ.*, 1 Jan 1898.
103 Yonge, C. M., "Victorians by the Sea Shore", in Quennel, Peter & Hodge, Alan (Eds.), *History Today,* Vol. 25, No.9 (London, 1975), p.603.
104 Matthew, Colin, p. 88.
105 *FJ.*, 18 June 1898.
106 *FJ.*, 3 June 1899.

ILL.12: THE LADY BETTY BALFOUR LADEN WITH EXCURSIONISTS

but the withdrawal of funding by a number of public bodies left the future of the trips uncertain.[107] The first day on which the trips ran, one boat going to Lough Derg the other to Lough Ree, attendance was very small despite the weather being '*most delightful*'. As a result a warning was issued that numbers would have to rise or the trips would cease.[108] There is evidence to suggest that the level of traffic on the river at the turn of the century was not substantial, to say the least, with many ships logs reflecting that the efforts of the Shannon Development Company were futile.[109] The company struggled on for another thirteen years but officially ceased to operate in 1914.

POPULAR ENTERTAINMENT

With the advent of the Victorian age entertainment became a more regular occurrence when the construction of purpose-built halls and theatres, as well as the spread of the rail network meant that towns could attract new plays and shows more easily. The spread of the railway network '…*much affected the structure and practices of the Victorian theatre*' through the growth in the number of travelling companies.[110] All throughout the early 19th century Athlone had a large number of visiting circuses, dramatic troupes as well as other forms of entertainment. From the number of newspaper reports dating as far back as the 1830s it is apparent that the arts were becoming more

107 *A.T.*, 25 May 1901.
108 *A.T.*, 1 June 1901.
109 Delany, Ruth, "The River Shannon, Lough Ree and Athlone", in Keaney, M. & O'Brien, G., *Athlone - Bridging the Centuries* (Mullingar, 1991), pp.31-32.
110 Booth, Michael R., *Theatre in the Victorian Age* (Cambridge, 1991), pp.16-18.

popular in Athlone, with more visits as well as greater local participation.[111]

Visiting circuses proved extremely popular in the early part of the 1840s. *The Athlone Mirror* reported that a 'Monster' circus (in reference to the number of animals and performers, as opposed to the presence of any monsters) visited the town and was greeted with such success as to stay on for a twelve-night run, which was subsequently extended to twenty-seven nights.[112] Miller's Equestrian Troop arrived in the town in July 1843 and enjoyed huge success; admission was just 1d, a price which led to large numbers being in attendance at each performance.[113] The mid-nineteenth century in general saw '*a multitude*' of circuses touring Ireland with a large number of them visiting Athlone.[114] The numbers visiting the circuses in the town were quite substantial with one, which arrived in 1852, drawing a crowd estimated at 2,500 for its performances at Scotch Parade on the east side.[115] The visit of 'Bell and Company's Gigantic Hippodrome' in 1858 was also deemed a great success in the local press such were the numbers of people who visited it.[116] The practice of offering different grades of tickets was advertised for 'Batty's Great Zoological Exhibition'. When it visited the town the cost of entry was 1s for ladies and gentlemen and 6d for the working class, which may help to account for the numbers that came to witness the performances.[117] The labourers and gentry were kept separate with the gentry's entry fee securing more comfortable seating. The 1870s saw the type and calibre of the performances at circuses grow, and these superior acts arrived in Athlone regularly with a report on 'Ginnet's Circuses (a former and future visitor) from June 1870: '*If we are to credit the unanimous voice of the press of Ireland, this company is far superior to any other travelling, both in the training of the horses and the talent of the artists.*' Schoolchildren were admitted at half the normal price with those children in the workhouse admitted free on a specified day.[118]

Acts with an international flavour were also seen in the town with 'Tannaker's Japanese' acrobats arriving in the summer of 1875.[119] Another well-known 19th century international circus to visit the town was 'Lloyd's American Circus' which boasted the famous Johnnie

---

111 *A.I.*, 20 Nov 1833, *A.I.*, 19 Feb 1834, *A.I.*, 22 Oct 1834, *A.S.*, 19 Nov 1834.
112 *A.M.*, 18 Sep 1841.
113 *A.S.*, 28 July 1843.
114 O'Brien, Brendan, "When the circus came to Athlone", in *Journal of the Old Athlone Society* Vol. II, No.6 (Athlone, 1985), p.114.
115 Ibid.
116 *W.I.*, 8 May 1858.
117 *W.I.*, 28 May 1859.
118 *W.I.*, 4 June 1870.
119 *W.I.*, 9 Apr 1875.

Patterson and 'Rosco the Clown'.[120] Its Mexican sister circus also performed in the town, as did 'Bakers American Circus' in 1894.[121] 'Bostock's and Wombwell's Menagerie' was billed to arrive soon after the circus with over 500 beasts in tow.[122]

Variations on the theme of spectacle came in the form of 'Howard's Diorama' which arrived in the town to present an audio-visual account of the Boer and Afghan Wars. This exhibit of the exotic scenes was viewed, probably exclusively, by the military and the gentry.[123] This embracing of technological innovation and exoticism was indicative of later Victorian thinking, which assisted in the development of 20th century innovations.[124]

Theatrically and musically Athlone was also quite well served during the Victorian period. The fact that the town had a garrison certainly exposed the more affluent classes to more theatre than they would normally have witnessed with the establishment of the garrison theatre in 1836.[125] The town itself does not seem to have had a purpose-built theatre until 1850. Prior to this, and on a few occasions after, most plays were held in makeshift theatres, such as O'Rourke's Hotel and Williams' Coach Factory.[126] This trend of using enclosed spaces for entertainment, be it in theatres or sporting venues, was part of the drive towards social change in the Victorian era – regulation of events was intended to produce a polite and civil society.[127] The number of visiting troupes in the town varied over the years, with just one visiting in the Famine year of 1846, while more regular visits occurred later in the century.[128] As the Victorian era progressed attitudes to the theatre changed, becoming more positive. Formerly the theatre was seen as being too bohemian and a source of low morality though positive advertising brought the more respectable middle and higher classes to halls and theatres around the United Kingdom.[129]

A number of music concerts also took place in a variety of venues around Athlone such as hotels and the Town Hall, which appears to be the most frequently used venue up to the 1890s. The spread of music in Victorian Britain began in the 1840s when teacher-training colleges began to teach music to students and they in turn passed on what they

120 *F.J.*, 15 Aug 1885.
121 *F.J.*, 10 Sep 1887, *F.J.*, 20 Oct 1894.
122 *F.J.*, 20 Oct 1894.
123 *W.I.*, 7 Jan 1882.
124 Saint, Andrew, pp.285–297.
125 *A.I.*, 9 Mar 1836.
126 *Athlone 1950* p.43, *W.I.*, 8 Nov 1851, *W.I.*, 5 Jan 1856.
127 Daunton, Martin, p.57.
128 O'Brien, Brendan, p.8.
129 Horn, Pamela, p.198.

learned, in the case of Ireland, mainly through private instruction.[130] The Royal Irish Academy of Music was opened in Dublin in 1848 and reflected '…*that mid-Victorian tendency to impose a coherent academic agenda upon the hitherto uncertain process of music education.*'[131] In the 1860s music-making of various forms began to grow in popularity among the lower classes of society, formerly it was considered mainly for the affluent.[132] Slater's Directory advertised that from 1870 onwards Athlone had at least three 'Teachers of Music' offering their services, showing the spread of the music phenomenon.[133]

Almost all of the concerts appear to have been popular, though not always of the highest quality with one held in 1872 causing a reporter from *The Westmeath Independent* to write: '*Because it was a charitable function the paper does not wish to be unduly critical but apparently the young man of the family who organised the function was less than talented.*'[134]

The makeup of the concerts varied; at times they were entirely English song-based affairs such as the Literary and Harmonic Society concert in October 1876. Concerts could also feature minstrels and comedic songs, as with the Athlone Instrumental and Vocal Musical Society concert of December 1878.[135] The town's larger societies such as the CYMS and YMCA generally held at least one annual concert for their members, with many societies having numerous concerts each year. The number of concerts staged in the town during one week in 1887 caused *The Freeman's Journal* to say that the inhabitants were in '*ecstasy*'; no matter what part of the town one visited the talk was of '*What did you think of the concert?*' and '*Never saw such concerts.*'[136]

The most important venue in which entertainment was staged towards the end of the 19th century was Longworth Hall, owned by the YMCA, which opened in 1891.[137] Music was heard there frequently, with a variety of reports concerning concerts published in the press.[138] The makeup of the audience was generally those from the upper strata of Athlone society, though on one occasion there was news of a trend towards a '*rough and disagreeable element*' being in attendance.[139] The

130 Flint, Kate, "Literature, music and the theatre", in Matthew, Colin, *Short Oxford History of the British Isles – The Nineteenth* Century (Oxford, 2000), p.248.
131 White, Harry, pp.102-3.
132 Best, Geoffrey, p.233.
133 *Slater's,* 1870, pp.4-7, 1881, pp.329-333, 1894, pp. 16-19.
134 *A.S.,* 7 Jan 1852, *W.I.,* 28 Dec 1872, *W.I.,* 4 May 1872, *F.J.,* 2 Jan 1873, *W.I.,* 28 Oct 1876, *W.I.,* 2 Mar 1878, *W.I.,* 8 June 1878, *W.I.,* 28 Dec 1878, *W.I.,* 19 Apr 1879, *F.J.,* 20 Jan 1882.
135 *W.I.,* 28 Oct 1876, *W.I.,* 28 Dec 1878.
136 *F.J.,* 26 Feb 1887.
137 *F.J.,* 31 Jan 1891.
138 *F.J.,* 2 July 1891, *F.J.,* 12 Sep 1891, *F.J.,* 31 Dec 1891, 21 Nov 1891, *F.J.,* 12 Dec 1891, *F.J.,* 5 Mar 1892, *F.J.,* 31 Dec 1892, *F.J.,* 29 July 1893, *F.J.,* 30 Sep 1893, *F.J.,* 30 June 1894, *F.J.,* 9 Nov 1895, *F.J.,* 21 Mar 1896, *F.J.,* 4 Dec 1897.
139 *F.J.,* 14 Nov 1896.

tradition of St Patrick's Day celebrations in the Hall appeared in 1896 when a concert of entirely Irish music was held.[140] St Patrick's Day celebrations were previously seen to be very Irish in nature, dissuading the more loyalist sections of Athlone society from becoming involved. The regulation of the entertainment on that day in a hall may have enticed some of the less staunch members to attend. As already noted the League of the Cross played many Irish songs on the feast day as did a number of the other local bands. The establishment of the Fr. Mathew temperance hall on the west bank of the river in 1897 caused the number of concerts held in the town to rise yet again, with the temperate members of the community seeking out alcohol-free entertainment. The Saturday night concerts held at the venue were said to have been a great success, with a number of other concerts held there throughout the last years of the Victorian period.[141]

THE EMERGENCE OF ORGANISED SPORT

The Victorian era in general saw some improvements in the living standards of the working-class and more particularly of the more affluent class and with this came the opportunity for more people '...*to share in the delights of a culture of consumption and leisure*'.[142] At the start of the nineteenth century many sports were in their infancy – played without rules and very disorganised. Towards the end of the century professionalism was introduced and codes of practice and conduct brought to bear on the sports.[143] This regulation came about as part of the Victorian mindset when it came to organisation – they wished to apply rules to as many facets of life as possible, social rules as well as rules for hygiene, war, education and of course rules for organised sport, a hallmark of the era.[144] Predictably, the Victorian period in Athlone saw the emergence of a large number of organised sporting events and bodies as well as the advancement of a number of those bodies that were already in existence.

Prior to the era the main sporting events in and around the town were yachting, horse racing, hunting and cockfighting.[145] The Athlone Yacht club was founded in 1770 as an amateur organisation and is still in existence today making it the second oldest yacht club in the

140 *FJ.*, 21 Mar 1896.
141 *FJ.*, 17 Dec 1897, *FJ.*, 10 Dec 1898, *FJ.*, 19 Mar 1898, *FJ.*, 15 Jan 1898, *FJ.*, 8 Jan 1898, *FJ.*, 11 Dec 1897, 4 Nov 1899.
142 Daunton, Martin, p.56.
143 Ibid.
144 Hart – Davis, Adam, *What the Victorians Did for Us* (London, 2001), p.158.
145 Murtagh, *Athlone to 1800*, pp.212-214.

world.[146] Professionalism in boating began in Britain during the 1830s and it did not take long for the allure of competitive boating to reach Athlone, which it did towards the end of the same decade.[147] The very first year of the reign of Victoria saw the establishment of Athlone Boat Club, which had a number of regattas on the Athlone and Lough Ree stretches of the Shannon during the 1850s and 60s with an article from 1862 describing how a successful regatta appeared:

> Yesterday, Wednesday, Athlone Regatta was held amidst the greatest excitement. The day was exceptionally favourable and the locality selected was well adapted for the purpose. The gay bannerets of the various yachts, the boats that studded the bosom of the lake and the snowhite [sic] tents and marquees along the shore, while multitudes of both sexes attired in holiday sheen, and the music that burst on the ear added to the scene.[148]

The staging of the regatta continued throughout the 1870s before a waning interest saw the club needing to be re-established in 1882.[149] The organisation gained the use of the Shannon Commissioners' premises in 1885 and the local press reported that it was usual for the club to hold a race every fortnight.[150] It appeared to encounter problems in 1887 when there was a major dispute over whether the employment of a local or military band would be best for the regatta. One man resigned from the committee in protest over the eventual decision to employ the services of the three local bands.[151] The makeup of the club's members must have been changing over the years to include more Catholics, for the local bands at the regatta were dominated by them and their inclusion instead of the British Army bands may have signalled a shift in power in the club. The presence of the town bands at the regatta did not become a tradition, however, with the army band in attendance at the next event.[152] The boat club was reported as being in good financial shape in 1888, with a small fleet of boats at the disposal of its members.[153] The club staged numerous regattas over the following decade, with the annual regatta generally being a good success, and was still in existence at the end of the Victorian period.[154] One travel writer

146 English, N. W., *Lough Ree Yacht Club 1770-1970 – A Memoir* (Athlone, 1970), p.3.
147 Mason, Tony, *Sport in Britain* (London, 1988), p.37.
148 *F.J.*, 28 Aug 1862.
149 Athlone Junior Chamber of Commerce, *So there's nothing to do in Athlone – A comprehensive guide to organisations societies & clubs* (Athlone, 1981), p.6, *W.I.*, 3 Sep 1853, *F.J.*, 28 Aug 1862, *F.J.*, 20 Aug 1864, *F.J.*, 19 Aug 1868, *F.J.*, 22 Aug 1870, *W.I.*, 16 Sep 1876, *W.I.*, 6 Sep 1879 *F.J.*, 6 July 1882.
150 *F.J.*, 9 May 1885, *F.J.*, 16 June 1886.
151 *F.J.*, 6 Aug 1887, *F.J.*, 20 Aug 1887.
152 *F.J.*, 3 Sep 1887.
153 *F.J.*, 19 May 1888.
154 *F.J.*, 16 Aug 1890, *A.I.*, 18 Aug 1900.

noted that in Athlone: '...*there is better boating kept up, both by civilians and military than I have seen in any other place, and the Shannon is constantly enlivened by numbers of sail and row boats.*'[155]

ILL.13: AN ENLIVENED SHANNON ON A RACE DAY

The town also played host to a number of horseracing events each year. The races were generally two-day events and gained most support from the local gentry.[156] Athlone had a history of race events stretching back to the 1730s and the 19th century was to see the tradition face both highs and lows. Those held in April 1868 were to be the last for twenty-five years, with the press describing the last three meetings held in the town as '*wretched displays*'.[157] Ballymore Races, twenty miles away (which were apparently set up by Athlone army personnel), were mentioned as the obvious choice to supersede the Athlone meet.[158] There were other races locally with both Moate and Taughmaconnell staging meetings during the lull in Athlone-based racing.[159]

The first revival race in April 1893 was described as a huge success, with beautiful weather and over 12,000 people in attendance.[160] Horseracing had undergone a great change in the nineteenth century. Easier travel afforded by the railways led to larger attendance and better competition. Also a move away from 'rowdyism' that had been associated with races helped its popularity to grow.[161] The races continued to be

155 Banim, Mary, p.203.
156 *Athlone 1947*, p.14.
157 *FJ.*, 30 Apr 1868.
158 *FJ.*, 12 Mar 1850, *FJ.*, 30 Apr 1868.
159 *FJ.*, 5 June 1886, *FJ.*, 5 Apr 1890.
160 *FJ.*, 29 Apr 1893.
161 Best, Geoffrey, p.223.

staged until 1897 when racetrack owners demanded high rents from the Race Committee which was unwilling to pay them.[162] The committee instead decided to try and reopen the Garrycastle races, held on the east of the town.[163] They had been closed in 1868 due to safety problems involving a disturbance between some of the patrons as well as falling revenue.[164] After a delay the races were eventually held in there in 1899.[165] The first was a great success, with the local gentry turning out in such numbers that the newspaper reported that, '*Garrycastle has again resounded with the mirth and merriment of a racecourse*'.[166]

Hunt meetings, one of the main local sports for the gentry in the 18th century, were still staged in the countryside surrounding the town during the 19th century. The years 1850–1870 were thought to be the 'greatest era' for hunting around Athlone, though the problems associated with a local land struggle led to a local Hunt Club being disbanded in 1872.[167] Another local club, which wished to continue as usual despite the agrarian tensions, the Westmeath Hounds, found its hunt in 1881 impeded by the presence of some 300 farmers who refused further passage.[168] As is the case today many associated fox hunting with the gentry. It was an elitist sport and considered very British. The sport did not become popular again locally until the late 1880s when agrarian problems began to subside.[169] A prominent local named Longworth was the only Athlone member of the Irish Game Protection Association – a body that dealt with the ramifications of new laws to do with trespass and hunting for the most part – in 1891, though this does not point to the decline in the sport locally.[170] A club was established in the 1890s called the South Westmeath Staghounds, which maintained a hunt pack into the 20th century.[171]

Evidence of cockfighting – another of the more popular 18th century pursuits – in the town during the Victorian period is also available with a report from 1849 detailing the obstruction caused by the cockfighters and their audience.[172] This sport was popular mainly with the working classes who organised virtually all of the clubs. A raid on a '*fight club*' in 1897 described how despite years of police attempts

162 *EJ.*, 10 July 1897.
163 *EJ.*, 10 July 1897.
164 *EJ.*, 27 May 1899.
165 *EJ.*, 17 June 1899.
166 Ibid.
167 Sheehan, Jeremiah, p.207.
168 *EJ.*, 10 Feb 1881, *EJ.*, 12 Dec 1881.
169 Sheehan, Jeremiah, p.208.
170 Conner, MacCarthy, *The Game Laws of Ireland with Irish Game Statutes Codified and Notes of Reported Cases* (Dublin, 1891), p.192.
171 *EJ.*, 2 Nov 1895, *EJ.*, 17 Apr 1897, *EJ.*, 16 Apr 1898, Sheehan, p.208.
172 *Athlone 1945*, p.23.

to stamp out the sport it was still popular locally with 'battles' staged frequently.[173]

Apart from the advancement of many sports that already existed in and around Athlone, the Victorian period was to see new games imported from Britain. One of these imports was the game of cricket and it appears that Athlone had a local club, apart from that of the army, from at least 1865 when they played Ballymahon in a match.[174] The members of the club appear to have been local Protestants with few typically Catholic names on the team sheet. During the 1860s the game was regaining popularity in Britain, rules were being set down and the game was seen as one where players could learn more about proper comportment from mixing with fellow 'gentlemen' players.[175] Though the game never reached the heights of popularity that it did in England, its presence in towns was believed to have helped the move away from uncivilised sports such as badger-baiting and pugilism, and was an important factor in the use of organised sport in developing a system of Victorian values.[176]

It has recently been claimed that cricket may have been the most popular sport among all classes in Westmeath during the period 1880–1895; on the face of it this appears to be possible. The author of this claim suggests that by reading newspaper reports from that period it is obvious that there were more on cricket than any other sport.[177] However, in the case of Athlone, the main local newspaper, *The Westmeath Independent*, was owned by local cricket enthusiasts, the Chapmans, who would certainly have included numerous extra reports about the sport. Also the idea that the sport was classless and most popular would lead one to believe that it was being played on the streets by the children of the working class, which would be hard to believe, for the equipment needed was not cheap and a luxury not many could afford.

The local Ranelagh School had a team, as did the garrison and the nearby regions of Clonmacnoise, Tullamore, Ballinasloe, Moate and Roscommon.[178] There are numerous reports of cricket matches that took place in and around Athlone towards the end of the Victorian era with the local woollen mills, brass band and RIC establishing clubs.[179]

173 *F.J..*, 22 May 1897.
174 *F.J.*, 21 Sep 1865.
175 Horn, Pamela, p.162.
176 Best, Geoffrey, p.231.
177 Hunt, Tom, "Classless Cricket? Westmeath 1880-1905", in *History Ireland*, Vol.12, No.2, Summer 2004 (2004), pp.26-30.
178 *F.J.*, 19 May 1866, *F.J.*, 6 Aug 1868, *F.J.*, 12 June 1875, *F.J.*, 21 July 1881, *F.J.*, 7 Aug 1886.
179 *F.J.*, 16 June 1886, *F.J.*, 7 Aug 1886, *F.J.*, 7 May 1892.

The Athlone Cricket Club expanded to include a Lawn Tennis Association around 1886.[180]

The game of tennis was invented in England in 1874 and became very popular there with both sexes amongst the upper classes.[181] It was only a matter of time before it reached Irish shores. The Athlone club played a number of tournaments and an annual report from 1886 stated that there were forty-five men and nineteen ladies in the Athlone Cricket and Lawn Tennis Club.[182] The Club appears to have broken away from the cricketers as the local press reported that the 'Lawn Tennis Club' had its first meeting of the season in a local hotel in May 1888.[183] The move does not appear to have lessened the frequency of tournaments.[184] The club allowed the local military to use the facilities regularly for a small fee, at times playing against them.[185] Garden Vale Lawn Tennis Club opened in May 1894, with news of another new club in April of the following year.[186] Towards the end of the 19th century the tournaments held at the Garden Vale Club had finals for gents, gents doubles, mixed doubles, ladies and ladies singles, though not all tournaments featured all categories.[187]

The sport of tennis was notable for one important reason, the participation of women. The mixed matches as well as the singles games allowed ladies to join in the sporting movement of the Victorian period. Most other sports were considered unladylike, therefore disallowing female entry. Along with many other things, the perceptions of women were changing during the Victorian period:

> Lawn tennis has taught women how much they are capable of doing and it is a sign of the times that various games and sports which would have been tabooed a few years ago as 'unladylike' are actually encouraged at various girls' schools.[188]

The first field game to gain some support in the town during the 19th century was rugby. The rules of the game had been published for the first time in 1846 and it soon started to become popular in Ireland. It was associated mainly with those of '*a superior social tone*'; soccer was believed to have enticed those of lesser social standing.[189] The main

180 *FJ.*, 24 July 1886.
181 Hart – Davis, Adam, p.162, Matthew, Colin, p.90.
182 *FJ.*, 28 Aug 1886, *FJ.*, 4 Sep 1886.
183 *FJ.*, 12 May 1888.
184 *FJ.*, 28 July 1888, *FJ.*, 6 July 1889, *FJ.*, 31 May 1890.
185 *FJ.*, 1 Aug 1891, *FJ.*, 31 May 1890.
186 *FJ.*, 5 May 1894, *FJ.*, 20 Apr 1894.
187 *FJ.*, 8 June 1895, *FJ..*, 6 June 1896, *FJ.*, 19 Sep 1896, *FJ.*, 18 Sep 1897, *FJ.*, 4 June 1898, *FJ.*, 17 Sep, *FJ.*, 2 Sep 1899.
188 Horn, Pamela, p.168.
189 Best, Geoffrey, p.229.

rugby team in the town was that of the Ranelagh School, which played a large number of matches.[190] This encouragement of rugby being played in schools was also the way in which the game had gained a foothold in England.[191] As noted previously the playing of games such as rugby was part of a 'Muscular Christianity', which saw participation in games as a virtuous and admirable pastime. The Ranelagh team was apparently quite good by 1891, having won the majority of the matches it played against other schools and clubs from different towns.[192] Athlone does not appear to have had a rugby team that played under the town's name on a consistent basis. However, there is one example where an Athlone rugby team did line out. It was on St Patrick's Day 1892, though the report records that most of the Athlone team were actually GAA players.[193] It appears that the popularity of rugby in Athlone persisted due to the presence of the garrison; the nationalist revival saw the game lose out to GAA in many other parts of the country that had no army presence.

Soccer became the most popular sport in the town towards the end of the 19th century and the main event was the foundation of Athlone Town F.C. in 1887. Described as *'conspicuous'* among *'new recreational institutions'* along with railway excursions, brass bands and music halls, soccer was to provide many people from different levels of society with an enjoyable and accessible pastime.[194] In Britain the sport had begun to take shape in the 1860s; the Football Association was created in 1863.[195] The Irish Football Association was founded seventeen years later in 1880.[196] From its foundation, Athlone Town F.C. grew at a rapid pace.[197]

> We are in a position to announce that O.R. Coote Esq., Larkfield, is organising a club under Association rules and already a large number of young men of the town have become members, the annual subscription being five shillings. Through the kindness of Mr S.Wilson, a suitable ground has been obtained, he having given his large field, the entrance to which is from Northgate Street, opposite the town hall.[198]

The first match under association rules, a friendly, took place in January 1887. A high standard of play as well as a sizeable crowd were

---

190 *F.J.*, 16 Mar 1883, 27 Feb 1886, *F.J.*, 6 Apr 1889, *F.J.*, 5 Feb 1890, *F.J.*, 8 Mar 1890, *F.J.*, 21 Mar 1891.
191 Matthew, Colin, p.89.
192 *F.J.*, 18 Apr 1891.
193 *F.J.*, 19 Mar 1892.
194 Horn, Pamela, p.8, Best, Geoffrey, p.220.
195 Daunton, Martin, p.56.
196 Matthew, Colin, p.89.
197 *F.J.*, 8 Jan 1887.
198 *W.I.*, 8 Jan 1887.

reported.[199] The first formal meeting of the members of the club took place in February 1887, at which time a decision was made that the colours for the club would be red and white.[200] The first official match that the club participated in was against Castlerea - established some five years earlier – during the second week in February. The game was played to a scoreless draw on the grounds at Ranelagh where a large crowd, many of whom were ladies, witnessed it.[201]

The team had a large number of matches against army teams and also included a number of army men.[202] Athlone F.C. won the Leinster Junior Cup in 1894 and 1895 though it appears to have played infrequently for the remainder of the Victorian era with newspaper reports becoming quite sparse.[203] There are reports of other soccer matches in the town on occasions such as sports days though the growth of GAA in Athlone may have provided some difficulties for those wishing to assemble teams.[204] Despite this there is evidence of local matches involving townlands, villages, schools and businesses such as Coosan, Glasson, Ranelagh School, Athlone Woollen Mills as well as the army playing civilians in impromptu games.[205] This widespread sporting interaction was believed to be central '...*to the creation of a regional or local identity within an increasingly integrated nation*', though the classes were still believed to have remained segregated for the most part.[206]

Perhaps the first mention of the GAA in Athlone concerned a hurling match that took place on Easter Monday 1886.[207] The sport was not reported on regularly, with little evidence of a high level of popularity, though this cannot be certain. Historians believe that hurling was a direct descendant of the village faction fight, which lost popularity during the Victorian period. The move towards more 'civilised' society saw faction fights branded as brutish affairs, though not all shared that view:

> And, sooth to say, it was not, after all, such a savage and bloodthirsty affair as the modern humanitarian might imagine. It may well be doubted, indeed, if in any other form of battle...could one have had such value in actual fighting with such little detrimental result.[208]

199 *F.J.*, 15 Jan 1887.
200 *F.J.*, 12 Feb 1887.
201 Ibid.
202 Lynch, Frank, *A history of Athlone Town F.C. – The First 101 Years* (Athlone, 1991), p.10.
203 Ibid. p.14–20.
204 *F.J.*, 12 May 1888.
205 *F.J.*, 26 Mar 1887, *F.J.*, 18 Dec 1888, *F.J.*, 17 Dec 1892.
206 Daunton, Martin, pp.56–57.
207 *F.J.*, 1 May 1886.
208 Conmee, Rev. John S., p.14.

A juvenile branch of the GAA was formed in July 1886, and to celebrate, the team marched through Athlone wearing green and gold kits.[209] The necessity for the townspeople to set up a senior GAA branch was reported in the press with teams coming from other parts of the country to play each other in Athlone.[210] There was a report of an Athlone football team playing Tullamore in April 1887, though the game was not regulated by GAA rules.[211] A GAA committee was established in the town by December 1889 when a report delivered stated that there were forty members in the club. It is fair to assume that the club had not been founded much earlier than this meeting as they only started to decide on the team colours by the end of business.[212] A president was elected one week later and the team colours confirmed as green with a white star on the left breast.[213]

After Athlone founded a GAA club Moate did the same.[214] With all of the groundwork in place the team began playing fixtures, one of the first being against Ballinasloe, who won by a single point. The return match showed the popularity of the game in the town with an '*immense*' crowd turning out to witness Athlone exact revenge.[215] During the 1880s, the United Kingdom had seen the growth of spectator sports, soccer and rugby being the most popular in Britain.[216] The popularity of the local team grew with that of the game itself and the town bands accompanied them to Dublin to play in a semi-final of the All-Ireland Club Championship in March 1893.[217]

The ready availability of cheaper bicycles in the early 1890s meant that it was only a matter of time before the town had a bicycle club.[218] The bicycle '*in all its modern essentials*' had been fully designed by the 1880s and a huge investment in production facilities in England had brought the price down.[219] The foundation of the Athlone Bicycle Club occurred in April 1892 and their '*first run*' was to Birr, Co. Offaly with a roundtrip time of just under seven hours.[220] A similar trip organised to Longford in 1893 took a '*full half-day*', with many other '*runs*' taking place.[221] The members of the club organised annual parties for both

209 *FJ.*, 3 July 1886.
210 *FJ.*, 4 June 1887.
211 *FJ.*, 16 Apr 1887.
212 *FJ.*, 4 Jan 1890.
213 *FJ.*, 18 Jan 1890.
214 Ibid.
215 *FJ.*, 15 Feb 1890.
216 Mason, Tony, p.38.
217 *FJ.*, 15 Mar 1893.
218 Daunton, Martin, p.57.
219 Murphy, Brian, pp. 692-693.
220 *FJ.*, 16 Apr 1892, *FJ.*, 23 April 1892.
221 *FJ.*, 8 Apr 1893, *FJ.*, 7 Apr 1894, *FJ.*, 9 June 1894, *FJ.*, 16 June 1894, *FJ.*, 13 Apr 1895.

themselves and invited guests. The first of these parties occurred in November 1893; formerly they had joined the Athlone Commercial Association at their soirees.[222]

The RIC on the Roscommon side of the town started their own cycling club in March 1893 and permitted a small select number of the public to join.[223] The YMCA also decided to open their own club in 1894, though it could be fair to assume that the move would have reduced numbers in the original club due to a membership overlap.[224] The pastime was to remain popular for the remainder of the 19th century. Apart from the more obvious health benefits, the opportunity of going for a cycle also provided the cyclist with a period away from the town, an excursion that would help alleviate the stresses of the mind and body caused by poor urban conditions.

The sports day phenomenon was also introduced into Athlone during the Victorian period. In the 1860s athletics were achieving massive popularity in Britain with the formation of athletics clubs and competitive events.[225] Originally athletics were considered to be exclusively for 'gentlemen' though their appeal meant that it soon became mainstream.[226] The main sports grounds were those at Ranelagh School where most of the large-scale sports days were held. The first was in 1883, with one held annually for a number of years. Some events such as the tug-of-war saw the participation of the army and the local police. The sports day in Athlone was quite inclusive with a number of representatives from both the town and further afield in attendance at the meetings where arrangements for staging the day were made.[227] The field sports that were becoming popular at the time were part of the 1888 sports day and hurling, Gaelic football and soccer matches were staged.[228] The list of events for the 1895 Athletics Day shows the large number of different newer disciplines introduced.[229] The local woollen mills also staged their own annual sports day, as did the League of the Cross and Bicycle Club while the army also held athletics days intermittently.[230]

One of the athletics days became known as Athlone National Sports Day, a name that did not seem to last much longer than two years, with

222 *FJ.*, 18 Nov 1893, *FJ.*, 14 Jan 1893.
223 *FJ.*, 25 Mar 1893.
224 *FJ.*, 4 Apr 1894.
225 Horn, Pamela, p.160.
226 Mason, Tony, p.37.
227 *FJ.*, 17 Mar 1888.
228 *FJ.*, 12 May 1888.
229 *FJ.*, 17 Aug 1895.
230 *FJ.*, 4 Sep 1886, *FJ.*, 25 June 1887, *FJ.*, 2 July 1887, *FJ.*, 2 June 1888, *FJ.*, 6 Aug 1883, *FJ.*, 18 Aug 1894,
     FJ., 28 July 1888.

employers in the town offering a half-day to their staff in 1888 so that they could participate. These games, whilst also played at Ranelagh, do not appear to have replaced the older Ranelagh sports days that happened just three months beforehand in June 1888 and again in 1889.[231] The Athlone National Sports Day held in 1889 was said to be a big tourist draw with the railways carrying large numbers of people to the town for the event.[232] The staging of sports days at Ranelagh and smaller venues around the town continued right through the 1890s.[233]

It appears that golf was introduced into town around 1892, with the establishment of Athlone Garrison Golf Club. Evidence of golfing tournaments during the remainder of the Victorian period is scarce though there are articles such as one from 1897 giving details of a competition between Athlone and Mullingar.[234] A course was built in the town on the site of the batteries on the west side that were erected during the Napoleonic wars. It consisted of nine holes, with games played mainly between the months of October and April when the grass was shorter and other sports took a winter break.[235] A number of other towns set up clubs during the last decade of the 19th century such as Birr, Mullingar, Tullamore and Moate and this meant that there was enough competition locally to ensure the growth of the game.[236]

TEMPERANCE

The temperance movement was one of the more influential social movements of the Victorian era. Its main aim was to bring about a society less dependant on alcohol, which many believed was at the root of slow progress in societal improvements. As already noted in relation to the army, one historian believes that the amount of drinking done by the poorer classes in the Victorian period has been thought of as an anxiety-based reaction, an attempt to alleviate the pressures felt under *'intolerable socio-economic circumstances.'*[237] Many people in Victorian society lived in economically depressed areas of towns and cities where they had to cope with appalling conditions, and few prospects of advancement. In many cases the local public house was the destination where they would attempt to 'drown their sorrows'. Even those for whom the socio-economic pressures may not have been as oppressive,

231 *F.J.*, 30 June 1888, *F.J.*, 6 July 1889.
232 *F.J.*, 17 Aug 1889.
233 *F.J.*, 5 July 1890, *F.J.*, 1 July 1893, *F.J.*, 30 June 1894, *F.J.*, 17 Aug 1895, *F.J.*, 22 Aug 1896, *F.J.*, 3 Oct 1896, *F.J.*, 27 Aug 1898, *F.J.*, 17 Sep 1898, *F.J.*, 16 Sep 1899.
234 *F.J.*, 6 Nov 1897.
235 Collins, Tom, pp. 16-18.
236 Ibid. p. 19.
237 Malcolm, Elizabeth, p.327.

the public house was still one of the main places to socialise, for the working classes it was the equivalent of '*symphony concerts and of literature*'.[238] The prominence of alcohol in people's lives and the debilitating effect this was believed to have on economic growth led to temperance movements cropping up all over Britain and Ireland and even as far away as America and Australia. A temperate society was idealised as one in which economic fortunes would improve, proper morals proliferate, and hence society improve as a whole. The temperance movements had to provide alternatives for people who gravitated all too readily to public houses; they had to change the habits of an entire generation.

In Ireland the temperance movement began in earnest in the 1830s under the guidance of Fr. Theobald Mathew, a Catholic priest. In general, the Catholic Church did not offer outright support to the temperance campaign in the country. At times Fr. Mathew was himself responsible for his fellow clergymen taking a dim view of the movement.[239] There were certain facets of his crusade that rankled many within the church – his use of a life-long abstinence pledge, the involvement of Protestants in the movement, the sale of temperance medals and Mathew's own behaviour.[240] Some believed that a fixed term pledge of, for example, five years was more than sufficient, taking '*man's weak nature*' into account.[241] The fact that alcohol was legally sold in Ireland coupled with the fact that it was lawful to consume it caused many problems when it came to declaring it an 'evil'. Many priests would remind those within the movement that the apostles in the Bible consumed wine and that if imbibed in moderation it was not generally a cause of ructions or iniquity.

In Athlone there were innumerable cases reported in the local press that dealt with the scourge of drinking, many outlining breaches of the peace, assaults, suicides and murders.[242] Rev. Strean, writing in 1819, laid the blame for many iniquitous acts seen in Athlone on public houses and, indeed more specifically, on Sunday opening:

> A species of trade this, by which, from the unreasonable number of such houses, and keeping them open on Sundays, a practice which is generally too little restrained, the morals of the peasantry are very much corrupted,

238 Horn, Pamela, p.63.
239 Malcolm, Elizabeth, "The catholic church and the Irish temperance movement, 1838-1901", in *Irish Historical Studies*, Vol. 23, No. 89 (Antrim, 1982), p.1.
240 Ibid.
241 Ibid. p.2.
242 *F.J.*, 6 July 1836, *F.J.*, 1 July 1845, *F.J.*, 22 Aug 1848, *F.J.*, 10 Aug 1872, *F.J.*, 22 July 1874, *F.J.*, 12 June 1878, *F.J.*, 31 Jan 1885, *F.J.*, 12 Sep 1885, *F.J.*, 28 Apr 1888, *F.J.*, 2 June 1888, *F.J.*, 9 June 1888, *F.J.*, 26 Jan 1889, *F.J.*, 30 Apr 1892, *F.J.*, 7 July 1894, *F.J.*, 4 May 1895, *F.J.*, 24 June 1899.

the day appointed to be kept holy and dedicated to the service of God is spent in every species of vice which the unrestrained abuse of spirituous liquors, and idleness are capable of producing, as intoxication excites the baser passions, and urges its unfortunate votaries to the most criminal acts which depraved hearts and ungovernable heads are capable of perpetrating, all or most of which might be prevented by a vigorous enforcing of the laws enacted for that very purpose.[243]

Strean even went as far as to say that Sunday drinking was leading to a surge in the number of illegitimate children as well as the '*murdering* [of] *same*'![244] As already mentioned in *chapter six*, drink played a prominent role in many of the most commonly reported crimes of the period. The temperance movement in the town blamed most of the transgressions on the consumption of liquor and they attempted to find entertainment without alcohol for people to dissuade them from visiting public houses. The success of the alternative entertainment hinged on a number of factors, one of which was the advertising of these events. The movement appeared to have the support of some of the local press with *The Athlone Sentinel* turning up to cover a '*large Temperance Tea Party*' held in October 1840.[245] It must be remembered that this report, and others like it, would not have been read by most of the working class in the town, who had low levels of literacy, and therefore, may not have reached those who could benefit most from it. The four-day visit of Fr. Mathew himself in September 1840 was said to have brought out '*vast multitudes*' of people on the streets with a variety of alcohol-free entertainments on offer. Interestingly it was noted that Protestants as well as Catholics took the abstinence pledge during Mathew's visit.[246]

When Daniel O'Connell visited Athlone for his 'Monster Meeting' in 1843 he asked all assembled there which of them were teetotallers, a question to which most of those assembled gestured in the affirmative. Jacob Venedey believed that the crowd would have caused disturbances at the meeting '...*if Temperance had not first spread its soothing blessings among them*'.[247] Venedey had written that whiskey was the Irishman's version of Indian firewater but that '...*the newly awakened sense of national identity among the peasantry made them conscious that it was one of the sources of their slavery*.'[248] By all accounts it appears that the movement was quite strong in the town. O'Connell was himself a former teetotaller, though

243 Strean, Annesley, pp.66/7.
244 Ibid., p.105.
245 Kerrigan, Colm, *Father Mathew and the Irish Temperance Movement 1838 – 1849* (Cork, 1992), p.76.
246 *A.S.*, 11 Sep 1840.
247 Kerrigan, Colm, p.123.
248 Bourke, Eoin, p.24.

he 'had' to resort to consuming alcohol again due to a medical condition, as apparently did many others of the period.[249] Fr Mathew became very wary of this reason for breaking the abstinence pledge, granting pardons from pledges on fewer occasions as the years passed.[250]

There is evidence that the temperance and repeal movements were more closely linked in the county than one might have expected. A number of reports from local magistrates regarding the link between the two spoke of how, in some instances, the members of the local repeal movement and of the temperance societies were the same, with others believing that the Ribbon Societies stemmed from the temperance/repeal societies.[251] This would not be in keeping with the general sentiment that the temperance movement, and the total abstinence movement in particular, were very Protestant in nature – the pledge on the cards issued by Fr Mathew actually contained a quote from a 'Protestant' King James version of the Bible.[252] Fr Mathew himself was a very vocal critic of all those who attempted to link his movement with that of O'Connell; indeed he complained about it to the point of '*antagonising all parties*.'[253] Herr Venedey also noted the '*military regularity*' of those people supporting the temperance movement, a regularity that he believed could only be bad for the union with England.

Alcohol was an important export from Ireland during the Famine years and huge volumes of the spirit were sent to England.[254] Athlone had two distilleries and two breweries in 1837, which were possibly the largest employers in the town up to the mid-Victorian era; the temperance movement may have affected their trade.[255] The movement was seen to be progressing well in the late 1830s and early 1840s, in Athlone, partially due to the influence and work of the Augustinians, though the Famine spelled the end of this, the first chapter in the temperance story in the 19th century.

After the Famine the mood in relation to the movement was somewhat different nationally. Those terrible events of the late 1840s were to alter radically the mindset of many of the citizens of Ireland, not just politically but also socially. A different set of standards was being drawn up as part of Victorian 'modern thinking': people's habits had to change to allow the society to develop in a positive manner and

249 Kerrigan, Colm, p.121.
250 Malcolm, Irish temperance, p.3.
251 Kerrigan, Colm, p.124.
252 Malcolm, Irish temperance, p.3.
253 Ibid., p.5.
254 Kinealy, Christine, p.35.
255 Lewis, Samuel, p.81.

temperance was to prove to be a large constituent in this push. Nationally, towards the end of the Famine, the Catholic Church was seen to be unsupportive of the movement in general; a synod in Thurles in 1850 ignored the question of temperance altogether. Also a large number of temperance associations in towns had not survived the Famine.[256]

A visitor to Athlone in 1850 spoke to a local man in an attempt to discover the state of the temperance movement and admitted that he believed '*Athlone never seems to have been very strong in this way*', even though it did have a temperance hall with 337 members.[257] The society that maintained the hall was in debt, though they did have a small library that subscribed to three newspapers. The person to whom he spoke had been a teetotaller for some time and was, according to the writer, a good example of what abstinence from alcohol could help one achieve:

> My informant was himself a good illustration of the value of the system. He confessed that if he had been a teetotaller ten years sooner he would have now been a rich man and worth £200! Previously to taking the pledge, he had spent not only all his earnings on drink, but had, according to the testimony of his wife, admitted by himself, wasted all his humble substance, his furniture and his clothes, on the same miserable object. He seemed now cheerful and happy, his little shop and room comfortably furnished, his wife and daughter neatly dressed, and more money made than was spent. He admitted that he had put by and preserved £75 since he had exorcised the evil spirit of his house.[258]

In contrast to the above account was one penned by a man named John Forbes who travelled around Ireland in the early 1850s assessing the state of temperance in the towns and villages. In Athlone he stated that there were only fourteen teetotallers, with towns such as Killarney and Galway apparently having a far healthier temperance situation.[259]

Nationally, during the early 1850s, there was a fall in the consumption of spirits, though some historians believe that the tax levied on whiskey in 1853 was more likely to have precipitated the fall, and evidence from the time shows a sharp fall soon after the government passed that law.[260] One of Athlone's distilleries, Robinson's, had closed in 1850 due to the death of the owner. The fact that it was not reopened may point towards a strong temperance movement in the

256 Malcolm, Irish temperance, p.5.
257 Forbes, John, M. D., p.206/210.
258 Ibid., p.206/210.
259 Malcolm, Elizabeth, p.152.
260 Cullen, Louis M., p.138.

town; prospective owners may have believed that there was not a sufficient market for the product. Another more modern belief was that the Famine had mostly blown away the somewhat subversive culture of violence, drunkenness and ignorance, leaving a more conformist, prosperous, 'religious' culture to take its place.[261] As stated above the Victorians were actively seeking to establish a culture of respectability.

Many believe that the over-consumption of alcohol in the nineteenth century, be it in Ireland or in England, was to some extent inevitable:

> The system of rule and regulation as to the times and occasions of drinking, pervades all branches of society in Great Britain – at meals, markets, fairs, baptisms, and funerals; and almost every trade and profession has its own code of strict and well-observed laws on the subject. There are numerous occasions when general custom makes the offer and reception of liquor as imperative as the law of the land.[262]

In this regard the push in some quarters in England towards Sunday closing caused the London Riots of 1855, for drinking on the Sabbath was seen as *'largely a working-class necessity.'*[263]

Whatever the real number of teetotallers in Athlone during the 1850s, the temperance movement in the town appeared to gain greater impetus from the 1870s onwards when the local Athlone Woollen Mills became profitable. In the intervening years the most common types of temperance societies in the country were Protestant-dominated, hence most of the working class was not involved. The main aim of these societies was to bring about legislation to restrict alcohol consumption in the country, most notably to introduce a Sunday Closing Bill.[264]

In England, the move towards closing on the Sabbath was gaining strength throughout the 1870s, with the cause becoming a force in the Liberal politics of the time. Some believe that the lack of success in the temperance drive was due to the radical nature of the proposals put forth, since many believed them impractical and impossible to implement.[265] The proprietors of the woollen mills, Gleeson and Smith, spent some of their spare time, and, later in the century, their money on advertising the virtues of temperance. These men, like the English temperance society activists '...*were well established and economically secure*'; and they had the time and money, to spend on the problem.[266] One example of involvement by the two men from the mills occurred

261 O'Farrell, Patrick, p.77.
262 Harrison, J.F.C., p.78.
263 Pelling, Henry, p.68.
264 Malcolm, Irish temperance, p.6.
265 Trevelyan, G. M., p.206.
266 Shiman, Lillian, Lewis, *Crusade against drink in Victorian England* (New York, 1988), p.246.

in 1871 when Gleeson chaired a meeting in the Town Hall where a diorama was presented in an alcohol-free setting. Again in this case the attendees were probably not working-class citizens, more likely they came from the local middle classes. *The Westmeath Independent* described the attendance as '...*most numerous and respectable – so large an assemblage was never before seen in the Town Hall.*'[267] The drive towards more organised work practices, typical of Victorian thinking, influenced the Operative Bakers of Athlone Association to outlaw any of their members from operating under the influence of drink. The decree from 1872 warned of a 6d fine per offence.[268]

During the 1870s bills were introduced in parliament in connection with the temperance movement. However, the legislation that was introduced to combat Sunday drinking was not judged a success in Athlone. The law stipulated that the townspeople could not drink in their usual haunts but only in those public houses that were three miles away or more. The publicans complained of the fall-off in business, whilst drinkers from Athlone just left to visit pubs the proscribed three miles away. In one case a funeral was described as far better attended than expected when the burial was heard to be in Drum, which had a public house.[269] In fact the main drinking day in Ireland was Saturday, especially at nighttime when the vast majority of arrests for drunken behaviour were made. The early 1870s saw the consumption of alcohol rise to its highest level during the nineteenth century where it accounted for 15% of total consumption of goods in the United Kingdom at the time.[270] The figure of course could not take into account the consumption of illicit beverages, prevalent in Ireland and Scotland, so even higher volumes were actually being imbibed.[271] However, the restrictions may have been working to some extent locally. The Westmeath Assizes recorded a drop in the number of drunkenness cases by sixteen from 402 to 386 in the period June 1872 – June 1873, when compared with the previous twelve-month period, yet the temperance movement were still unhappy with Sunday opening even with restrictions.[272] A meeting of temperance supporters in the Town Hall in 1874 issued the following statement:

> That, convinced of the fact that drunkenness is on the increase, and that this were greatly due to the intensity of the temptation to which all

267 *W.I.*, 11 Mar 1871.
268 *W.I.*, 31 Aug 1872.
269 *F.J.*, 4 Oct 1878.
270 Daunton, Martin, p.56.
271 Best, Geoffrey, p.240.
272 *F.J.*, 15 July 1873.

classes are exposed, especially in connection with the sale of Intoxicating Liquors on Sundays, this Meeting desires to express its conviction that a measure totally closing all public houses and beer-shops on that day, would be welcomed by all classes of the community, and would prove a powerful agent in diminishing the great evil so universally lamented.[273]

However, Sunday Closing did not happen at that time. A parliamentary vote rejected the Sunday Closing Bill due to a large vote from the English MPs against it, though it was favoured by the majority of the Irish members.[274] The English temperance societies or '*supporters of purity crusades*' attempted to sway the government in England with as little success, for they, like their Irish counterparts, saw drink as creating vice and iniquity.[275] The problem of drunkenness was, as already noted, seen as a working class problem. The upper classes did drink, though the depths of '*pain, misery, loneliness and boredom*' that the lower classes sank to caused them to reach for the bottle more frequently.[276] Ireland was granted a Sunday closure law in 1878 after a long struggle by the temperance groups, though it was seen to be limited and temporary.[277]

The temperance hall continued to offer an alternative and was to hold a number of concerts for the locals, most of which were successful. There was one pencilled in for most St. Patrick's Days – due to their reputation for being a day spent in the local public houses.[278] The Church of Ireland Temperance Society held a function in 1885 that attracted 200 of their 395 strong membership; this level of membership shows that a very high proportion of the Church of Ireland community in the town was teetotal.[279] The Athlone Methodist Temperance Society held a similar gathering in 1886 with their members numbering fifty-five, twenty-seven of whom were military men.[280] The strong showing in these two denominations in the town provided some proof to Catholic sceptics that temperance was '...a *Protestant-inspired movement with dubious political affiliations*.'[281]

The main Catholic moves in the temperance debate came around the same time and quite strongly, in the form of The League of the Cross. Like its counterparts, the League was an avid proponent of temperance in the town providing lectures on the virtues of abstinence and the

273 *FJ*, 5 Dec 1874.
274 *FJ*, 5 Dec 1874.
275 Daunton, Martin, p. 65.
276 Best, Geoffrey, p.241.
277 Malcolm, Elizabeth, p.249, Matthew, Introduction, p. 5.
278 *FJ*, 21 Mar 1885.
279 *FJ*, 12 Dec 1885.
280 *FJ*, 20 Mar 1886.
281 Malcolm, Irish temperance, p.7.

dangers of drinking staged in tandem with alcohol-free functions.[282] The sermons given by some of the clergy on the evils of drink regularly dealt with the effect that drink could have on the afterlife. One priest spoke of how a drunk could not receive the last rites and would therefore spend eternity in punishment.[283]

The League was originally founded in 1872 in England as an exclusively Catholic total abstinence society.[284] The Athlone branch was founded by a temperance activist, Fr. McGoey, in January 1885 and was, from the beginning, strongly committed to the cause.[285] An account by a stranger to the town describing New Year's Day 1889 said that '*drink did not hold sway*' either in the town or at a dance held by the League of the Cross which pleasantly surprised him, for the conviviality of '*the bone and sinew of the town*' was heartening.[286] The way in which the article was written would suggest that the League of the Cross was actually reaching a large number of working-class people; formerly it appears the other societies had not. Indeed, many clergymen saw another use of the temperance movement in both Ireland and England. It would, they believed, be useful: '*…as part of a campaign to raise the socio-economic status of Catholics and help integrate them into the existing society.*'[287] Some believed that the efforts made to change the mindset of the Irish people and the Victorians as a whole, through the promotion of temperance, education or other activities, really were an attempt to make the working classes become more suited to the society that was growing around them and to accept its values more readily.[288]

One problem with the temperance movement in Ireland amongst Roman Catholics was that the majority of them still lived in rural areas. In many cases priests were uncomfortable with attempts to force total abstinence on these locals. As one historian noted: '*Where homes were least homely, work most uncertain or disagreeable, people least able or willing to save, pubs or other drinking places naturally became social centres.*'[289] Whilst this comment referred to Britain, the harsh life of many in rural Ireland and in Irish country towns meant that this assessment would especially ring true here. It must also be noted that the importance of the local publican cannot be overestimated, since he was at times second in importance only to the priest in a small village or country area.[290]

282 *FJ.*, 22 Jan 1887, *FJ.*, 15 June 1889, *FJ.*, 28 July 1889, *FJ.*, 9 Aug 1890.
283 *FJ.*, 28 Sep 1878.
284 Malcolm, Irish temperance, p.9.
285 *FJ.*, 31 Jan 1885.
286 *FJ.*, 5 Jan 1889.
287 Malcolm, Irish temperance, p.9.
288 Harrison, J.F.C., p.135.
289 Best, Geoffrey, p.242.
290 Malcolm, Irish temperance, p.9.

Towards the end of the century, drink was finding itself in competition with other forms of social entertainment such as theatre and music though it was not until the 20th century that competition in the form of cinemas, radio and the motorised car brought about a wholesale change in drinking habits in the United Kingdom.[291]

With the rise in popularity of field sports in the late 1880s, the local clergy called for sporting events not to become associated with drinking, but to be played on the principles of temperance.[292] The Athlone Workingmen's Temperance Society was established in the 1890s, and again the purpose was to provide men with alternative entertainment so that the lure of the public house would not prove too strong.[293]

Athlone was visited by the leader of the World Temperance Movement in 1896. She was pleased with what she saw: the Irish had lessened their drinking to such a degree that the English were now, in her opinion, seen as far more intemperate.[294] Towards the end of the 19th century lectures on temperance were delivered more frequently to large attendances, and mainly '*fashionable*' people, were seen at most presentations.[295] The work of Fr. Cullen founder of the total abstinence movement, or Pioneer League, was providing returns for the movement as a whole. Cullen wished to '...*make Ireland permanently sober and Ireland permanently free.*' By saying this he was linking the struggle for national sobriety with that of national freedom, an attempted reversal of the associations with Protestantism that hindered the earlier movement of Fr. Mathew.

The temperance movement received its greatest boost locally with the news that William Smith of the Athlone Woollen Mills was to finance a temperance hall in the town dedicated to Fr. Mathew.[296] Throughout the Victorian period there were perhaps half a dozen establishments for those interested in the temperance movement, though, for a variety of reasons, none of these appear to have persisted for a long period.[297] The hall was opened to a large audience in Nov 1897 and was used as a tearoom and for concerts.[298] The construction of the hall and the general pace of the temperance movement caused some local publicans a certain level of anxiety.

291 Trevelyan, G.M., p.208.
292 *EJ*, 12 July 1890.
293 *EJ*., 12 Dec 1891.
294 *EJ*, 4 Apr 1896.
295 *EJ*, 24 Mar 1894, *EJ*, 26 Oct 1895, *EJ*, 14 Nov.
296 *EJ*, 19 Dec 1896.
297 Murtagh, H., pp.14-15.
298 *EJ*, 27 Nov 1897.

At a meeting of the Town Commissioners a memorial from the Irish Association for the prevention of intemperance caused a publican to call the organisers '*Temperance Shouters*'; he went on to state that they '*...draw larger income from the spirit trade than I do.*'[299] His views were condemned at the next meeting: it was pointed out to him that twenty-two members of the Association were Bishops, mostly Catholic.[300]

The local temperance movement again broached the issue of Sunday closing at a meeting in 1898 calling on the authorities to close all public houses on that day.[301] The movement in Athlone appears to have been winning the battle against drinking: a newspaper report on the celebrations held in the town on St. Patrick's Day stated: '*...not since the days of Fr. Mathew was there such temperance*'.[302] Smaller temperance associations had been founded near the town; the Drum association joined its Athlone equivalent in providing an excursion for members in July 1898.[303]

The level of success of the Fr Mathew Hall appeared to be quite high; at its first annual meeting in October 1898 membership had reached 694, with the café and concert venue described as very busy.[304] Concerts were held regularly so as to '*...maintain interest among members and supporters.*'[305] The café mainly offered tea as the alternative drink; the beverage had become very popular in the preceding twenty years, especially with women. In fact, its popularity in the United Kingdom as a whole, jumped massively in the 1870s and tea along with sugar led to a substantial growth in the import bill.[306] The hall held a large number of meetings and concerts and was still the main temperance hall in the town in 1900.[307]

As to the situation regarding temperance generally, a report from 1900 stated that it was unfortunate: '*...to find from grim and stern statistics that the Drink Fiend still stalks through the land with a vigorous step despite all that has been done to halt his onward march of destruction.*' The article went on to state that the temperance movement had accomplished much however, and that there was a '*bright and happy era of sobriety*' to look forward to.[308]

It is evident that the situation in England at the end of the Victorian

299 *F.J.*, 17 Apr 1897.
300 *F.J.*, 24 Apr 1897.
301 *F.J.*, 5 Feb 1898.
302 *F.J.*, 19 Mar 1898.
303 *F.J.*, 16 July 1898.
304 *F.J.*, 15 Oct 1898.
305 Horn, Pamela, p.250.
306 Murphy, Brian, p.639.
307 *F.J.*, 11 Nov 1899, *W.I.*, 20 Oct 1900.
308 *W.I.*, 11 Dec 1900.

era was quite different from that at the start: '…*drunkenness was no longer treated with the good-hearted tolerance of former times.*'[309] One estimate, considered inflated by most historians, stated that there were eight million teetotallers in the United Kingdom, and even if this number was exaggerated, there is no doubt that the temperance movement was one of the most influential.[310]

The availability of leisure time undoubtedly caused the number and type of recreational activities to grow. In the United Kingdom as a whole there was a great thirst for new experiences, new hobbies and new pastimes.

The establishment of societies in Athlone was very much in keeping with the Victorian trend towards creating respectable havens in which people could invest their energy. The societies exposed many to lectures, books and sports, which should ideally have brought about the intended improvement in character of the members. The appreciation of the arts through the medium of theatre can be seen to have grown considerably throughout the Victorian era. Plays were staged more frequently, and people viewed them in greater numbers than ever before. An increase in the number of circuses, due in part to better communications, gave the townspeople a greater exposure to entertainment, which became easily accessible and very popular. The better communications also gave rise to a tourism industry based around the river, which is still Athlone's main attraction.

The brass and fife and drum bands of the local garrison without doubt impelled many to join local bands leading to a growth in their popularity. The army bands certainly influenced what bands wore and how they performed. By the end of the Victorian era, the civilian bands in Athlone were becoming distinctly nationalist, and were the counterbalance to those in the garrison, which generally played on loyalist occasions.

The Victorian era saw an explosion in the number of sports played in Athlone. Some of the early sports from the 18th century were for the upper classes e.g. yachting, horseracing and hunting. These were seen to grow in the Victorian period, though not all at the same pace. Sports for the lower classes from the 18th century, such as cockfighting, were not seen as in keeping with the progressive and 'right-thinking' direction that Victorian society was taking and fell in popularity. Their replacements, soccer, Gaelic football and hurling were certainly more civilised, and all of them grew more popular as the years progressed. The

309 Shiman, Lillian, p.245.
310 Ibid., p.247.

games of soccer and rugby maintained their popularity through the presence of the garrison in the town and even cricket appears to have achieved a reasonable level of support due to the army.

One of the virtues of sport was that it provided a distraction for many people who would have spent their free time in public houses. Some sports were also thought of as good transmitters of culture, lower class men could learn how to be more gentlemanly through interacting brought about by participation with a social élite. Tennis provided women with a diversion from their traditional duties and was a useful step in the battle for sexual equality. Sport in the town became far more organised, with many new games imported from Britain, as well as some of the Irish sports, adopting the Victorian characteristics of associations operating under rules.

The growth and development of all of these forms of entertainment continued right into the 20th century and many people spent their free time engaged in updating and promoting them. The Victorian era to a large extent created many of the sports we play, or at least determined how we play them. It facilitated the evolution of music, theatre and societies providing much of the apparatus used by people in the 20th century for becoming involved in these pursuits.

By the end of the period alcoholic drink still featured very prominently in the lives of Athlone people. Alternative drinks such as tea were becoming more readily available though it would take a number of years for them to gain a larger consumer base. Of course the number of changes witnessed during the Victorian era certainly had some effect on alcohol consumption in Ireland: '*Economical, legal, social and recreational changes had a significant impact on drink consumption, all tending in the direction of diminishing it.*'[311]

311 Malcolm, Elizabeth, p.327.

Bibliography

Primary Sources

PARLIAMENTARY PAPERS, LOCAL AUTHORITY RECORDS AND PRINTED REPORTS

Addenda to the Census of Ireland for the year 1841; showing the number of houses, families and persons in the several townlands and towns of Ireland (Alexander Thom & Co., Dublin, 1844).

Athlone Common Council Minute Book 1804-1816 (Aidan Heavey Public Library, Athlone).

Athlone Town Commissioners Minute Book 1846-1847 (Aidan Heavey Public Library, Athlone).

Census of Ireland for the year 1851, part 1; showing the Area, Population and Number of Houses by Townlands and Electoral Divisions (Alexander Thom & Co., Dublin, 1852).

Census of Ireland for the Year 1851, Part VI – General Report (Alexander Thom & Co., Dublin, 1853).

Census of Ireland for the Year 1861, Part V – General Report (Alexander Thom & Co., Dublin, 1864).

Census of Ireland 1871, Part 1 – Area, houses and population: also the, civil condition, occupations, birthplaces, religion and education of the people, Vol. 1, Leinster (Alexander Thom & Co., Dublin, 1873).

Census of Ireland 1871, Part 1 – Area, houses and population: also the, civil condition, occupations, birthplaces, religion and education of the people, Vol. 4, Connaught (Alexander Thom & Co., Dublin, 1873).

Census of Ireland 1881, Part 1 – Area, houses and population: also the, civil condition, occupations, birthplaces, religion and education of the people, Vol. 1, Leinster (Alexander Thom & Co., Dublin, 1881).

Census of Ireland 1881, Part 1 – Area, houses and population: also the, civil condition, occupations, birthplaces, religion and education of the people, Vol. 4, Connaught (Alexander Thom & Co., Dublin, 1882).

Census of Ireland, 1881, Part II, General Report with Illustrative Maps and Diagrams, Tables and Appendix (Alexander Thom & Co., Dublin, 1882).

Census of Ireland 1891, Part 1 – Area, houses and population: also the, civil condition, occupations, birthplaces, religion and education of the people, Vol. 1, Leinster (Alexander Thom & Co., Dublin, 1891).

Census of Ireland 1891, Part 1 – Area, houses and population: also the, civil condition, occupations, birthplaces, religion and education of the people, Vol. 4, Connaught (Alexander Thom & Co., Dublin, 1891).

Census of Ireland, 1891, Part II, General Report with Illustrative Maps and Diagrams, Tables and Appendix (Alexander Thom & Co., Dublin, 1892).

Census of Ireland 1901, Part 1 – Area, houses and population: also the, civil condition, occupations, birthplaces, religion and education of the people, Vol. 1, Leinster (Cahill and Co., Dublin, 1901).

Distress Reports — Z series RLFC2/Z14282 10th Oct 1845, National Archives of Ireland (NAI).

Distress Reports — Z series RLFC2/Z14362 26th Oct 1845, NAI.

Distress Reports — Z series RLFC2/Z414 22nd Jan 1846, NAI.

Distress Reports — Z series RLFC2/Z5646 21st Mar 1846, NAI.

Distress Reports — Z Series RLFC2/Z5954 18th March 1846, NAI.

Distress Reports — Z series RLFC2/Z5942 22nd Mar 1846, NAI.

Distress Reports — Z Series RLFC2/Z5954 5th April 1846, NAI.

Distress Reports — Z Series RLFC3/1/1495 15th April 1846, NAI.

Distress Reports — Z Series RLFC3/1/3643 24th June 1846, NAI.

Dublin Almanac and General Register of Ireland, 1837 (Pettigrew and Oulton, Dublin, 1837).

Dublin Almanac and General Register of Ireland, 1848 (Pettigrew and Oulton, Dublin, 1848).

First Report of the Commissioners of Public Instruction — Ireland (William Clowes & Sons, London, 1835).

General Valuation of Rateable Property in Ireland, Union of Athlone, Valuation of the several Tenements comprised in that portion of the above named Union, Situate in the County of Westmeath (Alexander Thom & Co., Dublin, 1854).

General Valuation of Rateable Property in Ireland, Union of Athlone, Valuation of the several Tenements comprised in that portion of the above named Union, Situate in the County of Roscommon (Alexander Thom & Co., Dublin, 1855).

Godkin, James, *Education in Ireland, it's History, Institutions, Systems, Statistics and Progress from the earliest times to the present* (Alexander Thom & Co., Dublin, 1862).

Grimshaw, Thomas, et al, *Manual for Public Health for Ireland* (Dulin, Fannin and Co., Dublin. 1875).

Grimshaw, Thomas Wrigley, *Remarks on impending Sanitary Legislation for Ireland* (Browne and Nolan, Dublin, 1874).

Kane, Robert, M.D., *The Industrial Resources of Ireland,* 2nd Ed. (Hodges and Smith, Dublin, 1845).

Land Owners in Ireland - Return of owners of land of one acre and upwards in the several counties, counties of cities, counties of towns in Ireland in 1876 (Genealogical Publishing Co. Inc., Baltimore, 1988).

Lyons, John Charles, *The Grand Juries of the County of Westmeath from the year 1727 to the year 1853 with an Historical Appendix, 2 Volumes* (John Charles Lyons, 1853).

Mason, William Shaw, *A Statistical Account or Parochial Survey — Drawn up from the communications of the clergy,* (Faulkner Press, Dublin, 1819).

Moore, S. Arthur, *Sanitary Acts for Ireland* (Alexander Thom & Co., Dublin, 1848).

Observations of the provisional directors of the Mullingar, Athlone and Longford Railway on the report of the board of trade on railways proposed to be made in Ireland, Westward from Dublin (Webb & Chapman, Dublin, 1845).

Papers relating to Proceedings for the relief of the distress and State of the Union and Workhouses in Ireland 5th Series 1848 (William Clowes and Sons, London, 1848).

Papers relating to Proceedings for the relief of the distress and State of the Union and Workhouses in Ireland 6th Series 1848 (William Clowes and Sons, London, 1848).

Papers relating to Proceedings for the relief of the distress and State of the Union and Workhouses in Ireland 8th Series 1849 (Alexander Thom & Co., Dublin, 1849).

Papers relating to the Shannon Navigation Act 1874, HC 1875 (Alexander Thom & Co., Dublin, 1875).

Parliamentary representation: boundary reports (Ireland), H. C. 1831-32 (519), xliii, 23.

Report of the Commissioners appointed to inquire into the Municipal Corporations in Ireland (William Clowes & Sons, London, 1835).

Report of the Commissioners appointed to inquire into the State of Fairs and Markets in Ireland (Alexander Thom & Co., Dublin, 1855).

Report from His Majesty's Commissioners for Inquiring into the system of Military Punishments in the Army, with Appendices (W. Clowes and Sons, London, 1836).

Report of the Commissioners appointed to take The Census of Ireland for the year 1841, (Alexander Thom & Co., Dublin, 1843).

Report from the Select Committee on Bribery and Intimidation at Elections (London, 1835).

Report of the Select Committee on Outrages (Ireland) (Henry Hansard & Son, London, 1852,).

Reports and evidence relating to Shannon Navigation 1836-67 (Alexander Thom, Dublin, 1839-67).

Return of Outrages reported to the Constabulary Office in Ireland during the year 1861, with summaries for preceding years: and also, Return of Outrages reported by the Constabulary in Ireland during the month of April 1862 (Alexander Thom & Co., Dublin, 1863).

Royal commission of inquiry, primary education (Ireland), Vol. VI, Educational Census. Returns showing the number of children actually present in each primary school on 25th June 1868 [...] (Alexander Thom & Co., Dublin, 1871).

Report of the Select Commission on Industries – Ireland, (Henry Hansard & Son, London, 1885).

Second Report of the commissioners on public instruction, Ireland, (HC 1835, xxxiv).

Second report on the drainage and navigation of the River Shannon, 1867/8 (Dublin, 1869).

Slater's National Commercial Directory of Ireland 1846, 1854, 1870, 1881, 1894 (London).

Statement as to the decline of Trades and Manufacturers since the Union 1834-43, National Library of Ireland (NLI) MS 13629 (5)

The Parliamentary Gazetteer of Ireland, Adapted to the new Poor Law, Franchise, Municipal and Ecclesiastical arrangements and compiled with special reference [...], Vol.1 A-C (A Fullerton & Co., Dublin, 1844).

Thom's Irish Almanac and Official Directory/ Thom's Official Directory of the United Kingdom of Great Britain and Ireland, 1847-1902, (Alexander Thom & Co., Dublin).

The Irish Crisis of 1879-80, Proceedings of the Dublin Mansion House Relief Committee 1880, (Browne and Nolan, Dublin, 1881).

The Towns Improvement Act and Sanitary Reform in Ireland (Webb & Son, Dublin, 1861).

Vanston, George T.B., *The Law relating to Municipal Towns under the Towns Improvement (Ireland) Act 1854* (Edward Ponsonby, Dublin, 1900).

CONTEMPORARY ACCOUNTS AND TRAVELOGUES

Banim, Mary, *Here and There Through Ireland* (The Freeman's Journal, Dublin, 1892).

Bickerdyke, John, (Charles Henry Cook), *Wildsports in Ireland, with numerous illustrations* (Upcott and Gill, London, 1897).

Bradbury, John, *Connemara and the West Coast of Ireland, how to see them for six guineas*, (Simpkin and Marshall, London, 1871).

Conmee, Rev. S.J., *Old Times in the Barony* (Carraig Books, Dublin, 1979).

Conner, MacCarthy, *The Game Laws of Ireland with Irish Game Statutes Codified and Notes of Reported Cases* (Hodges Figgis, Dublin, 1891).

Cooke, John, (Ed.), *Handbook for Travellers in Ireland* (Edward Stanford, London, 1902).

Coulter, Henry, *The West of Ireland: its Existing Condition and Prospects* (Hodges and Smith, Dublin, 1862).

The Dublin Builder, Vol. IV, June 1st, 1862, no.59 (Dublin, 1862)

Edgeworth, Harold Butler (Ed.), *Maria Edgeworth, Tour in Connemara and the Martins of Ballinahinch* (Constable and Company, London, 1950).

Forbes, John, M.D., F.R.S., *Memorandum made in Ireland in the Autumn of 1852* (London, 1853).

Hall, Mr. & Mrs. S.C., *Ireland: Its Scenery, Character, &c.,* Vol. III (Jeremiah How, London, 1843).

Inglis, H.D., *A journey through Ireland during the spring, summer, and autumn of 1834*, (London, 1834).

Joly, Rev. John S., *The old Bridge of Athlone* (Dublin, 1881).

Lang, R.T., (Ed.), *Black's Guide to Galway, Connemara and the West of Ireland 19th ed.* (Adam and Charles Black, London, 1905).

Lewis, S., *A Topographical Dictionary of Ireland* (London, 1837).

Leaves from my notebook: being a collection of tales, all positive facts portraying Irish life and character. (Unpublished, nd., Aidan Heavey Public Library, Athlone).

Leigh, G., *New Pocket Road-Book of Ireland* [...] 3rd Ed. (T. Brettell, London, 1835).

Mahony, Jas., *Hand-Book to Galway, Connemara and the Irish Highlands* (James McGlashan, Dublin, 1854).

Moran, Malachy, *The Moran Manuscripts,* National Library of Ireland, MSS. 1543-7.

Murray, Rev. Hugh A.M., *A Friendly Question For a New Year* (Athlone, 1856).

Neave, Sir Digby, Bart, *Four Days in Connemara* (Richard Bentley, London, 1852).

O'Donovan, John, *Ordnance Survey letters for Roscommon, Westmeath, Longford, 1837/8* (N.L.I.).

Otway, Caesar, *A Tour in Connaught comprising sketches of Clonmacnoise, Joyce Country and Achill* (William Curry, Jun. and Company, Dublin, 1839).

Oxonian, An (Samuel Reynolds Hole), *A Little Tour in Ireland, Being a Visit to Dublin, Galway, Connemara, Athlone, Limerick, Killarney, Glengariff, Cork, etc. etc. etc., By an Oxonian – With Illustrations by John Leech* (Bradbury and Evans, London, 1859).

Porter, John Grey, *Some Calm Observations on Irish Affairs* (Hodges and Smith, Dublin, 1846).

Ritchie, Leitch, *Ireland, picturesque and romantic,* (London, 1838).

Russell, Maud Mary, *Sprigs of shamrock, (Irish Sketches and Legends)* (Browne and Nolan, Dublin, 1900).

Sime, William, *To and Fro, or Views from Sea and Land* (Stock, London, 1884).

Society for the Improvement of Ireland (M.H. Gill, Dublin, 1846).

Stokes, George T., *Athlone, the Shannon and Lough Ree,* with a local Directory edited by John Burgess (Alexander Thom & Co., Dublin, 1897).

Strean, Annesley, Rev. "St. Peter's Parish, Athlone", in Mason, William Shaw, *A Statistical Account or Parochial Survey – Drawn up from the communications of the clergy, Vol. III* (Faulkner Press, Dublin, 1819).

The Westmeath Coercion Act - Letter addressed by Rev. Dr. Nulty, Bishop of Meath to Right Hon. Benjamin Disraeli (Joseph Dollard, Dublin, 1875).

Thackery, William Makepiece, *The Irish Sketch Book* (1842), (Gill and Macmillan, Dublin, 1990).

The Westmeath Independent and Midland Counties Advertiser Almanac 1890 (Chapman and Co., 1891).

The Sermons, Lectures and Speeches delivered by his Eminence Cardinal Wiseman Archbishop of Westminster, During his tour in Ireland in August & September, 1858 (James Duffy, Dublin, 1859).

Venedy, Herr J., *Ireland and the Irish During the Repeal Year, 1843* (James Duffy, Dublin, 1844).

Wakeman, W.F., *Three Days on the Shannon* (Hodges & Smith, Dublin, 1852).

Weld, Isaac, *Statistical survey of the County of Roscommon* (Dublin, 1832).

Willis, Nathaniel Parker & Coyne, J. Stirling, *The Scenery and Antiquities of Ireland* (George Virtue, London, 1842).

Wriothesley, Noel Baptist, *Notes on a short tour through the midland counties of Ireland in the summer of 1836, with observations on the condition of the peasantry* (J.Nisbet, London, 1837).

NEWSPAPERS

Faulkner's Dublin Journal, 1800-1824
The Athlone Sentinel, 1834-1861.
The Athlone Conservative Advocate and Ballinasloe Reporter, June – September 1837.
The Athlone Independent or Midland Telegraph 1833-1836.
The Athlone Mirror and Westmeath and Roscommon Reformer, 1841-1842.
The Athlone Times, 1886-1902.
The Freeman's Journal, 1830-1900.
The Westmeath Herald, 1859-1860.
The Westmeath Independent and Agricultural and Commercial Journal (The Westmeath Independent and Midland County Advertiser) 1846-1901.

Secondary Sources

BOOKS AND ARTICLES

Acheson, Alan, *A History of the Church of Ireland 1691-1996* (The Columba Press, 1997).

Akenson, Donald Harman, *The Church of Ireland – Ecclesiastical Reform and Revolution 1800-1885* (Yale University Press, 1971).

Athlone Civic Week 1945-1951 (Aidan Heavey Public Library, Athlone).

Atkinson, Norman, *Irish Education – a history of educational institutions* (Allen Figgis, Dublin, 1969).

Anderson Graham, P., *The Victorian Era* (Longmans, Green and Co., London, 1897).

Athlone Junior Chamber of Commerce, *So there's nothing to do in Athlone – A comprehensive guide to organisations societies & clubs* (Athlone Printing Works, Athlone, 1981).

Bartlett, Thomas & Jeffrey, Keith, (Eds.), *A Military History of Ireland* (Cambridge University Press, Cambridge, 1997).

Beckett, J.C., *The Making of Modern Ireland 1603-1923* (Faber and Faber, 1966).

Beckett, J.C., *Confrontations – Studies in Irish History* (Faber and Faber, 1972).

Beresford Ellis, Peter, *A History of the Irish Working Class* (Pluto, 1985).

Best, Geoffrey, *Mid-Victorian Britain 1851-75* (Fontana Press, London, 1979).

Bew, Paul, *Land and the National Question in Ireland 1858-82* (Gill and Macmillan, 1978).

1739 – 1939 Bicentenary of Shamrock Lodge 101, Athlone (Athlone, 1940).

Bielenberg, Andy, *Cork's Industrial Revolution 1780-1880: Development or Decline?* (Cork University Press, Cork, 1991).

Black, Eugene C., (Ed.), *Victorian Culture and Society* (The Macmillan Press, London, 1973).

Booth, Michael R., *Theatre in the Victorian Age* (Cambridge University Press, Cambridge, 1991).

Bourke, Eoin, "'The Irishman is no lazzarone' German travel writers in Ireland 1828-1850", *in History Ireland,* Vol. 5, No.3, Autumn, 1997 (History Ireland Ltd., Dublin, 1997), pp.21-25.

Bowen, Desmond, *The Protestant Crusade in Ireland 1800-70* (Gill and Macmillan, Dublin, 1978).

Boyce, D. George, *Nationalism in Ireland* (Routledge, London, 1982).

Boyce, D.G., *The Revolution in Ireland, 1879-1923* (Macmillan, 1988).

Boyce, D. George, *Nineteenth Century Ireland – The Search for Stability* (Gill and Macmillan, Dublin, 1990).

Briggs, Asa, *Victorian People – A reassessment of persons and themes 1851-1867* (University of Chicago Press, Chicago, 1955).

Brown, Stewart J. & Miller, Daniel W., *Piety and Power in Ireland 1760-1960* (QUB, 2000).

Buckley, Gerry, *Millennium Handbook of Westmeath G.A.A.* (Leinster Leader, 2000).

Burke, John, *Athlone Woollen Mills* (Unpublished B.A. thesis, Humanities Department, Galway-Mayo Institute of Technology, 2002).

Butt, J., & Clarke, I.F., *The Victorians and Social Protest* (David & Charles, Archon Books, 1973).

Callanan, Frank, *The Parnell Split 1890-91* (Cork University Press, Cork, 1992).

Cannon, John, (Ed.), *The Oxford Companion to British History* (Oxford, 1997).

Carr, Peter, *The Night of the Big Wind* (White Row Press, Belfast, 1993).

Casey, Patrick, "Epidemic Opthalmia at Athlone" in *Journal of the Old Athlone Society* Vol. I, No.2 (Old Athlone Society, Athlone, 1970), pp.112-115.

Casserly, H.C., *Outline of Irish Railway History* (David & Charles, Newton Abbot, 1974).

Central Statistics Office, *Farming Since the Famine – Irish Farm Statistics 1847-1996* (CSO, 1997).

Chart, D.A., *An Economic History of Ireland* (The Talbot Press, Dublin, 1920).

Clare, Liam, *Victorian Bray – A Town Adapts to Changing Times* (Irish Academy Press, Dublin, 1998).

Clonown Local History Society, *Clonown, The history, traditions and culture of a South Roscommon Community* (Temple Printing, Athlone, 1989).

Collins, Tom, *Athlone Golf Club 1892 – 1992* (Alfa Print, Athlone, 1992).

Comerford, R.V., *The Fenians in Context – Irish Politics & Society 1848-82* (Wolfhound Press, Dublin, 1998).

Conlon, Patrick, "The medieval priory of Saints Peter and Paul in Athlone", in Murtagh, H. (Ed.), *Irish Midland Studies*, (Old Athlone Society, Athlone, 1980), pp.73-83.

Conlon, Patrick, O.F.M., "St. Bonaventure's Academy, Athlone", in *Journal of the Old Athlone Society* Vol. II, No.6 (Old Athlone Society, Athlone, 1985), pp.155-156.

Conlon, Patrick, O.F.M., "A note on the Augustinian priory in Athlone", in *Journal of the Old Athlone Society* Vol. II, No.7 (Old Athlone Society, Athlone, 2004), pp.205-207.

Connell, K.H., in McDowell, R.B., *Social Life in Ireland 1800-45* (Mercier Press, Cork, 1979), pp.80-92.

Connolly, S.J., *The Oxford Companion to Irish History* (Oxford, 1998).

Connolly, S.J., *Religion and Society in 19th Century Ireland* (Dundalgan Press, 1987).

Cooney, Dudley Levistone, *The Methodists in Ireland – A Short History* (The Columba Press, 2001).

Cosgrave, Art & McCartney, Donal, (Eds.), *Studies in Irish History – Presented to R.Dudley Edwards* (UCD, Dublin, 1979).

Crawford, E. Margaret, *Famine – The Irish Experience* (John Donald Publishers Ltd, Edinburgh, 1989).

Crossman, Virginia, *Local Government in 19th Century Ireland* (Queen's University Belfast, 1994).

Crossman, Virginia, *Politics, Law and Order in Nineteenth Century Ireland* (Gill and Macmillan, Dublin, 1996).

Crossman, Virginia, "The army and Law and Order in the nineteenth century", in Bartlett, Thomas & Jeffrey, Keith, (Eds.), *A Military History of Ireland* (Cambridge University Press, Cambridge, 1997), pp. 358-378.

Cullen, Louis M., *An Economic History of Ireland since 1660* (B.T. Batsford Ltd, London, 1972).

Cullen, Louis M., *The formation of the Irish economy, The Thomas Davis lecture series* (Mercier Press, Dublin, 1968).

Currivan, P.J., "Athlone as a Railway Centre", in *Journal of the Irish Railway Record Society*, Vol. 4, No. 20, Spring, 1957 (Ballyshannon, 1957), pp.209-212.

Curtis, T.B. & McDowell, R.B., *Irish Historical Documents, 1172-1922* (Methuen & Co., London, 1977).

Daly, Mary, "The Statistical and Social Inquiry Society of Ireland", in Kennedy, Kieran A., *From Famine to Feast – Economic and Social Change in Ireland 1847-1997* (IPA, Dublin, 1998), pp. 1-11.

Daunton, Martin, "Society and Economic life", in Matthew, Colin, *Short Oxford History of the British Isles – The Nineteenth Century* (Oxford, 2000), pp.41-78.

De Breffny, Brian, (Ed.), *The Irish People – the History and Cultural Achievements of the Irish People* (Thames and Hudson, 1977).

Delany, Ruth, "Athlone navigation works, 1757-1849", in Murtagh, H. (Ed.), *Irish Midland Studies,* (Old Athlone Society, Athlone, 1980), pp.193-204.

Delany, Ruth, "The River Shannon, Lough Ree and Athlone", in Keaney, M. & O'Brien, G., *Athlone - Bridging the Centuries* (Westmeath County Council, Mullingar, 1991), pp.22-33.

De Paor, Liam, (Ed.), *Milestones in Irish History* (Mercier, 1986).

De Paor, Liam, *The Peoples of Ireland* (Hutchinson, 1986).

Doggett, Maeve E., *Marriage, Wife-Beating and the Law in Victorian England* (Weidenfeld & Nicholson, 1992).

Doherty, J.E. & Hickey, D.J., *A Chronology of Irish History since 1500* (Gill and Macmillan, Dublin, 1989).

Donnelly, James S., *The Great Irish Potato Famine* (Sutton, 2001).

Donnelly, J.S. Jr & Miller, Kerby A. (Eds.), Irish Popular Culture 1650-1850 (Irish Academic Press, 1998).

Dudley Edwards, Ruth, *An Atlas of Irish History* (Methuen & Co., London, 1973).

Dudley Edwards, R, *A New History of Ireland* (Gill and Macmillan, Dublin, 1972).

Edwards, R. Dudley & Williams, T. Desmond (eds.) *The Great Famine – Studies in Irish History 1845-52* (The Lilliput Press, Dublin, 1994).

Duffey, Seán, (Ed.), *Atlas of Irish History* (Gill and Macmillan, Dublin, 1997).

Drudy, P.J., (Ed.), *Anglo Irish Studies* (Alpha Academic, 1975).

Drum Heritage Group, *Drum and its Hinterland*, 2nd Edition (Alfa Print, Athlone, 2003).

Encyclopædia Britannica, Vol. 29, 19th Ed. 2002.

Egan, Frank, *Athlone's Golden Mile 1920-1980 – Bridging the Gap* (Temple Printing Co., Athlone, 1980).

Englander, David, *Poverty and Poor Law Reform in 19th Century Britain, 1834 - 1914* (Longman, London, 1998).

English, N.W., "Athlone's "Ecumenical" Yeomanry Corps", in *The Irish Sword*, Vol. VII, No. 28, Summer (Dublin, 1966).

English, N.W., *Lough Ree Yacht Club 1770-1970 – A Memoir* (Athlone, 1970).

English, N.W., "Sisters of Mercy and Athlone Workhouse", in *Journal of the Old Athlone Society*, Vol.1, No.3 (Old Athlone Society, Athlone, 1973), p. 208.

Fallon, Michael et al, *A Sense of Place – Clonown, a County Roscommon Shannonside Community* (Temple Printing, Athlone, 2006).

Farrell, Mary, (Ed.), *Mullingar – Essays on the History of a Midlands Town in the 19th Century* (Westmeath County Library, 2002).

Feingold, William L., *The Revolt of the Tenantry – The transformation of local government in Ireland 1872-1886* (Northeastern University Press, Boston, 1984).

FitzGerald, Garret, "Transport", in Kennedy, Kieran A., *From Famine to Feast – Economic and Social Change in Ireland 1847-1997* (IPA, Dublin, 1998), pp.87-98.

FitzGerald, Michael, "Industry and Commerce in Athlone", in Keaney, M. & O'Brien, G., *Athlone - Bridging the Centuries* (Westmeath County Council, Mullingar, 1991), pp.34-46.

Fitzpatrick, Jim, *Three Brass Balls – The Story of the Irish Pawnshop* (The Collins Press, Cork, 2001).

Flint, Kate, "Literature, music and the theatre", in Matthew, Colin, *Short Oxford History of the British Isles – The Nineteenth Century* (Oxford, 2000), pp.229-251.

Flynn, Arthur, *History of Bray* (Mercier Press, 1986).

Foley, Tadhg & Ryder, Seán, *Ideology and Ireland in the Nineteenth Century* (Four Courts Press, 1998).

Foster, R. F., *Modern Ireland 1600-1972* (Allen Lane, The Penguin Press, 1988).

Foster, R. F., (Ed.), *The Oxford Illustrated History of Ireland*, (Oxford, 1989).

Foster, R. F., *Paddy and Mr Punch – Connections in Irish and English History*, (Penguin Books, 1995).

Gailey, Andrew, "Unionist Rhetoric and Irish local government reform, 1895-9", in *Irish Historical Studies*, Vol. 24, No. 93 (W.G. Baird, Antrim, 1984), pp.52-89.

Garnett, Jane, "Religious and intellectual life", in Matthew, Colin, *Short Oxford History of the British Isles – The Nineteenth Century* (Oxford, 2000), pp.195-222.

Garvin, Tom, *Nationalist revolutionaries in Ireland 1858-1928*, (Oxford, 1987).

Geary, Frank, "Regional industrial structure and labour force decline in Ireland between 1841 and 1851", in *Irish Historical Studies*, Vol. 30, No. 118 (W.G. Baird, Antrim, 1996), pp.167-194.

Gibbons, S.R., *Ireland 1780-1914 – Evidence in History* (Blackie and Sons, 1978).

Gillespie, Raymond & Moran, Gerard, *Longford – Essays in County History* (The Lilliput Press, 1991).

Gironard, Mark, *The English Town* (Yale University Press, London, 1990)

Godkin, James, *The Land War in Ireland* (1870) (Kennikat Press, 1970).

Golby, J.M., *Culture and Society in Britain, 1850-1890* (Oxford, 1986).

Graham, B.J. & Proudfoot, L.J. (Eds.), *An Historical Geography of Ireland* (Academic Press, London, 1993).

Grannell, Fergal, O.F.M., *The Franciscans in Athlone* (Franciscan Friary, Athlone, 1978).

Grierson, Edward, *The Imperial Dream – The British Commonwealth and Empire 1775-1969* (Collins, London, 1972).

Griffin, William P., (Ed.), *Ireland – A Chronology and Fact Book* (Oceana Publications Ltd, New York, 1973).

Griffiths, A.R.G., *The Irish Board of Works 1831-1878* (Garland Publishing Inc., London, 1987).

Grousset, Paschal, *Ireland's Disease – The English in Ireland 1887* (Blackstaff Press, Belfast, 1986).

Guinnane, Timothy W., "The Vanishing Irish - Ireland's population from the Great Famine to the Great War", in *History Ireland*, Vol.5, No.2, Summer, 1997 (Wordwell, Bray, 1997), pp.32-36.

Hanley, Lt. Col. M.K., *The Story of Custume Barracks Athlone* (Athlone, 1974).

Harkness, David & O'Dowd, Mary (Eds.), *The Town in Ireland – Historical Studies XIII* (Appletree Press, Dublin, 1979).

Harrison, J.F.C., *Early Victorian Britain, 1832-51* (Fontana Press, London, 1971).

Harrison, J.F.C., *Late Victorian Britain 1871-1901* (Fontana Press, London, 1990).

Hart – Davis, Adam, *What the Victorians Did for Us* (Headline, London, 2001).

Herlihy, Jim, *The Royal Irish Constabulary – A Short History and Genealogical Guide* (Four Courts Press, Dublin, 1997).

Hickey, D.J. & Doherty, J.E., *A Dictionary of Irish History 1800-1980* (Gill and Macmillan, Dublin, 1987).

Hill, Myrtle & Barber, Sarah, *Aspects of Irish Studies* (QUB, Belfast, 1990).

Holmes, Finlay, *The Presbyterian Church in Ireland – A Popular History* (The Columba Press, 2000).

Hooper, Glenn & Litvack, Leon (Eds.), *Ireland in the Nineteenth Century – Regional Identity* (Four Courts Press, Dublin, 2000).

Hoppen, K. Theodore, "National Politics and Local Realities in Mid-Nineteenth Century Ireland", in Cosgrave, Art & McCartney, Donal, (Eds.), *Studies in Irish History – Presented to R. Dudley Edwards* (UCD, Dublin, 1979), pp.190-227.

Hoppen, K. Theodore, *Elections Politics and Society in Ireland 1832 – 1885* (Clarendon Press, Oxford, 1984).

Hoppen, K. Theodore, *Ireland Since 1800 – Conflict and Conformity* (Longmans. 2nd Ed. 1999).

Horn, Pamela, *Pleasures and Pastimes in Victorian Britain* (Sutton Publishing, 1999).

Houston, C.J., "The Irish Diaspora: Emigration to the New World, 1720-1920", in Graham, B.J. & Proudfoot, L.J. (Eds.), *An Historical Geography of Ireland* (Academic Press, London, 1993), pp.338-365.

Howarth, Janet, "Gender, domesticity and sexual politics", in Matthew, Colin, *Short Oxford History of the British Isles – The Nineteenth Century* (Oxford, 2000), pp.163-190.

Hutchinson, Robert W., "Money and Banking", in Kennedy, Kieran A., *From Famine to Feast – Economic and Social Change in Ireland 1847-1997* (IPA, Dublin, 1998), pp.99-110.

I.C.A. Athlone, *Athlone – Glimpses and Gleanings* (Temple Printing, Athlone, nd.)

Inglis, Brian, "The Press", in McDowell, R.B., *Social Life in Ireland 1800-45* (Mercier Press, Cork, 1979), pp.93-105.

Ireland, Aideen, M., "The North Gate, Athlone", in Condit, Tom & Corlett, Christiaan (Eds.), *Above and Beyond – Essays in memory of Leo Swan* (Wordwell, Bray, 2005), pp. 461-472.

Jackson, Russell, *Victorian Theatre* (A&C Black, London, 1989).

Journal of the Old Athlone Society, 1965-2004 (Old Athlone Society, Athlone).

Jupp, Peter, "Urban Politics in Ireland 1801-1831", in Harkness, David & O'Dowd, Mary (Eds.), *The Town in Ireland – Historical Studies XIII* (Appletree Press, Dublin, 1979), pp.103-124.

Kapp, Yvonne, *The Air of Freedom – The Birth of the new Unionism* (Lawrence and Wishart, London, 1989).

Killen, John (Ed.), *The Famine Decade, Contemporary Accounts 1841-1851* (Blackstaff Press, 1995).

Keaney, Marian, *Westmeath Authors* (Mullingar, 1969).

Keaney, Marian, *Westmeath Local Studies – A guide to sources* (Longford-Westmeath Joint Library Committee, Mullingar, 1982).

Keaney, M. & O'Brien, G., *Athlone - Bridging the Centuries* (Westmeath County Council, Mullingar, 1991).

Keenan, Desmond, *The Catholic Church in Nineteenth Century Ireland – A Sociological Study* (Gill and Macmillan, Dublin, 1983).

Kelly, James, 'Select documents: The members of parliament for Ireland, 1806: two lists of 'parliamentary interests', in *Irish Historical Studies*, Vol. 34, No. 134 (Biddles Ltd, Norfolk, 2004), pp.198-229.

Kennedy, David, "Education and the People", in McDowell, R.B., *Social Life in Ireland 1800-45* (Mercier Press, Cork, 1979), pp.53-66.

Kennedy, Finola, "Family Life", in Kennedy, Kieran A., *From Famine to Feast – Economic and Social Change in Ireland 1847-1997* (IPA, Dublin, 1998), pp.123-133.

Kennedy, Kieran A., *From Famine to Feast – Economic and Social Change in Ireland 1847-1997* (IPA, Dublin, 1998).

Kennedy, Kieran A., "Industrial Development", in Kennedy, Kieran A., *From Famine to Feast – Economic and Social Change in Ireland 1847-1997* (IPA, Dublin, 1998), pp.75-86.

Kennedy, L & Clarkson, L.A., "Birth, Death and Exile: Irish Population History, 1700-1921", in Graham, B.J. & Proudfoot, L.J. (Eds.), *An Historical Geography of Ireland* (Academic Press, London, 1993), pp.158-184.

Kennedy, Liam, *Colonialism, Religion and Nationalism in Ireland* (W & G Baird, Antrim, 1996).

Kennedy, Liam, et al, *Mapping the Irish Famine* (Four Courts Press, Dublin, 1999).

Kerrigan, Colm, *Father Mathew and the Irish Temperance Movement 1838-1849* (Cork University Press, Cork, 1992).

Kinealy, Christine, *This Great Calamity – The Irish Famine 1845-52* (Gill and Macmillan, Dublin, 1994).

Kinealy, Christine, "Food Exports from Ireland 1846-47", in *History Ireland*, Vol.5, No.1, Spring 1997 (History Ireland Ltd., Dublin, 1997), pp.32-36.

Kinealy, Christine, *A Death Dealing Famine – The Great Hunger in Ireland* (Pluto, 1997).

King, Heather A., (Ed.), *Clonmacnoise Studies – Volume 1 Seminar Papers 1994* (Dúchas, Dublin, 1998).

Kissane, Noel, *The Irish Famine – A Documentary History* (NLI, Dublin, 1995).

Lane, Padraig, *Ireland* (B.T. Batsford Ltd., London, 1974).

Langrische, Rosabel Sara, "Athlone in the 1880s – Being extracts from the journal of Rosabel Sara Langrische", in *Journal of the Old Athlone Society* Vol. II, No.7 (Old Athlone Society, Athlone, 2004), pp.177-186.

Langrische, H.R., "A note on the author Rosie Langrische", in *Journal of the Old Athlone Society* Vol. II, No.7 (Old Athlone Society, Athlone, 2004), pp.186-187.

Larkin, Emmet, *The Roman Catholic Church and the Plan of Campaign 1886-1888* (Cork University Press, 1978).

Larkin, Emmet, *The Roman Catholic Church and the Modern Irish State, 1878-1886* (Gill and Macmillan, Dublin, 1975).

Ledbetter, Gordon T., *The Great Irish Tenor* (Duckworth, London, 1977).

Legg, Mary Louise, *Newspapers and Nationalism, The Irish Provincial Press, 1850-1892* (Four Courts Press, Dublin, 1999).

Lee, Joseph, *The Modernisation of Irish Society 1848-1918*, (Gill & Macmillan, Dublin, 1973).

Lee, J.J., "Education, Economy and Society", in Kennedy, Kieran A., *From Famine to Feast – Economic and Social Change in Ireland 1847-1997* (IPA, Dublin, 1998), pp.62-74.

Lenehan, Jim, *Politics and Society in Athlone 1830-1885 – A Rotten Borough* (Irish Academy Press, Dublin, 1999).

Lowe, W.J., "The Irish Constabulary in the Great Famine", in *History Ireland*, Vol.5, No.4, Winter, 1997 (History Ireland Ltd., Dublin, 1997), pp.32-37.

Lydon, James, *The Making of Ireland - From Ancient Times to the Present* (Routledge, 1998).

Lynch, Frank, *A history of Athlone Town F.C. – The First 101 Years* (Westmeath Independent, Athlone, 1991).

Lyons, F.S.L. & Hawkins, R.A.J. (Eds.), *Ireland under the Union – Varieties of Tensions, Essays in Honour of T.W. Moody* (Clarendon Press, Oxford, 1980).

Lyons, F.S.L., *Ireland Since the Famine* (Collins, 1982).

Lysaght, Charles, "Crime and Punishment", in Kennedy, Kieran A., *From Famine to Feast – Economic and Social Change in Ireland 1847-1997* (IPA, Dublin, 1998), pp.147-159.

Magnusson, Magnus, *Landlord or Tenant, A View of Irish History* (The Bodley Head, 1978).

Malcolm, Elizabeth, "The catholic church and the Irish temperance movement, 1838-1901", in *Irish Historical Studies*, Vol. 23, No. 89 (W.G. Baird, Antrim, 1982), pp.1-16.

Malcolm, Elizabeth, *Ireland Sober, Ireland Free – Drink and Temperance in Nineteenth Century Ireland* (Syracuse University Press, New York, 1986).

Malcolm, Elizabeth & Jones, Greta, *Medicines and the State in Ireland 1650-1940* (Cork University Press, Cork, 1999).

Marshall, John & Wilcox Ian, *The Victorian House* (Sidgwick and Jackson, London, 1989).

Mason, Tony, *Sport in Britain* (Faber & Faber, London, 1988).

Matthew, Colin, *Short Oxford History of the British Isles – The Nineteenth Century* (Oxford, 2000).

Matthew, Colin, "Introduction: the United Kingdom and the Victorian Century", in Matthew, Colin, *Short Oxford History of the British Isles – The Nineteenth Century* (Oxford, 2000), pp.1-36.

Matthew, Colin, "Public life and politics" in Matthew, Colin, *Short Oxford History of the British Isles – The Nineteenth Century* (Oxford, 2000), pp.85-132.

Matthew, Colin, "Conclusion, fin-de-siècle", in Matthew, Colin, *Short Oxford History of the British Isles – The Nineteenth Century* (Oxford, 2000), pp.293-299.

May, Trevor, *The Victorian Workhouse* (Shire Publications, 1997).

McCormack, John, *The Story of Ireland – The People and Events that Shaped the Country* (Mentor, 2002).

McCutcheon, Alan, *Railway History in Pictures – Ireland Volume 1* (David & Charles, Newton Abbot, 1969).

McDonagh, Oliver, *Ireland: The Union and its Aftermath* (George Allen and Unwin Ltd., London, 1977).

McDonagh, Oliver, *States of Mind – A Study of Anglo-Irish Conflict 1780-1980*, (George Allen and Unwin Ltd., London, 1983).

McDowell, R.B., *Social Life in Ireland 1800-45* (Mercier Press, Cork, 1979).

McDowell, R.B., "The army", in McDowell, R.B., *Social Life in Ireland 1800-45* (Mercier Press, Cork, 1979), pp.67-79.

McMahon, Sean, *Irish Quotations* (The O'Brien Press, Dublin, 1984).

Miller, David W., *Church State and Nation in Ireland 1898-1921* (Gill and Macmillan, Dublin, 1971).

Miller, Kerby A., "The Lost World of Andrew Johnston: Sectarianism, Social Conflict, and Cultural Change in Southern Ireland during the Pre-Famine Era", in Donnelly, J.S. Jr & Miller, Kerby A. (Eds.), *Irish Popular Culture 1650 – 1850* (Irish Academic Press, 1998), pp.222-241.

Mitchell, Frank & Ryan, Michael, *Reading the Irish Landscape* (Town House, 1997).

Moncrieff, M.C. Scott, *Kings and Queens of England* (Blanford Press, London, 1973).

Money, Tony, *Manly and Muscular Diversions: Public Schools and the 19th century Sporting Revival* (Charles Duckworth and Co., London, 1997).

Moody, T.W., et al, (Eds.), *A Chronology of Irish History to 1976* (Oxford, 1982).

Moody, T.W., *Davitt and the Irish Revolution 1846-82* (Clarendon Press, Oxford, 1982).

Morash, Christopher, *A History of Irish Theatre – 1601-2000* (Cambridge, 2002).

Morgan, Kenneth O., (Ed.) *The Oxford History of Britain* (Oxford, 1988).

Mosley, Charles, (Ed.) *Burke's Peerage & Baronentage, 106th ed.* (Genealogical Books, Switzerland, 1999).

Murphy, Brian, *A History of the British Economy 1740-1970* (Longman Group, London, 1973).

Murphy, David, *Ireland and the Crimean War* (Four Courts Press, Dublin, 2002).

Murphy, Desmond, *Derry, Donegal and Modern Ulster 1790-1921* (Aileach Press, Londonderry, 1981).

Murphy, Maureen (Ed.), *Annals of the Famine in Ireland – Aesnath Nicholson* (Lilliput, 1998).

Murray, A.C., "Nationality and local politics in late nineteenth-century Ireland: the case of County Westmeath", in *Irish Historical Studies*, Vol. 25, No. 98 (W.G. Baird, Antrim, 1986), pp.144-158.

Murray, Patrick, "Fr. John Conmee: a portrait of the rector", in *Journal of the Old Athlone Society* Vol. II, No.6 (Old Athlone Society, Athlone, 1985), pp.94-99.

Murtagh, H. (Ed.), *Irish Midland Studies*, (Old Athlone Society, Athlone, 1980).

Murtagh, Harman, "Old Athlone", in Keaney, M. & O'Brien, G., *Athlone - Bridging the Centuries* (Westmeath County Council, Mullingar, 1991), pp.11-21.

Murtagh, H., *Irish Historic Towns Atlas Volume VI - Athlone* (Royal Irish Academy, Dublin. 1994).

Murtagh, Harman, "Athlone", in Simms, Anngret & Andrews, J.H., (Eds.), *Irish Country Towns* (Mercier Press, Dublin. 1994), pp. 154-165.

Murtagh, Harman, *Athlone History and Settlement to 1800* (Old Athlone Society, Athlone, 2000).

Newsinger, John, *Fenianism in Mid-Victorian Britain* (Pluto Press, London, 1994).

Newsome, David, *The Victorian World Picture* (John Murray, London, 1997).

Ní Bhrolcháin, Máire, "Is Ireland Underpopulated?", in Kennedy, Kieran A., *From Famine to Feast – Economic and Social Change in Ireland 1847-1997* (IPA, Dublin, 1998), pp.23-37.

Nicholson, Shirley, (Ed.), *A Victorian Household* (Sutton Publishing, 2000).

Ní Mhuiríosa, Máirín, *Réamhchonraitheoirí – Notaí ar chuid de na daoine a bhí gníomhach I ngluaiseacht na Gaeilge idir 1876 agus 1893* (Clíodhanna Teoranta, Baile Átha Cliath, 1968).

Nolan, Matt, *Mullingar, Just for the record – A Window on the Millennium* (Crigeán Press, 1999).

Norbury, James, *The World of Victoriana* (Hamlyn, London, 1972).

Norman, Edward, *A History of Modern Ireland* (Penguin, 1971).

Nowlan, Kevin B., "Travel", in McDowell, R.B., *Social Life in Ireland 1800-45* (Mercier Press, Cork, 1979), pp.106-118.

O'Brien, Brendan, "When the circus came to Athlone", in *Journal of the Old Athlone Society* Vol. II, No.6 (Old Athlone Society, Athlone, 1985), pp.109-115.

O'Brien, Brendan, "Earliest memories of the Theatre in Athlone", in *Journal of the Old Athlone Society* Vol. I, No.1 (Old Athlone Society, Athlone, 1969), pp.35-38.

O'Brien, Brendan, "Athlone's Repeal Demonstration", in *Journal of the Old Athlone Society* Vol. I, No.2 (Old Athlone Society, Athlone, 1970), pp.108-109.

O'Brien, Brendan, "The Tholsel of Athlone", in *Journal of the Old Athlone Society* Vol. I, No.3 (Old Athlone Society, Athlone, 1973), pp.190-194.

O'Brien, Brendan, "Early Days of Garrison Theatre in Athlone", in *Journal of the Old Athlone Society* Vol. I, No.4 (Old Athlone Society, Athlone, 1974), pp.275-280.

O'Brien, Brendan, "They once Trod the Boards in Athlone", in *Journal of the Old Athlone Society* Vol. II, No.5 (Old Athlone Society, Athlone, 1978), pp.6-10.

O'Brien, Brendan, "Amateur drama in Athlone: some early records", in Murtagh, H. (Ed.), *Irish Midland Studies*, (Old Athlone Society, Athlone, 1980), pp.229-238.

O'Brien, Brendan, "Some Aspects of Municipal Government in Athlone", in Keaney, M. & O'Brien, G., *Athlone - Bridging the Centuries* (Westmeath County Council, Mullingar, 1991), pp.79-91.

O'Brien, Brendan, *Athlone Workhouse and The Famine* (Old Athlone Society, Athlone, 1995).

O'Brien, Donal, *Athlone – a visitors guide* (Alfa Print, Athlone, 2003).

O'Brien, Gearoid, (Ed.), *Athlone Tourist Trail – A Signposted Walking Tour* (Athlone Chamber of Commerce, Athlone, 1985).

O'Brien, Gearoid, "Athlone Newspapers", in *Journal of the Old Athlone Society* Vol. II, No.6 (Old Athlone Society, Athlone, 1985), p.147.

O'Brien, Gearoid, *St Mary's Parish, Athlone – a History* (St Mel's Diocesan Trust, Longford, 1989).

O'Brien, Gearoid, *John McCormack and Athlone* (Old Athlone Society, Athlone, 1992).

O'Brien, Gearoid, *Athlone in old picture postcards* (European Library, Zaltbommel, 1996).

O'Brien, Gearoid, *Athlone in Old Photographs* (Gill and Macmillan, Dublin, 2002).

O'Brien, Joseph V., *William O'Brien and the Course of Irish Politics 1881-1918* (University of California, 1976).

O'Ciosáin, Niall, *Print and Popular Culture in Ireland 1750-1850* (Macmillan Press, 1997).

O'Connor, John, *The Workhouses of Ireland – The fate of Ireland's poor* (Anvil Books, Dublin, 1995).

O'Day, Alan & Stevenson, John, *Irish Historical Documents since 1800* (Gill & McMillan, Dublin, 1992).

O'Donnell, Patrick, *The Irish Faction Fighters of the 19th Century* (Anvil, 1975).

O'Donoghue, Bernard, *Oxford Irish Quotations* (Oxford, 1999).

Ó Gráda, Cormac, "The Rise in Living Standards", in Kennedy, Kieran A., *From Famine to Feast – Economic and Social Change in Ireland 1847-1997* (IPA, Dublin, 1998), pp.12-22.

O'Farrell, Padraic, *The Book of Mullingar* (Topic Newspapers, Mullingar, 1987).

O'Farrell, Padraic Col., "Athlone – A Garrison Town" in Keaney, M. & O'Brien, G., *Athlone - Bridging the Centuries* (Westmeath County Council, Mullingar, 1991), pp.62-78.

O'Farrell, Patrick, *England and Ireland Since 1800* (Oxford, 1975).

O' Ferrall, Fergus, "The Church of Ireland: a critical bibliography, 1800-1870", in *Irish Historical Studies*, Vol. 28, No. 112 (W.G. Baird, Antrim, 1993), pp.369-376.

O'Grada, Cormac, *Famine 150 – Commemorative Lecture Series* (Teagasc/UCD, 1997).

O'Grada, Cormac, *Ireland – A New Economic History* (Oxford, 1994).

O'Keefe, Peter & Simington, Tom, *Irish Stone Bridges – History and Heritage* (Irish Academic Press, 1991).

O'Leary, John, *Fenians and Fenianism* (Irish University Press, 1969).

O'Neill, T.P., "Rural Life", in McDowell, R.B., *Social Life in Ireland 1800-45* (Mercier Press, Cork, 1979), pp.40-52.

O'Sullivan, Donal J., *The Irish Constabularies 1822-1922, A Century of Policing in Ireland* (Brandon, 1999).

O'Tuathaigh, Gearoid, *Ireland before the Famine 1798-1848* (Gill and Macmillan, Dublin, 1990).

O'Tuathaigh, Gearoid, "Life on the Land", in Kennedy, Kieran A., *From Famine to Feast – Economic and Social Change in Ireland 1847-1997* (IPA, Dublin, 1998), pp.38-49.

Orel, Harold, (Ed.), *Irish History and Culture – Aspects of a People's Culture* (Wolfhound, 1979).

Owens, Gary, "Nationalism without Words, Symbolism and Ritual Behaviour in the Repeal 'Monster Meetings' of 1843-5", in Donnelly, J.S. Jr & Miller, Kerby A. (Eds.), *Irish Popular Culture 1650-1850* (Irish Academic Press, 1998), pp.242-269.

Parnell, Anna, *The Tale of a Great Sham* (Arlen House, 1986).

Parsons, Gerald, *Religion in Victorian Britain – 1 Traditions* (Manchester University Press, Manchester, 1988).

Paseta, Senia, *Before the Revolution – Nationalism, Social Change and Ireland's Catholic Elite, 1879-1922* (Cork University Press, Cork, 1999).

Pelling, Henry, *Popular Politics and Society in Late Victorian Britain*, 2nd Edition (Macmillan Press, London, 1979).

Percival, John, *The Great Famine 1845-51* (BBC, 1995).

Poirteir, Cathal, *Famine Echoes* (Gill and Macmillan, Dublin, 1995).

Porter, Andrew, "The empire and the world", in Matthew, Colin, *Short Oxford History of the British Isles – The Nineteenth Century* (Oxford, 2000), pp.135-155.

Prill, Felician, *Ireland, Britain and Germany 1870-1914, Problems of Nationalism and Religion in Nineteenth Century Europe* (Gill and Macmillan, Dublin, 1975).

Proudfoot, L.J., "Regionalism and Localism: Religious Change and Social Protest, c.1700 to c.1900", in Graham, B.J. & Proudfoot, L.J. (Eds.), *An Historical Geography of Ireland* (Academic Press, London, 1993), pp. 185-218.

Proudfoot, L.J., "Spatial Transformation and Social Agency: Property, Society and Improvement, c.1700 to c.1900", in Graham, B.J. & Proudfoot, L.J. (Eds.), *An Historical Geography of Ireland* (Academic Press, London, 1993), pp. 219-257.

Quane, Michael, "The Ranelagh Endowed School, Athlone", in *Journal of the Old Athlone Society* Vol. I, No.1 (Old Athlone Society, Athlone, 1969), pp.23-34.

Quane, Michael, "Athlone Classical School and Athlone English School", in Journal of the Old Athlone Society Vol. I, No.2 (Old Athlone Society, Athlone, 1970), pp.90-99.

Rees, Jim, *A Farewell to Famine* (Arklow, 1994).

Rees, Rosemary, *Poverty and Public Health 1815-1948* (Heinemann, Oxford, 2001).

Reid, Michaela, *Ask Sir James* (Hodder & Stoughton, London, 1987).

Roche, Desmond, *Local Government in Ireland* (Institute of Public Administration, Dublin, 1982).

Royal Arch Chapter 101 Athlone 1850-1950 (Athlone, 1951).

Royle, S.A., "Industrialisation, Urbanisation and Urban Society in Post-Famine Ireland c.1850-1921", in Graham, B.J. & Proudfoot, L.J. (Eds.), *An Historical Geography of Ireland* (Academic Press, London, 1993), pp. 258-292.

Saint, Andrew, "Cities, architecture and art" in Matthew, Colin, *Short Oxford History of the British Isles – The Nineteenth Century* (Oxford, 2000), pp.255-288.

Searby, Peter, *The Chartists* (Longmans, London, 1967).

Sexton, Seán, *Ireland Photographs 1840-1930* (Laurence King, 1994).

Sheehan, Jeremiah, *South Westmeath – Farm and Folk* (Blackwater Press, Dublin, 1978).

Sheehan, Jeremiah, *Westmeath: as others saw it* (Jeremiah Sheehan, Moate, 1982).

Shiman, Lillian Lewis, *Crusade against drink in Victorian England* (St Martin's Press, New York, 1988).

Simms, Anngret & Andrews, J.H., (Eds.), *Irish Country Towns* (Mercier Press, Dublin. 1994).

Simms, Anngret & Andrews, J.H., (Eds.), *More Irish Country Towns* (Mercier Press, Dublin. 1995).

Smith, Gus, *Festival Glory in Athlone* (Dublin, 1977).

Smyth, William J., "The Making of Ireland: Agendas and Perspectives in Cultural Geography", in Graham, B.J. & Proudfoot, L.J. (Eds.), *An Historical Geography of Ireland* (Academic Press, London, 1993), pp.399-436.

Snell. K.D.M., *Letters from Ireland During the Famine of 1847* (Irish Academic Press, 1994).

Spiers, E.M., "Army Organisation and Society in the nineteenth century", in Bartlett, Thomas & Jeffrey, Keith, (Eds.), *A Military History of Ireland* (Cambridge University Press, Cambridge, 1997), pp.335-357.

Stern, W.M., *Britain Yesterday and Today* (Longmans, London, 1969).

Swift, Roger & Gilley, Sheridan, *The Irish in Victorian Britain* (Four Courts Press, Dublin, 1999).

The Making of Athlone Tweeds and Serges, Ireland (Healy's, Dublin, 1910).

Thomson, David, *England in the Nineteenth Century <1815-1914>* (Penguin Books, London, 1950).

Trevelyan, G.M., *English Social History – A Survey of Six Centuries, Chaucer to Queen Victoria* (Book Club Associates, London, 1973).

Trevelyan, G.M., *Illustrated English Social History: 4* (Pelican Books, Middlesex, 1964).

Tunney, John, *Leitrim and the Great Hunger, Poor Law Famine and Social Decline in County Leitrim 1831-1851* (Unpublished Report, 1994).

Turner, M., "Rural Economies In Post-Famine Ireland, c.1850-1914", in Graham, B.J. & Proudfoot, L.J. (Eds.), *An Historical Geography of Ireland* (Academic Press, London, 1993), pp. 293-337.

Turner, Michael, *After the Famine – Irish Agriculture 1850-1914* (Cambridge University Press, 1996).

Vaughan, W. E. & Fitzpatrick, A. J., *Irish Historical Statistics – Population 1821 - 1971* (Royal Irish Academy, Dublin, 1978).

Vaughan, W.E., *Landlords and Tenants in Ireland 1848-1904* (Dundealgan Press, 1984).

Vaughan, W. E. (Ed.), *A New History of Ireland V – Ireland under the Union 1, 1801 - 70* (Clarendon Press, Oxford, 1989).

Walker, B.M. (Ed.), *Parliamentary Election Results in Ireland 1801-1922* (Royal Irish Academy, Dublin, 1978).

Welsh, Frank, *The Four Nations – A History of the United Kingdom* (Harper Collins, 2002).

Went, Arthur E.J., "Five eel spears from the Shannon basin.", in *Journal of the Old Athlone Society* Vol. I, No.4 (Old Athlone Society, Athlone, 1974), p.247.

Went, Arthur E.J., "Eel Fishing at Athlone, Past and Present", in *Journal of the Royal Society of Antiquaries of Ireland* Vol. 5, lxxx pt.2 1950 (JRSAI, Dubline, 1950), pp.149-155.

Whelan, Brendan J., "Changing Work Patterns", in Kennedy, Kieran A., *From Famine to Feast – Economic and Social Change in Ireland 1847-1997* (IPA, Dublin, 1998), pp.111-122.

White, Harry, *The Keeper's Recital – Music and Cultural History in Ireland, 1770 - 1970* (Cork University Press, Cork, 1998).

Wiley, Miriam M., "Housing, Health and Social Welfare", in Kennedy, Kieran A., *From Famine to Feast – Economic and Social Change in Ireland 1847-1997* (IPA, Dublin, 1998), pp.50-61.

Wilson, A.N., *The Victorians* (Hutchinson, London, 2002).

Wilson Foster, John, *Recoveries – Neglected Episodes in Irish Cultural History 1860-1912* (UCD Press, Dublin, 2002).

Winstanley, Michael J., *Ireland and the Land Question 1800 - 1922* (Methuen, London, 1984).

Wohl, Anthony S., *Endangered Lives – Public Health in Victorian Britain* (Dent, London, 1983).

Woodham Smith, Cecil, *The Great Hunger* (Hamish Hamilton, 1962).

Woods, James, *Annals of Westmeath* (Athlone, 1977).

Yonge, C.M., "Victorians by the Sea Shore", in Quennel, Peter & Hodge, Alan (Eds.), *History Today*, Vol. 25, No.9 (London, 1975), pp.602-609.

Index